WEST AFRICAN CHALLENGE TO EMPIRE

Western African Studies

★forthcoming

West African Challenge to Empire

Culture and History in the
Volta-Bani Anticolonial War

Mahir Şaul and Patrick Royer

Ohio University Press
ATHENS

James Currey
OXFORD

Ohio University Press
Scott Quadrangle
Athens, Ohio 45701

James Currey Ltd
73 Botley Road
Oxford OX2 0BS

10 09 08 07 06 05 04 03   5 4 3 2

Published in the United States of America by Ohio University Press,
Athens, Ohio 45701

Library of Congress Cataloging-in-Publication Data
Saul, Mahir, 1951–
    West African challenge to empire : culture and history in the Volta-Bani anti-
colonial war / by Mahir Saul and Patrick Royer.
    p.   cm. — (Western African studies)
    Includes bibliographical references (p.) and index.
    ISBN 0-8214-1413-5 (cloth : alk. paper) — ISBN 0-8214-1414-3 (paper : alk.
paper)
        1. Anti-imperialist movements—Africa, French-speaking, West—History—
20th century. 2. Africa, French-speaking West—History, Military—20th century.
I. Royer, Patrick Yves. II. Title. III. Series.

DT532.5 .S38 2001
966'.0314—dc21   2001037449

British Library Cataloguing in Publication Data
Saul, Mahir
    West African challenge to empire : culture and history in the Volta-Bani anticolonial
war. - (Western African studies)
    1. Anti-imperialist movements - Africa, West 2. Africa, West - History, Military -
20th century
I. Title II. Royer, Patrick
966'.0314

ISBN 0-85255-474-5 (James Currey cloth)
ISBN 0-85255-479-6 (James Currey paper)

Contents

APPENDIX

Illustrations

Foreword

THIS BOOK WAS WRITTEN ON TWO CONTINENTS about a third one. Its seed was sown in 1997 in a meeting of the two authors in Orléans, France, where one of them was spending the year as a research fellow in the newly created ERMES/ IRD institute. After many years of anthropological fieldwork in Burkina Faso, what had until then been a passionate side interest for both of them found a focus when they decided to write a joint paper on the Volta-Bani War. Work on the idea started in earnest after Mahir Şaul returned to the United States. Soon the collaboration revealed, however, that there was much to learn and much to explain on the topic. The original paper became unwieldy, but this only fanned the researchers' enthusiasm to embark on a more ambitious project. Circumstances dictated the division of labor. Having conducted fieldwork among the Sambla people who participated in the anticolonial movement, Patrick Royer checked and rechecked the documents in the archives of France, unearthing in the process hitherto unsuspected riches of information. Mahir Şaul relied on his fieldwork among the Bobo, archival research conducted years before in France and Côte d'Ivoire, and a trip to the Marka villages in the course of the writing of the book. Ideas matured and older analyses sharpened and acquired new clothing as drafts of chapters traveled back and forth across the Atlantic in the form of electronic files. The text went through numerous stages of rewriting as details accrued to it and the authors struggled to find a happy medium between the conflicting aspirations of presenting little-known historical details and providing an interpretative study.

Our debts to people in West Africa, France, and the United States who helped us by giving us copies of crucial documents, guiding us, and providing hospitality, critique, and inspiration are too many to enumerate here. What we owe to fellow scholars finds partial expression in the notes and bibliography. The archival centers that hosted us are listed in a separate section. Over the years, Patrick Royer received grants from the Wenner-Gren Foundation for

Anthropological Research and from the Centre d'Etudes Africaines at the Ecole des Hautes Etudes en Sciences Sociales (Paris); Mahir Şaul benefited from the generosity of the National Science Foundation, the Wenner-Gren Foundation, the Fulbright-Hays Program, the Program for the Study of Cultural Values and Ethics at the University of Illinois, and the John D. and Catherine T. MacArthur Foundation. Steven Holland drew the maps and restored the illustrations from old material.

Note on Spelling and Maps

THE SPELLING OF THE HUNDREDS of place-names encountered in this work presents multiple challenges. The orthography is not always consistent from one document of the period to another; furthermore, a name may not correspond to the name that people in the locality today give to the place, or it may be only one among several names. For the large cities and cercle headquarters, we have kept the spellings found in colonial documents, which in almost all cases are also the current official spellings given to these places on today's maps. For the villages, we have used the colonial names, but simplified the spelling by replacing the French *ou* with *u* (or, in initial position, *W*), avoiding doubled consonants, and so forth, thus approximating for the benefit of the reader in English the pronunciation of the forms found on the documents.

Many of the maps illustrating the chapters in this book are based on the maps accompanying the reports preserved in the archives; they are either redrawn from them or they transpose the information the maps contain, adding or subtracting features. The mechanically reproduced village maps will be recognized from the hand lettering. In the Volta and Bani region, one finds villages with similar or identical names, sometimes not far from each other; moreover, some of the villages mentioned in this book do not exist today. Many places mentioned in the text would have been impossible to locate without the source documents. In redrawing, checking, correcting, and adding features and place-names to the maps, we have used the 1:200,000 maps of the Institut Géographique National.

For the names of African personalities, we have adopted the same principle as in village names; that is, we kept the names found in the colonial documents but simplified the French spelling to facilitate pronunciation. In a few cases, those in which we have found out much more about a person through fieldwork in the community of origin, we have substituted or added the more accurate name by which fellow villagers would recognize the person.

Introduction

IN THE FINAL MONTHS of 1915, the prominent residents of eleven villages in the Volta region of French West Africa gathered around a shrine to take an oath and declare war on the colonial administration. Thus started the Volta-Bani war, one of the last and bloodiest confrontations of the colonial occupation of West Africa. This book presents a historiographic account and an anthropological interpretation of this extraordinary series of events. It provides simultaneously a cultural and sociological analysis that reconsiders the historical ethnography of the region, the context for the colonial encounter, and a chronological narrative of the political and military realities of the anticolonial movement.

The anticolonial leadership taking the initiative for the war had not gone into this dangerous affair blindly or in a fit of anger. They had calculated their odds well and had undertaken a tremendous effort of preparation. They were well armed, they knew the art of fighting, they had confidence in their spiritual agencies, and as it turned out they were also geniuses of military tactics and strategy. They defeated the first expeditions that the administrator of the cercle (province) of Dedougou hastily arranged with the means at his disposal. They also defeated the larger military column that was put together by the governor-general of French West Africa, which included companies from other parts of the colony and an artillery unit.

World War I was raging in Europe, and the military apparatus of the colonial government had been reduced to the absolute minimum. The government's inability to crush the opposition confirmed the claims of the anticolonial partisans that the time had come to force the French out of the region. The movement spread. By

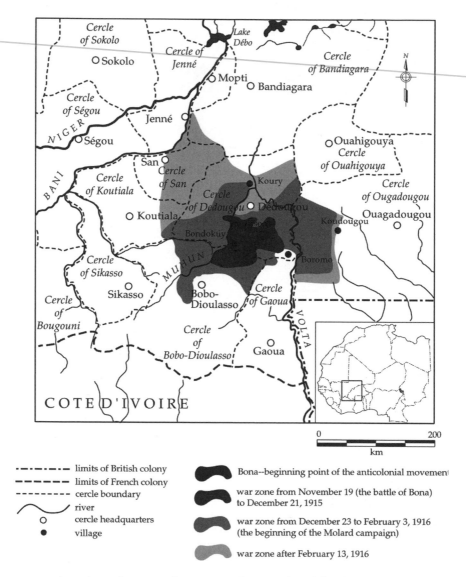

Map 1. The Volta and Bani conflict zone. Redrawn and modified from a map included in the Picanon report (ANSOM 2762).

January 1916, hundreds of villages had taken up arms in the cercles of Dedougou and Bobo-Dioulasso and in the Koudougou residency of Ouagadougou. That month, the government-general of French West Africa gathered most of its available military resources in the war zone into one column and launched its offensive, "a repression effort without precedent in the history of the French Soudan."[1]

On February 14, 1916, the column embarked on a campaign of repression by systematic destruction, and slightly more than a month later, on March 23, it returned to its headquarters in Dedougou, having exhausted most of its ammunition. The anticolonial combatants interpreted the column's return as a defeat, and the movement entered another phase of expansion. In March it spread to the cercles of Koutiala, San, and Bandiagara, all between the Muhun (the former Black Volta) and Bani Rivers. It covered an area of about one hundred thousand square kilometers inhabited by Marka, Bwa, Samo, Fulbe, Tusia, Sambla, Minyanka, Bobo, Lela, Nuna, and Ko communities. It put at risk what a French report called "our very domination in the whole of the Niger Bend region."[2]

In April, bolstered by new regiments, brought with great difficulty from all over French West Africa, and fresh munitions and supplies, two separate columns started a second campaign against the anticolonial forces. Laying waste wherever they went, they managed by the end of July to destroy the strongest centers of opposition in the cercles of Dedougou and Bobo-Dioulasso, and in the Koudougou region. The Marka leadership that had initiated the war started to waver. Many of them were killed or imprisoned; some of them surrendered. But the war picked up in the Bani valley, and some of the original leaders were able to join the conflict there. By mid-September, these movements were quelled, communication between San, Koutiala, and Dedougou was reestablished, and the opposition collapsed into isolated confrontations.

For the French, the final episode of the movement was the destruction of Lahirasso in the cercle of Bobo-Dioulasso in February 1917. But whereas the war can be said to have had a formal beginning with the public declaration in which the core of the anticolonial leadership announced its opposition, it did not have an end of the same sort. There was no treaty—no agreement binding all participants. Each village or ward or even a fraction thereof surrendered separately. As some areas capitulated, other areas continued the fight with even more ferocity. Some communities submitted to force in the course of the repression, but later took up arms again. The staunch determination of the anticolonial partisans had such a horrendous effect on the French that even after all enemy centers and all organized opposition was destroyed they still could not believe that the resistance had truly ended. For years afterward, in every dry season they feared that violent opposition would resurge.

THE SCOPE OF THE WAR

The scale of this anticolonial war raises several questions: How were the resisters able to marshal such tremendous resources and what kind of society was it that made this mobilization possible? How did this society articulate with the occupying colonial forces? Such questions pose many challenges to the conventional understanding of the historical ethnography of this region and some accounts of the establishment of the early colonial state.

The year-long confrontation in the Volta-Bani region brought the colonial administration up against approximately a thousand villages, representing a population of between eight hundred thousand and nine hundred thousand people. This was about 8 percent of the total population of French West Africa, which was estimated at eleven million at that time.[3] There were four distinct arenas to the war. In the principal arena—the cercle of Dedougou—for many battles the anticolonial party was able to gather fifteen thousand to twenty thousand soldiers at the height of the war, from February to June, when successive engagements were only one or two days apart.

These forces were heavily armed with flintlock muskets, gunpowder, an abundance of projectiles for muzzle loading, and arrows. Some of this armament was purchased from craftsmen and traders; some of it was produced locally. The blacksmiths took to manufacturing arrow tips, projectiles for muskets, and gunpowder. Much of their work was done privately as the arms market took off with the beginning of the preparations. In "Nienegue" country (southern Bwa) some communities organized a large-scale industrial effort outside market channels, bringing the blacksmiths together in secret places to mine and smelt the iron ore. Nor were the blacksmiths the only nonfighters on whose contribution the war effort depended. During the year, a large number of fortress walls were built and rebuilt, entire villages being partly reerected after having been razed. This construction activity required the collection of materials and the transportation of water and dirt across long distances in the dry season. Foodstuffs and animals were also transported and stockpiled. These arduous tasks were performed by women and children—participants who are often omitted from war histories, except when they become casualties or captives.

As in many other anticolonial confrontations, there was a total lack of parity between the weapons of the two sides. The anticolonial side had superiority in numbers, but the colonial troops had the superior firearms. Many of the battles left hundreds of dead on the opposers' side, but only a few on the colonial side. In the most extreme case, on May 6, in the battle of Boho, in the cercle of Bobo-Dioulasso, more than two thousand people lay dead on the ground by the end of the day. The total number of people killed in the entire war is impossible to determine with accuracy, in part because not all official reports listed enemy casualties and also because between major battles many poorly documented confrontations took place between anticolonial forces and villages that either refused to join the opposition or supported the administration. We estimate that the deaths on the African side were at least thirty thousand. In the areas of heavy fighting—that is, in the cercle of Dedougou and the northern half of Bobo-Dioulasso—several villages lost more than half their populations. Because losses were particularly severe among men between the ages of eighteen to thirty-five, the distortion introduced into the demographic structure of the population was felt for years afterward.

Again as in some other anticolonial wars, there is an anachronistic "modern feel" to the Volta-Bani war. The repressive activity of the French took the form of a total war, as opposed to the familiar war of the trenches of the World War I period. During and after the war, the colonial army deliberately targeted women and children as captives and hostages. With its auxiliary forces, it destroyed food reserves and ripening crops and prevented the establishment of farms. It carried off herds to feed its own soldiers and to bring to heel the indomitable enemy. It poisoned the wells and in other ways kept people from reoccupying the deserted villages. All these activities added casualties to those on the battlegrounds. Such "collateral damage" was not accounted for in administrative reports but was recorded in casual remarks and preserved in oral memory. Mortality was so high that the living were often unable to bury the dead. In some places, bodies lay exposed for months on roads, in fields, and in clearings.

On the French side also, the number of forces mobilized was extremely high, compared both with most of what had preceded in African colonial history and with all that was yet to come up to the middle of the century. About five thousand soldiers participated in the French colonial columns, approximately half of whom were *tirailleurs*—that is, enlisted African soldiers of the French colonial army who had been recruited in other parts of West Africa. The rest were "auxiliary soldiers," mounted and infantry, provided by African chiefs allied to the colonial government, and a smaller number of guards who were hired by the cercle administration. Six cannons and four machine-gun units supported this army. In addition, an even larger number of carriers and other nonfighters were recruited for support services and logistics. This was "the largest number of men and the most powerful armament that had been used to that day in French West Africa."[4] It should be remembered that for the capture of the fortress of Sikasso in 1898, the greatest military feat in the French conquest of West Africa, the colonial army was less than one-third that size (Méniaud 1935, 89; Griffeth 1968, 141). Most of the territory of the Volta region that constitutes Burkina Faso today was occupied with fighting forces of a few hundred.

THE ANTICOLONIAL LEADERSHIP

The 1915–16 Volta-Bani War was a "primary resistance" movement, to use a common expression first suggested by Terence Ranger. We should not imagine, however, that it mushroomed spontaneously among all these populations that participated in it, or that it resulted from religious fervor or mystical ties between its participants. What brought the heterogeneous anticolonial party together was a political project: to end colonial occupation. The Volta-Bani War had neither pamphlet writers, labor-union organizers, mission-educated elite, nor decorated officers, but it had the equivalent of all of these in a cadre of very remarkable people. The movement struck a chord with the readiness and desire of the majority of the population where it spread, but there can be little doubt that it was also the initiative of a restricted group of leadership that conceived the movement and carried it through. We have the names of many, but not all, of these leaders. In the vast area of war operations, several of them led an itinerant existence, and sometimes they cultivated an air of mystery and secrecy about themselves, thus making it difficult to match archival information with oral accounts.

The single most important figure in the conception and planning of the movement was Yisu Kote, of the village of Bona. It is risky to venture strong affirmations with so much that needs to be reconstructed from an imprecise record, but it seems fairly safe to claim that without him this movement either would not have come into being or would have been something different. Yisu first urged his cousin Yike Kote (who held the office of *perenkie,* head of fighting-age young men) to convince the customary authorities of Bona and of nearby villages that were historically allied to Bona to convene and discuss a declaration of war on the white man. Today in the villages of the bend of the Muhun River, Yisu Kote is remembered as tirelessly visiting each village, wearing two cords made of hibiscus fibers, the conventional badge of accomplished warriors—one wrapped around his head and the other hanging from his neck. He also carried a whistle, which was the ceremonial paraphernalia of fighting-age grades. Yisu exhorted the population to join the fight, threatening the waverers with retaliation and mystical misfortunes. In colonial records, he appears as "the fetishist of Bona," a dark and distant presence in the horrifying events that were taking place. It is important to note that Yisu was no appointed officeholder in the formal structures of the village of Bona or in the small, original alliance around it. His position of preeminence was his own creation, resulting from his personal vision, conviction, and strength. Important historical factors added to this personal aura, as explained in chapter 5, but these should not make us lose sight of the fact that it was he who mobilized them with exceptional qualities to forge the emblematic role that he played in the movement.

Siaka, of Datomo, was a war leader in Pompoï, Kopoï, Bagassi, and Pa, and in Nieneguc country in the south. The other commanders of the military action included M'Bien Nienzien, of the village of Tunu; Tara, of the village of La; Wani, of Cheriba; M'Bwa, of Bagasi; and Domba, of Banu, who directed the war in the Yankasso-Tiga-Cheriba region and, later, in the Nuna country to the east. Among the leaders of the southern Marka zone was Abdulaye Ba, a "young Fulbe chief"; Tembe, the famous general of the Nienegue of the cercle of Bobo-Dioulasso, who was killed early in March 1916 in skirmishes with the passing Amalric company; and Beniamu, the leader of the Dampan ward in Bondokuy. When the movement entered its second phase, it spawned some territorial organization and developed a kind of ranking of its leaders. Batieri, of Sanaba, on the west bank of the Muhun River, led the spread of the movement to the Bani valley, and the Muslim leader Adama Dembele, of the village of Kula, emerged as the critical figure in the north of the cercle of San and in the south of the cercle of Bandiagara; Dasa, from the region of Bona, took charge of the southern part of the cercle of San. In the residency of Koudougou, to the east, two leaders from Marka country, Dahuda and Lasana, were very active; a third, Yombie, of local origin, who had been a groom for a Mose chief, or *naaba*, became a legendary figure.

These people had uncommon gifts to improvise and innovate, to keep the movement alive in its various phases. Their work stamped its course at different levels. First, they engaged in remarkable diplomacy and propaganda to convey their vision of the possibility of this movement. They went to the villagers using alternatively and simultaneously arguments of different orders, ranging from the immediate hardships resulting from colonial interference to the deepest anxieties and fears of the population, such as the taking away of their young men for the porter columns and recruitment for the French army. They stressed the chances for successful military action, the promising omens of trusted and venerated shrines, and the historical prestige of the fighters of the Bona alliance.

They proved also to be remarkable military leaders, learning from experience, diffusing innovations, and coordinating the various parts of the movement. The French officers in charge of the repression observed that, despite different traditions, settlement patterns, and population densities, there was a common strategy throughout the vast territories that participated in the war. This sense of unity was due largely to a mobile leadership that actively took charge of the battles in widely separated zones. The tactics were also flexible. The battle leaders constantly came up with new ways to disorient the French and make the best of their own limited-range firepower.

The movement leaders cleverly exploited their initial military successes. They used terror as a deterrent, forcing those who hesitated into compliance by threatening them physically as well as with the prospect of being left alone in a country abandoned by the defeated colonial troops. Such activity minimized the support that the wandering colonial columns received in the countryside. Without matching, numerically, the barbarism of the colonial army's collective punishments, the anticolonial partisans celebrated victories with sometimes bloody and cruel ritualized performances. Their propaganda was ingenious. After the second battle of Bona — one that was disastrous for the French — they paraded in all villages the seized personal effects of the European officers and colonial army material, a practice repeated thereafter following every successful engagement.

The exhibition of colonial objects was intended to overcome the widespread sense in the region of French invulnerability. Worldly success, knowledge, and the favor of suprahuman agencies are intricately enmeshed for local people, and the French superiority in the battles of the initial conquest period was interpreted as a sign of French mystical inviolability. To counter that sentiment, anticolonial partisans targeted with particular ferocity the few French officers who commanded the colonial units. Scores of partisans got themselves killed by deliberately venturing close in order to make a more decided hit on a white man. In fact, very few of these Frenchmen were killed, although several were wounded; the few fatalities, however, were exploited out of all proportion as central victories, and in the remote parts of the war scene they spread as exaggerated rumors that all the Frenchmen in Dedougou had been killed.

This leadership was carried out in an ethos and context very different from those modeled on recent European armies, with hierarchical command and centralized budget and supplies. The anticolonial forces of the Volta-Bani were made up of volunteers — peasant farmers who came to the battlefield with their own weapons and supplies and who stayed together as long as they each individually believed in the cause. For as long as they trusted their leaders, they would follow instructions even when to do so put their lives at risk. That a high degree of discipline, so startling and even flustering to their French opponents, was achieved in catastrophic engagements is a measure of the command of this leadership.

In the biographies of some of the leaders of the movement we find elements that are familiar from the historical ethnographic sources for this region —

elements associated with men of the precolonial warrior stratum: for example, the leadership of the perenkie organization in Marka country; *sofa* status, of captive origin in the service of leaders combining warfare and trade; and Muslim clerical status in an environment of non-Muslim practice and orientation. What was novel in 1915–16 was that most of these leaders recognized the higher rank of the small circle of leadership in the area of Bona. Leaders in other places sent sacrificial animals for the shrine of Bona and symbolic shares of the spoils; in turn, these local leaders received from the leaders in Bona declarations of recognition, countergifts that expressed this recognition in tangible ways, and objects of mystical support from the central shrine.

This kind of ranking among the leaders of a vast region did not exist in earlier social organization, at least, not in this way, but the fact that it emerged in these unusual circumstances forces us to reconsider how these societies have so far been described in the literature. The Marka leadership of Bona even seems to have adopted elements from the hegemonic language of the fledgling colonial administration. They declared, for example, that they would replace the French and impose taxation, and Yombie is said to have announced that after the victory he was going to take up residence in Ouagadougou. There are similarities, in all this, with other primary resistance movements, if not with resistance in general. At times the leaders appear as if they desired colonial office without colonialism. It is indeed a matter of curiosity to think what might have happened had the movement succeeded beyond the initial phase of anticolonial struggle.

None of this, however, should make us forget the fervor with which most of the population participated in the movement and the loyalty they felt to the cause. One of the movement's most striking symbols was the collective effort in parts of the cercle of Dedougou to transform the colonial roads into farms by sowing millet on them, "because they no longer had a use for them."[5] Roads stand as the emblem of the colonial period. The drudgery of the labor expended on them enters all stories of that time. Until the end of the colonial period, all roads were built and maintained with requisitioned manual labor. But to what end? The roads did not make much sense as economic initiative, especially in the early period before the cars came, as Erdmute Alber points out in an imaginative essay (2000), and they cannot be fully accounted for as a military measure, either. One way to understand this impulsive road-building project is to connect it to the colonial officers' need to restructure "wild" space, and as tangible proof of their determination to reach and rule the locals. They were also monuments to the coercive apparatus that extracted the human resources that were necessary to build them. How significant, then, was the countersymbol that emerged from the peasant logic!—to erase the roads from the landscape by planting them with millet and sorghum, the staple crops of the region.

WAR, COLONIALISM, AND ANTHROPOLOGY

Much attention is given in this book to the military aspects of the confrontation, going beyond their connection to sociopolitical organization. Chapter 6 describes the first critical battles that set the war on its course, and in chapters 7 to 10 we look at the different phases and arenas of the war. We show the particular antecedents that conditioned the anticolonial opposition in each one of these arenas and we provide as accurate as possible a chronology of the main engagements. This is the contribution of our book to local historiography. We also discuss overall strategy and the questions of supply and draw the implications for the understanding of the type of society that produced this war effort. In chapter 7, which deals with the main arena of the war, there is an extensive commentary on the strategy and tactics of the two sides and the conduct of battle. This attention to detail is in part a burden imposed on this work for being the first comprehensive account on the topic; in the scattered literature, even the main outline of an overall chronology has not previously been available. The war was a pan-regional phenomenon, and when it is thus understood, and when the military effort and ingenuity that went into it is recognized, some previous assessments are likely to change.

A more general reason for laying emphasis on the military facet of the anticolonial movement is that much of what has been said about political organization in precolonial Africa and on resistance movements has military implications and corollaries. Classical anthropology remained aloof to the domain of warfare,[6] and the recent turn toward history in anthropology, despite the growing fascination with colonialism as part of it, continues this tradition. A bridge has not been built between the humanities and military history, although a new military history exploring the relationship between war and society in a more profound manner emerged almost twenty years ago (Vandervort 1998).

An older "anthropology of war" is relevant to our theme. This field of study developed in the United States in the 1960s in the favorable environment provided by the antiwar movement. Many studies then employed a comparative approach, surveying world cultures, which was fashionable at the time, to identify variables that promote war or inhibit it. Much of value can be found in the large body of research that has thus been generated. More recently, the War and Society series published under the general editorship of S. P. Reyna and R. E. Downs is rich with extended monographs.[7] The focus of this book does not make it easy to engage with the comparative earlier portion of this literature. Its questions were mostly formulated on the basis of an abstract conception of war, and they engaged the researchers in the path of paradigmatic explanations. We are concerned here with the different project of providing a historical account that focuses on specific social practices, colonial conventions, the day-to-day decisions of the actors, and interpretations based on contingent as well as permanent factors. Works that compare the relationship between society and warfare within a circumscribed ethnographic and historical setting have been more inspiring for us. Among these stands out a collection that includes several contributions on our geographic area of research (Bazin and Terray 1982).

Anthropological work on African political organization relies heavily on the contrast between noncentralized political systems and kingdoms. Despite many criticisms directed from a variety of angles, political analysis in Africanist anthropology often falls back on this dichotomy, and the history of colonial occupation and resistance cannot escape it. It was once believed, for example, that "states" in Africa, because of their large armies, offered the stronger resistance to Europeans (Crowder 1971, 3). This is no longer recognized as true. Our problem is that, when presented as a form of political organization that can stand by itself, the segmentary model inhibits a more comprehensive understanding of the history of the west Volta. It blinds researchers to broad regional processes that shaped local histories and that stem not from kinship but from alliances across large distances, carried out through couriers, letters, oaths, and contracts. This shortcoming cannot be remedied by simply recognizing that the so-called noncentralized societies, too, can offer serious resistance. The dichotomy still acts on perceptions. It is sometimes imagined, for example, that resistance in "tribal" societies was spontaneous, uncoordinated, or even a suicidal "let me deal a blow and then die" kind of reaction. This was not the case in the west Volta, and so the question becomes: How, some twenty years into the colonial period, did the so-called acephalous societies of the west Volta organize the effective anticolonial opposition that is described in this book? And why were they difficult to "penetrate" in the last decade of the nineteenth century? What was the social pattern, what were the resources? Posing a model of "segmentary political systems" does not provide answers that are valid for this region.

Michel Izard (1993, 1997, 1999) interprets the conquest of the west Volta region and the 1915–16 events in contrast to the Mose of Yatenga, on which he has extensively written. He thinks that in the west Volta a difference existed between a narrow community space and global space. When foreign aggression provoked a transition to a war situation, global space took over, and the segmentary communities united and acquired, temporarily, a form comparable to state formations. The military successes of the acephalous-type societies are due to a combination of great mobilizing capacities and diffuse decision making. Pushing this analysis even further, we can break more clearly from the segmentary/centralized dichotomy. The organizational capacity that became manifest in the time of war was not created out of nothing; it persisted at other times in other ways. Village alliances were the building blocs of this organization, and networks of big men across large distances formed enduring ties between some of them even when large-scale foreign aggression did not exist.

In fact, the view that aggression was often "foreign" is an unfortunate hangover of the notion of "segmentary" political organization, and of the rarely explicitly stated correlate assumption of inherent peacefulness. Before the arrival of the French, much of the aggression was not "external" at all, but only a new configuration of forces that were already present in the locality, even if only in dispersed form. An event or personality provided the spark that ignited a movement sweeping communities *as if* it were a foreign power, realigning former parochial animosities and absorbing them into a larger entity in the form of a regional front between two gigantic opponents. Even the French colonial occupation, although certainly triggered by unconnected events in distant Europe, can be read not as totally "foreign" but as a catalysis that gave new shape to local hostilities. In chapters 1 to 3, we reformulate in this light the nineteenth-century political organization of the west Volta societies and provide a brief account of the initial French occupation. The 1915–16 anticolonial movement arose from the social foundation that made the initial penetration and early colonial control of the west Volta difficult for the French. This analysis of precolonial society provides the ground for interpreting the purposes, desires, and resources of the anticolonial partisans of the Volta and Bani regions.

At the outbreak of the Volta-Bani War in 1915, the French had tenuously occupied the area under discussion for about seventeen years. They had been able to collect some taxes, levy forced labor, and had recently even started to recruit conscripts for the famous French Black army, a practice that loomed large in subsequent explanations of the origin of the war. This initial French occupation removed some of the largest players in the regional political realm, but as we explain in chapter 3, it did not immediately dissolve the precolonial social formation. The administrative and later ethnological view that this region was made up simply of juxtaposed villages, all equivalent and similar, all fending for themselves, is a byproduct of this elimination or subjugation of major political leaders. However, connections between villages persisted along with the long-term links and the political culture that allowed for broader mobilization.

In 1916, the French commander of the principal column of repression, Colonel Molard, wrote: "These populations . . . in a sense were never conquered by arms, but attached, so to speak, to the bloc of French West Africa simply by their consent."[8] This consent was not obtained freely, but by the practice or threat of violence. Still, Molard's words echo those uttered by the principal orator in the fateful meeting that took place in the village of Dahuan, in the last week of November 1915, to seal a broader alliance against the French (a meeting we describe more fully in chapter 5): "The whites came to our country. We let them, thinking that they would behave like the Fulbe, that is without interfering in our business." For the people of the country the French were powerful but distant intruders. The communities bowed to them as one bows to force, as they had done to other powerful actors before. But this was only a temporary expedient. They did not in the same act surrender sovereignty. Throughout the region, what is comparable to the European notion of political sovereignty lay in complicated arrangements of first occupant and shrine that were not always homologous even to the settlement pattern in villages.

The colonial newcomers, however, had refused to behave according to this code. They had not been content simply to enjoy the contingent advantages of superior force expressed in the idiom of alliance, which implied respect of local autonomy and some minimal reciprocal gestures of solidarity. Instead, they had insisted on the full trappings of territorial control. The second element of the situation, which is fully expressed in other contexts, is that the French superiority of force had, according to appearances, now eroded. But the French continued to act as superior, expecting from the villagers the loyalty of subjects to legitimate authority. The difference between yielding intermittently to force, which was the local reading of the brief colonial experience at this point, and accepting subjecthood, which was the French presumption, explains many early colonial episodes in West Africa. The initial French occupation looked to the village communities of the west Volta like a weak state (the villages and the alliances they formed) being blustered by a strong state. Being compelled by a foreign power is not the same thing as accepting to become a province in its state apparatus. Where the French thought administration, the locals saw gunboat diplomacy, if not outright banditry. The colonial assertions of territorial control and government did not have their counterpart in local perception. In this important sense, the defeat of the Volta-Bani movement in 1916 represented the true conquest of this territory.

It follows that the habitual distinction made in the literature on colonialism between "resistance," designating opposition to conquering armies at the time of the initial European occupation, and "rebellion," describing opposition after the conquest is completed, is not very pertinent to the events we describe here. In many West African settings, the difference between "conquest" and the following stage of "pacification" has meaning only from the perspective of the international agreements that the colonizing European powers made among themselves at the outset of the scramble for Africa. The word *rebellion* veils the magnitude of the violence of 1915–16, which dwarfed that of the initial penetration of the late nineteenth century. More importantly, it clouds the issue of legitimacy by implying that the communities had at some earlier moment resigned themselves to the occupation. A proper understanding of the motivations of the African leadership that launched the war in November 1915 rests on recognizing that this was not the case.

The people of the west Volta region remember the 1915–16 events as a war among autonomous parties, not as a rebellion against higher authority. In the Marka areas within the bend of the river, whence the original leadership cadre came, people remember these events as Bona-kele, the War of Bona. In the Bwa language, they are remembered as *hyen,* in the Nuna language as *twa,* in Bobo as *kun,* in Sambla as *kaa*—all words that can be translated as *war,* but not, appropriately, as *revolt* or *rebellion.* We follow the same usage. In the rare instances that we use the expressions *rebellion* or *insurrection* in this book, we do it to signal the perspective of the colonial power.

THE ETHNIC PUZZLE

The land between the Nazinon (formerly, the Red Volta) and Bani Rivers supplies a bewildering multitude of ethnic labels and language names. For this kaleidoscopic reality, early colonial administrators used belittling words: *anarchy* or *poussière*—a dust cloud, or sprinkle, of peoples.[9] The anticolonial movement originating in Bona very quickly crossed the linguistic, religious, administrative, and geographic boundaries by which the people of this area have been classified by outsiders. On the face of it, there is no reason why this should be surprising. The emphasis put on ethnicity, however—first in the colonial mindset, later in anthropology, and finally and derivatively in history—transformed the expansion of the movement into an intellectual problem that demands an explanation. If the Bwa, Marka, Bobo, Lela, Nuna, Sambla, Tusia, Minyanka, Fulbe, and so forth are each assumed to have a different worldview and therefore a distinctive political organization, how is it that people from all these backgrounds collaborated so closely on this occasion?

That puzzle is a perfect example of the burden that Africanist anthropology has inherited from nineteenth-century frames of reference. The more sociologically oriented approaches of the interwar period had made some progress in relativizing the significance of tribes and ethnic groups in the discourse of Africanist anthropology, but in recent years ethnicity made a comeback under different guises, despite the protests of some historians. Terence Ranger writes, for example, that

> far from there being a single tribal identity, most Africans moved in and out
> of multiple identities, defining themselves at one moment as subjects to this
> chief, at another moment as a member of that cult, at another moment as part
> of this clan, and at yet another moment as an initiate in that professional
> guild. These overlapping networks of association and exchange extended
> over wide areas. (Ranger 1983, 248)

In the Volta region, ethnicity did not come into play in the nineteenth-century village coalitions and larger hegemonic projects described in chapters 1 and 2. The effective sets of social action were much smaller, sometimes kinship clusters, and often, as we have seen in the case of the village, the groupings of them by agreements and pacts. The village leagues brought together people of different ethnic groups. Villages themselves were often multiethnic. People of different ethnicities intermarried, went to the same marabouts for charms, or sacrificed to the same earth shrine. As a consequence, descent groups, one of the most enduring elements of identity, could be multiethnic. At times, members of a community might be enemies of a neighboring community who spoke the same language as they themselves did, while swearing oaths of mutual assistance with people living far away and who spoke a different language. We have little evidence that there was awareness of a shared overarching ethnicity in the sense that it becomes the topic of anthropological monographs, and the presence of a language bond did not automatically generate solidarity or common interest. When it did, such language-bound solidarity was limited to the most local arena, where acknowledged common origins gave one sector of the community a basis to oppose another sector of it. Ethnicity itself was unstable. The rubrics used in written descriptions create a false sense of homogeneity. For example, as we explain in chapter 9, the label Marka applies to groups that are very different in the Volta region and in the San valley. People who are Bobo now will tell you that their ancestors hailed from places where different languages are spoken; and a Samo earth shrine custodian can announce that his ancestor was a brother of the founder of that other village that is well known to be Marka. As trained anthropologists, we might perceive in such comments contradiction that needs to be smoothed out, but our local interlocutors are likely not even to understand what causes our problem.

It is possible that even phrasing the issue as shifts and changes in ethnic identity profoundly distorts the reality as it was lived in the nineteenth century. We simply do not know what labels such as Bobo, Marka, or Bwa might have meant at that time, and attempts to smooth over inconsistencies by presuming that some people have dropped out of one of these categories to assume another come out as contrived inferences based on the present. We can be certain that ethnic categories did not cover the social space exhaustively, because at some level this is true even today. There were interstitial cross-ethnic or non-ethnic groups. This was the case, for example, for the Blacksmiths and the bards, the endogamous groups of craft specialists on which there is a vast literature. It was also true for people torn out of their communities. Thus some people were primarily blacksmith, trader (*jula*, written with lowercase), Muslim, or slave; all these are categories in a matrix of reference altogether different from ethnicity. Ethnic categories were not nonoverlapping either. One could be Marka and Samo simultaneously, or Marka and Bwa, as well as Bwa and blacksmith, or Marka and Muslim.

The small bodies of hereditary and endogamous craft groups adapted to different cultural settings without deeply identifying with any one of them and/or/because they were perceived as radically different. In some respects, groups of fighters who joined a farm community were likewise defined primarily by an occupational choice. But when as newcomers they settled into an area, they established affinal links with other people in the community, perhaps engaged in the exchange of shrine offices, and in this way they went through a process of peasantization. Consequently they assumed local ethnic color. Such military groups that had become part of village life, and the fighting traditions they maintained, were essential to the 1915–16 anticolonial movement. Approaching political organization with the conventional lens of ethnicity has had disastrously limiting consequences for scholarship in this historical setting.

The understanding of the Volta-Bani War has suffered from this limitation.

A fixation with ethnicity encouraged a partial view of the conflict. The best-known authors who have written about it did so in studies of particular ethnic groups in the region. It has been called the Bwa Rebellion because the most widely read discussions of the war happened to be lodged in books concerning the Bwa. The Bwa made the largest sacrifices for it, but the movement did not start among the Bwa, and not all Bwa were on the anticolonial side. People of Gurunsi, Marka, Bobo, Sambla, Tusia, Samo, Minyanka, and even Fulbe origin participated on both sides in the war. Volunteers did not participate in the anticolonial movement as members of particular ethnic groups, but only as members of an extended family, a village ward, or a community of allied villages in a restricted area. Linguistic or other cultural boundaries define neither a natural vessel for political organization nor a particular barrier to be crossed. We propose to replace the view of ethnicity with an analysis of nodes of power and of the links between these nodes.

INTENTIONS AND STRUCTURES

One of the difficulties in giving an account of such a war is to overcome the overwhelming sense of the unfolding of the inevitable. In addition to the general problems that historiography presents in this regard, we are influenced by many images—both verbal and cinematographic—linked specifically to the African colonial past. What level-headed analysis can totally discard the terrible spectacle of helpless natives mowed down by the fire of a machine gun wielded by a small company of white men wearing tropical helmets? Or the drama of a quasi-medieval army, chanting, wearing turbans, and bearing swords, confronting a self-assured, disciplined company armed with cannons and wearing uniforms? Under the influence of such images, opposition to white rule can be explained only by factors such as the hold of mystical fanaticism, irrational rage, or—in a more sociological parlance—misplaced trust in a "charismatic" leader. Explanations of that type are very far from giving a sense of what happened in the Volta and Bani regions in 1915–16. The misleading images of native helplessness hinder us in the search for the objectives of the anticolonial fighters, in uncovering the cool reasoning with which they carried out the war strategy, and their serene assessments. These images also blind us to the sheer terror that struck the hearts of the French and to the lack of trust that, for most of the conflict period, the colonials had in their own weaponry.

The defeat of the anticolonial movement was not inevitable, at least not on account of the disparity in the arms technology. The possession of sophisticated rifles was not the main reason for French triumph in the end. The anticolonial fighters took these weapons into account when they planned their strategy, and they succeeded in partly neutralizing the weapons' effect by drawing on superior numbers, tactical resourcefulness, and their spirit of sacrifice. The latter was based on accepting as a given that they would suffer casualties in much greater numbers than their opponent.

The primary goal of this book is to provide an intelligible narrative of this dark episode that brings out the thoughts, intentions, and perceptions of the actors. We try to understand and convey the subjective dispositions of the African actors who were on the anticolonial side by examining the traces of self-expression they have left behind. But we are also interested in the European actors. Historians of colonialism will not find the inclusion of European subjectivities to be a great novelty, but the burgeoning field of colonial anthropology still has not found a totally satisfactory way to balance the two sides of the colonial divide in its interpretations.[10]

We see ourselves as part of a growing contemporary drift that signals itself by the use of the words *agency* and, more recently, *historicity.* Nonetheless, we use these and other fashionable expressions sparingly, because, once their novelty has worn off, they can become clichés, anesthetics that cloak older attitudes, instead of contributing to clarity or imagination. Our commitment is to understanding the events of the past not as enacted cultural scenarios or the instantiation of social positions, but as contingent decisions in response to novel situations. Whatever part "structures" play in these decisions, they do so by shaping the biographies of the actors and their mutual expectations. The actors experience the events in which they participate mostly as strings of intended or meaningful acts, the articulation of which a historical anthropology, as much as history *tout court,* has as its first obligation to recover from the record. By this we mean nothing very mysterious — only that as we try to reconstruct the past we will present the events resurrected from the documents as intelligible; that is, with the minimal requirements to achieve what, in daily human interaction, we mean by the word *understanding.*

By the same token, we also agree that human desires, intentions, and assessments — whether of the past or of the present — are not primary givens; they are grounded in historical and social contexts, the "ghosts of the past generations" that the living bear on their shoulders. Thus we have an ear for the poststructuralists, who announce the illusory character of the subject, as well as for the older sociological traditions that proclaimed the same thing. Human intentions also emerge in the crossroads of contingencies, conjunctures, as only one of the determinants of—to use an expression popularized in Louis Althusser's writings—overdetermined outcomes. Finally, purposes and intentions do not constitute the last word of history. It is in the case of very few people, if of any at all, that the future becomes what was intended or desired by those who fashioned it. Still, if a sociocultural event is to be understood, it must be understood first as linked series of intended acts. No talk of charisma, mystical participation, symbolic analysis, or social structural causality can replace this rung in the ladder of comprehension.

In the opening remarks to the account of another war, Marshall Sahlins wrote: "What is generally called 'event' is itself complex: at once a sui generis phenomenon with its own force, shape and causes, and the significance these qualities acquire in the cultural context" (Sahlins 1991, 45). Revisiting with the optic of an anthropological theory a terrain well explored before by "good historians," he explains that the decisive actions and subjective dispositions of his actors were relatively autonomous, not simply expressions of the larger system. The structures and relations of higher order do not specify the unique circumstances or individual biographies through which their history is worked out. History needs to be understood as the "synthesis of the heterogeneous," the intersection of different causal series of events, the coincidence of different chains of determination. Sahlins's own polemical stress on structure and culture may conceal the profound wisdom in these remarks. We underline his passing remark that notions such as culture and structure are ultimately "evident oversimplification."

One way to bend these unwieldy notions into more usable instruments is to replace them with memories, sketches, prophesies, all rehearsed, shared, and communicated in narrative form. "Any anthropology that takes seriously the idea of human agency," says J. D. Y. Peel (1995, 584, 606), "will be concerned with how the narratives-as-lived are shaped by narratives-as-told." These narratives do not always come in recognizable discursive form; some local traditions are more tight-mouthed when it comes to verbal communication than others. But the kernel of self-understanding is at least implicitly present in the very use of language. We prefer to rest our conceptual apparatus on such self-understanding and resist the temptation to take flights of interpretation without mooring in it.

In the conclusion, we discuss how with this war the populations of the west Volta region and of the Bani valley contributed to the emergence of two separate colonial territories that eventually became the independent nation-states of Mali and Burkina Faso. The agency of African populations in the definition of colonial boundaries is not as frequently debated as the role of different metropolitan interests. More generally, researchers neglect the transitory period that lies between the initial conquest before the turn of the twentieth century and the high period of colonialism (between the two world wars). Yet this is a time of significant transformation in which one can discern more clearly the agency of segments of the local population and of individual local colonial administrators—more clearly, that is, than in the subsequent period when the institutions and practices had already solidified.

COLONY, POSTCOLONY, HEGEMONY

In the period following political independence, the historians of Africa whole-heartedly celebrated the anticolonial movements. Soon afterwards, however, a growing awareness of the heterogeneity of precolonial society and of class issues gave these studies a much more sober tone (see Isaacman and Isaacman 1977, 34). At the same time, and independently, a new style of writing on colonial matters was emerging. It possessed literary flair, and it privileged South Asia. In the last decade, this stream of publications established a strong junction with what is often called cultural studies. The publications that place themselves under this sign are now so numerous and varied, and cover so many areas of the world, that it is difficult to say something generally valid about them as a field of research. This flood, perhaps attributable in part to the pressures for conformity in the academic marketplace, now seems to enter the unavoidable ebb phase. We will simply try to identify a few strands in this trend as a reference and counterpoint to the present work.

The influence of Michel Foucault, in books written mostly in the 1960s and documenting in nineteenth-century Europe the development of institutions that invaded and regimented the lives of the citizenry in the name of more humane and efficient organization, is evident in much recent historiography. One also finds a strong imprint of feminist scholarship—for example, that showing homologies between political subordination in the colonies and issues of class and gender in the metropole. A smaller number of studies inspired more directly from Derrida infuse conceptual criticism into sociological studies. One common ground between the studies that show such a wide range of theoretical influences is a particular use of language and an expository style that consists in collating what is thematically incongruous while resisting the urge to establish theoretical or interpretive connections. For the originating authors, the language of irony and wit was tied to an epistemological stance, but it seems now to be emulated like a fashion, to become the hallmark of what is vaguely called postmodernism. Fredric Jameson (1991, 198) remarked that the moral and political urgency of the earlier models has now given way to a "new stridency . . . combined with celebratory accents," which for our purposes can be extended to the troubling embrace of the expression *postcolonial* itself. We find that this language and style of montage turn writers away from conceptual effort and precise articulation.

One particular strand in this recent output has a pedigree in the tradition of history writing, which came out of India by way of Australia. This body of work, which is the strongest influence on "postcolonial studies" of our day, was initially known as "subaltern studies," after the title of a series of yearly volumes that began in 1982. It privileged the study of popular uprisings and less violent kinds of oppositions of the colonial period, taking issue with colonial historiography and also with the anticolonial nationalist history that replaced it. A connection between the resistance studies of the 1960s and this subaltern literature has been established in the comprehensive and sensitive review of Cooper (1994). While the claims to originality are open to debate, we do find ourselves close to some members of this school. G. Bhadra (1988), for example, writes in the conclusion of a study of the Indian mutiny of 1857 these pointed words that could serve as an epigraph for our own study:

> The recognition of the strength and weakness of these rebels would be a step forward in understanding their role beyond stereotyped categories and formulae . . . they [cannot] be merely described as faceless elements in an omnibus category called "the people." To seek after and restore the specific subjectivity of the rebels must be a major task of the new historiography. That would be a recognition of the truth that, under the given historical circumstances in which he lives, man makes himself. (1988, 175)

Inspiration from Antonio Gramsci permeated these works until literary poststructuralism became predominant. But does the increasing frequency of references to this brilliant Italian thinker-activist of the interwar period show that he is a carefully studied source, or simply a dashing accessory to the text? Kurtz (1996) argues that the way *hegemony* is commonly used in recent anthropological writing has little bearing on Gramsci's subtle concept, while Roseberry (1994) insists that it should not be understood simply as perception, confusion, or indoctrination. The propensity to quote without a close reading of the source is aggravated by indifference to the circumstances under which the work was created.

Gramsci wrote during the time when colonialism was established and consolidated in Africa, but this political reality was not his principal preoccupation. His insights on the elusive nature of hegemony and inconstancy of class were grounded in his revolutionary aspirations, which were at odds with the popular support that the populist Mussolini regime received in Italy. These circumstances of his country were very different from the conditions of colonial domination.

Gramsci confronted the realm of domination by consent, education, mass rallies, and the social engineering of nation building, in contradistinction to the colonial situation of 1915 West Africa, which we assimilate to what Max Weber called *Macht.* Transposing Gramsci's analysis mechanically to early colonial settings would surely be a case of misplaced generalization. A. R. JanMohammed (1985) reasonably proposed to distinguish in colonial history at least two phases: first a "dominant" phase of military subjugation and coercion, and then perhaps a "hegemonic" phase which may involve partly shared representations.[11] Compare this now with the introduction to a collection of essays in anthropological history, in which Nicholas B. Dirks (1992) presents a seamless colonial hegemony as simultaneous consent and resistance. Gramscian concepts are hybridized with the inconsonant notion of culture, and the distinction made by JanMohammed disappears from view. We risk being dazzled with a homogeneous category of colonialism, where resistance becomes a faintly perceptible space both within and against colonial culture. The 1915–16 resistance in the Volta, in contrast, belonged to a period of juncture, a "heterogeneity" in its full sense. Fledgling colonialism disrupted many people's everyday life, but still functioned outside of it. People's cultural vision and political project were not molded by those of colonialism.

The word *subaltern* inspires in us a commentary that is parallel to the one we made on *rebellion,* above. For the first decades of colonial occupation, subaltern is improper as a collective designation for West Africans in opposition to Europeans. There were undoubtedly subalterns among the Africans, as there were among the Europeans, and we will elaborate upon this in various parts of our account. But the conquering armies led by Europeans found themselves up against armies led by Africans who saw themselves as the Europeans' equal, if not their superiors, even though they had to take account of great differences in armament. The local people did not assimilate the colonial occupation as subjugation, and in fact this occupation was very tenuous, as explained in later chapters. The violent encounter that generated colonialism in West Africa was as complicated a social phenomenon as the class processes of early-twentieth-century Europe, but it was so in different ways, and we should not overlook the differences.

THE VOLTA-BANI WAR IN HISTORIOGRAPHIC DISCOURSE

The postindependence period in Africa was a time for valorizing the anticolonial struggles of the past, and such projects absorbed most people writing in the developing field of African history at that time. Reflecting this climate of opinion, Asiwaju and Crowder wrote (1977, 2): "Armed confrontation with colonial rulers . . . is perhaps the best studied aspect of protest against colonial rule, no doubt because of its greater dramatic appeal." Eventually, historians began protesting against the fixation with large-scale risings at the expense of smaller-scale oppositions and other forms of protest (for example Tosh 1974). We seem to have come now full circle. The tide has turned, and we hear complaints that there is too much "small" opposition, too much "passive resistance" or protest by semiotic detour, at the expense of what was dramatic and what needs to be told first. The general knowledge of large-scale West African oppositions to colonial rule is still sketchy, and largely dependent on random factors leading to the production of theses and books in this or that part of the West African subcontinent. New fads in scholarly writing, focusing on colonial discourse rather than on organization and confrontation, may be taking us further away from filling the gaps.

In our case, we have even more compelling reasons to return to the "large-scale." The 1915–16 Volta-Bani War was a seismic event in West African colonial history, but it remains virtually unknown in the English-language literature. In a journal intended for use in African colleges and universities, a 1977 survey article entitled "West African Revolts during the First World War" mentions the 1915–16 Volta-Bani War only with the laconic phrase "revolts against forced recruitment in . . . Dédougou, Bobo-Dioulasso, Ouagadougou in the Upper Volta" (Osuntokun 1977, 10). The same issue of the journal includes an article on the much smaller-scale uprising in the Borgu districts of French Dahomey. The landmark volume edited by Rotberg and Mazrui (1970) makes no mention of the Volta-Bani War, neither in its introduction nor in the sections "Resistance to Conquest" and "Rebellions." Sixteen years later, the introduction to another landmark volume, edited by D. Crummey (1986), makes no reference to it either. We note that the Volta-Bani War is not the only blind spot in this literature. Also missing from the surveys are the Baule wars, in what is now central Côte d'Ivoire (Weiskel 1980; Chauveau 1987), and the other serious military challenges that shook the French colonial administration between 1916 and 1918, first in the area of the current Burkina-Niger border and then in the Ahaggar region of the central Sahara.[12] It is as if in the pages of history books the thousands of anticolonial

fighters of the Volta-Bani War and of these other struggles have fallen victim
once again, this time to the invisible language barrier between French and English that still divides postcolonial Africa.

The literature by French scholars, however, also lacks mention of the Volta-
Bani War, when one looks beyond the small circle of specialists of Mali and
Burkina Faso. An illustration is the authoritative synthesis of African history by
Catherine Coquery-Vidrovitch (1988), which has one chapter entitled "State
Resistance" and another, some forty pages long, entitled "Revolt and Resistance." The "violent revolt . . . in Western Volta" is mentioned, in half a sentence, as a "local peasant revolt" in reaction to forced conscription in West
Africa, whereas the Maji-Maji in Tanganyika (1905–7), the Kongo Warra war
in Central Africa (1927–32), the Mau Mau uprising of Kenya (1952–56), and
the 1964–65 rebellions in Zaïre are described as "Mass Movements." In terms
of scale only, going by the numbers provided by the author, the Volta-Bani War
was by far more massive than any of these other movements. The text reports
12,000 deaths in the Maji-Maji conflict and perhaps 10,000 in the Mau Mau;
this is about one-third the number of those who fell in the Volta-Bani War.
More than 350,000 are said to have participated in the Kongo-Warra war. This
is again about one-third of those who participated in the Volta-Bani War. We
are aware that caution is needed in a simple comparison of numbers; one finds
different estimates in different books, and it is not always clear what is being
counted. Our figures for the Volta-Bani War deaths are conservative estimates
that include only those who fell in the battlefield, and participation was measured on the basis of the colonial census figures of the cantons and cercles in
question. The point is not to decide, once and for all, which was the most murderous anticolonial war in Africa; on the contrary, we suggest that comparative
statements about the scale of these movements are necessarily provisional, because there is simply too much that has not been written about. With all that,
still, the conclusion of the author that "West Africa . . . never in the twentieth
century underwent large-scale peasant revolts comparable to those in Central
and East Africa" (1988, 205) is certainly very rash, even in light of what has
already been published.

One reason the Volta-Bani War is so little known in the scholarly literature
is the attitudes of successive governments that ruled over these territories. First
the attitude of the French colonial government: Because the Volta-Bani movement occurred during World War I, and had in fact its genesis in the conditions
of that larger war (as we explain in chap. 4), the French government kept secret
what happened in that part of their colonial empire, from their own public as

well as from the rest of world. This was the time of strong Allied propaganda against Germany. The German territories in Africa were attacked and taken over by joint British and French forces, with the loud justification that Germany was unfit for the "civilizing mission," atrocities in the suppression of the South West Africa and Tanganyika insurrections being given as evidence. Any news about trouble in their own territories would expose both Britain and France to the charge of self-righteous hypocrisy. France especially had good reason to fear exposure. The violence in the suppression of the Volta-Bani opposition probably surpassed German actions in either of the above-mentioned conflicts.[13]

A lecture by Albert Lebrun, deputy and former minister of colonies, delivered in Toulouse in June 1916, the most violent moment of the Volta-Bani War in all its fronts, illustrates the point. His speech was entitled "The Colonial French Effort." In it he declared that the colonies of France "in complete unanimity . . . have all sided with the metropole," and he listed all the loyalist manifestations coming from Algeria, Morocco, Tunisia, and Indochina. He did acknowledge "some attempts at local rebellion," but these were not significant either in their causes or in their effects. "France should be legitimately proud," he concluded, "of the support that all her subjects have given her" (Kaspi 1971, 381). Thus what was a "repression effort without precedent," according to the panic-stricken governor-general in Dakar, was downgraded to an attempt at local rebellion by the politicians in Paris.

The second moment in the perpetuation of the amnesia on the Volta-Bani War was 1960, the year of independence for French colonies. The team that took Upper Volta to independence, unlike some of its counterparts elsewhere in Africa, was not consumed with anticolonial fervor. These Roman Catholic mission-trained intellectuals were not all of the same mind or supportive of each other, but they were deferential to France. The Volta-Bani War did not come to the front stage of national consciousness under the politicians of the first two decades of independence. The situation was not exactly the same in Mali, the second nation-state that partakes of the heritage of this movement. But both in Mali and Upper Volta (the former Burkina Faso), the Volta-Bani anticolonial war concerned areas that were marginal in terms of the symbols mobilized to forge a national identity: ancient Mali and the heritage of the Bambara of the middle course of the Niger, in the first case, and the Mose kingdoms, in the second. In fact, in both countries large numbers of people who identified strongly with this national identity came from places that participated on the side of the French in the repression of 1916. At the same time, the local authors who wrote about the war all identified strongly with the populations that became minorities in their

respective nation-states, and in their literary efforts there was a stance of opposition to the nucleus that controlled the new states. Even today, people may read
a tinge of regionalist subversion in glorifying the opposition of 1915–16.

We should add that among the populations of the villages that participated
in the anticolonial movement and were decimated by the repression, the memory
of it today is not necessarily a reason for jubilation. The descendants of particular
famous leaders may betray a discrete pride in their family association, but the
more widespread recollection of the war is that of a tragic disaster or an error of
catastrophic proportion. It is also common to encounter a reticence to remember
the war at all.

This attitude has complicated roots. The memory of the expectations with
which people participated in the movement at the time is hard to preserve after
the brutality of what actually transpired. The celebratory outlook of the movement and the persisting disillusionment among its participants' descendants today are linked by a view of human agency that stresses efficacy in the world and
leaves little room for the brooding contemplation of martyrdom. An intervening
factor is the current hold that the notion of progress has in the hearts and minds
of the local people. It strengthens the ambition for personal success and breeds
further contempt for failure. At another level, the local attitude toward the memory of the anticolonial war perdures because of the indifference of successive re-
gimes to raise this event into a positive moment of the national past.

To return to the world of the script, for the reasons we explained the Volta-
Bani War remained buried in military reports and administrative documents for
many years. It is through military history, albeit the type that eulogizes the
officers of the colonial army, that the war made its way to print. Colonel Mangeot's training manual (1922), written for the colonial officers, includes illustrative references to the Molard campaign. A history prepared for the 1931
Colonial Fair in Paris gives a brief description of the war.[14] A longer description, which is obviously based on military field reports, is found in General
Duboc's history of the French conquest of West Africa (1938).

An article written by a schoolteacher, Ibrahima Maiga (1937), from what
is now Mali, on the battle of Tominian, has a different character, because it includes local stories and memories. This is the earliest piece we have seen on any
episode of the war written by a member of the local intelligentsia. But it was
published in one of those colonial journals that encouraged the literary output
of young African educators and it does not make a break with the perspective
of the government. After this article comes a long silence, and then the first literary and scholarly references begin in the years following independence.

The first work on the Volta-Bani movement in postindependence times, and probably the most influential of all, was published in 1962 by an outstanding Burkinabe writer, Nazi Boni, while he was in self-imposed exile in Dakarand. Boni was a Bwa, and his rich and evocative book, which is part fiction and part chronicle, is set in the Nienegue region.[15] Boni's novel inspired most of the authors mentioned below, and we should mention that the anticolonial movement of the west Volta and Bani regions came to be known under the misleading name of the Bwa rebellion largely due to the influence of this work.

Among the historians of recent times, Jean Suret-Canale has precedence in drawing attention to the significance of the Volta-Bani War as an anticolonial movement. In a book that is the first critical reappraisal of colonialism in French West Africa by a historian, he lists it among the resistances to the colonial administration during the years of World War I (Suret-Canale 1964). In a footnote, he states that he is preparing a separate book on the subject, but unfortunately this project seems not to have come to fruition. The main source that made the movement known to French West Africanists was the acclaimed Bwa ethnography of Jean Capron (1973), circulated and quoted as a mimeographed thesis before the printed version. The section on the anticolonial war was part of the introductory chapter dealing with the history of the San region, and it provided the first synthesis of ethnographic observation and a few difficult-to-find local publications on the topic.

Two local studies of the Volta-Bani War were published in 1970 in the same issue of the journal of the National Research Center in Ouagadougou. One of them was the text of a graduation thesis for the National School of Administration written by Blami Gnankambary (1970), a Bwa professional. It combined data from archival documents from the cercle of Dedougou with information obtained from oral sources in the Bwa villages within the bend of the Muhun River. The second article was by Father Jean Hébert (1970), who also published many other pieces on Voltaic history. Although very important for their time and a primary source for many later studies, caution is advised while reading these two articles. Neither of them provides references. Father Hébert's piece incorporates unacknowledged long quotes and paraphrases from official documents, without warning for qualifications that might be introduced on the basis of other documents of the period. Gnankambary's thesis harbors also a few errors, which seem mostly to have been introduced at the typing stage, but which may disorient readers unfamiliar with the setting. Some of the small inaccuracies in these two publications have found their way to many other publications that have relied on them. Another *maîtrise* thesis, longer than Hébert's and

Gnankambary's articles, was written in France by Pascal Toe (1970). It relies heavily on the two important reports that were produced by Jules Vidal and Edouard Picanon, inspectors of the colonial administration, before the heat of the events had dissipated. It shares the flaws of unacknowledged references and uncritical copying, but of the sources mentioned here it includes the most comprehensive event history. Another National School of Administration thesis remained as a typescript, largely unknown. Written by Siaka Sombie (1975), the narrative of this text seems to be based on the diary of the administrator of Dedougou, as well as on the thesis of Gnankambary, but it also includes significant small details from oral sources, which bring out the role of the Marka leadership of Bona in the organization of the movement.[16]

The chapters in the books that two French historians published in the 1980s are more solidly bedecked with scholarly apparatus. The first, by Marc Michel (1982), on the topic of military conscription in French West Africa, includes a chapter on the West Volta War based on a wider range of archival and oral sources. The second book, Anne-Marie Duperray's historical monograph on the Gurunsi (1984), broadened the understanding of the movement outside of the bend of the Muhun River.

We are not surveying here all the more recent work that contains some discussion of the events we write about below, but we will mention two unusual efforts. Lazoumou Seni published a small pamphlet in a government press in Burkina Faso in the years of Thomas Sankara's revolutionary government and a separate brief article elsewhere; both works are based on a longer manuscript (Seni 1981 and 1985). The second recent source is a booklet printed in Jula in the adult-literacy series of the rural-development extension services of Bobo-Dioulasso and Dedougou, produced by a team that made use of a few of the sources mentioned above, adding some new oral narratives that they collected in villages (Bobo Julaso ni Dedugu Serepeya 1995). The booklet, which is distributed in the villages, is the only published source on the war accessible to young farmers who are literate in Jula.

OUR SOURCES

Our sources for most of the events as well as the ideas guiding the action of the protagonists include colonial documents, field reports of the officers, letters and justificatory texts by the administrators, and a few more encompassing general documents commissioned by the government. The research was mostly carried out in archives in France (Aix-en-Provence and Paris) and, secondarily, in Burkina Faso and Abidjan (see archival sources). Moussa Niakate provided a service to the scholarly community by making available an important collection of documents from the archives of Bamako.[17] On the African side there are memories, stories, comments, and attitudes, most of which are recorded in the local sources we mentioned above. They do not add up in volume to the mountains of colonial paperwork, nor are they of a nature to allow for a direct comparison. In addition, this book's two authors have separately conducted long stretches of fieldwork, mostly in areas of the former cercle of Bobo-Dioulasso, even though much of it was not directly focused on the 1915–16 war. During the writing of the book, one of the authors also conducted a rapid survey on the memories of the war in the former cercle of Dedougou. It is the essence of the labor of historical interpretation to tread through this uneven material.

The colonial documents, we would like to point out, are not univocal. The mass of archival material presents a diversity of information and points of view that is unsuspected before engaging in its study. We owe this to the sheer number of people who wrote the documents, the different motivations for producing them, and the disagreements and conflicts among the colonial personnel. Archival materials are far from representing a "colonial mind" that can be distilled easily. The colonial records also include direct and indirect voices of African protagonists, as depositions, observations, and as arguments used by different colonial parties to support controversial points. We strive to undo the stereotypical colonial actor as we do that of the native or the anticolonial partisan. We hope that our study, based in extensive fieldwork and archival research, will strengthen the growing ties between anthropology and history by encouraging the combining of the work methods of the two disciplines.

CHAPTER I

The West Volta in the Nineteenth Century

WHEN OPPOSITION STARTED IN NOVEMBER 1915 in Dedougou, the French administrators were unprepared for this kind of event, not only in a military way but also conceptually. Their first responses failed because they had an inadequate view of local society, although they also carried a strong conviction that they knew all about it. The colonial view of politics in western Volta derived from the French experience in eastern Senegal and around the upper and middle course of the Niger. In these regions, they had clashed with well-known Muslim leaders who had brought together large armies to oppose them. The conquest of the Volta, both east and west, had been relatively easy.

On closer inspection this comparison does not hold in every respect. The opposition to the French in the Samo and Bwa zones of the Volta region, though it did not produce big-name enemy leaders like Ahmadu Seku or Samori, was fierce. Despite numerous setbacks, including the most striking one — the anticolonial war of 1915 — the early colonial view that society in the west Volta was fragmented, politically divided, "anarchic" in the sense of weak, persisted. It also influenced the social-science literature that came into being after 1960.

The idea of a "disorganized" west Volta region finds pithy expression in a 1902 report from Bobo-Dioulasso. The administrator first complains of the difficulty in making the villagers do anything because they cannot reach consensus on any issue. Then he draws from this an optimistic conclusion: "Because people do not know to band together to obey, we can surmise that they

30

will also not know how to rally into threatening masses to resist us. They have too many conflicts of interest among themselves for that."[1]

This perceived fragmentation was partly an illusion created by the multiplicity of ethnic labels and partly the result of the French conquest itself. The regional links and flows had been disrupted when the French destroyed, or absorbed as allies, the most significant local political actors. In this area, after the occupation the French were observing a "part society" that could no longer operate as before, because broader organizational linkages were fractured. The generative principles of those structures, however, were still alive, and the inability to see them behind the interminable village meetings had a heavy cost for the French in 1916.

THE INVENTION OF THE VILLAGE IN THE WEST VOLTA

The ethnographic works written on parts of the vast zone between the Muhun and Bani Rivers present the village as the outstanding unit of sociopolitical organization. We will present first this view and a brief analysis of what these villages are like, and then show why an exclusive focus on the village encourages a narrow view of community life.

The villages of the populations described under the rubrics of Bwa, Bobo, Marka, Minyanka, Samogo, or Gurunsi impress outsiders first with their architectural style. Until a very recent past, these were large, compact settlements, with populations ranging from one thousand to seven or eight thousand, sometimes enclosed within a freestanding defensive wall. When there was no enclosure, houses shared side walls to form rows, the thick back walls of which served the same purpose. These walls were tall and crenellated, continuing above the level of the flat roofs. On the inner side of the exterior wall, people could stand on the roofs, which they used as parapets. The entire complex presented the appearance of a fortress and had a manifest defensive purpose. Socially, these villages included heterogeneous populations with complex forms of self-administration. Multiple hierarchies existed side by side, cross-cutting each other, grounded in generation and age seniority, in anteriority of settlement, and in the custodianship of shrines.

A milestone study that brought to wider awareness the significance of the village in the social topography of this region was a comparative essay written by J. Gallais (1960). He noted in this work that in an extensive portion of West Africa defined by the large bend of the Niger River, between the drier zones of the Sahel and the fringes of the forest, the village is the typical form of settlement, independently from ethnicity or linguistic affiliation. The village, he further postulated, is not only a physical arrangement, but a distinct form of sociopolitical organization. In this characterization, Gallais was in fact continuing a theme of the colonial administration, which saw the village as a collectivity with "a soul, a mind of its own" (Royer 1996, p. 116). In his exposition, Gallais took note of the contrast that the anthropologists commonly make between centralized and segmentary societies. At the edges of the band of territory he defined—that is, among the Mose in the east and on the borders of the Niger in the west—one finds historically political forms that could be called kingdoms. But in the between areas, one finds nothing of the sort—only villages, autonomous settlements, with no political tie to connect them to each other. They were just placed side by side, and the entire region was dotted with them, "like a mosaic of monotonous color."

The village differed from the classical segmentary system of anthropologists in that kinship was not the dominant principle on which it stood. Kinship did not govern membership in the community or shape the form taken by administration. The village was a distinct territorial and political organization. What made the villages of this region somewhat similar to the segmentary lineages of the anthropologists was that they constituted the outer limit of political regulation. Villages, like segmentary groups, resulted in a pattern of minuscule social scale. Village society was a kind of acephalous social organization, even though nonrelatives lived together in large agglomerations. Gallais's notion of village altered the contrast between segmentary and centralized political systems, resulting in a tripartite classification of African societies—segmentary lineage, village, and centralized/kingdom—which took hold of the literature in the 1960s. Of the three, the village was the most useful descriptive tool for those who worked on the western Sudan.

Gallais proposed a continuum to take account of the variability in the constitution of villages, presented somewhat as a microevolutionary series, at least in concept if not in actual history, but most importantly with each step corresponding to a particular modality of political organization. At one end was the "galactic settlement," large domestic groups of thirty to fifty adult members living each in a stand-alone compound separated from its neighbors by farms and unoccupied land. A thick grid of footpaths connected the compounds within a radius of about five hundred meters, and this conglomerate constituted a ward. Several wards, in turn, were recognized as a village. This pattern is described for the Kabre of northern Togo and the Dagari of southern Burkina Faso.

The middle of the continuum was a more concentrated form of habitat where the compounds constituting the ward were built next to each other. The wards themselves were still separated by empty spaces, and the radius of this semidispersed village could extend to two kilometers. This pattern is typical of Minyanka country and of the Dogon. Finally, at the far end of the continuum, was the fully clustered village. Not only the compounds but the wards, too, were built near each other, and the result was a town with a bustling social life. The population often numbered more than a thousand.

Around the Muhun River, which was the center stage for the war of 1915–16, the villages fall somewhere in between the second and third patterns identified by Gallais. It is not always simple, however, to assign a village to one or the other of these types, and here one encounters the limits of this typology. In some cases, the wards of a village were separated only by a narrow path; in other cases they were built at a distance of one or two kilometers (see the village maps drawn by colonial authorities—4 and 5 in chap. 5, and 7 to 17 in chap. 7). Many villages possessed a kernel made up of wards close to each other, and then one or two distant outlying wards. Gallais's essay was a fresh departure, opening up the topic of political organization to new vistas beyond the acephalous/centralized dichotomy, but the promise was only half fulfilled. Absorbed into ethnology with essentialist assumptions, his village types were turned into cultural traits. The ethnic titles given to the types of settlement implied that they were the result of unchanging ethnocultural preferences and not of the historical development depending on contingent factors.

The wards and villages of the Volta region have actually been more transient in form than is implied in this ethnographic version, and they therefore cannot possess the conceptual centrality that we might be tempted to attribute to them. An entire ward of a village could move closer to or away from other wards, or its population could simply migrate to another village. Common in the region are artificial hills representing old ruins, and there are also many former village shrines that sometimes still receive occasional ritual attention from descendants of former inhabitants. Names of old settlements that have disappeared bestrew the bush: they are among the first landmarks an outsider trying to find a path in unfamiliar territory is likely to be taught.

Although the massiveness of the architecture conceals this constant shuffling of settlement sites, the history of successive moves is sometimes inscribed in the very physical structures. One such architectural element can be seen in the thick posts that support the heavy roof terraces and the rooms built on top of them. Such timbers—tree trunks selected from a handful of tree species that give resistant wood—constituted valuable inherited property, and when a house was abandoned or destroyed the posts were carefully salvaged; thus, many posts carry traces of the settlement past in their soot-covered surfaces. Ask an elderly man about the posts in his house and you are likely to hear a long story. He may explain that they came from the house of his father, which was at such and such a place, who in turn inherited them from *his* father, who lived in yet another place. Great uncles and aunts may get into the story, and you will be given a string of place-names that indicate the peregrinations of his ascendance in the last two or three generations and that can take you to the middle of the nineteenth century. The family telling the tale do not need to be "foreigners," immigrants, or other category of transients; on the contrary, probably they will present themselves as "owners" of the village or as a member of a senior group in it. The multitude of place-names is not the sign of marginal experience for an uprooted minority but of the large degree of spatial mobility that is characteristic of the majority.

This high mobility and the mutations that settlements undergo from one type to another are the result of strong fissiparous tendencies within the villages. Far from being the stable social entities they are sometimes assumed to be, the villages are ridden with strife and tension. The villages were composite units, and so were the wards within them. A ward was divided into distinct residential areas, which we can call neighborhoods. Each neighborhood had a core population made up of people who migrated into the ward together. Later-arriving client groups often augmented this core. The neighborhoods of a ward carried proper names and maintained their separate identity for several generations. If conflict were to erupt in the village, these neighborhood groups were generally the parties pitted against each other. It was such conflicts that motivated people to move from one ward to another, or even to a different village. If they grew in numbers, the people of a neighborhood could decide to separate themselves from the parent community, move out, and organize themselves as a separate ward. In this manner, over time not only the physical layout but also the internal configuration of a village changed. Some villages lost constituent segments, while others, conversely, gained them or integrated the existing ones more tightly.

The neighborhoods themselves consisted of smaller segments. They were agglomerates of unrelated groups that stayed together essentially by political agreement, such as a pact made among the ancestors or a host/guest arrangement. These smaller groups had proximate origins in a nearby location, although they might also declare remote origins in a faraway place. The pacts accounted for the solidarity and explained the ranking within the neighborhood.

The smallest segments within the neighborhood are generally presented as patrilineal descent units, making the ward a collection of small, unrelated descent groups. In certain parts of the Volta region, especially in its southern half, people acknowledge both matrilineal and patrilineal sets. Then the pattern fits what has been well described in the literature as double descent. The small agnatic groups in a neighborhood have descent ties with people in other wards and other villages. These are not always mobilized for social and political purposes, or are mobilized only in a small, circumscribed zone where communication across villages is frequent.[2] But the effective constituents of a ward were in fact not these small descent groups but larger social units referred to in most languages of the region as "houses." A house includes several domestic groups collaborating in farming and ritual matters, perhaps even holding collective claims to territory. In most cases, the households constituting a house are not all related to each other by descent. The house can be seen as a confederation of unrelated lineage segments. At the same time, people may recognize patrilineal and matrilineal ties, and these segments may consider themselves to be so related to other segments in different houses, in different wards, and in different villages.

The picture is further complicated by bilateral ties among people who belong to different cells within the house. It was common, for example, for a nephew to be adopted in his maternal uncle's household and end up as an adult member there. This kind of integration was into the household and did not replace or obliterate the patrilineal identity rooted in a chain of filial successions; it did not make the adopted man or his descendants agnates of the uncle's line. Such nonagnate relatives were sometimes married to one of the "daughters" of the house, duplicating ties and reproducing them for the next generation. A house can form around a core that is presented as a true descent group; the core agnates would be the first to arrive (as is explained in a story given below), and they then attract other individuals and families as clients. The clients then constitute the house's periphery. Alternatively, a house may result from a foundational pact among two or three small lineage segments.[3] It was also possible for a house to form without a descent-defined core element, starting with an amorphous social aggregate.

Oral accounts in parts of the Volta region suggest that, two or three hundred years ago, people in this area lived in smaller and more dispersed settlements.

Thus, Gallais's typology may actually correspond to historical development as well as to synchronic observation. The instability of settlement in the past is revealed in fuzzy toponymy today. A name can be presented as both that of a ward and, in another context, that of a village in its own right.[4]

The standard narratives of village foundation recognize and sanction the heterogeneity of the village. In many of them, the settlement starts with two hunters. At first, the two hunters do not know each other. When they meet, they argue about the right of first arrival. One of them deceives the other to concede this right.[5] These stories confirm rank differentiation among the oldest families of the village, but they also indicate that the ritualized village space requires at least two unrelated partners.[6] At one level, they ground the privileges of first-comers; at another, they affirm the structure of the village and the joint interests of the founding houses against those who arrived more recently.

The sequence of arrivals is an important piece of knowledge shared by most people in the village. The heterogeneity of the village community reveals itself also in what is taken into consideration in this ranking. A house is ranked according to the seniority of its leading segment. A house, including its more junior cells, is ranked in the public space of the village according to the seniority of its leading segment. From the outside, all the free members of a house are treated as substitutable for each other. The sequence of arrival in the village corresponds to the distribution of politico-ritual tasks among the houses of the village. Each house can then negotiate the allocation among its constituent social cells of the politico-ritual tasks that it holds. If status differences correlate with the possession or custodianship of ritual tasks, this differentiates family lines only within the house. In the public space of the village, all members of the house share in the burden and glory associated with holding such offices or ritual tasks.

Each new group that arrives to settle in the village brings with it particular skills, special worldly and ritual competencies. Some of these were put at the disposal of the rest of the community. Such adoptions lead to modifications in the ritual topography of the village by accretion. As the mystical patrimony of shrines and cults changes, so do the celebrations associated with them, and every village has a different ritual calendar. Where blacksmiths and bards existed, they became clients to one of the established houses. Some people were incorporated into the houses as captives, but they had possibilities for social enhancement after a generation, even though no acknowledged way could reverse their inferior ritual status. One mechanism that improved their lot was the assumption of offices of common interest, which their original freemen custodians found too onerous or dangerous in its proscriptions. The transfers of shrine offices also tied the village community together.

Despite this symbolic exchange, on the whole villages were delicate constructs. The boundaries between their constituent elements did not dissolve easily. Villages were vulnerable to periodic crises and could lose entire segments. When internal tension combined with external pressure, a village could explode along the existing fault lines. Oral histories in the west Volta report many village names that survive only in memory, as points of origin of particular groups, no longer locatable on a map with certainty. Capron coined the phrase "a civilization of villages" for this area. On the basis of these memories, it would perhaps be equally appropriate to call it "a civilization of vanished villages."

To understand the external pressures on the village, we need to turn to a discussion of extravillage ties. We review here two different kinds of ties that are most relevant to the 1915–16 anticolonial movement: ties in the ritual domain and ties of a political nature.

RITUAL TIES AMONG VILLAGES

Various sorts of ritual ties exist among the villages in the Volta region. We focus here on only one of these, the type that derives from settlement history. We explained that among people of various ethnic origins, a widely shared cultural element is the formal recognition of a founding house in every village. Similarly, in a particular area people recognize a founding *village*. The founding village of an area is the one that was established before all the others. The founding house of this village is considered anterior, and senior, to the founding houses of the other villages in the zone.

In order to show how the shrines come into existence and how the circumstances of their genesis connect them to each other, we will outline here the standard discourse about a presumably unpopulated and wild area. Settlement in a territory depends on successful contact with the spirits of the land; hence, the recognition of anteriority and seniority is grounded in the relationship between people and natural and mystical resources. The first settlers founded the original village because they were successful in establishing such contact by discovering the initial shrine. Later settlers asked the custodians of the same shrine to intercede on their behalf with the spirit, and the descendants of the later settlers now still depend on the custodians of the initial shrine. The settlement history, which is recorded in stories, establishes, therefore, a kind of parish of earth spirits, focused on a shrine that constitutes its central point. This "parish" stretches toward an ill-defined boundary at the periphery. The people who hold this first shrine become "owners of the earth" for the entire zone, and as villages come and go, these shrines become the relatively constant references in the landscape.

As an area becomes populated, more recently founded villages gain autonomy from the first village by establishing new vegetation shrines. Around a more recent shrine, a new parish will develop, based on the territory of the new founding village. The original shrine retains seniority over later shrines and its custodian continues to perform functions essential to the well-being of the entire region. The memory of the sequence in which the villages were founded thus provides a basis for a ritual hierarchy among the earth shrines and also preserves the entire set of villages as a socioreligious unit. This is a shadowy reality, however, and is not always manifest; it will have only weak political content. The significant point for us is that such dormant seniority of an old shrine can become a support for a regionwide project, if the project is motivated by other considerations as well.

In most Marka villages, the shrine that "rules" over the territory is called *suru.* This shrine is often located in a grove on the outskirts of the village. The person in charge of this shrine is called the *masa,* a word that in the languages of the Mande family has a set of strong connotations. In the Manding language it combines the meanings of both political and ritual function, the social referent leaning toward one pole or the other in different parts of West Africa (see Royer 1996, chap. 3 for a full discussion). In Marka ethnography, *masa* could be translated, without too much distortion, as "custodian of the earth." But the masa is also the symbolic axis of the village and is also spoken of as its ruler. Each village has its own masa, but the masa of the first suru shrine has ascendancy over those of the other villages of the area.[7]

As an example, we can look at the territory that lies south of the portion of National Highway 14 in Burkina Faso between Koudougou and Dedougou (map 2). This small area has special relevance to our discussion because the villages of Bona, Datomo, Tunu, and Yankaso, from which came the initial leadership of the anticolonial movement, are part of it, as is Safane, which became an ally of the colonial government and turned against them. This territory can be identified as lying in a quadrilateral measuring forty kilometers north to south and twenty kilometers east to west. A small plain, drained by several seasonal waterways that flow northeast by north toward the Muhun River, the area includes a cluster of about fifty villages. Relatively empty zones of slightly more heavily wooded savanna separate this zone from similar clusters of villages to east and west.

The oldest village of the cluster is Banu, which is known as Masa-du koro (old masa village). The masa of Banu today still performs periodical ceremonies over the suru shrine of his village, which are said to bring rains and prosperity to all the other villages of the cluster. For this reason, it is also said that Banu "rules" over the other villages.[8] In the following discussion, it will be clear that, even in the nineteenth century, this "rule" had little political content, and no relationship to defense alliances.

The masa of Banu did, however, act as intercessor in some economic and social contexts for the villages of the plain. In cases of land conflict, they came to him as the final arbiter. He had no way of enforcing his decision, but his judgment on these matters carried weight. Also, where there were markets, their smooth operation depended on the will of the agencies of the earth; therefore, it was necessary for the masa of Banu to perform ceremonies for them. The five-day cycle market of Safane, for example, could not open until a representative of the masa of Banu arrived.

The type of association that formed around the senior village of Banu, although backed by strong ritual sanctions and anxieties, appears toothless when compared to unions formed by smaller sets of villages with defensive purposes. This second type of union is now only a memory in the region, but late-nineteenth-century explorers commented upon them as a living reality. Gustave Binger learned about them from his hosts in the part of his trip through Nienegue (southern Bwa) country, and he described them as village confederations.[9] In recent ethnographic works, these village unions are referred to as leagues.

DEFENSIVE LEAGUES

In the southern sector of the plain defined by Banu's ritual preeminence, at the end of the nineteenth century twelve villages formed such a defensive league (see map 2). This league became known to colonial observers because it was led by Bona and formed the kernel of the anticolonial movement of 1915. Commandant Maguet, the administrator of Dedougou, wrote in his report on the origins of the war:

> Bouna still effectively rules the villages that the administration included in
> the canton of Datomo because they are of its family headed by Yssou. Bouna
> maintains all over Marka country the authority deriving from its earlier

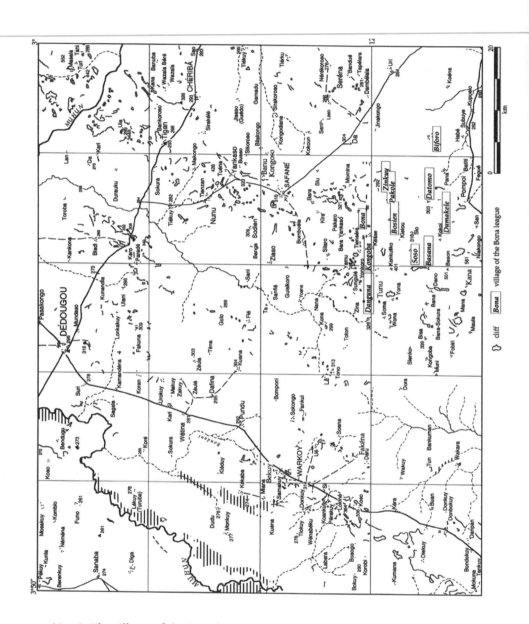

Map 2. The villages of the Bona league.

successes against the Ko population, and especially against the marabout of
Ouahabou, who wanted to subjugate the villages of the Volta [Muhun River]
bend to Islamic domination, but was after much effort driven back toward
Leo, and also against invaders coming from beyond the Volta who rushed to
the help of the defeated marabout, but who after having come as far as Safane
were thrown back to the other side of the Volta river, thanks to the Marka
coalition. In these happy events, Bouna played the principal role.[10]

The mid-nineteenth-century events to which this passage refers—the battles
with the marabout of Wahabu (Ouahabou, in the original) and his Zaberma allies from the south—will be explained in chapter 2. This information on the
coalition led by Bona, deriving from Maguet's report, was first presented in
print by Hébert (1970, 18).

According to the list provided by the present-day elders of the village, the
coalition of Bona included eleven other villages: Kongoba, Datomo, Bosien,
Pakole, Zinkuy, Sokurani, Dumakele, Soso, Danguna, Basana, and Biforo.[11]
Based on this list we can make a few observations on the relationship between
the political ties of "league" and the ritual connections explained above. First,
the villages in this confederation are fewer in number than those under the ritual
jurisdiction of Banu. Second, the overlap between the two sets is only partial.
The confederation of Bona includes villages belonging to two separate areas of
ritual jurisdiction: most of the twelve belong to the "parish" of Banu (although
Banu itself was not part of the confederation), but a few others belong to another parish. In this second group we find the village of Danguna, which itself
had a suru shrine of great reputation, acting as focus for another set of villages
that constituted a ritual circle similar to the one formed around Banu. In other
words, while Bona was ritually under the authority of Banu, as a military-
political leader it had a following among villages that were not part of the same
suru parish. Among its junior partners was Danguna, which possessed a shrine
that was focus for a different ritual circle. The political league that Bona led
thus straddled two parishes.

In November 1915 the anticolonial leaders of Bona and the other villages of
its league were able to articulate these different kinds of ties. To gather the extraordinary assemblies that launched the war, they mobilized first the connections around the shrine of Banu and then those around the shrine of Danguna.
They were thus able to forge an alliance for the anticolonial cause that was much
broader in scope than the original league around Bona. Without this broader participation from the very beginning, which made possible the military resistance

to the French in Bona and then in Yankaso, it is hard to imagine that the anti-colonial movement would have snowballed the way it did.

Local traditions assert that Bona's leadership came after that of another league that was lead by a village that no longer exists (Blegna 1990, 39–40). This village—called Son-non, according to some people, and located between Fakena and Dora—was destroyed in wars with its neighbors.[12] Son-non's "clans and lineages" were dispersed and became founders of new villages. The village of Tunu, which seconded Bona as leader of the league, was founded by a lineage from Son-non. The village of Danguna, which was already prominent as a military center at the time of Son-non, became another secondary leader of the league under Bona. In fact, Ble, Yaho, Tunu, and the villages located in the hilly zone to the south were allied as a subconfederation under Danguna's leadership. It is noteworthy that Danguna—the site of the prestigious suru shrine mentioned above—and Tunu allowed Bona, as their ally, to straddle the villages of two distinct ritual areas.

A third league to the west of this area was under the leadership of Tena. It included Komo, Fie, Kuana, and Dafina. According to Fabegna Koulibaly (1970, 44–45), the first Marka village in this zone was Gnemere, which no longer exists. Lead by the Konate, who were supported by professional fighters invited from elsewhere, Gnemere dominated in its heyday the entire area within the bend of the Muhun River. Gnemere was eventually destroyed by some kind of curse, and its leading families moved to Kerebe, where the Konate military prominence continued. At this point, a new category of actors enters the scene. A Muslim cleric and his student came to settle in Kerebe. He built a famous school and a mosque surrounded with miraculous narratives of holiness which brought to Kerebe a prestigious Islamic center.

In these traditions we find the principle elements of the regional political configuration: 1. A village with an outstanding military reputation as the leader of client villages constituting a confederation; 2. A leading house that exercises leadership for several generations and outlives the existence of its original village; 3. Groups specializing in warfare and invited to settle in a village by its leading families; 4. Finally, an Islamic cleric who founds a religious sector in a village of non-Muslim founding families and who contributes by providing mystical services and his reputation for knowledge.

These traditions also suggest how the different confederations were loosely linked by the existence of different ties among member villages. These ties created possibilities for interrupting rivalries and creating broader unions. As in the internal constitution of a village, some intervillage ties were strong and survived periods of tension, although their meaning changed over time; others were more transient and arose in response to contingencies. For example, on separate occasions and in different villages we were told that the founders of Banu and Safane were classificatory brothers. These comments were perhaps motivated by the desire to overcome a tension between these two towns, because some bitterness remains from having joined opposite sides during the anticolonial war of 1915–16. The rift needs to be patched up, but as explained above, Banu and Safane were already part of the same ritual cycle, and the legacy of the war has not changed this link. The talk of brotherhood is not now without a practical counterpart: the prominent families of Safane who currently have a member in the parliament assisted Banu in gaining redress for wrongs dating back to the aftermath of the anticolonial movement.

Membership in the military alliances was not permanent. The driving force behind each confederation was the hegemonic ambitions of its leading village or villages. Looked at in another way, there were two strata of villages in the region: a minority of strong villages, which became the leaders, and the rest, which were the clients. The game of domination and intimidation took place among strong villages, but they dragged into it the weaker villages that followed them. In the course of time, the benefits and losses of these rivalries changed the relative strength of villages. A defeat made a strong village lose followers, and the followers often joined the winner's side. The fluidity of the membership of a confederation went together with, and amplified, reversals in fortune.

Other factors gave village confederations some historical continuity. Once they emerged, the confederated blocs constituted a structure of opposition that self-perpetuated. The most important villages often survived their client villages and constituted the enduring core of rival camps, while the weaker partners had a more ephemeral existence. Also, when a once-powerful leading village was destroyed, another village rose to fill its place by gathering around itself the discombobulated clients of the former. When Gnemere disappeared, Kerebe succeeded to its vacated position; Bona's leadership was, according to Blegna's account, a continuation of the position of Son-non.

The possession of a prominent shrine did not guarantee a village military superiority. As already seen, Bona's rise was not hampered by its ritually junior status, compared to Banu. Another example of the contrast between these different varieties of rank is found in the zone around Durula. The founder of this village, Pamba Soare, by force of arms compelled the dignitaries of Kerebe, who were his ritual superiors, to take an oath of alliance with him. He also subdued his original hosts in the village of Sa. Thus, the Soare, "last comers to the region, became the absolute masters, even though their village was the most recently founded one" (Koulibaly 1970, 46).

Ritual preeminence and military superiority were grounded in different considerations. At the same time, the ascendancy of centers that were militarily better endowed did not render obsolete the ties based on ritual seniority. At particular historical conjunctures, it was possible for the two planes of ranking to reinforce each other. The leaders of the anticolonial movement seized this possibility in 1915. Before launching their broader campaign, they organized their first decisive meetings at the suru shrine of venerated Danguna (chap. 5).

Since affiliation with a league was sometimes imposed on its weaker partners by threats, the ranking of villages within the league was an important part of the social landscape. Then a league could be more or less strong, compared with other leagues. It could take a more aggressive stance and try to dominate other villages—for example, destroy a leading rival village to absorb its clients. Alternatively, it could take a more defensive stance. The balance of power shifted quickly in this local game, partly because villages maintained their autonomy. Even the weakest village was ultimately an independent agent, and its population had to make decisions after a long series of palavers. A weak village could be bullied, but it did not thereby lose its distinctive political identity. It did not dissolve within a political structure dominated by the strong. By deciding to join a league, a village affirmed its political independence, because entering a pact is engaging in an act of diplomacy. This pact could be revoked, and a village changed allegiance when it faced new pressures or found new opportunities.

The ups and downs of the Marka village of Fobiri in the second half of the nineteenth century illustrate this possibility (Blegna 1990). Initially, Fobiri and many other villages were set against Yaho, which, as mentioned above, was a strong village following the leadership of Danguna. Yaho attacked Fobiri to punish it for sheltering refugees from a village it had destroyed. As a result of these conflicts, Fobiri was deserted and repopulated eight times. By the end of the nineteenth century, Yaho managed to subdue most of its opponents and reduce them to the status of clients. This was the case with Fobiri, too. But the villages of Mamu and Bondo still opposed Yaho, which now put them in a position of being enemies of Fobiri and some other former allies. When the French arrived in this region in 1897, this was the situation that they found.

North of the area that we have discussed so far, in the surroundings of Dedougou, we find the same instability in village alliances (a history known thanks to the accounts written down by Jean Cremer, shortly before the devastation of the anticolonial war of 1915).[13] Three strong villages appear as the leaders of the contending leagues: Dedougou, Pasakongo, and Kari. In the beginning, Dedougou "owned" Fakuna and Longakuy. But Longakuy left Dedougou and joined Pasakongo following a fight between one of its men and a man from Fakuna. Dedougou responded by attacking its former client, which did not receive the support it hoped for from its new ally. Longakuy was overwhelmed and reentered the orbit of Dedougou. Leading villages promoted good relations among their followers and also received some tangible benefits of leadership. Following the reconciliation, when Longakuy brought to Dedougou the customary sacrificial chicken, Dedougou asked Longakuy to take the chicken to Fakuna as an apology and to repair the damaged ties. Fakuna, in turn, brought this chicken, plus a goat of their own, to Dedougou (Cremer 1924, 130–31).

The gifts that a village leading a coalition received from its followers were often disguised as sacrifices for rituals and oaths. But the value of these gifts was also small, and it is hard to imagine that they constituted the main motivation for spending so much energy on politics. The dominant villages were respected and feared. Most conflicts between members of these dominant villages and people of other villages were resolved to the advantage of the former because of the fear of reprisals: a reputation for strength was thus the more important gain. Benefits that were even greater were obtained from the warring activity itself: booty or captives in conflicts with enemies or from perpetual low-scale banditry. Villagers with strong fighting companies could also attack and loot caravans that did not belong to a strongman with whom they were associated. In the politics of supremacy, palpable benefits were at stake, but there is no evidence that land itself was taken or that political dominion was instituted.

This regional configuration affected the internal affairs of the villages. The claims and threats of competing strong centers provoked dissension, and even splits, in weaker villages. Within each of the villages, the leading houses were near equals. Decisions were taken by the consensus of the elders representing the houses, and it was not possible to impose conformity within the village. The threat of force could not be used as long as the village functioned as a community. A group within a village could take the initiative and engage in a course of action without the approval of the rest; thus, it could put at risk all the other groups. A segment of the village could dissociate itself from the rest and even participate in intrigues against its other segments. Villages could be drawn into messy conflicts by the unilateral acts of a small minority. Then again, a village in trouble with outsiders could use lack of consensus as an excuse to open negotiations. As a strategy rather than as a result of disorganization, part of a village could take an aggressive stance while the other part acted conciliatory. In hard confrontation with

outside forces, there was often a party in reserve, ready to step forward if developments were unfavorable and try to save what they could by blaming those who
had started the confrontation. This strategy did not always work because all parties
were aware of how internal dissension was manipulated; hence, again, the risk for
all villagers who were drawn into confrontations they were unable to stop.

Intervillage associations and leagues were not limited to the Marka and Bwa
areas within the elbow of the Muhun River; they were also found outside of this
zone and in different linguistic and ethnic settings. Françoise Héritier (1973),
who worked in the region lying north of the river, provided a detailed study of
a broad union that collected a large number of Samo villages around the *dondana*
shrine in the village of Go. She described how, within this broad ritual union,
smaller sets of villages established military alliances, very much like the situation
within the bend of the Muhun River. Hubbell (1997, 110, 145) also writes of
the unions that emerge around dondana shrine villages. He explains that the
smaller military confederations contained, in the nineteenth century, the predatory activities of the war chief Usman Umaru, who was based in Luta. In his
Bobo ethnography, Le Moal (1980, 37) briefly mentions that the villages were
in the habit of forming confederations with each other and some of them also
built mutual relations of support with strong war and trade leaders, such as those
in Dokuy and Barani. He notes that the organized nature of the 1915–16 war
can be understood by reference to these confederations.

The politics of village alliances did not exhaust the type of links that existed
above the village level. The village leagues could become part of a broader movement when a military center acquired an uncommon level of strength and engaged
in more ambitious political projects. Well-documented instances of this are few for
the west Volta region, and consequently historians and ethnographers tend to
imply that whenever such broader movements emerged they were due to some
"foreign" disturbance imagined as a "conquest." The next section shows how hegemonic ambitions could result from the internal working of village league politics. The activities of powerful leaders who cannot be considered "foreign," such
as the Karantao or Gandiari (discussed in chap. 2), were extensions of, or simply
better documented cases of, the type of process described in this next section.

THE INSTITUTION OF WAR

Villages in the Volta region were diverse, because in the course of time each
community absorbed different kinds of groups. Some of them were warfare

specialists, and some of these people were organized as bands. As they roamed around seeking adventure, they would engage in small-scale predatory activities at the expense of the farmers, trading the proceeds of their activities. They were usually a motley collection. Some might be free volunteers, brought together by a forceful leader, but a successful band could acquire captives or purchase slaves, thus increasing the number of fighters. Captives could also be set to farm work to feed their masters. Sooner or later, such bands settled down, affiliating themselves either with a village that invited them or with a more imposing military leader. After that the military band would go through a process of "peasantization" as leaders acquired wives and children and established extensive farms and houses. The settled guests would assume the ethnic traditions of their hosts and exchange spouses with them. They became a house, in the sense used above, and in time its core would take the form of a descent group that perpetuated itself, but despite these accommodations these guests were encouraged to retain their specialization in warfare.

The village of La, which played a pivotal role in the war of 1915–16, is an illustrative example of the complex evolution of specific communities within this framework. La now includes some people who declare themselves to be Bwa and others who consider themselves Marka, but it was founded by a group originating in the village of Satiri, carrying the patronymic Traore. Satiri is culturally Bobo, but is more specifically dominated by the Zara, people of Bobo speech, who claim Jula-Mande origins and who are associated with trade and fighting. At some point in the past, in a period of intense fighting with the neighboring villages of Fakuy and Sokongo, the Traore of La asked the Tambure, who are described as a band of warriors who possessed horses, to settle down with them. Today the Tambure of La are divided into two branches: one of these supplies the masa of the village; the other branch alternates with the founding house of Traore in filling the office of perenkie, the head of the fighting-age youth in the village (see below). La also had an important contingent of Bwa blacksmiths.[14] The remarkable activity of these blacksmiths can be gauged from the two large slag mounds found in the old location of the village. The pattern of recruitment to the offices of masa and perenkie is particular to the village of La and the result of its particular history; it is not representative of the region.

Cheriba, another prominent village of the 1915–16 war, offers a contrast to La. Cheriba also participated in the nineteenth century in wars against the Karantao. It is divided into two sections, including in all a total of nine wards. One section is led by the ward Masabe, which, as its name implies, supplies the masa. Of the four remaining wards of this section, one is Marka, two are Nuna, and one houses the traders of the masa, Masabe Zulaw. The second section of the village is led by the ward Tinabe and includes two other Marka wards and one Nuna ward.

According to oral accounts, Cheriba suffered from raids by outsiders. Rumor maintained that these raids were facilitated by insider collaborators, people who owned horses and wealth in the village and who were suspected of colluding with the raiders. At some point, the masa settled a group of Mose people at the outskirts of the village as a buffer against these marauders. Then another military group was invited to the village. The latter did not engage in agriculture but kept a stock of weapons, spent all their days practicing martial arts, and trained the youth of the village in the art of fighting. The farming population of the village contributed food to supplement what the fighters' slaves produced. Thanks to these arrangements, Cheriba was strong militarily and led a confederation, which at some point included twenty-one villages.[15]

The inclusion of fighting groups and the concern with defense had implications for the internal organization of the village. The strongest communities became militarized, their farming population becoming part-time soldiers, and many other communities emulated the pattern. Youths were trained for physical endurance, and cycles of initiation were punctuated by ceremonies that regulated adult life. The shrines and masquerades linked to the complex of practices centered around initiation lends an aura of exoticism to the cultures of the west Volta, but this impression is misleading: many elements of this complex are mimetic transfers from Islam, indicating that the ceremonies had a connection to warfare and defense (Saul 1997a). Among the Marka, juveniles are recognized as adults when the first member of their class marries. Then they all become *kambele,* the fighting men under the authority of a small set of adults. This organization cuts across the distinctions between the houses and descent groups that are the constitutive elements of the ward and village. The age groups and their training and education was the arena where the diverse groups displayed trust in each other to participate in the common political project of the village. At the head of the class of kambele is the perenkie, who operates under the authority of the masa. A council, called the *perendew* (the children of the peren) assists him. All men of the community were integrated into this structure, and this gave the entire community a military tilt. The distance between the horse-riding professional warrior and the peaceful farmer was not very large.

Depending on the historical particulars of each village, the way the masa and perenkie are chosen differs from one community to the other. We saw that in La the office of masa was entrusted to one section of the Tambure, who were professional fighters, but this is uncharacteristic for the region. Warrior groups were usually not offered the office of masa; in most cases, the older houses of the village retained this office. The perenkie almost always belonged to a ward different from that of the masa. According to the explanation given in Cheriba, for example, a long time ago in that village the perenkie was selected from the same ward as the masa. But the "foreigners" (more recent settlers) of the village thought that the masa abused his authority. In order to prevent them from leaving the village, the founding houses decided to break the concentration of powers and transferred the office of perenkie to one of the Nuna wards of the village, where it is still held today. In Banu, where the office of masa carries more responsibility because of the significance of its suru shrine, the masa always comes from the founding house of the village. It is passed from father to son, and consequently the other five wards of that village are excluded from it. In Bona, the offices of masa and perenkie alternate between the wards of Kimaabe and Dawabe, with the condition that the two should not come from the same ward at the same time. The smaller ward of Blaabe serves as enthronizer, but is not able to supply either office.

In most cases, warrior groups integrated in the villages remained subordinate to the founding houses that invited them there. The founders maintained the control of the important protective shrines and central cult activities. But when warrior groups prospered, they were tempted to establish their own separate villages. Many people who adopted the patronymic Kulibali in the west Volta region are descended from professionals organized as military corporations, and some of these Kulibali also founded villages.

Warrior groups that prospered and were popular as allies among many villages could develop ambitions beyond the horizon of the initial village where they were lodged; they could thus embark upon greater adventures. It was in this manner, in the eighteenth and nineteenth centuries, that the groups generally considered under the rubric of Watara put their stamp on the history and ethnic composition of the west Volta (Şaul 1998). Their zone of operations seems to have extended in the late eighteenth century as far north as Jenne. The part of the Volta region that lies within the bend of the Muhun River produced its own pan-regional warrior leaders, although an exact chronology is difficult to establish from oral sources.

An important leader of this type, Ikie Zina, reported by Koulibaly (1970, 40–45), seems to belong to the period before the nineteenth century. Ikie, born in the village of Dafina, left his home place in bitterness as a young man and offered his services to the chief of Gnemere. Ikie returned to Dafina to destroy the village with an army made up of men given to him by his new chief, then took its inhabitants as captives to Gnemere. Ikie waged wars in areas to the west and north of the Muhun River and in places that are now in Mali. Gnemere became an important center in the region because of Ikie's activities. Since early colonial times, the term *Dafina*, which stems from association with Ikie, has underlined the Marka identity of the area within the Muhun bend, but consonant with the region's hybrid layering it is said that Ikie was not Marka. Descendants of Ikie appear today as dignitaries in many villages and occasionally as village founders.

In the nineteenth century, two ambitious hegemonic projects that prompted villages to forge alliances wider than the framework of local leagues were carried out by Muslim clerics. These men diverged from the adjunct role that the clerics generally assumed in symbiotic relationships with dominant villages and powerful war houses. They adopted instead a model of political action that sought legitimacy in the Hijaz, the heartland of Islam. The house of one of these men played an important role in colonial expansion. In the next chapter we turn to these events and to the origins of the French occupation.

CHAPTER 2

The Muslim Houses
of the Volta and the Beginnings
# of French Occupation

IN THE SETTING OF THE WEST VOLTA, Muslim and non-Muslim are rarely discussed together, an unfortunate outcome of academic specialization. But nineteenth-century Muslim clerics and their associates — the topic of this chapter — were the allies or opponents of the intervillage associations described in chapter 1. Muslim and non-Muslim were not two separate, internally coherent sectors of local society. The west Volta region remained predominantly non-Muslim until the 1930s, but during the nineteenth century it received many immigrants, some of whom were Muslims, including clerics and scholars. A number of them arrived from the west and the north, via Jenne; others came from the south, whence they brought a remote Malinke influence. Whatever their origin, they spoke varieties of the Manding language, although some of them traced their ultimate origins to places where Manding was not the language.

For the rest of the population, Muslims served primarily as ritual specialists. They supplied charms and amulets to villagers, and one domain for which these were sought out was warfare. The clerics also acted as emissaries and arbitrators, administered oaths, and became counselors to people who could afford their services. Because they traveled frequently, they brought to local areas news of the wider region and of the world, and shaped opinions. In these ways the clerics were complementary to the houses of warriors and traders. Although the occupation of Muslim cleric tended to remain in the same families, partly because of the lengthy formal education necessary to qualify for it, the boundaries were not drawn hard and fast. Most members of families of clerics (called by the French, indiscriminately, *marabout*) participated in trade, and some became career warriors.

Muslims provided access to the medium of writing for others. They carried out correspondence for themselves and also for rich men and military leaders, allowing a broader use of "the paper as messenger and the pen as tongue."[1] The travel accounts of French explorers of the end of the century bear witness to the importance of the written word for regional diplomacy and safe travel in the West African savanna. Although conversions were few, and were more than compensated for by backsliding, because of these exchanges Islam had a profound cultural influence in the Volta region, recognizable today in more or less muted forms in the vocabulary, beliefs, and practices.

The most renowned scholars had international connections. Many of them traveled to the Levant and Arabia on pilgrimage. The importance of the Hijaz in establishing and maintaining contacts and spreading new ideas within the premodern Islamic world is coming into sharper scholarly focus, and the history of western Sudan both benefits from and contributes to this new awareness. The Muslim clerics also traveled within West Africa, in their youth to study with a master and in their mature years to visit other scholars. Mentor-student relations or spiritual comradeship among clerics from different areas facilitated transregional alliances.

A Muslim cleric who was an immigrant usually settled in a host village with a large group of people, including family members, students, many domestics, and captives. Renowned clerics had extensive farms that were worked by students and slaves. When the Muslims grew in numbers, they tended to move away from the public life of the village to create a distinct neighborhood in the ward or a separate ward in the village. They remained "guests" of particular dignitaries or founding houses of the village, but this arrangement gave them greater freedom to organize their lives according to their own principles.

Because they were clients of non-Muslims, the Muslims of the west Volta did not constitute a political interest group and could not present a common front. When conflict arose, every Muslim dignitary followed his own host and patron, as was the case also with traders and war specialists. Rivalries and ambitions also divided the clerics among themselves. Some large villages even contained two separately organized and rival Muslim communities. In the literature of the Volta region, one commonly encounters phrases such as "important Muslim village." It is therefore important to stress that there were no "Muslim villages" as such, a point of great relevance in understanding certain dynamics of the anticolonial movement of 1915–16. In some villages, a Muslim presence was highly visible, either because there was a large community of Muslims or because a cleric of great reputation lived there. But in those villages, too, the founders and important dignitaries holding the reins of public affairs remained committed to non-Muslim practices, even if they used the services of the Muslims, while considering them subordinate allies.

In 1904, when a French lieutenant, Gondalma, organized a crackdown against the Muslims in the cercle of Koury (renamed the cercle of Dedougou after 1911), he interrogated more than 180 marabouts. Gondalma wrote that at that time there were more than fifty-five villages with a significant Muslim presence. The more important of these were Biforo, Boromo, Dabulara, Danu, Dalono, Dedougou, Jinakongo, Durula, Lanfiera, Nunu, Wahabu, Wele, Uri, Safane, and Sono (Kote 1982, 7). In all of these centers, with the exception of Wahabu, the Muslims were subordinate as "guests" to non-Muslim "hosts."

WAHABU

The case of Wahabu is unique in the west Volta. In the mid-nineteenth century it was the sole attempt at a broader hegemonic political project led by a cleric. Launched by Mahamudu Karantao, it was similar to but smaller in scale than the near-contemporary movements of Usman Dan Fodio and Mohammed Bello in Sokoto and Seeku Amadu in Masina. As in those better-known historical examples, Mahamudu's wars have been described as jihad — that is, religiously motivated struggle. It is important to note in the following discussion, however, that Mahamudu did not clash only with non-Muslims, and that he also had solidarity with some non-Muslims.

Mahamudu Karantao was born in Durula from a line of Muslim clerics from Timbuktu who traced their ancestry further to the Middle East.[2] After studying under a famous teacher in Durula, he went to live in Pura to participate in the gold trade.[3] As was to be expected from a person of his background and disposition, he also undertook study and prayer trips to other Islamic centers in the Volta region, developing friendships and animosities that shaped his later life. Then he heard "the call from the east" and embarked on a long journey. His pilgrimage travels included two separate visits to Mecca and Medina, with a visit to Jerusalem, the second sacred city for Muslims, in between.[4]

When he returned to West Africa, Mahamudu resumed trading in gold between Safane and Pura. Finally, he settled down in the town of Dobakoro, where he established a school. At this point he seems to have manifested

Fig. 1. The oldest mosque in Durula as it stood in June 1998. The mosque is said to have been built by Sidi Karantao, Mahamudu's father, in the first half of the nineteenth century.

greater ambitions. He gathered around him people of various origins — Marka and Winye (Ko) volunteers from the vicinity, Dagari men from Wa in the south, and Mose mercenaries from the north — and launched his first successful attacks against Boromo. Other villages rallied around him. He held the allegiance of most southern Winye villages, but the growing scale of his activities led to broader resistance, drawing people from further away. The mostly Marka villages of Da and Jinakongo led an alliance, including the northern Winye villages, against him (Jacob 1997, 293). The renowned Muslim clerics of these two villages became the nucleus of the opposition, balancing Mahamudu's spiritual authority. It is said that Mahamudu was tempted to attack Durula, his birthplace, but he refrained from doing so when his former mentor miraculously showed to him an army of spirits protecting it (Kote 1982, 86).

The rise of Mahamudu was finally halted in an inconclusive attack against Sokongo, which was fiercely defended by a large number of fighters from a number of villages (on Sokongo see chap. 7, pp 189, 185). Then he suffered a defeat against Bagasi. Mahamudu withdrew to a small village, which he renamed Wahabu and ruled as the head of a vast domestic unit. While his influence diminished, he maintained a reputation for holiness in the region, and he also retained worldly influence over three nearby centers—Boromo, Koho, and Nanu—that were controlled by captains who commanded large contingents of soldiers.

Even in his time of greatest glory, Mahamudu did not try to convert the mass of non-Muslims around him. The villages that recognized his superiority without resistance were left alone.[5] His religious strictures were directed against those who already claimed to be Muslims. In the circles that claim Karantao's heritage today, this lack of insistence on conversion is likened to the similar attitude displayed by the Prophet and his close associates in the seventh-century Arab conquests, which is an exemplary period and source of symbolism for the Karantao. (In the most common interpretation, tolerance of the followers of "the religions of the book"—that is, Christians and Jews—is commendable for a Muslim ruler. In other eras and places, the exemption has been extended to people of other religions, such as Zoroastrians and Buddhists [Kote 1982, 69].)

The descendants of the opponents of Mahamudu saw in his activities thirst for wealth and power. Gustave Binger (1892, 1:416), who passed through that region fifty years after the events described, reflects this opinion in his account. In the 1960s, Nehemia Levtzion (1968, 150) was told by the Muslims of Safane that Mahamudu fought "Muslims and pagans indiscriminately." Twenty years later, Blamami Kote (1982, 64) was told again—by both the traditionalists of Boromo and some Muslims of Safane—that Mahamudu had an ambition to dominate rather than a religious purpose. Louis Tauxier, however, reported that Mahamudu's aggressive campaigns started only when the original residents of Boromo decided to chase him and his students away from Dobakoro.[6]

Taking account of these divergent views, we can try to elucidate some characteristics of Mahamudu's project. Although the Karantao partisans were ruthless against their defeated enemies, they do not seem to have been interested in chasing people away in order to occupy their territory, nor in securing a regular flow of tribute or taxes. There was no attempt to impose administration. As in the similar case of Watara leaders of the Bandama-Volta region, it is evident that dominion over a territory was not Mahamudu's purpose. Apart from his school and religious activities, he maintained companies of armed men led by subordinate commanders. Fighting was undertaken in part to obtain captives and goods of value. Mahamudu's activities cannot be described as conquests. Fighting activity and trade brought the returns that were needed to sustain his military apparatus. The leisure required for study and for training as well as the means to pay for luxuries—books, papers, cloth, rugs, firearms and gunpowder, and other goods, both local and imported—were all obtained in exchange for captives. Firearms and powder were especially important to Mahamudu, who pioneered their widespread use in his region. Nonetheless, the religious motivation cannot be disentangled from the rest of his project. Gustave Binger (1892, 1:427) wrote in Boromo in 1888 that the dominant Mose merchants of that town had come from Yatenga and Ouagadougou "by conviction"—that is, because they were Muslim and were attracted to the Islamic community that Mahamudu had created around him.

There is the question of how much Mahamudu's ambition derived from local models versus extralocal ones. Frontal attacks against stockaded villages were costly, and since a military outfit could not rely only on this type of activity, the small-scale military entrepreneurs of the Niger-Volta region generally avoided high-profile provocations to well-organized villages. Also Mahamudu's partisans indulged in genocidal executions—for example, against the defeated inhabitants of Bole—that are not consistent with the purpose of gain.[7] In some other respects, Mahamudu followed the local style of leadership. He was the strategist and inspiration of the political movement he founded, but he was no autocratic ruler. As in the case of Seeku Amadu in Masina, a council of dignitaries took the decisions in Mahamudu's circle; he voiced opinions but did not give orders.[8] He seldom took part in the fighting personally; his troops were led by his brothers and subordinate fighting chiefs, which is consistent with a widespread west Sudanic pattern (Jansen 1996). Mahamudu also developed his campaign by carefully nurturing alliances with strong villages and powerful leaders and, when possible, taking advantage of their relations with other communities to win wider support.

Mahamudu started his campaign with the support of some people in his native Durula and of the villages situated east of the Muhun River. Dedougou and Pasakongo had first followed Kari to oppose Mahamudu Karantao, but later they capitulated (Cremer 1924b, 145). The Bwa villages of Masala, Sokuy, and Buron joined him under varying degrees of coercion. Kerebe and the large group of villages in its orbit became his followers, and the warrior establishment of Kerebe (mentioned on p. 42 in chap. 1) became the backbone of his army. Some of these ties survived until the twentieth century. In 1916, at the height of the war against the French, La and some other Bwa villages in its vicinity went to Wahabu to obtain war charms from Mahamudu's successor.[9] The Muslims of Wahabu supplied them, although they were officially on the French side and the sworn enemies of the core leadership of the anticolonial movement.

The issue of whether or not to support Mahamudu divided village communities and the Muslims in the region. In Cheriba, internal fighting broke out because, whereas the ward of the masa opposed him, the other wards supported him. In Datomo, the Dao Muslims supported Mahamudu but the other Muslims joined the rest of the population against him. In Jinakongo, the Konate Muslims put their ritual expertise in the service of the enemies of Mahamudu and assumed a leading position in the alliance against him.[10] The Bwa villages of Pundu, Kari, Warkoy, Bondokuy, Samakuy, Bekuy, and Ikonkuy were also part of the leadership that fought against Mahamudu and suffered great destruction. These memories were vivid in 1915 when these villages participated in the anticolonial movement.

A second moment of the Karantao movement came after Mahamudu's death. His successor Karamoko Moktar led an expedition to the south, where he received the support of the Jan of Pura and of some Puguli. He established his influence on Diebougou. In Jinjerma, however, he was defeated by the united forces of other Puguli and Dagara villages.[11] There, he formed an alliance with a Zaberma leader and took him and some of his men back to Wahabu for what turned out to be an eventful episode.

The Zaberma loom large in the descriptions of the troubled final two decades of the nineteenth century in Gurunsi country. Although a considerable amount of information is available on them, they appear generally as peripheral figures — marauders, bands, or raiders who lacked the dignity of being treated as either communities or rulers. Yet they seem to be not much different from the Karantao or other leaders in the broader region who combined commerce, warfare, and Islamic learning.

THE ZABERMA ALLIES

The core of the people who came to be known as the Zaberma were Muslim merchants hailing from the region east of Niamey, who terminated their peregrination in what is now northern Ghana and took to Islamic learning.[12] They also served as mercenary commanders to the political contenders of the area, using their personal following as an army and making widespread use of firearms. This combination of trade and fighting, considered antinomic in other contexts, is a common career pattern in the western Sudan (Şaul 1998). When the Zaberma became stronger, they organized expeditions in all directions from their bases in Sati and Leo, now in southern Burkina Faso, becoming in the

1890s the most important political force. While the activities of the Zaberma in what is now the Burkina Faso–Ghana border region are relatively well known, this is not the case for their adventures further north, around Wahabu-Safane and beyond the Muhun River. Oral traditions and ethnographic accounts from this region differ from the version repeated in most books, both in historical detail and the way they depict the Zaberma.

The received version stems from Louis Tauxier, who gathered accounts about the Zaberma, c. 1905, the earliest to be committed to writing if we exclude Binger's contemporary notes from 1888. According to Tauxier, the Zaberma leader Babato was invited by Moktar Karantao and went north with a force of five thousand, including one thousand mounted men. He attacked Safane but was defeated by a wide coalition of villages (Tauxier 1912, 410; Levtzion 1968, 142; Duperray 1984, 60; Kote 1982, 100). Moktar himself was later defeated in a confrontation against forces of the village of Da and the Muslims of Jinakongo.

In contrast, oral sources from within the bend of the Muhun River and in the Suru valley suggest that the Zaberma leader who was active in this region was Gandiari, not Babato. In our own inquiries, we discovered that the name of Babato provokes no response, whereas the name of Gandiari is volunteered without prompting.[13] Traditions recorded by other researchers go in the same direction. The Winye (Ko) of the Boromo region also remember the name of Moktar's ally as "Gazani" (Jacob 1997). In the Suru valley, villagers described the incursions of "Gãzari" to researchers who were not informed of these historical events and were not inquiring about them (Quéant and de Rouville 1969, 34). In May 1888, Binger was also told in Boromo that the warriors of Gandiari, including people of all nationalities, were moving back and forth in the countryside (Binger 1892, 1:427–28). The passages in Mallam Abu (1992, 87–88), which have been interpreted as referring to Babato's activities around Safane are obscure, because none of the place names can be identified. The "Guni" people that Babato is said to have defeated in Bobo country are hard to link with any known group, and *Bobo* itself is a notoriously vague label that may mean very little when used by someone unfamiliar with the northern Volta region.

Abu Mallam's description of Gazari's sojourn in the Volta is more extensive than this obscure reference to Babato (1992, 102–3). He mentions the town of Banu and also Gazari's ally Alhaji—"on the other river bank"—who was defeated by the people of Kayoro. While Kayoro cannot be identified, the ally Alhaji is mentioned once again at the end of the manuscript as Alhaji Mahmudu, who wrote valuable amulets for Gazari (1992, 110–11).

It seems that the desire to identify a "succession" of chiefs has deformed the history of the Zaberma. Succession allows for only one Zaberma leader at a time, provoking endless discussion about who replaced whom, at what date.[14] The Zaberma used honorific titles among themselves, but it is clear from Mallam Abu's account—and circumstantially from other accounts close to the sources— that there was no clear political hierarchy among them. Among the Zaberma, two important social positions existed: free men—the people who originally came from Jerma country, who were merchants and also Muslim clerics—and then, as elsewhere, captives. Some of the latter were soldiers, and some of them ("captains") held command positions. The free men of Jerma origin were equals, even though there were differences of wealth and military muscle among them. The evidence for this fundamental equality is the disputes among them reported by Mallam Abu. The captives belonged to individual Jerma men, not to an overall Zaberma political organization. A Zaberma political body with some chiefly office and a homogenized or ranked category of subjects is an illusion that misrecognizes simple solidarity among independent free Jerma men operating as freelancers. Gandiari and Babato overlapped throughout most of their careers and evidently were independent operators, as were some other Jerma men of free status in the lower Volta and Upper Volta.[15] This revision sheds light on the characteristically noncentralized nature of the leadership in this region, which nonetheless could result in the emergence of translocal blocs in opposition to each other.

In the traditions of the Safane region, Gandiari is described not as a conqueror—a kind of Genghis Khan sweeping the land with his wild horsemen—but as a merchant, as in Mallam Abu's written account. He came peacefully, albeit deceptively, to develop connections and trade relations with other important people. For a period, he settled down with his entourage in Cheriba and had friendly contacts in many other important villages. People say that he manifested his aggressive intentions only after he was well established and strong enough to receive support from local allies. This description is familiar. It is precisely the terms in which his Winye adversaries describe Mahamudu Karantao's stay in Dobakoro early in his career (Duperray 1984, 58). Trade, military strength, and low-level banditry were not mutually exclusive; on the contrary, they were elements of one single vocation. They allowed for a sustained spiral of growth and enrichment, bringing the successful actors to a position of strength from which they could contemplate larger-scale military challenges. When this level was reached, the leaders' relations with some villages deteriorated, but the expanded movement was possible only with the continuing support of at least some villages.

The armed men of people like Karantao and Gandiari were not, therefore, unknown faces erupting suddenly on the horizon. They were mostly locals. Even when the top leader, as in the case of the Zaberma, was truly born in a foreign land, most of the fighters were from areas surrounding the action. Some of them were slave fighters owned by rich men, but others were free local volunteers. Movements like the one initiated by the Karantao followed preexisting social "fault lines," although in the end they stimulated new conflicts that could transform the political scene in unanticipated ways. But local people saw these developments, too, as an extension of prior, smaller-scale conflicts and rivalries.

A direct link existed between the anticolonial movement of 1915–16 and the wars that set some villages of the Safane area against the Karantao and their Zaberma allies. The opposition leadership in both cases came from among the same set of people, according to administrator Maguet in the report already quoted in chapter 1.

> Douan, Yssou's grandfather, was the commander of part of the Marka forces. The authority of the fetish of Douan, the very same one inherited by Yssou, was considered sacred and infallible as an oracle. . . . What was more natural for these primitive populations other than thinking that since they had won over large, imposing forces with a great reputation such as those of the marabout of Ouahabou and his allies, they would be successful against us who were few in number, and that the infallible fetish would guarantee them victory [?][16]

Toward the end of the nineteenth century, another Muslim cleric arose, further north in the Suru valley. Named Ahmadu Deme, he is better known as Al-Kari.[17] The French action against him heralds the period of initial colonial occupation and shows how this occupation also followed the fissures of local life, transforming them at the same time.

AL-KARI OF BUSE

Al-Kari was born in Buse and studied in Lanfiera, where he came under the influence of Mamadu Sanogo, known as Karamoko Ba (the great scholar). He furthered his studies in the Masina region, made a pilgrimage to the Hijaz, and returned to West Africa about 1887 to establish a school in Buse. He advocated religious war, despite the disapproval of his former teacher Karamoko Ba, and asked his many partisans to stock muskets in preparation. Al-Kari launched his war in May 1892 and gained prestige and captives, which were exchanged for horses, firearms, and gunpowder.

Al-Kari took advantage of prior alliances in the region but ended up polarizing people for or against him and thus imploded these alliances. According to Michel Izard and Françoise Héritier (1958, 6–7), in the late nineteenth century there were three major leagues in the Suru valley, each including a mix of Marka, Samo, and Pana villages. Many of Al-Kari's first supporters came from one of these leagues—the one that included We, Buna, Nyasa, Debe, Toma, and Buse.[18] Not all villages of the league went to his side, however; Turukoro, also in the same league, became an enemy and early target for Al-Kari. After Al-Kari's victories, many villages in the area put aside their old rivalries and united in opposition to him. Suru and Gasan provided the leadership. Along with Jere, which was a client of Gasan, these villages became havens for refugees. This struggle was continuing when, in 1894, French colonial troops made their first incursion in the area and abruptly ended Al-Kari's career.

This particular French intervention deserves commentary because it precedes the principal French occupation by two years. The antagonism between Al-Kari and the Muslim leaders of the Masina who had made peace with the French seems to have played in triggering it. Al-Kari's main opponent, Adama Gnôbo Sidibe—known by the nickname Widi—was to become an important figure of the early colonial phase (see pp. 238ff.). As an ally of Tijani Tall in Bandiagara, Widi acquired fortune and returned to his native land to build, in 1875, the town of Barani as his headquarters. He prospered by organizing raids and taking part in commerce, especially as an intermediary in the trade of captives for horses. In those years, there was hot conflict in Minyanka country and around Sikasso in the south, increasing the supply of captives, while horses came from Yatenga and other parts of the Sahel in the north. Widi started the market of Warkoy, which became the principal trade center for captives in the west Volta. However, Al-Kari, as intermediary, trading slaves for guns in its western gateway, played a strategic stranglehold role (Hubbell 1997, 132), and both Widi and his patrons in Masina disliked the Muslim leaders of the Suru valley.

In 1893 the French entered Bandiagara and installed Aguibu, a son of El Haj Umar, as "king" of Masina.[19] Widi entered into Aguibu's orbit of influence. At this time, the French field commanders, feeling restrained by the metropole in staging campaigns at the pace they desired, tried to circumvent this by using "African conquerors" as surrogates. After installing Aguibu in Bandiagara, Commandant Louis Archinard instructed him, in writing, to make war only against two named enemies of France. One of them was Al-Kari.[20] It is hard to determine to what extent Aguibu's decision to attack Al-Kari was motivated by his understanding that the French expected him to do so. The origin of Al-Kari's bad reputation with the French was his refusal, in 1890 and 1891, to give audience to two French explorers, Dr. Crozat and Lieutenant Colonel Monteil. Al-Kari had also sent a letter of reproof to the marabouts of Masina who had given letters of introduction to these two Frenchmen. But because Widi and his Tukulor allies importantly shaped the opinion of the French after 1893 by being the main source of information for them, it is difficult to know whether this was the only reason that the French turned against him.

In any case, Aguibu first dispatched his clients Dawuda Ngiro and Usman Umaru of Luta against Al-Kari, but they returned with heavy casualties. He then sent Widi, who also was repelled. The new French officer in Bandiagara decided to organize an expedition in retaliation, but in the two encounters in May 1894 he, too, was defeated. The commander of the region, Captain F. J. H. Quiquandon, seized the opportunity of this humiliation to get around an instruction that had been issued by the newly appointed civilian governor of the Soudan to suspend all combat operations. He sent to Buse a larger column of regular tirailleurs commanded by Captain Bonaccorsi, two field guns, and Usman Umaru and Widi as allies. The column marched at great speed, took Buse after a fierce day-long battle, killed Al-Kari, and returned to its base. The bulk of Al-Kari's army under the command of Al-Kari's brother was spared because it was not stationed in the village, but they decided to leave the area immediately.[21] The elimination of Al-Kari changed the volatile political conditions of the northern Volta region. The rapprochement between Suru and Gasan — in opposition to Al-Kari — ended, and when the French returned three years later, this time to occupy the territory permanently, Suru and Gasan chose opposite sides.

Bonaccorsi's campaign against Al-Kari marked the beginning of a long and tight association between the French and the Sidibe House of Barani, headed then by Widi. After Widi's death in 1901 the alliance continued with his son Idrisa. Remembering the early colonial period, people living within the bend of the Muhun River make more frequent references to Barani than to the colonial army itself. In Samo country, too, the locals remember the French repressive action of 1897 as the work of Widi, rather than the French. When the anticolonial movement started in the cercle of Dedougou in 1915, Idrisa Sidibe became the main ally who supported — and to some extent guided — the response of the colonial army. Between these two events there was another development, to which we now turn: the French occupation of the west Volta.

THE BEGINNINGS OF FRENCH OCCUPATION IN NORTHERN VOLTA

The occupation of the Volta came at the tail end of the French expansion in western Sudan, in feverish competition with the British and conducted with meager resources and wavering commitment from the metropole. The French columns first skirted the Volta basin at its northern edge. Only in the final months of 1896 did they have their first confrontations with the population of Samo country. In the following two years, the French advanced to the south with relatively small and rapidly moving contingents. They defeated the local resistances they encountered but left behind large expanses of territory that they had not even visited. These lands were nonetheless claimed for France. Conspicuous in the history of this advance is the absence, in the area of Bona or elsewhere, of any engagement with the populations labeled Marka.

The expansionist phase had in fact started in 1881, when Colonel Desbordes marched a French column into the Upper Senegal Valley and displaced Ahmadu, one of the successors of Al-Haj Umar.[22] For the following eighteen years, periods of aggressive advance and of calmer consolidation alternated, the latter imposed on the field commanders by the metropole. In the lull between aggressive campaigns, with ambitions greater than the means at their disposal, the French commanders pursued a diplomacy of exploration missions to establish protectorates further east. Three of these diplomatic-exploration-intelligence missions reached the Volta region between 1888 and 1891. They were led by G. Binger, Dr. F. Crozat, and J.-L. P. Monteil. Together they yielded a handful of treaties, which ultimately proved to be of limited usefulness, and a wealth of information,[23] which shaped the expectations of the French when they finally arrived with an army. One of the important discoveries was that some Watara leaders in the Kong and Bobo regions (more about them in chap. 3) and the Muslim leaders of places such as Wahabu, Boromo, Durula, and Safane had a friendly disposition.

In 1890, Commandant Archinard initiated new confrontations with the successors of Al Haj Umar. Segou was captured in April 1890, and after that the cities of Mopti, Jenne, and San came relatively easily under French domination. Many former Tukulor enemies became French allies. Finally, in April 1893, Archinard entered Bandiagara, the major city in the region commonly known as Masina.

During the nineteenth century, two waves of political turbulence had swept through the Masina region. In the 1830s, Seku Amadu had led a movement in the name of Islam that fought mostly with non-Muslim Fulbe but brought in its wake a strong sense of Fulbe Islamic identity. Then in 1862 the

Tukulor of Al Haj Umar, who belonged to the novel Tijaniyya brotherhood of Islam, entered Masina and displaced the successors of Seku Amadu. Some of these successors moved with their dependents and herds into more inaccessible places, to the north of the Niger valley or across the Bani River into northwestern Volta. When the French arrived in these territories, the powerful Tukulor houses of Masina were still struggling with rivals, such as Ba Lobbo, who were successors to Seku Amadu.

The French Pound allies and resisters within the camps of both the Tukulor and the successors of Seku Amadu. Among the allies were Widi of Barani, Usman Umaru, a Tukulor of the Ciem family, and Salum Sangare, who was based in Dokuy and had close ties with a large number of Bwa and Bobo villages in that area. This realignment did not dissolve the older enmities between the two camps. On the contrary, it complicated matters by giving new life to even older rivalries within each camp, family oppositions that had been temporarily submerged during the conflict between the Tijani partisans of Al Haj Umar and his Qadiri opponents. The colonial career of Usman Umaru under the French, for example, was cut short because he was executed by Aguibu.

After another temporary halt, French colonial campaigns resumed in 1895. Archinard was now director of defense in the Ministry of Colonies,[24] and the French policy objective was to unite France's coastal territories with their recent acquisitions in the Soudan and to reach as far as possible into Central Africa. The attempt to march north from their Ivory Coast colony was frustrated because of the resistance of the Baule peoples in the hinterland and the presence, since 1894, of the formidable army of Samori further north. The British and German advances northward from the Gold Coast and Togoland colonies could be blocked only by moving south from the newly conquered Masina.

Within this horizon, the French command targeted Ouagadougou, which was coveted by the British. Captain G. M. Destenave, the resident of Bandiagara, went to Ouahigouya in May 1895 and signed a treaty with Naaba Baogho. But in Ouagadougou, Mogho Naaba Wobogo (Bakari Kutu) remained hostile to the French. In August 1896, Lieutenant P. G. L. Voulet attacked Ouagadougou, forced Mogho Naaba Wobogo to flee, and used the city as a base for his operations in Mose and Gurunsi countries. The roads used for the flow of supplies from San to Ouagadougou traversed the lands of the Samo north of the bend of the Muhun River. Large and frequent French supply convoys requisitioned porters and food from the villages of the Suru valley, thus provoking the first resistances to the French in this region.

An important confrontation started in November 1896, when Widi, in charge of a convoy carrying munitions and supplies for the French, crossed to the east bank of the Suru River. He met strong resistance, and around Gasan a large army forced him to take refuge in the nearby village of Suru. Voulet, an impetuous man, was in Ouahigouya. He set out immediately to rescue Widi and the convoy, but fierce opposition slowed down his movement—a challenge, by his own account, greater than anything he had encountered in Mose country. It took him five days and two major battles in the villages of Wele and Boare to reach Gasan, which he attacked and occupied after a day-long battle and five hundred enemy killed (see map 18, p. 210).[25] This defeat broke the spirit of the villages in league with Gasan, and resistance dwindled. But Voulet was not satisfied. The resistance had been organized around large villages that were fortified to stand a battle and had been chosen as gathering points for the rest. These villages included Kamina, Kumbara, Jere, Yaba, Sono, Lesere, Basan, and Tongo (Kambou-Ferrand 1993b, 177 n. 379). Lieutenant C. P. J. Chanoine, second in command of the column, thought that the complete pacification of this area could be achieved only if a large military column with artillery went through the countryside and systematically destroyed such villages (Kambou-Ferrand 1993b, 130). This sort of vengeance became the dream of many frustrated French commanders, but generally they did not have the troops and equipment needed to indulge in it. It was applied fully only in response to the uprising of 1915–16.

Foreshadowing 1915 in a different way, Voulet became convinced that there was some kind of Muslim conspiracy behind the coordinated agitation of Suru valley villages, and that Karamoko Ba (Mamadu Sanogo), of Lanfiera, was involved. Karamoko Ba had hosted the French explorers Crozat and Monteil, distanced himself from the militancy of Al-Kari, remained neutral when Buse was attacked, and continued a friendly diplomacy with the French. All of this notwithstanding, Voulet vented his rancor on this easy target. He brought Karamoko Ba to a summary trial, with Widi acting as a prosecutor of sorts, accusing the man of having corresponded with the dreaded Samori. Karamoko Ba was condemned and executed.

This incident became an icon of colonial miscarriage of justice since Karamoko Ba's son later became a prominent colonial chief and the colonial administration posthumously repealed the judgment and returned Karamoko Ba's reputation. The incident no doubt shows Voulet's violent disposition and lack of diplomacy, which perhaps made him play more eagerly to the rivalries among his African associates. Widi especially was jealous that Destenave had declared Karamoko Ba the Islamic authority for the region, thus instituting a kind of diarchy that limited his ambitions. It is perhaps true that Voulet's act ultimately hurt French interests by scaring the other French supporters, but to single out this incident in terms of justice or its miscarriage is to be blind to the gross realities of the colonial occupation.

It would be more profitable to look at these events in terms of what they can reveal about local political diplomacy. It is very likely that Karamoko Ba was indeed carrying out correspondence with Samori, as some of his successors today believe.[26] Far from being surprising, this would accord with what we know of diplomatic relations between the Muslim clerics of the Suru valley, the towns within the Muhun River bend, and Sia (Bobo-Dioulasso). A man such as Karamoko Ba would have concerns that would justify some connection with Samori. All local associates of the French played a double game in that epoch. At about the same time or shortly afterwards, it was found that Widi not only corresponded with Samori, but also supplied him with horses, at the very moment the French were preparing the ultimate assault against him. The French learned of this when Widi's rivals in Fio captured the horses and the inculpating correspondence written in Widi's hand and denounced him. The French commanders chose to ignore the incident (Person 1975, 3:1790 n. 100). This one example gives an idea of the degree of perfidy—from the perspective of the Muslims of the Suru valley—that Widi manifested in the Karamoko Ba affair. It is also possible that Karamoko Ba was providing amulets and advice to some resistant villages that were close to him, as did the Karantao of Wahabu in 1915, even though officially they were pro-French and benefiting from the repression.

From these intense tragedies of the colonial encounter we can derive a conclusion that will cast a great deal of light on the organization of the 1915–16 movement. The new regional configuration brought about by the French occupation transformed local alliances, forcing them to become part of a vast regionwide dual opposition. But the particular ties making up the previous alliances did not all disappear. Solidarity among smaller sets of local actors overrode the more general ties established within the temporary broad alliances that were imposed by the circumstances. This was an essential characteristic of the rise and fall of broad political currents in the savanna. Despite the force with which the tide came, it was short lived and had limited carrying power. In the *longue durée,* political life remained multicentric and liable to swift reversals and oscillations.

J.-M. Kambou-Ferrand (1993b, 131) suggests another lesson of the Karamoko Ba incident. Subsequent correspondence between Voulet and Destenave reveals that these two men were not friends. It is possible that Voulet, by killing the man in Lanfiera who was Destenave's protégé, also wanted to deal a blow to his superior. If correct, this illustrates that colonial developments were influenced not only by the conflicts among the African associates of the French but also by the rivalries among the French officers, which were not of an altogether different nature. The repressive actions of 1916 and the interpretations made of them at the time will give us reason to return to this point.

Fighting between French forces and the Bwa and Samo villages on the supply roads to Ouagadougou continued after the Voulet expedition. In January 1897, Destenave came to this area with an important column to establish order and lay down the beginnings of administration. First he spent almost a month in Luta, where the French protégé Usman Umaru was experiencing major difficulties. We know little about this period, except that he engaged in battles with Kare-Mangal, Simbara Bumba, and Yaba (Kambou-Ferrand 1993b, 188–90).

During this early phase of colonial occupation in Samo country, the rivalry between the large villages of Suru and Gasan shaped the confrontations. Gasan, which was the object of Voulet's wrath in 1895, again in 1915 became an important support of the anticolonial movement in this area, whereas Suru remained loyal to the French—not by opposing the anticolonial movement, but by wavering. Later in the colonial period, the two villages competed to become the headquarters of the canton and also to promote their own markets. Today these two villages are practically merged because urban expansion has eaten away the small empty distance between them, but the rivalry between their leading families continues.

The attitudes toward Al-Kari show that since the nineteenth century the relations between these two villages have gone from hostility to collaboration and then back again. Although Suru is now predominantly Marka, and Gasan is Samo, they are said to have been founded by two brothers. In Gasan, some of the most important ritual functions are carried out by the Yeye house, which hails from Suru, although the masa comes from an originally Samo house. Together with many other villages of the area, the two are integrated in a ritual circuit that is based upon a shrine called Zonkoro. These ties, of course, by themselves do not explain the choices of the two villages in the past hundred and twenty years or so, but they provide a template within which people can establish new relationships.[27]

The experiences of the French in the Suru valley included the emergence of a broad alliance of a military nature against them. In 1897, Commandant Destenave thought that some Samo villages were working to realize such an alliance: "The example set by the Samo has encouraged the Yatenga on one side and the Bobo on the other, and already these three regions have started to organize an alliance of sorts to resist our authority; emissaries have even been sent to the Habe community of Masina to involve them in this movement" (Hubbell 1997, 72). Although the author who quotes these lines is skeptical about the existence of the types of links Destenave describes, there is no reason to think that Destenave invented them.

What is described in the above quotation is not an alliance of a "tribal" sort (that is, one that is based on kinship or that tries to unite all members of one ethnolinguistic community); it is the type of association that organized the opposition against the Karantao or Gandiari in the precolonial period, but also the support that these two figures enjoyed in the region. Such movements did not unite all the people in one region or all the people of one ethnicity. They were political projects that brought a sector of the population together around a particular shared goal for a limited period of time. Under their influence, some former enemies made common cause and fought side by side; other local conflicts survived but were rechanneled as the former rivals now fought with each other in a new situation, on either side of a larger conflict. The broader alliances were achieved by extending the logic and the practices of the small intervillage confederations, but they took them from the local level to the level of the region and transformed them. Destenave's description of 1897 fits perfectly well the way the anticolonial movement started in 1915.

In 1897, when the French moved south in the Volta region they confronted Britain in an exaggerated example of what Hargreaves (1985, 190ff) called the "steeplechase." The context for this game was shaped by Samori, Babemba, and other local actors. These origins of French expansion set the parameters of the political system that followed and determined the character of the colonial administration until 1915.

French Expansion to the South

In 1897, the French command in Masina created a new administrative region called Niger-Volta (see map 3). This was to conquer the territories south of the Muhun River, stem the British advance toward the gold-producing Lobi country, and watch the movements of Babemba of Sikasso, who while still nominally an ally was making overtures to Samori. Organizing the supply trains from San to Ouagadougou was among the Niger-Volta administration's tasks. The head of the new region, Commandant Valet, started by launching a campaign against Bwa villages in the north—a campaign Destenave had intended to wage but had not been able to carry out. Before reaching his destination, Valet clashed again with Samo villages and battled between February and April 1897 with the villages of Diedu, Yegere, Niankoro, and Sono.[28] This campaign ruined Valet's health and he was repatriated. On April 23, his second-in-command, Captain L. Hugot, initiated one of the most important confrontations of this occupation period in the region—an attack supported by a cannon against the fortified village of Masala, where resisters from "twelve to fifteen villages at least" had gathered (Hugot 1901; Boni 1962, 221). The purpose of the attack was partly to facilitate the task of the small detachment that Captain G. M. Cazemajou was to lead south to Lobi country (Person 1975, 3:1872; Kambou-Ferrand 1993b, 218)— the first time that the French military were to cross the territory of Marka villages within the bend of the Muhun River.

The French moves once again had followed the alignments of the preceding period. Masala had been an ally of Passakongo, in a three-way rivalry setting it against Kari and Dedougou (Cremer 1924b, 131–48). When the French entered the scene, Dedougou sided with the French, while the opposition gathered around Masala. It had played a similar role once again in the past, during the resistance against the Karantao. When, in a bloodbath, Hugot destroyed that town and took from its inhabitants enough cattle to supply his troops for one year, Dedougou emerged unscathed and triumphant. Many villages that had previously joined Dedougou's rivals returned to become its clients again. Dedougou benefited from its early association with the French throughout the colonial period, and in 1911, when the headquarters of the cercle was moved for a second time, Dedougou was chosen as its new location. Masala, on the other hand, became one of the important centers of resistance in 1915–16.

Cazemajou's expedition to the south started with a visit to Wahabu. On April 22, 1897, he signed a treaty with Karamoko Moktar, recognizing him as "king of Wahabu" and proclaiming under French protectorate "all the territories that [Karamoko] or his successors could conquer" (Duperray 1984, 124).[29] The French used the regional ties of the Karantao to make alliances with local strongmen against resisting villages and to beat the British in treaty making. Further south, Cazemajou clashed with Dagari villages, but was well received by the warlike Jan. He signed another treaty in Diebougou in May. As he had only a small expeditionary force, he deemed it prudent to return north because Samori's son Sarankenyi Mori had destroyed the British column of Captain G.-C. Henderson in April.

When Commandant P.-C. Caudrelier arrived in Sono in May as Valet's replacement, he discovered that the successive blows dealt by Voulet, Des-

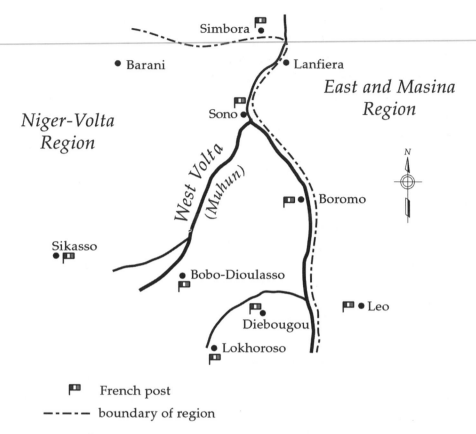

Map 3. The creation of the East and Masina region, 1896–98. Modified from a map in Commandant Destenave's "L'occupation et l'organisation de la Boucle du Niger," Publication du Comité de l'Afrique Française, Gouvernement du Soudan Français, 1898.

tenave, Valet, and Hugot to the Samo and Bwa villages north and south of the Muhun River had not sufficed to conquer the region. Only Dedougou sent a delegation to express its loyalty, while in Warkoy there were serious war preparations against him. He established three military posts. Their location shows that Caudrelier was concerned more with rapidly extending French presence to the south than with quelling the seething opposition in the north. The northernmost post was in Boromo, near the landing on the Muhun River, where boats from Sono arrived with supplies for Mose country.[30] The second post was in Leo, where Caudrelier sent Hugot to watch the British and Sarankenyi Mori. The third was in Diebougou, under the command of Captain Braulot. Caudrelier instructed both officers to avoid conflicts with the local population and with the detachments of Samori's son Sarankenyi Mori's army, and in fact a prohibition against battle was in force for the entire Niger-Volta region. In a letter of December 3, 1897, Destenave wrote: "it will be easier later to suppress the resistances when the situation will not force us to conserve all our forces to meet a possible complication in the south" (Kambou-Ferrand 1993b, 227). The "complication" was the possibility of a confrontation with Samori himself. Despite these instructions, fighting was unavoidable. Hugot found himself at war against the Zaberma leader Babato, who enjoyed the protection of the British. The posts could survive only by pillaging the region, and villages also resisted the recruitment of porters; others abandoned their houses and ran away from the roads.

The occupation of what became the cercle of Bobo-Dioulasso followed from decisions taken against Samori and the British. In August, in the midst of a campaign against villages that disrupted the convoys between Sono and San, Caudrelier learned that the Braulot company, which he had sent south to take possession of the city of Bouna, had been annihilated by the soldiers of Saran-kenyi Mori.[31] Fearing that this might be the beginning of a large-scale offensive by Samori, the next day Caudrelier left for the south with all the soldiers he had with him, on his way also taking along the garrisons of Boromo and Diebougou. He arrived in Lokhoso on September 10 and started to reinforce the town. A few days later, Widi of Barani joined him with auxiliary troops.

Events took a different course from what Caudrelier had anticipated, however. Samori went on the defensive. He immobilized his son's army in Bouna and then withdrew it to the southwest (Person 1975, 3:1930ff). At the very same time, in Europe, preparations for an agreement between France and Britain to fix the mutual boundaries of their newly acquired African territories entered their final phase. The French government wanted only to consolidate its existing positions vis-à-vis the British and was not interested in beginning an uncertain war with Samori. The French field officers' calls for vengeance were ignored, and the government issued strict orders that hostilities not be provoked. Forced thus into inactivity in the south, Caudrelier decided to march north in search of action in order to boost the morale of the large column that had gathered under him.[32] (Most of these soldiers—not only the "auxiliaries" but the regular tirailleurs troops, too—were mostly motivated by the prospect of war booty.) This campaign in the north met with little resistance because Samori's voluntary restraint had created a power vacuum.

On September 25, 1897, guided by the subordinates of Pintyeba, the column arrived before Sia (Bobo-Dioulasso). Pintyeba, a Watara leader based in Kotedugu, had appealed to the French because he feared Samori. In contrast, in

Sia the Tunuma ward leaned toward Samori; it had prepared for defense, but surrendered after the loss of more than eighty men in a battle lasting a few hours (for a summary of the sources, see Person 1975, 3:1914, 1963). Three days after the capture of Sia, Caudrelier and all of his soldiers left for Diebougou. The first post in Bobo-Dioulasso was established only two months later, on November 23. The commander of the post, Lieutenant Sagolz, had few troops, but following Caudrelier's advice he united forces with Pintyeba, who staged systematic attacks on the northern territory lying within the bend of the Muhun River to collect food supplies that were sent south to the French posts on the Komoe River. Sagolz also organized a campaign to Dokuy and opened a shorter supply road between San and Bobo-Dioulasso through Bwa country.

After British forces occupied Wa and Bouna, in January 1898 Caudrelier returned north to Sono and organized another punitive expedition against the confederated Bwa villages, which had effectively stopped the French convoys heading for Boromo. Caudrelier's forces suffered heavy casualties in Bagasi (an important center of resistance again in 1916), but he took the town. He returned to the south and convinced the British commander, Northcott, to let him reoccupy part of Wa until the treaty in preparation in Europe resolved the matter. This triggered the final and strangest form of territorial rivalry: the establishment of several British and French military posts cheek by jowl in neighboring villages. Early in 1898, Caudrelier and his associates were forced to relieve Kong, which a small detachment from the post of Leraba had unwisely captured, to find itself soon afterwards besieged by Sarankenyi Mori. Reorganizing the new small posts of the Komoe-Leraba area, Caudrelier managed to receive the support of both the local Watara leaders and their antagonists, the Gwen villages of this area, which until then had been allied to Samori (Person 1975, 3:1936–38).

A decisive development in April 1898 was the French decision to capture Sikasso, a preliminary to the final confrontation with Samori (which was being delayed until the signature of the treaty with the British). Caudrelier had transferred his headquarters to Bobo-Dioulasso in March to participate in this campaign. As the French forces massed around Sikasso in April, Caudrelier created two columns to operate in the upper Muhun in order to cut Babemba's lines of supply and reinforcements from Samori. The Sambla villages west of Bobo-Dioulasso and the Syemu, Senufo, and Minyanka villages between the Muhun and Bani Rivers thus met for the first time with French forces.[33]

Two principal forces dominated the politics of this area. One of them was Sikasso, controlled first by Tieba and then by his successor Babemba, who had enjoyed the support of the French, when they were allies against Samori. The second was the various Watara houses (among which there was no unity). After 1894, Samori's men were added to the picture as a third focus of power. Each one of these forces had its own allies and foes scattered throughout the area. The Watara dignitaries of the region of Kong as well as those of the Volta area suffered when Samori destroyed Kong and pursued them in his northerly advance. The Watara elders gloomily accepted the de facto leadership of Pintyeba, who had had the good fortune of being far distant, both from Sikasso and from Samori's line of advance, and who had sided with the French early enough not to endure losses. Resistance to Caudrelier's columns came mostly from villages that had small garrisons of soldiers belonging either to Babemba or to Samori.

Sikasso fell on May 1 after a siege of two weeks. Samori ceased to be a factor by withdrawing west of the Bandama River. The convention between the British and the French was signed on June 14, 1898. The borders of the two powers were set at the eleventh parallel and the Muhun (Black Volta) River. Even though for a few more years disagreements of detail continued, the scramble for the Volta region had ended, and the major lines of colonial West Africa were drawn on the map. The task that lay ahead for the French was "pacifying" the populations within these borders who had not been party to the convention. As Caudrelier returned to France,[34] the commander of the Sikasso column, Colonel I. H. Pineau, took over what became the Volta region (the hyphenated name, Niger-Volta, was now dropped). After a lengthy expedition to supply Kong, Pineau arrived in the residence of Bobo-Dioulasso on June 21.

The next chapter provides an overview of the institution of the colonial regime and how pacification turned out to be not a brief phase but a state that lasted about two decades. The colonial officials reconciled their ideal of political control with the reality that they were unable to achieve it with stopgap measures—measures that in fact occasionally bordered on delusion.

CHAPTER 3

An Incomplete
Colonial Occupation

IN THE FIRST DECADE OF THE TWENTIETH CENTURY, colonial rule in the west Volta region greatly differed from standard accounts of colonialism. The prototype of French "direct rule" became a reality mostly in the interwar period, and even then existed only in certain areas. After the first five years, popular resistance to French occupation subsided not because the colonial administration achieved fuller control over the countryside, but mostly because the colonial administration lowered its expectations and modified its tactics, moderating its drive for political control with a part-fiction of rule. Colonial rule was satisfactory in the areas near the posts, and ignoring the rest of the country made possible relatively uneventful careers for administrators. In this chapter, we describe the early institutions of colonial rule, from the hot-conflict period at the turn of the century to the eventful years of opposition during World War I.

THE TERRITORIAL ORGANIZATION

After arriving in Bobo-Dioulasso as the new commander of the Volta region, Colonel I. H. Pineau undertook its territorial organization along the lines suggested by Caudrelier and Lieutenant Governor Audéoud. He divided this broad region into eight "cercles" (administrative circles, or provinces).[1] In the center was the cercle of Bobo-Dioulasso, the largest in area and population. In the northwest, Bobo-Dioulasso bordered the cercle of Minyanka, which included the city of San but whose new capital was the smaller but more centrally positioned Koutiala; by 1915 this cercle had been divided into two cercles, each with its own headquarters, in San and Koutiala. North of Bobo-Dioulasso lay the cercle of Volta Supérieure, with headquarters in Sono. The headquarters of Volta Supérieure were shifted to Koury in 1899, and to Dedougou in 1911, the name of the cercle changing each time to that of its capital city; the boundaries were also modified. In 1903, the surroundings of the town of Koudougou—the area east of the Muhun River—was annexed to the cercle of Bobo-Dioulasso, but this was later separated again and made into a residency of the cercle of Ouagadougou. These named administrative areas, with the addition of the adjacent zones in the north belonging to the cercles of Jenne and Bandiagara, became the stage for the war of 1915–16.

Pineau explains in his report (p. 10) that the delimitation of the cercles constitutes a transition from indirect to direct rule. The new organization changed the position of the French commanders in the region; the former "residents" would now be called administrators. In the 1880s, the French had spread their influence in the Bani region by making treaties with a few major military leaders. At that time, the resident was an officer sent as an ally and adviser, accompanied by only a small contingent of soldiers. The most famous of them had been the resident of Sikasso, F. J. H. Quiquandon, who volunteered advice and participated in some of Tieba's campaigns, but did not take independent military action.

After 1893, during the campaigns of expansion beyond the Bani, the officers commanded relatively important military forces and started treating the African allies as subordinates, rather than equals. They stopped supplying them with firearms and restrained them from independent raiding activity, which constituted their main source of income. The chiefs now only provided auxiliary troops to the conquest columns; in return, the officers turned a blind eye to looting and captive-taking during authorized battles. When Voulet drove Bakari Kutu out of Ouagadougou and then declared his brother Mogho naaba, the commander of the column appeared as both king breaker and kingmaker. In 1897, Caudrelier declared some of his allies "heads of state." In this context, *state (état)* meant a unit within the administrative structure, a subdivision of the cercle, but these heads of state lacked autonomy. The 1898 convention with the British had eliminated the need to justify the colonial occupation, and the French ignored treaties made with Africans, or at least no longer referred to them. Individual chiefs were maintained in position only because of administrative efficiency. The new administrative texts provided grounds for such action without bothering to establish legal continuity with the claims of the protectorate phase. Kambou-Ferrand (1993b) points out that if the treaties made with African "kings" and "chiefs" in the earlier period were to be accepted as legal, the establishment of cercle administration amounted to a coup d'état by the French colonial army against the established (proto)colonial order.

The title of chief, or head of state, was bestowed upon African subordinates not only in recognition of their help in the campaigns but also as an expedient to control the population. In December 1897, Caudrelier reprimanded the commander of San for being an advocate of Bwa villages: "Why are you against placing Dokuy under the Fulbe chief Widi? I don't see the advantage we would have in accepting anarchy by multiplying the number of independent villages." And again, a month later, to Sagolz in Bobo-Dioulasso: "It is necessary to back the chiefs to avoid anarchy, but not to tolerate their extortion" (Person 1975, 3: 1964).

It soon became clear, however, that many appointed chiefs had very limited powers. They had influence not over a majority of the population but only over a small portion, connected to them by an old pact, as kinsmen, or as the captive population of their agricultural hamlets. The majority could be made to obey only by coercion, and the chiefs did not possess sufficient military force for that.

Models of Native Society

The early colonial administrators used two different models to make sense of the responses of the population to coercion: a historical-political model of conquest and a cultural model of ethnic group specificity. These two were connected and could be drawn upon by the same person — sometimes in the same breath — but they pointed to alternatives in administrative policy.

The cultural model is signaled by the use of the French word *races,* which is best translated as "ethnic groups." Starting with the late-nineteenth-century explorers of the Volta region, colonial records display elaborate lists of ethnic groups. The lists were highly speculative and confused in the beginning because little was known of the peoples described, especially in the matter of language. But the effort was pragmatic rather than scholarly, and observation of custom and lifestyle compensated for lack of philological mastery. The main source of information were African allies and informants, who in the west Volta came mostly from among Manding-speaking people of trader or warrior backgrounds. Through them, elements of prior African classifications entered the French schemes. West African regional identities had more to do with location, political relationships, shrines, or professional status than with language or patterns of culture, but the former transmuted into cultural traits when recorded by the officials.

The recognition of *races*—and the linked notions of *tribus* and the more belittling *peuplades*—led to the doctrine that Pineau called "the autonomy of races." Ideally, each tribe would be a canton, related tribes would constitute a subdivision, and the cercle itself would correspond to the *race*. At the beginning of his report, Pineau writes: "Before determining the mode of administration that is suitable for the Volta region, it is indispensable to study, at least in summary fashion, the character of the different races that make it up" (3). Thereafter, he uses the words *canton* and *tribu* interchangeably. The problem was that the *races* were not organized as political corporations, and many of them did not occupy a territory exclusively. The chiefs that the French chose as allies were not representatives of these cultural groups but owed their influence to different political processes. Their supposed subjects did not constitute homogeneous lots. The problem was resolved by rank—ordering the groups on the assumption that a few of them had conquered the others in the past.

The French officers ranked the West African groups from "intelligent" to "primitive." The biology implied in this ranking was of Lamarckian variety, accepting improvement by effort rather than unchanging genetic inheritance. One of the most salient traits was clothing. In many parts of the Volta, men and women wore scant clothing or none at all (see fig. 7, p. 214), while others living among them or next to them had elaborate textile traditions. Such practices entered local consciousness as central components of self-identity and became a matter of political positioning. Those who had migrated recently from the west wore clothing, and clothing was also part of an Islamic way of life. This correlation confirmed to European eyes that clothing was a sign of civilization. Locally, cotton cloth was also associated with war. Professional fighters wore a cotton frock treated with substances believed to make their wearers invulnerable (see image on the cover; at least, they wore them in battle, even if otherwise they went naked, like many others). Although the wearing of clothing, like other practices, was not a stable cultural trait or the exclusive possession of a linguistic-cultural category, there was enough coherence for French officials to think of it as such.

Another consideration for ranking was the reaction of populations to the colonial conquest. Warlike populations who organized resistance were "primitive." This judgment introduced incongruity into the ranking. In the conquest scheme, it was assumed that the Manding speakers were superior. The Fulbe—who were supposed to be of Hamitic, or mixed-white, origin—were even higher. These two groups, it was assumed, had imposed themselves on the less-astute "paleonegritics." This generalization was based on a few episodes of political conflict of the late nineteenth century that were known to the French. In fact, in these conflicts it was not entire ethnic groups that were pitched against each other. The parties were not even ethnically homogeneous. Important war leaders led mixed crowds, including their own slave soldiers and those of their associates, free volunteers, and members of allied villages. Regardless, colonial authorities seem to have used the schoolbook version of the Roman and Germanic invasions in early Europe as a template for understanding the Volta region.

There was a problem, however: if "intelligent" peoples had subjugated the weak paleonegritics, how could the latter also be more warlike? We have not found anyone who articulated this paradox at the time, but contrasting evaluations followed from it. Being warlike could indicate either a higher or a lower civilization. It depended on the supposed motivations of the resisters. If people refused to submit simply because they were stubborn and impervious to the values and advantages of a higher civilization, it meant that they were primitive. The circularity of the argument is astonishing, but French officers thought differently of enemies such as Samori or Babemba. These latter may have been "cruel" and "bloody," but they were not called primitive. The colonial officials did not all have the same political values. There were a few, like the author of the 1903 monograph of the cercle of Koury-Boromo, who sided emotionally with the partisans of "anarchy," comparing the resisting Bwa to the tribes of Gaul, except that they had not found their Vercingetorix.[2] The presence of high and low tribes, however, was not questioned. In the 1898 report, Commandant Pineau lists the Samos, the Nienpegues, the Bobos, Dagaris, Kos, Lobis, and Pakhallas among the warlike primitive populations, and the Fulbe, Dioulas, Senufos, and Minyankas as the more intelligent, peaceful, industrious, and capable of assimilation.

The people called Marka were placed close to the high end of the ranking in this period. Pineau described the Marka of the Minyanka cercle as intelligent and those of the Volta Supérieure as docile. The French forces seem to have had very few clashes with these Marka communities. The reason was partly their geographic location (they were far from the French convoy routes) and partly the close relations some of them entertained with Muslim houses, all of which, except Buse, had accepted the French without fighting.

There is, however, the more complicated conceptual issue of what was meant by Marka in these early French writings. West of the Bani, Marka referred primarily to Muslim populations of mixed origin who spoke the same Manding language as that spoken by the pagans called Bambara. Meillassoux underlines the heterogeneity of this category and the misrecognition involved in considering the Marka originally an ethnic group rather than a professional category (1991, 56). In the west Volta region, some people consider *Dafing* and *Marka* to be synonymous, others do not. The population that speaks Manding dialects in the west Volta is very heterogeneous, although more engaged in farming than the people called Marka west of the Bani. The Marka of the Volta consist of migrants who arrived at different times from different places. At the turn of the century some migrations were yet very recent. In 1888, Binger encountered around Wahabu immigrants who had arrived from Kaarta and Bakel (more than 1,100 km away) so recently that they gathered around his men to find out about their former villages and acquaintances they had left behind (Binger 1892, 1:421). Other migrations had occurred several generations before. Some immigrants were already Muslim when they arrived, but most were not. There were conversions among the latter, while some of the former apostatized to fit better their adopted community. Immigrants often became clients and had to adjust to the customs of their hosts. Some immigrants belonged to the blacksmith and bard endogamous groups that cut across linguistic boundaries. The incorporation of slaves was another factor in the mix. Consequently, it is not surprising to discover contradictory definitions of Marka.

According to Maurice Delafosse, who wrote his major, three-volume work using cercle monographs compiled by or on behalf of administrators, the Marka were "warrior and conqueror occasionally, but more often of peaceful disposition . . . less attached to the soil than most blacks, and more likely to leave their country of origin. They engage in agriculture especially by making their slaves or vassals work, but they prefer to deal with trade or with crafts such as weaving and dyeing themselves" (Delafosse 1912, 1:341). In the monograph of the cercle of Bobo-Dioulasso, written after the anticolonial war, the Marka-Dafing are listed as agricultural populations and are demoted, along with the Senufo, to the group of "primitive tribes."[3] A study from the 1950s makes quick reference to their mixed racial origin, and declares that "the Marka are an ethnic group that has a long time ago blended with the local population; they have no special type, appearance-wise they are indistinguishable from other groups."[4] The farthest point to which the pendulum of opinion swung is a more recent article on the 1915–16 War: "The Marka like the Bwaba have profound attachment to the soil of birth and are all agriculturalists. There seems to be little respect for commerce, and generally it is limited to the strictly local exchanges that are necessitated by daily food needs" (Gnankambary 1970: 56).

The Marka of Delafosse imperceptibly merge into the category of people known as Jula—*Jula* being another elastic and puzzling rubric. Today, any person who is transient to the local community and trades for a living is called Jula. The people who are called Marka officially are designated by some of their neighbors as Zaza, the word *Zaza* being similar to *Zara*—people of Bobo speech who are mostly traders. Both *Zaza* and *Zara* seem to be variant pronunciations of *Jula*. *Dafing*, for some local interlocutors, is simply the word used by the Jula of Kong and Bobo-Dioulasso for their counterparts who have settled further north in the Volta region.[5] The French considered the Jula to be associates of the colonizing project. The identification worked both ways: the industrious, bourgeois-like Jula were good, and those who were good were Jula.[6] For the Frenchmen in those initial years, the Marka also were, like the Jula, for the most part Muslim—traders, clothed, and perpetual colonial associates.

The idea that superior *races* had conquered the region and could now help the French administer it had so many faults that Pineau had many misgivings about "indirect administration." One was that the chiefs often drove their supposed subjects to rebellion, causing more military expenditure than savings. Pineau recommended that some—but not all—of the allies of the conquest period be provisionally maintained as chiefs, both as a recognition of their past services and in order to take advantage of their influence in certain parts of the region. This seems to be a concession to his predecessor Caudrelier, who had blind faith in rule through these African leaders. The outcome was a mixed system. Some cantons were directly attached to the cercle; others were grouped into *états*—territories placed under an African subordinate ruler: the "head of state."

NATIVE HEADS OF STATE

Top-down historical accounts of French colonial doctrines are likely to miss the complexities that the French faced in West Africa when they appointed chiefs. Conklin (1997), for example, establishes the important point that a few years before World War I assimilation had been abandoned by the colonial administration as emphasis was laid on having colonized Africans evolve within their own cultures. Then, however, she makes a serious misinterpretation of French chiefly policy (pp. 109–19, 178–79). Assuming that the "great" African chiefs were a precolonial—rather than a colonial—elite and that "traditional chief" is a unitary and unproblematic category, Conklin interprets Governor-general Clozel's instructions to name chiefs with locally grounded genealogies as a departure from his predecessor Ponty's *politique des races*. In practice, *politique des races* meant abandoning the "conqueror" model of local history and the faama-type chiefs *("chef d'etat"),* modifying canton boundaries to correspond to assumed ethnic boundaries, and acknowledging the legitimacy of local cultures. Clozel's fascination for local culture and rebuke of "foreign" potentates in favor of "indigenous" chiefs was clearly a continuation of Ponty's chiefly policy. The *chefs de race* was, for Clozel, to belong "to the same ethnic group as his subordinates" and "follow the same religion as the majority of them."[7] These words could have been written by Ponty and also show that a concern with Islam was an important factor (see p. 97). The *races* policy of Ponty had nothing to do with being for or against "the African elite." It was a response to the dilemma of "native command," based on a divergent reading of the African past and present (tribes with distinct cultures versus conquest states), by an administration beset with cost considerations. This section deals with the "great chiefs" of the early period in the west Volta, the people that the *races* policy and Clozel's instructions later targeted for elimination. The reform that eventually removed them in Bobo-Dioulasso, the chiefs who replaced them, the role some native employees played in these decisions, and the little that the majority had to do with all this are discussed on pp. 114–19.

In the cercle of Volta Supérieure there were three subordinate rulers. The most prominent was Widi Sidibe of Barani, whose domain consisted of at least eleven cantons. Widi fell out of favor after Caudrelier's departure in 1898, but when Widi died in 1901 his son Idrissa, whom Ponty in 1905 took as the example of a rapacious great chief, succeeded him. The second most important "head of state" was Salum Sangare, who was given the area around Dokuy. This included nine cantons. The Tukulor Seydu Amadu had some thirty Samo villages around Simbara-Bumba (Diallo 1997). Like many other strong colonial chiefs at that time, the three soon started quarreling over jurisdiction and the collection of taxes. Commandant Pineau arbitrated but could not stop the rivalry. The three states were dissolved in 1905, and thereafter in the cercle of Koury (later Dedougou) the cantons were directly administered (Hubbell 1997).

In Bobo-Dioulasso, too, three states were created and placed under important Watara leaders who had been French allies since the beginning of the Volta campaign. Pintyeba was given fifteen cantons.[8] When he died in 1901, his son Karamoko replaced him. Tieba Nyandane, who was the senior elder of one major branch of the cluster of Watara houses, was given nine cantons.[9] Tieba died in April 1904 and was replaced by his "cousin" Dafogo. The third state was given to Mori-fin; it included eleven cantons.[10] Other important Watara leaders (e.g., Yamori, Baratu, and Badioli) were made chiefs of other independent cantons. When Dafogo died in 1912, his state was dissolved. Ponty in 1905 had already decided to abolish the Watara states, but Karamoko's and Morifin's survived until 1915, when Maubert with the blessing (and perhaps prompting) of Clozel put it into execution—one of the preliminaries of the 1915 movement.

The états did not constitute continuous stretches of territory and cantons were added or taken away from particular states when taxes came short or when they staged armed opposition. Cantons also were split or amalgamated. Major chiefs had a weak relation to their territories, both in the cantons directly attached to a cercle and in those that belonged to a head of state. A head of state would appoint personal dependents and domestics as chief of a canton. In 1903, Captain Desallais wrote:

> They call canton chief one of their parents who live in Bobo, or one of their *sofa* (slave soldiers), who habitually transmits the orders to that canton rather than to another. These men usually live in Bobo with their chief. For example, in the house of Pintie Ba, the same sofa is canton chief of the cantons of Faramana and Komonos, which are 140 kilometers away from each other. This man also lives in Bobo, which is 50 kilometers to the closest one of the two cantons.[11]

Not all chiefs appointed by the French at that time had been important figures in precolonial times although all were given their positions partly as "recompense." Some of them had been simply low-level colonial collaborators. One example is Karfalat, the chief of Kari in the Volta Supérieure, and also at some point of the cantons Sokongo, Warkoy, and Bondokuy. Born in a Ko village near Boromo, he had worked as a porter and guide for the French columns. All these important chiefs, irrespective of how they achieved their fortunes, kept sizable private armies, consisting of the sofa of the disbanded armies of the precolonial leaders defeated by the French. Karfalat was allowed to build a patrol made up mostly of soldiers discharged from the colonial army.

In contrast, to French administrators who succeeded each other at an amazing pace, the major African chiefs and the interpreters and senior guards remained permanent features of the cercles. Some of them developed considerable skill in manipulating the cercle administration. Behind the backs of novice administrators, they fought major battles over influence, coveted positions, and wealth. Even in cercle headquarters where French presence was firmly established, local people thought that the white officials were the instruments of the African personnel, rather than the other way around (See about Diaman Bathily, p. 115).

From the beginning, administrators held contrasting opinions about the utility of maintaining the heads of state. In 1902, Captain Marandet advocated dissolving the states in the cercle of Bobo-Dioulasso. But when he left in 1903, the reverse was done: all the "independent" villages—that is, those kept up to that point outside of the three states—were attached to the states.[12] The following year, this decision was cancelled and the states were reduced to their former size. The performance of Watara leaders was disappointing, stated a 1903 report:

> Generally they manage to recruit in their state the porters and workers that we need, without needing too much of our help . . . also they can provide us reasonably well with construction materials. Finally, but with much greater difficulty, they assist us in the collection of taxes, in the villages that accept to pay such tribute. Nevertheless, there are in their états a very large number of villages where they can obtain neither porters nor materials or taxes without our intervention.[13]

In 1905, the administrator of Bobo-Dioulasso explained to the governor of the colony why the tax revenue was low:

> All these chiefs have little or no authority at all, and the little of it that they have is limited to a few villages. Many villages do not recognize these chiefs. . . . We cannot, each time we need to collect the tax of a stubborn village, force a group of thirty or forty soldiers to endure the fatigue of a fifteen-day walk. . . . Other [villages] are absolutely implacable. It is perfectly useless to even visit those . . . it is better to not even try, our prestige would suffer too great a blow.[14]

Collecting the head tax was the principal activity of the administrators. There were two reasons for the emphasis on taxes. First, administrative costs were met from the local budget, and therefore tax revenue was important. Second, the successful collection of taxes was the measure of the power of the administration and the chiefs. In the two decades following colonial occupation, tax revenue rose exponentially, because it had started from zero. But the administration had varying degrees of control in the different parts of the region, and the progression was uneven among the cantons.

The French officials also complained about the cupidity, cruelty, and inefficiency of the chiefs. The administration punished many chiefs, but many were later returned to some other position of authority. Despite the wish of some administrators to eliminate the important chiefs, the local leaders had remarkable longevity in the system. Youssouf Diallo (1997) argues that this was because, ultimately, they provided significant military assistance. They served as guides in punitive expeditions, and supplied armed men, of which the administrators were always short. For example, the chiefs of Barani and Dokuy gave mounted auxiliaries, for which there was no substitute, even though doubts on their value existed during the 1915–16 war. Thus the relation between the French officers and the local chiefs continued to have the appearance of a military alliance.

Accordingly, the chiefs acted somewhat like the precolonial war leaders, the *faamaw*. For example, Karfalat, accompanied by a large retinue of bards and musicians, met a French captain visiting Koury in 1899 and tried to present him with gifts, including two horses and three head of cattle. The irritated officer refused the gifts. But the French implicitly accepted this model of partnership. In 1899, one-third of the tax collected in Bobo-Dioulasso by the major chiefs was returned to them as compensation, and the officers were aware that the chiefs were in fact collecting much larger sums in goods and services from the villages they were able to subdue. The collection of head taxes had animated the slave market of Subakaniedugu, where Mori-fin and his agents sold, to traders heading for the Ivory Coast, captives given to them as payment.[15]

"Ruling over the Footpaths"

Realizing that it was impossible to control the population with the soldiers available, the administration adopted a policy of avoiding major clashes. The administrators responded only to acts of opposition that were easy to suppress. True domination of the region was put off to a distant future. Colonial rule was to be broadened only gradually. The treaty with Britain had eliminated competition among the European powers and so tenuous territorial control did not worry the politicians in Paris. The administration's modest target was laid out in Pineau's report of 1898: "Pacification, actually conquest, is not finished in many places, and will be achieved slowly, as the [military] posts gain more terrain by spreading their influence, at the same time as they try, to the extent it is possible, to avoid action that would necessitate the use of force."[16] This last clause did not mean that only peaceful means would be used; it said only that post commanders should avoid large-scale confrontations — ones that could not be put down with the limited personnel at hand and that would result in the embarrassing and costly measure of bringing in reinforcements. Pineau explained how this was to be achieved: "When there are a few especially rebellious tribes, a few quickly and vigorously dealt blows will strike a salutary fear that will hasten the pacification process, without making it necessary to engage in military operations that are both murderous and expensive."[17]

The type of military post mentioned here was the centerpiece of the French strategy of limited and partial occupation. It consisted of about twenty regular tirailleur troops, commanded by a French officer who was sometimes seconded by another Frenchman. These posts thinly covered the territory, and the colonial administration allotted the troops and its few French officers with careful consideration. The posts communicated with an administrative center that had a more important garrison and a cannon. Pineau's report provided for a company of regular soldiers to be deployed in each cercle, divided between the headquarters and one or two other permanent posts. A platoon of cavalry and a mobile artillery unit, to be stationed in Bobo-Dioulasso, would serve all the cercles in the region. In addition, the cercle administration had a small unit of guards, paid from the local civilian budget.

The policy of avoiding military confrontations, reliance on threats and negotiation where control was difficult to achieve, and ignoring strong centers of resistance brought forth increasing reliance on the doctrine of *apprivoisement*—"training," or "domesticating." The use of this term in reports expresses a resignation to limited political control and recognition of the partial nature of the conquest.

The villages around the posts bore the full burden of occupation. They were subject to taxation, recruitment of porters, and labor corvées for the construction of roads and administrative buildings. They constituted the area of immediate impact of colonial rule. The further from the post, the less influence the administration had. At the periphery were areas where the post commander organized punitive expeditions when convoys and caravans were attacked. Beyond the periphery were large areas where colonial influence was naught. It was believed that by widening the zone of influence around each post, such areas would eventually be brought completely under political domination. This idea was expressed with the figure of *tâche d'huile* (oil stain), found in Pineau's report and then in many other documents: it pointed to an occupation that spreads like a drop of oil to cover a larger area. The "oil stain" doctrine had been first advocated and applied by General Gallieni in Tonkin and in Madagascar: the initial military successes were to be followed by the establishment of a network of small military posts throughout the territory. The oil stain was the broadening of the area of control around each post, with an increase in the number of posts to follow as more troops became available. The last point was partly achieved by recruiting among the subdued inhabitants of the previously resisting territories.[18] The strategy of oil stain was considered to have been successfully implemented by Governor-general Angoulvant during his "pacification" of the Baule region in Ivory Coast between 1909 and 1915.

Contrary to this official expectation, in the Volta area the oil stains did not spread uniformly. Instead, periods of aggressive colonial initiative alternated with periods of retrenchment. This was often due to heightened village opposition that reversed a prior trend toward submission; the oscillation corresponded to the different personalities of administrators or to changes in local perceptions. The stagnation in the growth of political control after the initial occupation is documented in many reports of the first decade of administration. Some areas were targeted for punitive campaigns year after year, because either their location near roads or posts made their subjugation imperative or the personality of the commanding officer or colonial chief attracted a spectacular opposition that could not be ignored. The troublesome areas that are mentioned in Pineau's report are the same ones found in the reports of 1913. In time, a list of "especially rebellious tribes" became part of the folk wisdom of colonial administrators. Areas that were not mentioned in the reports were not necessarily more subdued; some were simply left alone. Administrators were reluctant to mention in a report trouble in an area that had not been mentioned in previous years, and they chose to ignore such places as long as the tiniest amount of symbolic taxation was forwarded from them.

Successive colonial administrators accepted that, even after having completed a punitive expedition, they had only limited impact in that part of the countryside. For example, after completing an exceptionally murderous repression campaign against the Samo of Yatenga in February and March 1900, Commandant Buvet wrote: "The resistance of the Samo cannot be broken with a single blow of force. It needs to be won in the long run, with patience and a lot of tenacity" (Kambou-Ferrand 1993b, 374).

In the southern part of the Volta region, the Lobi, Wile, and Pakhalla populations, likewise, were to be penetrated "little by little," over a "long time" and with "patience and tactfulness." That is, except when it became "indispensable" to stage a punitive expedition because the colonial troops had been attacked or mail was interrupted. The westernmost part of the Volta region, the famous Tierla, including the three cantons of Beregadougou, Nafona, and Dramandougou, that was inhabited mostly by M'Boing (Gwen) and Karaboro populations, became larger in 1903 by the addition to the cercle of four more troublesome cantons ceded from the cercle of Sikasso. This area, where no officer had gone since the movements of Caudrelier in 1898, was considered "in full rebellion."[19] In 1903, Captain Marandet, the administrator of Bobo-Dioulasso, organized a six-month expedition during which he relied on, instead of using force, a mix of intimidation and negotiation in village "meetings." He considered his campaign a great success, but the following year a new subdivision was created in Banfora to watch over this area.[20] The report of 1904 still described Tierla as "imperfectly submitted."[21] From then on, this area was pretty much left on its own, and it is frequently described as one of the tribes "in love with their independence." The Tierla and surrounding cantons did not participate in the war of 1915–16, but they were in a state of extreme agitation in 1913, which according to many observers contributed to the environment in which the movement of the cercle of Dedougou was planned.

In the border zone between the cercles of Bobo-Dioulasso and Volta Supérieure, the "Nienegue" and the "Bobo" were the most famous rebellious tribes. These two rubrics cover another heterogeneous group of populations: the Bobo were sometimes differentiated into Bobo Oule and Bobo Fing. The former, now called Bwa in the ethnography, speak dialects of a language of the Voltaic family, whereas the latter speak dialects of a Mande language that is distinct from Manding (that is, Jula or Bamana).[22] The political situation at the turn of the century was, of course, very complicated and had little to do with ethnicity in this sense. Some Bwa and Bobo villages had ties with Fulbe and Watara war leaders and with the Karantao, as explained in chapter 2. Widi had ties with the Bwa village of Warkoy, but the connection did not keep this village in the colonial fold. At the end of the nineteenth century, the Zara houses of Sia (Bobo-Dioulasso) and their Watara allies (from bases in Koroma and Bosora) also waged war against a strong confederation of Bwa villages led by Sara (Binger, 1892, 1:395–407). These conflicts continued into the early colonial period and explain the removal and addition of the canton of Bereba to the state of Tieba Watara. In 1904, the cantons of Nienegue, Bereba, and Siankoro qualified as "completely nonsubmitted."[23]

The government-general in Dakar was more concerned with keeping its expenditures low and its budgets balanced than with responding to the frustration and ambitions of the cercle administrators. Indulging in obsessive fantasies of getting back at these defiant populations, the administrators made repeated requests to the lieutenant governor for larger forces of repression, but they were turned down. In 1904, for example, the administrator of Bobo-Dioulasso requested permission to engage in three punitive expeditions, two supposed to take place simultaneously in December. The largest, meant to give a "good and just lesson" to the Bwa populations of the cantons of Nienegue, Bereba, and Siankoro, would be placed under a captain's command and include one hundred tirailleurs, a cannon, and fifty infantry and cavalry auxiliary soldiers. The second column was for Tierla and would include thirty tirailleurs and auxiliary soldiers. After the completion of these missions, a third expedition would be sent to the canton of Nanergue, in the northwest of the cercle, and the surrounding area in the state of Mori-fin.[24] Authorization for all three expeditions was denied. Administrators were allowed to conduct only carefully planned "police and tax collection rounds" in the "good season"—that is, between January and May, when rivers and standing pools shrink. In these expeditions, the villages on the path of the column that had been abandoned by the frightened inhabitants were destroyed: the grain and valuables found in them were carried away. When the villagers had the courage to stay in place, or if they had been caught by surprise, they were asked to pay a tax in animals, cowry shells, and grains. They had to feed the troops stationed near the village until payment was made. The villages that offered strong resistance were often rewarded in their effort; either they were completely ignored or invited to negotiate, which generally resulted in a tax reduction.

In the most abstract analysis, the colonial administration in the Volta region was a predatory system with the sole purpose of making the population pay for the cost of its presence. In those early years, it managed to drain completely the few areas that it could subdue and to weaken a few others by periodically sending in punitive columns. But it had little effect on many other areas. As can be gauged from the steadily rising curve of tax receipts, the zone of impact of the posts gradually increased from the early years of the century until 1914, but it still left out many areas. The transformative impact of this early colonial administration on the regional political structure of the west Volta was limited. The populations of the region maintained most of their late-nineteenth-century political and economic organization. Village autonomy was maintained, and in some cases even broadened by the elimination of some of the major regional leaders—this despite the colonial administration's use of subordinate chiefs. What Henri Labouret wrote in 1914 was true not only for the cercle he administered, Lobi, but also for large areas of the cercles of Dedougou and Bobo-Dioulasso: "We really rule only over the footpath on which we are traveling at the moment, and over the post that we occupy."[25]

CHAPTER 4
Before the Storm

THE ANTICOLONIAL MOVEMENT WAS BORN in the special conditions of 1914 and 1915. The overwhelming subjective reading of the situation was that the creeping growth of colonial domination had ended and the administration's control of the countryside was receding. This chapter shows how the environment of World War I inspired this interpretation in the two critical cercles of Dedougou and Bobo-Dioulasso, and how the actions of the administrators of the two cercles contributed to it. In the final months of 1914, both cercles had new administrators. The first four sections of this chapter present the scandalous developments in Dedougou that were later related in government reports to the birth of the anticolonial movement. The final section takes up the activities and reforms of administrator Henri Maubert during the same period in the cercle of Bobo-Dioulasso. The situation prior to the beginning of the anticolonial war in the cercles of San and Ouagadougou is described in separate chapters.

THE COLONIAL ADMINISTRATION IN DEDOUGOU: MAGUET AND HAILLOT

Edgard Maguet, the new commandant of the cercle of Dedougou, took up his position late in August 1914, arriving from Sikasso, where he had served since 1911. Maguet was a product of the famous colonial school in Paris. He had been initiated into colonial service in the finance bureau in Bamako. When he arrived in the cercle he was about thirty years old and had received so far only glowing evaluations from his superiors. Shortly after his arrival, he was promoted to the rank of administrator third-class, continuing his track record of quickly paced preferment. Maguet projected less charisma and inspired less fear than Maubert, his gun-wielding, larger-than-life counterpart in Bobo-Dioulasso, but he seems to have been more calculating. He responded to the agitation stirred by the news of the world war with selective repression, perhaps to regain a sense of control, but also with an eye to obtaining promotion.

Maguet's subordinate, Haillot, played an important hand in the events that happened in the cercle. He had already served under Maguet in Sikasso, and the two men got along well, despite their different backgrounds. Haillot was a few years older than Maguet, and although he was less educated he played the role of mentor to his superior because of his longer colonial service. His chief qualification was that he belonged to a family that had produced several officers.[1] During the years Maguet spent in school, Haillot had served in the marine corps, from which he was discharged at the rank of corporal. Whereas Maguet had entered colonial service as an entry-level administrator, Haillot began at the humble rank of clerk. But in the remote parts of the colony where there were very few Frenchmen, these differences mattered little. Maguet praised Haillot's work and made him his executive assistant. Haillot actually carried out most of Maguet's decisions that will be reviewed here. When, after the anticolonial war, the shocking severity of their joint rule went beyond rumors in the hallways of Dakar and was exposed in detailed reports, Maguet pointed his finger at Haillot. But the evidence showed that little was done without Maguet's intimate knowledge.

The Maguet-Haillot team created in the cercle of Dedougou two series of incidents, separated by five months, that are reported in the documents as "affairs." These two affairs targeted different sets of people but decimated them equally with extreme physical abuse. It is astounding that both sets of victims were people known as allies of the French. Something about these "affairs" defies comprehension. The voluminous administrative documents about them enables one to guess what motivated one of these affairs, but the other remains a puzzle. Another unexpected twist to these affairs is that their victims did not all side with the anticolonial movement when it started. The connection between the "affairs" and the anticolonial movement is fuzzy, and at the end it contains a paradox. The next two sections focus on the contribution that the affairs had on the growing popular perception that colonial force had become vulnerable.

The affair of the marabouts was a harsh crackdown against the Muslim clerics and dignitaries of the cercle of Dedougou. The religious men were charged with planning and promoting a general uprising against the French. The event is remembered in the region as "the gathering of the marabout."

THE MARABOUT "CONSPIRACY"

Administrative inquiry into what became the marabout affair started early in December 1914 in the cercle of Ouagadougou. A few Muslim clerics had been arrested in the Koudougou subdivisions of the cercle of Ouagadougou and charged with spreading seditious rumors. Some of these people were visiting from places as far away as the cercle of Jenne. In the atmosphere of intense suspicion of Islam that the world war promoted, the administrator of Ouagadougou, Henri d'Arboussier, visited Koudougou to inquire further about the matter. During this visit, Laarle Naaba Pawitraogo, the Mose chief who was appointed to head this subdivision, told him that there was a broader Muslim conspiracy prepared against the French. It included the Muslims of Leo—and, most importantly, the imam of To and the clerics of Boromo and Wahabu, in the neighboring cercle.[2] As discussed in more detail in chapter 10, this was the network of Amaria, an early military ally who had played an important pro-French role in the rivalry with the British at the end of the nineteenth century. Amaria had just triumphantly returned from the joint British-French campaign against German Togoland, where he had led his irregular soldiers.

The few people who were first arrested on the basis of charges made by the laarle naaba denied the allegations, but the interrogators became convinced that there was a foundation for the accusation. They discovered connections among the Muslims of Ouagadougou, Dedougou, Dori, and San. They reported their suspicions to the administrators of these other cercles, with the recommendation that they inquire further into the matter.

This information came to Dedougou in December 1914, when Maguet was conducting an expedition to the troublesome area of Sami and Perive. He asked Haillot, left in charge of the headquarters, to summon to Dedougou the major Muslim dignitaries of the region. Haillot went to the villages of Cheriba, Jinakongo, Tunu, Datomo, Wahabu, and Safane to ask the Muslim dignitaries what they knew about this. Nothing, they answered. Haillot, not satisfied, decided to extract confessions by torture.[3]

The Muslims, as we saw in chapter 2, were a heterogeneous group who offered their services as ritual specialists to villages and to their hosts. Each village confederation, each important political leader, each party in a conflict—all had their own Muslims. Confrontations between power centers and village confederations often placed the clerics in opposite camps. Far from constituting a united political bloc, Muslim dignitaries were also divided by serious rivalries among themselves and by memories of past conflict. Retrospectively, it is baffling that people such as the Karantao of Wahabu, the Sere of Safane, and the leaders of Jinakongo — all of whom, not so long ago, had warred against each other — could find themselves facing Haillot's inquisition as coconspirators. It is unimaginable to us that a Karantao would have attended a funeral service conducted by the imam of Safane; nearly the only thing these people had in common was that they had all sided with the French when the latter arrived in the region — and that was the only reason why hostility among them had become dormant. Maguet, however, did not like the Muslims. On visits to Muslim communities around Dedougou he had felt uneasy, and he did not think they were loyal to France. He gave his approval to Haillot's action.

The interrogations turned on the issue of a letter, in Arabic, that it was claimed announced the arrival of the Mahdi (a Muslim equivalent of the Messiah) and called the believers to rise against the Christians. It was reported that this letter had been read by the imam of Safane, Abdoulaye Koïta, during the funeral of a venerated man, then copied at different Muslim centers and circulated.[4] The Muslim dignitaries told Haillot that a letter existed, but that it was only about the bad harvest, the short rainy season, women who refused to get married, and diseases that would strike the population. The circulation of letters between Muslim communities across large distances was not unusual. Some of these letters had an apocalyptic tone since they exhorted people to mend their ways. Funerals provided the opportunity to read such public messages and give advice to the Muslim community. Most likely, it is such an occasion that became the basis for the charges of first the Laarle naaba in Koudougou and then of Haillot in Dedougou.

In his later investigation, the inspector-general, Picanon, concluded that a letter did exist, and that it was read in the mosque of Boromo by a seventy-two-year-old Dagari-Jula man, Siribu Senu, whom he had interviewed. No letter was read in Wahabu, and it is not clear whether a letter was read in Safane. The letter that Picanon found is a document of Qadiri origin written in the form of a dream. It explains that Mohammed implored God through the intermediary of the angel Gabriel not to destroy humankind, promising to send Abd al Qader al Jeylani to reform people (see fig. 2 and the appendix for the French translation by Paul Marty). The letter consists mostly of a litany of ways in which humans erred (at a time unspecified in the letter), and it makes a number of prescriptions by which

Muslims could show repentance.[5] There is no mention of the Mahdi, of the French, or of Christians, nor anything that could be remotely taken as incitement to rebellion. In fact, there is no reference to the present in this letter, the only connection being what an audience might have inferred from the extensive list of ways in which people may go astray. The inquiry in the cercle of Ouagadougou uncovered two more letters in Arabic, but they, too, lack any sign of instigating insubordination (see chap. 10). If there were more grounds other than these letters for suspecting conspiracy, none was presented in the trials that followed, and later in colonial circles a quiet consensus emerged that the charges in Dedougou were concocted by Maguet's entourage. "From the very beginning of the inquiry on the marabouts," wrote Picanon in his report, "it is not possible to think that Haillot believed in a conspiracy, but he continued it to seek personal success."[6]

When Haillot failed to find tangible evidence to support serious charges, he had the clerics, their sons, their relatives, and other members of their households publicly whipped, tortured, and jailed. Under duress, some people gave false confessions, like a son of Moktar Karantao who, in the midst of a feigned execution, said that he would take Haillot to the weapons hoard of his father. Once in the village, he could not show this hoard and was tortured again for lying. These acts were performed in public, junior dependents and loyal followers watching the suffering and humiliation of the venerated men. The canton chief of Safane, Suleyman Sere, was only whipped, but the Karantao family was less fortunate. Two of its younger sons died under torture, as did two of its adult soldiers. According to Picanon's report, between December and February nine Muslim leaders died during this inquisition, including the canton chief of Datomo. Copies of the Koran and other Islamic manuscripts were gathered and burned in public. Many Muslim leaders, including M'Pa Karantao, the successor of Moktar (d. 1910), were kept under dreadful conditions in jail, where epidemics and mistreatment killed many inmates. The house and grain stores of M'Pa Karantao were burned down while he was imprisoned.

The investigation ended with a three-day trial that started on February 27. The verdict was given on March 2, and twenty people were condemned to prison sentences. The heaviest sentences (ranging from ten to twenty years) were given to Abdulaye Koïta, of Safane; M'Pa Karantao and Lansane Senu, of Wahabu; Abdulaye Wattara, of Boromo; and Isu Dao. In April 1915 there was another wave of arrests and another trial on related charges, this time in the cercle of Ouagadouguou. At the end of the anticolonial war, to reward the Muslim families for the support they gave to the administration, the convicts of the Dedougou trial were pardoned. The sentences of the Ouagadougou trial, however, were never cancelled.

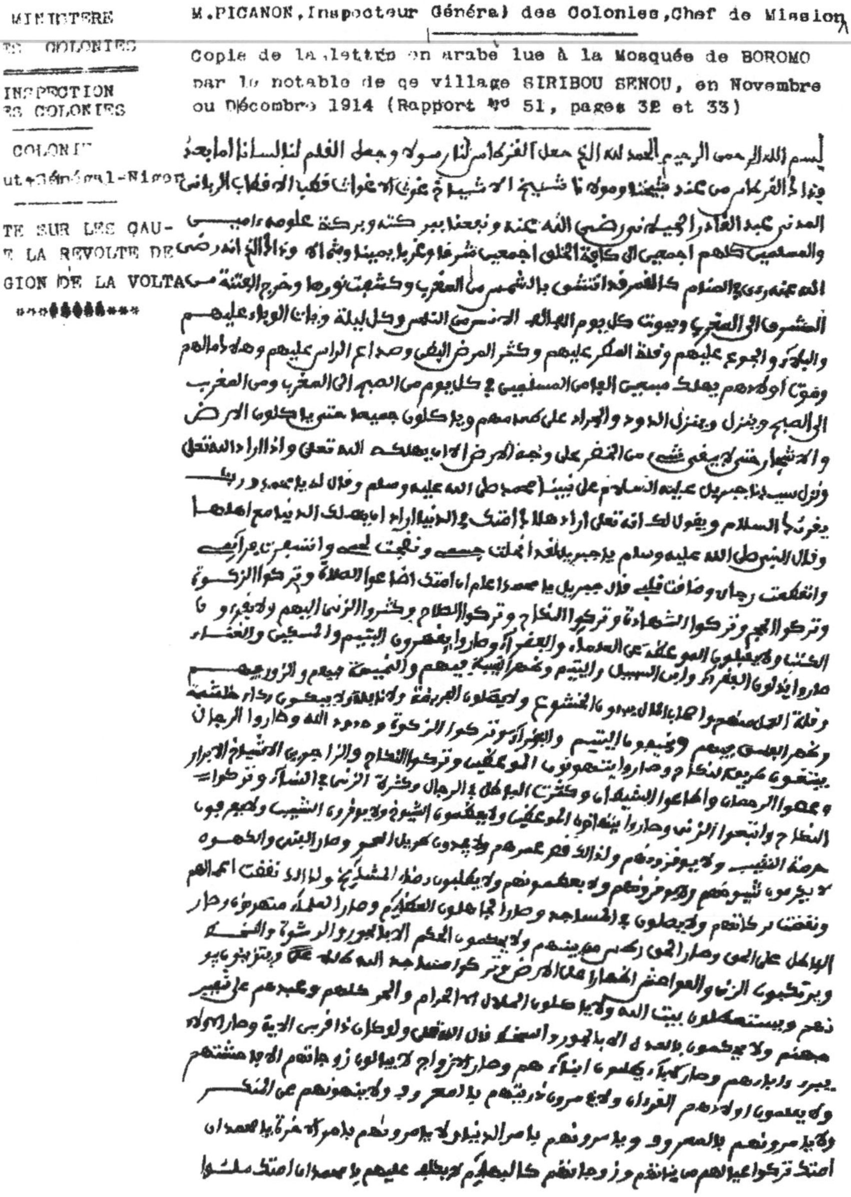

MINISTERE
DES COLONIES
INSPECTION
DES COLONIES
COLONIE
Haut-Sénégal-Niger

M. PICANON, Inspecteur Général des Colonies, Chef de Mission

Copie de la lettre en arabe lue à la Mosquée de BOROMO par le notable de ce village SIRIBOU SENOU, en Novembre ou Décembre 1914 (Rapport No 51, pages 32 et 33)

TE SUR LES CAU-
E LA REVOLTE DE
GION DE LA VOLTA

Fig. 2. Copy of the letter in Arabic used in the Dedougou trial. See the appendix for a translation into French.

الأرض بالخير ولا يحمدون ولا يحمدون الله لا بجور ولا الملوان ولا يطلبون الله تعالى بالنوافل
ولا يكثرون الصيام رمضان ولا يعبدون الله عبها ولا يطلبون النوافل لليلهم وينكاثرون بكثرة سوال
ولا صراخ واصولهم حنين يبروا العطا برولا ينوبون الى الله ولا يكثرون صيام الله وشهر النبي
وشهرهم وان من الرجال يدخل القوم بهوم لند ﻉ النهار ثم يبكر بالطعام بالزنى ثم بينها مع
زاينتها ومنهم من يدخل ﻉ القوم ثم يخمس ﻉ فيه الغيبة والنميمة والزور ويتكلمون ﻉ المسا
جد بكلام الدنيا يا محمد قلوبا منك افسى من الصفا أو الحجارة يا محمد ان اصنك لا يبعدون النكا
على الحفيفة وكل نكاحهم اليوم يكون أصله على الزنى ويبصرون على استبراء ﻉ زوجاتهم
ومن يكون نكاحه على الزنى بيجسد بشرح بشرط النكاح ولا يعلمون حرمة النكاح و لا
يعطفون حدود نكاح ولا شروكمه وصار العلماء من اصنك لا يبتلحون الناس الحلال وصار
المتعلمون لا يكلبون علمهم له الله نيا ولا بحر قون العالم الا جسى صرت وانتشرت
العشر والنصراني منهم وليبر الناص منهم يا محمد غنيار صاروا ويبصرون على الفقرا ء
واليتيم والمساكين وكانوا كاليهود والنصراني ولا يفبلون الشباعة ولا يباليون المزن
ولا يتبعر ونها ويبفنون انهم موجودون ﻉ الدنيا على الحنت العظيم ولا ينوبون منه ويذوبون
ثم يبحرون منه ويفلعوا بارهامهم ولا يبلعونهم ﻉ الارحام يا محمد من مات من صما اصنك
خلفك مسمرون ﻉ الامر حرموا ظلهم الله ولكن كانوا انفسهم يظلمون وبحر النبي
صلى الله عليه وسلم ﻉ الفبر حتى اضفريت صنارة الفبور وصار اهل المدينة بنكرون الفبر حتى
كخواء الفيامة فد فامت وفال النبي صلى الله عليه وسلم ارجع الى ربي وفل لهم امايهطلهم
وبجري مى بشعر عة لربه ثم فلا النبي صلى الله عليه وسلم ارجع الى ربي وفل لهم امايهطلهم
ساعة ان ارسل اليهم رسول انا جعلوا نعيمة يبعير منهم من صلا حرهم والله جعل ما
شكرى وارسله النبي حاوه م عبد الدفا در الميلاد نعينا الله بمر كته وفال يبهب ربهم المشترى
الى المغرب بان وجه كل نصر ذ الح الزى بيهلك سريعا وذ الكالزى انتى ما الحبيجة اعاة ذا الله
منها وبونا ول النبي صلى الله عليه وسلم ارسلت اليكم رسالة بعد رسالة ولا يزيدكم شيا الا
نبورا وفال عميد الغا در الميلاد بسا اردكم ان نحيبه الله عن تلك الوبأ وبلبغرا داية الكرسى
سبع مرات وسورة آ خلاص اثنى عشرة صرة ﻉ عصف حلا بريفة وبختبط ذ ذ الى ويعلفها على
نوبسه ويبكون الخانبين اجرتهم لا نحا لا ينبع موجود كا موجود ثم الصليون صورة الا
خلاص البه صرة مع رامى الرسول الح صرة ومذطا كالله ليبعد به م وانت فيهم وما كان الله
معذبهم وهم يستغفر وما سبعين ﻉ باب المسا جد الصباح و المسا سبعة ابا م
من احجد ان السبت وسلطان البلد يتصد ق العمر والبعر مع الفميص ﻉ يعطى ه
للامام وينهد ه طا حب كل ﻉ ار اربع واوصى خبز او الجسر ﻉ بذ جمه ﻉ ة او ه وينتصد ى
كل رجل فميصه وجفيه الفقرا والمساكين ومائة ودع وينتصد ه كل رجل بجا مبعة
ودع وكل نسا ة اربع و ﻉ م و صا لم بجد هولا لستد ة وجمافة بلينتصد ى بفد رها
فتنة او مصدفة بد جح البلد و العذ اب وما شاو بليبعطله وصى بشر و بلينتر
كنته انا ربكم نحنر من الحلميين انتم الفقراء الى الله والله غنى حميد

Fig. 2 (continued).

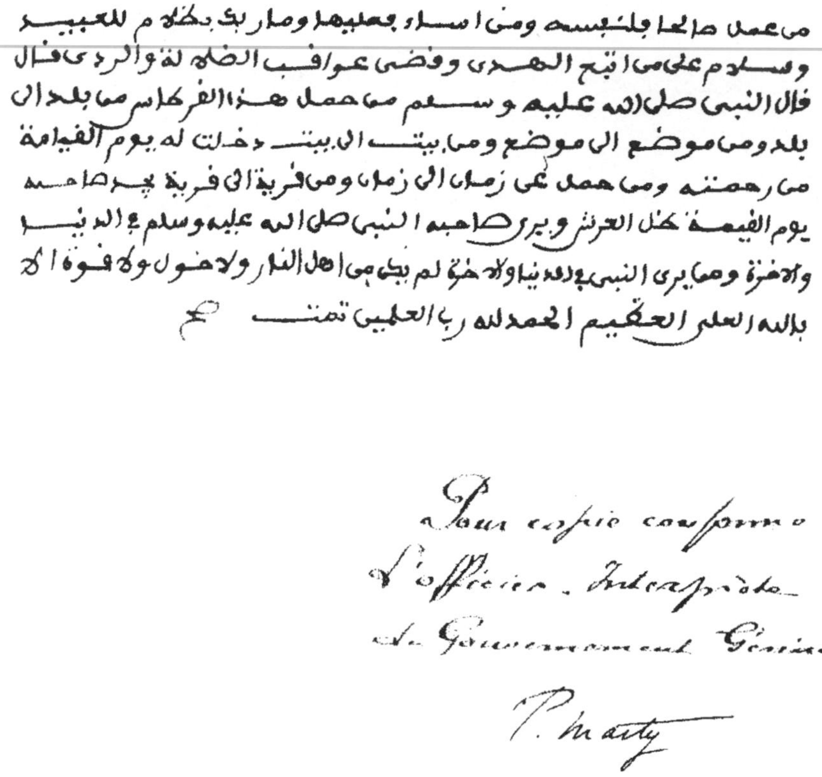

من عمل صالحا فلنفسه ومن اساء فعليها فمار بك بخلا م للعبيــد
وسلام م على من انج الهــدى وفضى عواقـب الظلم لة وألرد ي فـال
فال النبى صلى الله عليه و ســلم من حصل هـذا القرطاس من بلد ان
بلد ومن موضع الى موضع وما بيتــه الى بيتــ دخلت له يوم القيامة
من رحمته ومن حمل على زمان الى زمان ومن القريذ الى فريذ يمرضاحبه
يوم القيمــة كل العزن ويبر ز صاحبه النبى صلى الله عليه وسلم ع الد يــا
والاخرة ومن يرى النبى ولده نياولاه خية لم يبك من اهل النار ولا حنول وله فــوة ا لا
بالله العلم العظيم الحمد لله رب العلمين تمنـــ

Fig. 2 (continued).

Examining how the first denunciations reached the colonial administrators, Anne-Marie Duperray (1984, 175–80) proposed that the Muslim plot was a stratagem that the traditionalist Mose chiefs of Ouagadougou devised to eliminate some of their Muslim rivals within the cercle. The chief target was Amaria of Leo, who was abruptly eliminated at a time when most people thought he was at the apex of his popularity; jailed in May, he was dead shortly afterwards, under obscure circumstances.[7] The charge that had originated as part of the factional struggles among local chiefs in Ouagadougou had crossed the borders of the cercle of Dedougou to become a vehicle for Maguet and Haillot's ambition.

The ease with which the administrator of Ouagadougou adopted the conspiracy story, and with which Haillot and Maguet in Dedougou were able to carry out their investigation and punctuate it with convictions, had to do with the climate of opinion at that time. The suspicion of "Muslim fanaticism" had never died in French colonial circles, despite close collaboration with Muslim dignitaries, clerics, and warlords in Masina and then in the Volta region. In 1906, William Ponty, as lieutenant governor of Haut-Sénégal-Niger, instituted the systematic surveillance of all Muslim leaders, using yearly updated files. When Ponty became governor-general of French West Africa, he embarked on a more determinedly anti-Muslim course. An example was the 1909 move away from paramount chiefs, who were the precolonial allies, toward the "policy of races" — that is, reliance on small cantons with chiefs recruited from more humble origins; this, in effect, amounted to the removal of the Muslim collaborators of the early occupation period. In 1911, Ponty wrote to Clozel, who was then the lieutenant governor of Haut-Sénégal-Niger, that maraboutic propaganda was "the hypocritical facade behind which are sheltered hopes of the former privileged groups and the last obstacle in the way of the complete triumph of our civilizing work."[8]

When in November 1914 the Ottoman Empire entered World War I as an ally of Germany, suspicion of Muslims in West Africa reached new heights. In 1898, Kaiser Wilhelm II had proclaimed himself "Protector of the Islamic World." The Ottoman sultan claimed to be caliph of all Muslims, and the government in Constantinople (Istanbul) tried to exploit his prestige in its war effort. The French fear that subversion in the name of the caliph would reach the interior of West Africa with the help of German propaganda conducted from their colonies was not totally unfounded. In December 1914, the British authorities discovered in the Adamawa region of Nigeria a letter in Arabic that had been written by a Muslim from German Kamerun. German propaganda was based on the five *fatwa*, or authoritative religious opinions, that the Ottoman government had obtained to ground their declaration of war. The propaganda targeted the Muslims of Nigeria. In addition, materials were prepared in English and French to incite desertions among the French tirailleurs and the northern Nigerian recruits fighting with the British forces in Kamerun (Norris 1990: 14, 19, 21).

These German attempts turned out to be ineffective, and no echo of them reached the Volta region. Even without the pamphlets prepared by the German Nachrichtenstelle für den Orient, the local Muslims were certainly aware of the Ottoman alliance with the Germans and that the Ottomans supported the Sanusi war in the Sahara. Any indication, however, that they felt loyalty to the Ottoman caliph and actively opposed the French colonial administration is lacking. In Teneni, near San, a search in the house of a Muslim leader yielded the portraits of Empress Augusta Victoria and the Ottoman crown prince, Yusuf Efendi.[9] The French took this as incriminating evidence of collusion with the enemy power. But in the cercle of Dedougou, between Bona and Safane, the investigation

yielded not even evidence of this indirect nature. On the contrary, during the war
the major Muslim houses of the Volta were anxious to manifest their loyalty to
the French.[10]

The crackdown of the early months of 1915 achieved the opposite of what
its planners thought it would do, and this is the aspect of the affair most relevant to our topic. Instead of stamping out an anti-French conspiracy, it resulted
in the virtual disappearance of an entire set of French allies from the political
scene of the cercle of Dedougou. The elimination on the Karantao served particularly a village confederation that had been their enemy in the nineteenth
century. Its leaders came mostly from the villages of Bona and Tunu. The unexpected blow that was dealt to their Muslim opponents in the area and the disarray into which World War I had thrown the colonial administration of the
cercles left a power vacuum, which they saw as a unique opportunity. As we
briefly mentioned in chapter 2 and will explain in detail in chapter 5, they became the people who started the anticolonial war.

THE AFFAIR OF THE GUARDS

The opening salvo for the second campaign of Commandant Maguet, known as
the "affair of the guards," was an inquiry begun in July 1915 into the miscon-
duct of certain guards. The guards remained in the employment of the cercle for
years, and even if initially they had been foreigners to the area, they had set local roots—by marrying into the community and leading huge compounds with
many domestics and dependents. They were few in number and constituted an
important component of the early native colonial elite. The reports that Maguet
and other officials wrote about the extortions and the cruelty of some of the
guards in his cercle provide one of the few glimpses we have, from the official
side, of what the workings of colonialism at that time meant in everyday life. We
have little reason to doubt the veracity of these charges. What is hard to understand is why Maguet started this investigation.

Maguet wrote in a report during the investigation that his suspicion was
aroused when he noticed that the lavish lifestyle of the guards could not be supported by their salaries.[11] They left on administrative duties without money or
food and returned with horses and goods. At night, the villages that they had
recently visited sent them convoys of porters carrying gifts. The expenditures of
the guards sustained the growing market for luxury consumer goods (such as
sorghum beer, meat, and clothing). If villagers made a complaint against a chief,

interpreters and guards assumed control of the case, and the information invariably turned out to be either vague or impossible to corroborate. Even conflicts among guards that were brought to Maguet's knowledge were resolved immediately after one party declared that he would open his mouth on what other guards did when they set off on rounds. It was as if the administration harbored a parallel, invisible world of relationships and references. Maguet ended his report by saying that, because a blanket of silence was thrown on every lead he had found, he had to conduct the investigation with great discretion, to reassure potential witnesses and not to alert the guards and interpreters.

Discretion and witness security were the exact opposites of what happened, according to what is revealed in Inspector Picanon's later report.[12] During August and September, hundreds of canton chiefs, village chiefs, and village dignitaries were dragged to Dedougou, interrogated under torture, and jailed in order to extract from them confessions that they had indeed given gifts and bribes to guards. Dissatisfied with what they had obtained, administrative agents went to villages and humiliated and tortured hundreds of other interrogatees. The punishments ranged from routine public whipping to fumigation in a closed room. Many old and infirm people were interrogated, and several of them died as a consequence. As in the marabout situation, the chief agent of execution was Haillot. In the resulting trial on October 19, 1915, twelve guards were sentenced to prison, or fined, and ordered to make restitution.[13] But these punishments were negligible compared to the suffering endured by many other villagers during the interrogations.

Why did Maguet and a few of his subordinates decide to act against some guards and interpreters in their cercle? As Maguet himself pointed out later, when the matter turned against him, abusive guards were not peculiar to his cercle. The practices were so widespread that some of the accused guards in fact used this as a line of defense: in the surrounding cercles, they said, it would not be possible to find a single guard who had not stolen or coerced gift payments. Why, then, go to such lengths to torture and humiliate aged dignitaries allied to the administration if the purpose was to protect them from extortion? A cruel irony permeated these actions. During his expedition to the villages of Sami and Perive in December 1914, Maguet had stopped in Warkoy, where complaints were made against the canton chief. After a cursory investigation, Maguet decided that the complaints were unfounded and severely punished the people who made them. Eleven months later, the same canton chief was called to Dedougou by Haillot and lashed until he admitted that he had collected money in his village to pay the guards.[14]

The conduct of Maguet and his associates does not incline one to think that he was motivated by genuine concern for justice. Policing practices did not improve even in the course of the inquiry. The expeditions organized to gather the facts and witnesses for the campaign were sent out, as usual, without money or food, with the expectation that they would be supported by the villages they visited. Wards and villages made payments simply to shorten the stay of the interrogators and to ransom individuals threatened with deportation to De-dougou as potential witnesses for the case. In fact, as special envoys of the commandant on extraordinary assignment, the inquisitors dropped all pretense and indulged in open ransacking on a scale rarely seen before.

Karama Tamini, the interrogated chief of Warkoy, explained in a deposition how the procedure was conducted:

> Around September 1915, I was called to Dedougou by order of Mr. Haillot. . . . [He] accused me of having raised among the population a sum of money so that I could give gifts to the guards. I denied this. Then the interpreter Yoro Caye, who is here present, took me to the prison. I had to take off my cloths, my robe and my pants. As I was lying on the ground face down, two guards held my feet, and the interpreter Yoro Caye started hitting me with a rope or a leather strap.[15]

Nouye Yedan, chief of the village of Yona in the canton of Safane, later testified:

> One and a half or two months before the rebellion, Ako Diallo asked [the chief's] brother Yore Yedan, who was then chief, what gifts were made during the construction of the colonial compound of Safane to the guard Alandou Zanzolo, who was overseeing the work. He answered that no gifts were made. Then the guard said to him: "Even if you did not give anything, you have to say that you gave something." Yore answered that he was not lying. He was beaten by Ako with a braided cord and then with a stick. He was unable to recover from these blows and died about the time when the rebellion started.[16]

In the village of Balave, in order to extort confessions and money eight old men were shut in a room with smoking charcoals to which hot peppers were added. One of these men died that evening. Picanon's report said that twenty-one people died during these interrogations placed under the responsibility of Haillot.

Maguet, who personally participated in village interrogations, pursued this investigation with dogged persistence; it is as if he had a personal vendetta against some of the employees of the cercle. But his personal investigative team also included native agents. The guard Alamasson and the interpreter Yaro Gaye were two of the most prominent. Aka Diallo, known locally as Tiefin, was also very active. He conducted much of the witness hunt in the villages with the vague and transitory title of *agent politique*. Tiefin was the brother of Maguet's African mistress.[17] It is evident that the group that carried out the campaign was a close-knit coterie consisting of a few French officials and a few Africans who had personal ties to them.

Later, the inquiry of Inspector Picanon also revealed financial fraud. Maguet and his French subordinate in the residence of Boromo, Combes, regularly withdrew sums from the special budget of the cercle—sums that did not require accounting. Maguet and Combes composed false receipts and claimed to have made payments to recipients who, when asked, denied having received them. These offenses were frequent and systematic, suggesting prior example and experience. Picanon felt compelled to raise the disturbing question of whether such practices were not more widespread in the colony than was imagined.

While we can continue to wonder what in the tiny colonial stratum of Dedougou could explain the motivations for this campaign, the broader consequences of the affair for the anticolonial movement are fairly clear. The witness hunt of Maguet and his associates occurred only one or two months before the beginning of open anticolonial opposition in the cercle. And this opposition started precisely in the area where the investigation had focused. The investigation teams for this affair had visited almost all the major villages that gathered around the anticolonial leadership of Bona. Yet not every one of the victims of Maguet's inquiry sided with the anticolonial movement; on the contrary, many of them participated with enthusiasm in the government repression.

A contrast emerges on this score between simple village chiefs and dignitaries, on the one hand, and the small number of people who were given the title of canton chief, on the other. The majority of village chiefs humiliated in this affair did indeed join the ranks of the anticolonial fighters. Some of them, such as Domba Ye, of Yankaso, even became important leaders of the movement. However, the chiefs of the cantons of Warkoy, Tunu, and Datomo chose the side of the administration. The chief of Safane went even further, becoming the crucial procolonial actor in the events that set off the war. These people walked with the colonial officials who had tortured them only months or weeks before, in opposition to the anticolonial crowds that included their fellow village members.

To understand this better, it will be helpful to say more about the position that canton chiefs occupied in the colonial administration. In those years, village chiefs were not yet truly colonial appointees. Their tasks consisted of maintaining the colonial compound in good order, organizing the supply of cooked food for a visiting colonial company, responding to the visitors' questions, and conveying their orders to the villagers. Very often they were younger brothers or sons of elders with significant ritual authority in the village community who wanted to keep an eye on relations with the outside without subjecting themselves to the indignities of direct contact.

In contrast, the canton chief was a person who had been selected by the administrator or his native helpers. The position of canton chief involved some risks. Chiefs were exposed frequently to the whims of colonial personnel and many received punishment for being unable to fulfill the requests made of them. But the position also carried tangible benefits—a salary, a percentage of the collected tax, the support of the administration in cases of difficulty, access to some free labor. While most people who had witnessed the pain and humiliation of elders during the interrogations responded favorably to the emissaries from Bona who invited the villagers to join the anticolonial movement, the canton chiefs were given little choice. Even if they wanted to reconsider their commitment to the colonial regime, the villagers left them out. Not only were village proceedings kept secret from them, the canton chief also almost immediately became the favorite target of mob activity when people crossed the line from passive sympathy to active participation in the movement.

Another important contribution of Maguet's two "affairs" to the rise of the anticolonial movement was a strengthening of the perception (already suggested by other observations such as the withdrawal of soldiers) that the colonial order was going through a terminal convulsion. To help appreciate the persuasive force of this spectacle, we turn to local attitudes toward the French.

At the deepest level of local discourse, the French were seen only as the blind instrument of a transcending order—the way some would view a natural disaster that would scathe some people but not others. In the inexplicable swings of colonial policy, the local population found not the thread of consistent human purpose but the unpatterned moves of a suprahuman agency for which the French were but tools. Colonialism was not seen as a collective calamity—because the misfortunes of particular individuals caught up in these events could be explained, and the explanation was often that they were retribution for a transgression on the part of the victim. The downfall of French allies, therefore, even if it was by the hand of the French, was a providential occurrence. Rot had taken hold of all these men who had defiled themselves by collaborating with the white man, and, like a disease, it was corroding the colonial stratum from the inside.

This understanding was also amenable to a more explicitly political spin. Led by Bona, the villages of the canton of Datomo rejoiced at the disappearance of their perpetual enemies—the Karantao—and took note that there was greater freedom of action for them. Now most of the guards too were either in jail or dismissed, and the canton chiefs had been humiliated. Some political space had opened up, and it could be filled with proper initiative and intelligent action. The conscription campaign, curious as it may seem at first, also led to an optimistic prognosis for a movement of opposition.

THE CONSCRIPTION CAMPAIGN OF NOVEMBER 1915

The drafting of African men to the colonial army was one of the distinguishing practices of French colonialism.[18] Until the end of the nineteenth century, the enlisted African soldiers recruited by the French—the tirailleurs—were a "voluntary" (i.e., not conscripted) mercenary force (see fig. 3). They included many of slave descent, for whom the former owners were generally compensated (Echenberg 1991). As these troops came increasingly to be used as an expeditionary force to defend the far-flung French Empire, it became clear that the growing need could not be met by the old rough-and-ready techniques of recruitment, and in 1912 partial conscription *(voie d'appel)* was enacted. During World War I, General Mangin, the major advocate for a larger, so-called Black Army,[19] was promoted to the rank of general, and black soldiers were now deployed not only in North Africa but also to face Germany in continental France. An expanded Black Army necessitated a broader base of recruitment.

Conscription in the West African territories was uneven. Rates of recruitment varied greatly according to various factors in different colonies, mostly the willingness of the communities to provide volunteers and the ability of the administration to take them by compulsion. Some groups—such as the Tuareg and the Fulbe—were left out of recruitment, others contributed heavily. When the world war began, the quotas of recruits to be raised in West Africa were increased and it became necessary to extend the draft to regions that had hitherto been spared.

The draft came to the cercle of Dedougou for the first time in 1915. The first levy took place in March. The second came six months later, following a

Fig. 3. Tirailleurs. Drawn by G. Bruyer from an old photograph and printed in Jacques Méniaud, *Les pionniers du Soudan,* vol. 1, p. 67 (Paris: Société des Publications Modernes, 1931).

decree on October 5 that enjoined the conscription of fifty thousand more men from West Africa. The March campaign proceeded without major crisis in the cercle of Dedougou, but it caused serious disturbances in other parts of Haut-Sénégal-Niger. The most important opposition took place north of Bamako, in the Beledougou region. A man named Diose, assisted by Samba Jara, started an armed movement that spread quickly to Gumbu, Nioro, and around Banamba. It was put down before the end of March by a column that set out from the nearby base in Kati. The Beledougou uprising was like a rehearsal for the Volta-Bani War; besides the numerous similarities in leadership and the way the movement grew, the news of Beledougou became an important encouraging factor for Africans in the Volta region.

The civilian colonial cadres in West Africa—from the level of the governor-general in Dakar down to the cercle administrators—loathed military conscription. This is abundantly documented in all kinds of reports and public announcements, including the later insistence of civilian inspectors that conscription and conscription alone had caused the 1915 uprising in Dedougou. The draft came on top of a drastic regime of surplus extraction, and even when it did not provoke opposition, it took away part of the active population. At a time of personnel shortages, the campaign itself commanded all the attention of the administration and brought to a halt all other activities. But the colonial government could do little about this, especially in the midst of a war with Germany.

Upon receiving from the metropole the total levy for West Africa, the governor-general in Dakar divided up this figure among the colonies under him. The governors and lieutenant governors of each colony in turn divided the number they received among their cercles. The cercle administrators broke down their allotment into a number of recruits from each canton. The native canton chiefs were given the actual duty of gathering the conscripts, while in each cercle a mobile company of tirailleurs made the rounds to ensure smooth operation. The canton chiefs requested the villages under them to provide a specified number of candidates. Although these allotments were supposed to be based on estimated population figures, at the local level, as at the higher level, other factors came into play. Groups privileged by the administration were given a lighter share of the burden, while villages that could be intimidated contributed disproportionately larger shares. The census figures, themselves largely fabricated, were adjusted up or down to keep up appearances. The recruitment campaign facilitated new forms of abuse; bribes and favors reached new heights because guards and other native employees could discharge their duties with greater or lesser leniency.

Most villages responded to conscription with strategies to lessen the burden laid on them. Which young men were to be presented to the recruitment agents was a matter of life and death for families within each village, and the campaign rekindled many dormant and ancient hostilities. It set off a struggle among the houses of each ward and sometimes even split houses and kinship groups. Public meetings turned into shows of intimidation, and behind closed doors people turned to aggressive secret rituals to save their dependents at the expense of those of their neighbors. The various subterfuges and delays slowed down the campaign.

The first to be sacrificed to the conscription campaign—as to other impositions—were people of slave descent and members of other subordinate groups, but in heavily subordinated communities, years of portage service, roadwork, and other administrative corvées had already eroded much of that layer. The preeminent houses in these villages had already lost most members of the subaltern groups on which their privileges depended. Many of the senior houses were now threatened with having to send young members of their core kinship groups, the less-well-placed houses having already lost a good number of theirs. Very often, the community tried to circumvent the imposition by providing old and sickly candidates in the hope that they would be rejected and sent back.

The administration asked each village to supply three or four times the number of men actually required for conscription. The canton chief gathered the candidates from the villages and took them to the cercle headquarters. A selection committee, headed by a doctor, selected the conscripts of each village from among the candidates it had provided. Besides the general health and age appearance of the candidates, some weight-to-height formulas had been developed to expedite the process. Once the requirement of the cercle was filled, the rejected candidates were allowed to return to their villages. The conscripted men were sent on foot under the supervision of armed guards to Kati, the military headquarters of Haut-Senegal-Niger. They made the trip under horrendous conditions. They were not given uniforms and they slept unsheltered, without blankets, in roadside camps.[20] In the savanna, the early dry season is cool, and because local clothing for young people was next to nothing, it was not uncommon for recruits from Dedougou and Bobo-Dioulasso to die from cold.

In the November 1915 campaign, the canton of Datomo, which as we have seen included the village of Bona, had to supply a total of thirty-six conscripts. Bona itself had a population of only about four hundred. In the previous recruitment, in March, Bona had provided two candidates, but the selection committee had rejected both.[21] (Since March, this area had also been compelled to provide a thousand porters to go with the troops sent to invade German Togoland; none had yet returned. We do not know if Bona supplied any of the porters.) In November, Bona was asked to provide four candidates, only one of which was to be drafted. By mid-November, most of the recruitment in the cantons of Datomo and Tunu had been completed. The village of Bona had provided three men, but the canton chief found none of them acceptable.[22] He sent them back and asked the village to provide other candidates. It was at this point that the refusal of Bona took a defiant turn.

Before proceeding with the story of Bona, we will consider the meaning local people gave to the conscription campaign under the circumstances of those months. As in many other parts of the colonial empire, periodically a special situation raised the hopes that the French were about to leave. The beginning of World War I, and the measures that the French took in the colonies as part of the war effort, was one of these situations. Villagers closely followed the news of the war and debated the chances of France against Germany. Early in 1915, the

French missionaries in Bwa country wrote, "The natives are interested in the news of the war in an extraordinary manner. . . . France was done for . . . . The Germans were triumphant. All the whites in the colony had to be killed" (Prost 1971, 106).

The departure of the few Frenchmen in the colony following the massive call-up in France had great influence on the way people locally understood what was happening. The French civilians who were called to active duty departed in the course of 1914, and the vacancies they left behind disrupted many services. For example, the Banfora agronomic station that had opened in 1904 had to close down. Many of the missionaries had to leave too, forcing the shutdown of some recently established mission posts, which were very sparse to begin with. The colonial administration was already understaffed before the call-up. The cercle of Dedougou, which had a population of about 300,000 and an area equivalent to a few metropolitan French departments put together, was administered by only four Frenchmen, two of whom were normally assigned to office work.[23]

To local eyes the colonial government truly appeared, then, like a system ruled by a small group of privileged Africans, with only a few, rarely seen Europeans behind. With the war mobilization, the government started to withdraw these Africans as well. The tirailleurs troops were concentrated in selected bases in West Africa, or sent to other colonies and to Europe. In the cercles, smaller numbers of guards replaced these troops. The brigade of Bobo-Dioulasso, the largest military base in the Volta and Bani regions, was withdrawn in August 1914. It left with some fanfare for Kati.[24] The neighboring cercles, too, were emptied of their tirailleurs units. At the beginning of the conscription campaign, some tirailleurs were returned to these cercles, to help carry out the recruitment. Dedougou then received a handful of them under Lieutenant Taxil. In the cercles of Ouagadougou and Fada— two immense administrative units covering an area that includes today more than half of the population of Burkina Faso—the only military personnel left were fifty tirailleurs assigned to the recruitment commission. The August 1914 campaign to occupy German Togoland, carried out jointly with British forces from the Gold Coast, drained further the posts of the Volta region.[25] Besides officers, guards, and porters, local chiefs were asked to contribute to the effort by raising auxiliary troops from among their followers and leading them to the front, as in the case of Amaria mentioned above (p. 91).

The conscription campaign, coming in the wake of this apparent evacuation of the country, provided proof to local people that the French were extremely

weakened. This extraordinary effort made them think that France had no army
left to defend herself against Germany and was desperate. "The major recruitment campaign which took place in the last months of 1915, totally unusual and
unprecedented, appeared to them as another proof that we no longer had any
soldiers, since we were forced to have recourse to such procedures," wrote Governor Antonetti in his report of a visit. "Our force was broken."[26]

The perception of the weakening of France was not unique to the west Volta.
It was shared in other parts of the French colonial empire and caused in those
years a spate of unconnected uprisings. A chain reaction effect ensued, the earlier
movements adding to the perception that the colonial empire was falling apart.
Besides the earlier Beledougou uprising already mentioned, simultaneous with
the Volta-Bani War was the end of the truce with the Tuareg in the cercle of Dori,
and the larger unrelated Tuareg war in the Sahara (where the borders of Algeria,
Libya, and Niger meet today) which, under the blessing of the Sanusi, received
support from the Ottoman and German governments. The Baule resistance in the
Ivory Coast had ended before the start of the world war, but sequels to it in 1914
in the southern part of the cercle of Bobo-Dioulasso will be described in the next
section. The continuing oppositions on the border with the cercle of Koutiala
became bolder. Toward the end of the rainy season of 1915, when the anti-
French stirrings in the cercle of Dedougou were taking a more definite organizational shape, many signs confirmed the view that an armed movement against
the French had a good likelihood of success. This reasoning was not devoid of
factual basis, and the leadership in the canton of Datomo was able to make a
persuasive case that swayed the opinion of the majority.

Maubert and Chiefly Policy in the Cercle of Bobo-Dioulasso

In the neighboring cercle of Bobo-Dioulasso, the situation in 1914 and 1915
was also very volatile. It was shaped as much by power struggles between local
strongmen as by the personality of colonial administrators. In October 1914,
Henri Maubert replaced Georges Chéron, who had been appointed the year before as the first civilian commandant of the cercle of Bobo-Dioulasso.[27] Maubert
represented a different style from Maguet. He had started as a clerk in the general administration in Dakar and had worked his way up. He was forty-four
years old and a protégé of Lieutenant Governor Clozel, who had appreciated his
energetic actions in Fada N'Gourma (eastern Burkina Faso).[28] The mutual dislike
and rivalry between Maubert and Maguet had an impact on their decisions at

critical junctures and at the end of the anticolonial war turned into a battle of incriminations.

The first report that Maubert sent to his superior conveyed a rather bleak view of the cercle:

> The tirailleurs have left. In Bobo there are only two or three unfortunate white people who keep quarrelling with each other, assisted only by a few guards who are barely dressed. The emissaries of the commandant are chased away and abused, the jula (itinerant traders) are ransacked, markets refuse to pay the taxes. . . . The populations of the cercle of Bobo have never been subjugated. Military officers and cercle administrators just came by and left. Then came Mr. Chéron, young assistant-administrator. In order to remain in Bobo alone and to reign as absolute master, he did not hesitate to falsify the truth, to lead his chiefs to misconceptions, and has thus precipitated the course of events.[29]

These were not words of a dispirited man. On the contrary they portended a radical turn that came about as much by Maubert's personal disposition as by the force of circumstances. Chéron belonged to the first generation of administrator-ethnographers. He had a doctorate in law, a diploma from the School of Modern Oriental Languages, and was a correspondent of the Academy of Colonial Sciences.[30] Maubert saw himself as a man of action and was eager for recognition. He maintained that his predecessor had created the impression of calm by ignoring serious cases of insubordination. Maubert's energetic temperament found full expression in the conditions of this time, a period of extraordinary challenge to colonial rule coupled with severe shortage of administrative personnel. It gave him the opportunity to take bold actions, which according to him later curtailed the spread and severity of the anticolonial movement. His detractors claimed that he also provided the one single move that contributed more than any other to flare up the spirit of resistance.

To this day, Maubert is remembered in the cercle as Tasuma, a sobriquet that means Fire in Jula. His violent character comes in view in this name which traveled with him to his later appointment in Senegal. In a hearing presided over by Chief Inspector Vidal one of the guards who accompanied the administrator on his military expeditions testified: "The commandant asks everyone, native chiefs and personnel, to always be next to him. If someone does not answer at his first call, he becomes furious and insults the person. The commandant always yells very loud when he gives orders. Everybody is frightened."

According to another witness, what mattered to Maubert was that "everyone be frightened by the force, whichever way it might manifest itself." When his interpreter tried to warn him that his attitude caused tension, Maubert replied that he knew the natives well and that he knew how to deal with them.[31]

The impetuous temperament of Maubert is therefore amply documented, but these testimonies may create an exaggerated impression of his personal flaws if we forget that they were gathered at a time when Maubert had been recalled and was facing charges of abuse of power. Some of his actions indicate more generally a state of mind prevalent in the colonial administration. He was blamed, for example, for forcing people to organize strange ceremonies of welcome when he visited the villages during his rounds. Guards were sent before his arrival to round up all the inhabitants and make them come on the road to greet him—men with a military salute and women by clapping their hands. This practice was not the product of his megalomania; it was in fact nothing more than standard procedure, which a commandant of the cercle had introduced with an order only seven years before that date.[32]

From the first day he took office Maubert went on an uninterrupted series of repressive campaigns. In November 1914, a few days after his arrival in his new post, he received an order to help the administrator of the cercle of Koutiala who was mired in a conflict in the canton of Nampela. Maubert went to this border region and reported that he found a country in open rebellion. The rebels were, according to him, "almost all former soldiers of Babemba," the famous *faama* of Sikasso who had been eliminated by the French in 1898 (pp. 72–73). The people of this region, Maubert noted, had declared that "The time has come for us to gain back our freedom. Let us refuse all orders, even under constraint, no more work of any kind, no more of this coin money for which we have no use whatsoever, and to prove our determination to free ourselves from the yoke of the past, let us destroy all the colonial compounds."[33]

Although Maubert's writing style is evident in this declaration, the passage does reflect the widely shared hopes and expectations that became the foundation of the 1915–16 anticolonial movement. Maubert seized 4,107 guns in this campaign and brought the rebel leaders to Bobo-Dioulasso where his tribunal sentenced them to various prison terms. In January 1915 Maubert led a campaign to the Nienegue cantons at the northeast of his cercle, Kumbia, Bereba, Wakuy, and Sara, which refused to pay taxes. Again he brought many leaders back and sentenced to prison terms twenty-three of them and seventy-two others for acts of violence. In a noteworthy comment on these events, Maubert indicated that "these fetishists were obeying, without knowing it, to a watchword coming from nearby religious centers . . . spread by Muslim Jula. Allusions to the European war leave no doubt on this."[34] We do not know whether this reflected the implication of Muslim leaders in the Nienegue area or Maubert's desire to compete with Maguet whose reputation was improving as the "Affair of the Marabouts" unfolded. Maubert wrote many other statements showing that he considered Islam a threat, or that he thought that his superiors considered it so. Whatever the case may be, Maubert claimed that he had restored order in this region. Ten months later however, the Nampela and Nienegue regions that he visited became staunch strongholds of the anticolonial movement.

In 1914 Maubert discovered that Subaganiedugu and Diefurma near the subdivision headquarters of Banfora were also in a state of insurgency. The anti-colonial movement of 1915–16 did not extend to this southern region, but these events are of interest here because their political and ritual organization resemble in many ways the beginning of the anticolonial movement in Dedougou.

> It is now without doubt that the M'Bouin, Karaboro, and Turka tribes had planned for November 30 (first day of the indigenous year) the general massacre of the Jula, who by miracle escaped death, and that they were even talking about paying a visit to the Whites in Banfora. . . . In different *sanga*— meetings during which animals were sacrificed—the M'bouins [Gwen] and Karaboro . . . had decided the killing of the people devoted to our cause and an attack on Banfora.[35]

The substitution of the vague tribal labels for the names of actual leaders or villages was consistent with Maubert's alarmist style but also indicates the scope of the movement. Its principal leader was Yoye Karama, an important religious and political figure. Yoye Karama had led the opposition against the French during the conquest of 1898–99. When the struggle proved fruitless he became a mediator with the French who named him chief of the canton of Banfora, a transformation from resister to collaborator that was rather common in the history of the colonial conquest. Yoye Karama was the "master of the earth" for the region of Banfora (his lineage claims to be the first to have settled in the land), and the "owner" of a cult called Poilongo. The shrine of the Poilongo takes the form of a large spear (*poilongo* meaning spear), which Karama claimed had been sent to him from the skies.[36] The regional appeal of the powers of the Poilongo provided the focal point enabling Karama to confirm his leadership.

Karama's initial projects were foiled because of events that took place in the Tusia village of Yogofereso. As early as June 1914, that village had become a refuge to many runaways and by December 1915 it had grown into a major resistance center of one hundred free standing reinforced compounds.[37] Twice in December 1914, the people of the village assailed and chased away the guards sent by the administration. They also made a pact with the people of the villages of Nianaba and Tusiana to kill Mintapri Watara, the chief of Tusiana, on December 22.[38] On that day, however, only the people of Yogofereso came forward, allowing Mintapri to escape and alert Maubert. The next day Maubert attacked Yogofereso. The village lost seven men and Maubert brought some of the leaders back to Bobo-Dioulasso where four of them received life sentences.

This punitive action served as deterrent to the other movement of revolt that was brewing. Informants told Maubert that three days before his attack on Yogofereso, a meeting was initiated by Yoye Karama in the village of Diaraba-koko. Representatives from all of the region's villages took the decision once again to attack Banfora and kill the agents and allies of the French. But the news of the repression in Yogofereso frightened them, and the attempt failed. Regardless, people everywhere maintained an attitude of open defiance towards the colonial administration. In January 1915, the Resident of Banfora reported to Maubert that the people of the village of Tusiana "ignore the orders they are given, in spite of the exemplary punishment inflicted to their neighbors of Yogofereso."[39] West of Tusiana, the Turka villages of Musodugu and Diomo declared that they would greet the Administrator with arrows.[40] In the political report for January 1915, Maubert acknowledged that the whole southern region of the cercle had again entered in open rebellion.

That rebellion was put down in March 1915. Maubert maintained that the colonial administration had "run a grave danger."[41] He convicted Yoye Karama and 148 others to prison sentences ranging from five to twenty years. Karama died in the Bobo-Dioulasso prison on April 9. Maubert reported that "the consternation among the M'bouin [Gwen], Karaboro, and Turka people at the news of his death gives a just and precise idea of the formidable influence of this great fetishist. . . . With Yoye Karama disappears our deadliest and most dangerous enemy."[42]

Maubert's military campaigns resulted in a sizable population of inmates in the Bobo-Dioulasso prison, killing or imprisonment being the only means of punishment available to the colonial administration. The administration was concerned, the lieutenant governor of Haut-Sénégal Niger noted at a later point, that other penalties such as fines would have been perceived by the population as a form of exchange, the purchase of the right to steal or kill.[43] At the same time, prisoners constituted a precious source of free labor. In Bobo-Dioulasso, the houses and vegetable gardens for the Europeans and the new prison erected in 1914 were all built by the prisoners. The growth of the prison population under appalling sanitary conditions led to astounding rates of mortality. According to the inquiry conducted by inspector Vidal, of the 360 inmates in the Bobo-Dioulasso prison who had been convicted of "attempted rebellion" between November 1914 and March 1915, 283 had died before October 1915. The cause of these deaths was never clearly established. The French doctor of the cercle, who had antagonistic relations with Maubert, concluded that they were due to the advanced age of those put in jail. Maubert supposed that many of the deaths were caused by dysentery. The idea that some prisoners chose to commit suicide rather than remain in jail also circulated in the reports, which gave the officials comfort because of its romantic implication that those incarcerated preserved their moral freedom.

During his campaigns Maubert pursued an iron policy of disarmament, a critical facet of his tenure. He reported that in his first three months as administrator of Bobo-Dioulasso he confiscated a total of 18,156 firearms, 1,000 war axes and picks, and hundreds of thousands of bows and arrows. He also destroyed a large number of Strophanthus plants from which arrow poison was made.[44] Disarmament was not standard policy in the colony, because the possession of weapons by the subjects was not illegal. Maubert later pointed out that his foresight in this matter was a great contribution to the suppression of the insurrection in his cercle. While the benefit there was in gathering bows and arrows is open to debate, because private individuals and communities were able to engage in a feverish production regime in 1915 to compensate for it, it is probably true that the collection of firearms at that time seriously curtailed later the ability of the anticolonial fighters, especially in the northern and the Nienegue regions of the cercle. After the 1915–16 War, disarmament became a permanent feature of cercle policy and was extended to the cercle of Dedougou.

The most important political action of Maubert, with consequences extending far beyond the year of the anticolonial movement, was his reshuffling the indigenous chiefs in his first months of service. It resulted in the exclusion from power of the first allies that the French had made during the occupation of 1897.

As explained in chapter 3, in the wake of the occupation the French had created states *(états)*, large territorial units, and appointed friendly African military leaders to head them. This was perceived as a sort of "indirect rule," but it is important to note that judicial powers, separate budget, or administrative autonomy were not recognized for these states. Cercle administrators, with the approval of the governor, were able to reshape these units and dismiss their heads at will, without a need for new legislation. In 1897, Commandant Caudrelier created three states in the cercle of Bobo-Dioulasso, placed under the command of the elders of important Watara Houses, with the assumption that this would constitute a more cost-effective way of subduing the populations of the newly occupied territories, who were as yet unaware that they had become colonial subjects.

When the subjugation of the populations turned out to be more difficult than anticipated, divergent opinions emerged among administrators, at both low and high levels, as to the utility of maintaining these African leaders. The *politique des races* view of William Ponty and his successor Clozel advocated forming smaller territorial units defined on an ethnic basis.[45] In the cercle of Dedougou, the states were disbanded in 1905 (Hubbell 1997), but in Bobo-Dioulasso nothing came of this policy for many more years. The state under Dafogo, successor to Tieba Nyandane Watara, had been suppressed upon his death in 1912, but the other two states survived into Maubert's term of office. Four months after his arrival, Maubert dissolved them and proceeded to overhaul the canton chiefships. He presented this change as an imperative of the *politique des races,* and obtained the full support of Lieutenant Governor Clozel.[46] The conscription campaign of April 1915 provided the opportunity. The men recruited by Morifin Watara escaped from the gathering center in Bobo-Dioulasso. Mori-fin replaced them with handicapped and elderly men.[47] The Sambla today say that he had made a deal with village dignitaries that he would send only unfit candidates. To find new candidates, Maubert turned to Si-Boro, whom he had named chief of the newly created Sambla canton in December 1914. Mori-fin was dismissed and jailed for eight days and Maubert appointed Si-Boro and his brother as temporary administrators of the state of Mori-fin. On grounds of similar malfeasance, Maubert dismissed the other important Watara leaders, including the other head of state, Kobana, leader of the Watara house in Kotedugu.

The influences that played on these decisions are difficult to recover in full detail. Lieutenant Governor Clozel was a supporter of the *politique des races,* and he had appointed Maubert to Bobo-Dioulasso. Local power struggles also fit the vivid world of intrigue described by A. Hampate Bâ (1987). The intense rivalries around canton chiefship unleashed by Maubert's reform allow us to discern their rough outline. What is somewhat left out of the picture in Hampate Bâ's story is that the network of French colonial officials was as deeply divided by discord as that of the senior indigenous officials who had created around themselves patronage groups that became factions in competition. It was when the local cliques were able to seize upon the rivalries between the West Africa–wide French coteries that the Byzantine artifices of cercle politics became animated.

One such senior official in the cercle of Bobo-Dioulasso was Diaman Bathily, the interpreter of the cercle. He had arrived in the cercle's capital city with Colonel Pineau in 1898, and his long tenure was so exceptionally successful that he had been made a chevalier of the Légion d'honneur. When Bathily died on April 15, 1918, in Bamako, stripped of his power and glory (see below), the administrator Mornet wrote of him: "In the eyes of the natives Bobo was his private kingdom. The cercle administrators who succeeded each other at short intervals came only to strengthen his authority or to give satisfaction on his desire for vengeance on his enemies."[48] Maubert did not, in fact, remove all the Watara. He left in office Mo Ture Watara, canton chief of Lorofereso, who according to a later administrator was "among the clients of Diaman Bathily."[49] It seems that Maubert removed from office the Watara who were not clients of Bathily.

At the same time that he was changing the native chiefs, Maubert started a procedure against Sadia Sylla, another powerful native clerk of the cercle. Sylla was the interpreter of the subdivision of Banfora. He was accused of rape, abduction, extortion, usurpation of power, and misappropriation of public funds, during a "census campaign" (which was indistinguishable from a *tournée de police*—a police operation) organized immediately after the Karama affair. Again, as in the Dedougou affair of the guards, there is no reason to question that these charges were well founded, but it was a heavy list of accusations to make, even with supporting evidence, against a person like Sylla, so centrally positioned in the colonial administration. There can be little doubt that they reached Maubert's ears through the offices of Bathily. Maubert sentenced Sylla to fifteen years in prison.

After removing the two heads of state, Maubert dismissed the canton chiefs that they had appointed (who, as explained in chapter 3, were figureheads selected from among the head of state's servants or soldiers) and the chiefs of the independent cantons. The new chiefs with whom he replaced them were suggested by Bathily and became the interpreter's protégés.

The profile of these new colonial chiefs did not quite match Maubert's claim that they were different from the "foreign" Jula chiefs before them and the true representatives of the ethnic group in the canton to which they were appointed. Several of these new chiefs were simply subordinates of the Watara leaders who had been just discharged, and it was while working in this capacity that they had come to the notice of the cercle headquarters. Si-Boro, who was appointed to the

Sambla canton, for example, had as a young man entered the service of Mori-fin as a sofa—a man of arms of servile status. He had been an orphan, the son of a Fulbe man and a Sambla woman from Bwende, giving him matrilateral links to that village, which was a common occurrence for Watara dignitaries and the people in their employ. The men who were appointed as chiefs of the canton of Kote-dugu, Zezuma and his "cousin" Basabati, were previously subordinates of Kara-moko (son of Pintyeba) and represented the canton in his name when he was the head of that état.[50] In the canton of Bobo-Dioulasso, Maubert dismissed Kele-tigi, who was the elder of the Zara house of Sangbeleluma, which had held the canton chiefship since 1898, and appointed a young man, Suro (Konyagamu), from the different Zara house of Yo Ziri.

If the administrative reform of Maubert was a questionable success in terms of the objectives of the politique des races, it did manage to change the character of the group of African chiefs in the cercle. The Watara chiefs and other promi-nent figures from precolonial days had joined the French in the early chaotic years of French occupation in pursuit of their own projects. They never fully committed themselves to the colonial interests and resisted the attempts of the administration to make them bureaucratic underlings. Maubert's new appointees owed their ascendancy exclusively to the administrator. They did not look back to days of independence and greater prestige, as did the Watara, but only for-ward, to possibilities of enrichment as colonial chiefs. To register their freedom from their former Watara masters and their newly found fortune, Zezuma and Si-Boro adopted new patronymic names—respectively, Millogo and Traore.

The rivalry between the old and the new cadres turned to rancor after the Volta-Bani War. On January 30, 1918, the day of the Ramadan festival, a mas-sive fight broke out in Bobo-Dioulasso between the members of the Zara house of the old chief and that of the new one.[51] This was only the surface manifes-tation of the competition that was carried out more effectively by other means. The deposed chiefs started an "unrelenting struggle" against the new canton chiefs by scheming with their allies in the villages to make it impossible for the new chiefs to comply with the demands of the administration.

The reversals in chiefly appointments after Maubert's departure are worth reviewing because they shed light both on the political alignments within the French administration and on the local political struggles that had shaped Maubert's own decisions and how arbitrary they must have appeared to the vil-lagers. The official recall of Maubert to Bamako in March 1917 after the anti-colonial war tolled the end of interpreter Bathily's glory. The instruction given to Hummel, who replaced Maubert for two quarters, warned him of Bathily's ability to stop any complaint from reaching the administrator. It also advised caution with the *agents politiques,* who were the clients of the canton chiefs and of Bathily.[52] Presumably taking his cue from this warning, Muller, who came after Hummel, made one substantial recommendation during his brief tenure: the removal of Bathily from the cercle.[53] This was carried out in June 1917.

Muller's successor, Fernand Froger, went further. With the approval of the acting lieutenant governor, Périquet, who had asked him "to maintain some generosity" toward the deposed Watara leaders,[54] in January 1918 Froger started a systematic campaign to undo Maubert's reforms. He replaced Mo Ture as canton chief of Lorofereso with Kobana Watara, from the house in Kotedugu. He appointed Baladian Watara (a successor to Tieba Nyandane) in place of Soma Viguie as canton chief of Karankaso-Vige, where Baladian had a following among the warlike Tiefo and Vige communities.[55] Then Froger started a large-scale investigation against Anzumana, canton chief of Subaganiedugu and an important former client of Bathily, accusing him of rebellion. Many other people were arrested as accomplices, including the canton chief of Kotedugu, Zezuma, and his associate Basabati, who was also Anzumana's son-in-law. He replaced Zezuma with Kwese, from the house of the former canton chief of Bobo-Dioulaso. Froger was building another case against Suro Sanou, the new canton chief of Bobo-Dioulasso.

At this point, Périquet left. Maubert, who was facing charges in Bamako, tried to protect his appointees by writing a letter denouncing Froger. The large amount of detail in this letter shows that Maubert followed closely the developments in Bobo-Dioulasso and had good sources of information there.[56] The new lieutenant governor, Charles Brunet, took a course opposite to that of Périquet and Froger. He formed a commission to look into the Anzumana affair and he replaced administrator Froger. With this broader involvement, the charges against Anzumana did not have the same success as those that Maubert had made against Karama; Brunet dismissed them. The new administrator of Bobo-Dioulasso appointed by Brunet, Mornet, released Basabati and afterwards returned Zezuma and Anzumana to their cantons as chiefs. The movement against Anzumana, he discovered, was orchestrated by the Watara in Bobo-Dioulasso. Mornet also acted against another influential person in the city: the imam Mama Sanou, who was generating public support for accusations against the canton chiefs Zezuma and Suro. Mornet reprimanded him and threatened him with deportation.[57]

The bitterness and intrigues between the factions in the city continued for many years. Changes of canton chiefs, however, became less frequent with the constitution of the colony of Upper Volta in 1919. Most of the chiefs mentioned above remained in office until their deaths and were replaced by their sons, thus becoming the founders of the little colonial dynasties that continued to influence local politics well into the postindependence period.

After this excursion into the Wangrin-esque drama of native chieftaincy in Bobo-Dioulasso, what can be said of administrator Maubert's role in the rise of the anticolonial movement in 1915 and its growth? His massive disarmament campaign probably did, as he claimed, put the anticolonial movement in his cercle at a disadvantage in 1916. The consequences of his administrative reforms are more difficult to determine. Maubert claimed that his new chiefs, being closer to the native *races,* would give the French "at last a grip on the indigenous mass and information on its feelings toward us, its real needs and desires." These chiefs not only failed to warn Maubert of the anticolonial aspirations of their subjects, they also were among the first targets to be attacked in 1916. The Sambla villagers of his canton called Si-Boro *bila-mo-sera* (pillage master). Less than a year after Maubert's reforms, Bobo-Dioulasso was isolated in a region up in arms and the commandant had to draw contingency plans to evacuate the city.

The new chiefs, and even those who had failed to obtain office but were still hopeful, did help Maubert with the suppression of the anticolonial movement, raising auxiliaries, where they could, in the villages and heading them enthusiastically in action (see chap. 8). Maubert wrote in his last report before he departed: "It is a duty for me to recall their loyalty and admirable devotion that made it possible for us to hold out against the rebellion from 27 November 1915 until 29 March 1916, the date of arrival of the Molard column in the cercle; they saved from certain disaster the canton and the surrounding areas."[58] This praise was not exaggerated. The support of the chiefs was critical because for many months Maubert had to face the anticolonial forces in multiple fronts with weak local resources.

The flip side of the reform, however, was that the dismissed chiefs, who still commanded considerable resources and connections with certain villages, were alienated during the anticolonial war and remained indifferent. They may even have acted against the administration. Maubert reported that Mori-fin Watara had given a few firearms and advice on military matters to the Sambla insurgents. When Maubert confronted him, Mori-fin said it had been a token gesture to stem the threats of the rebels to his family and his property—parenthetically, a notable expression of expectations of mutual support between precolonial "big men" and the villagers. It can be surmised that Mori-fin and the other dismissed leaders did not very actively support the anticolonial movement, despite these expectations, because if they had the French would have eventually learned about it. Still, it is also evident that what Maubert gained in support for the suppression from his new appointees, he lost in the lack of involvement of the deposed Watara chiefs.

The question about the reforms is what impression they made on the population watching from the sidelines. Maubert's reforms, more so than Maguet's moves against the Muslims and the guards in Dedougou, must have looked to the people to be a pointless exercise resulting from the struggle between the small cliques of the colonial establishment. In a way, however, the removal of the powerful chiefs was also the manifestation of the reign of the arbitrary, of the precariousness of colonial fortunes, and of the confused and impulsive character of administrative decisions. Those were conclusions concurring with a view that was spreading in parts of the cercle of Dedougou—that the French were losing their composure.

The most decisive impact of Maubert on the development of the anticolonial movement was not in any of his actions described so far, but in something he did later. This was his expedition to Bondokuy, in November 1915, to rescue the village chief, an expedition decided on after he learned that Maguet had been beaten in Bona. Maubert's desire to outdo his younger, astute counterpart in Dedougou was a strong motivation.

CHAPTER 5
The Call to Arms

IN THE DAYS AND MONTHS PRECEDING the first battles of the 1915–16 Volta-Bani War, a number of little-known events occurred in the Marka villages that started the anticolonial movement. This chapter traces the movement's beginnings back to those events. The sequences are important to clarify what the principal actors thought in those days, the factors that shaped their perceptions, and the mood that prevailed in the area. We show how political mobilization was achieved within and among the villages in that fluid political arena where negotiation, rather than authority or compulsion, occupied the central spot. The village leagues were reactivated and coordinated, while shrines and institutions such as the masa and the perenkie provided the medium. Thus the exercise in anthropological microhistory offers a synthetic interpretation of the proximate origins of the anticolonial war. The last section of the chapter adds an exploration of the narrative self-understanding of the movement.

PLANNING THE WAR

The chief of the canton of Datomo, M'Pa Adama Nianu, went to Bona on November 14 to gather the candidates for the colonial army from the village.[1] The leaders of the village told him that the candidates were not ready, that he should continue his journey to the other villages, and that the selected young men would join him later, in his home village. Two days later, the promised young men not having arrived, the canton chief returned to Bona. It is at this point that Yisu Kote, who was singled out in our introduction as the key figure in the anticolonial movement's origins, enters the narrative. It seems that when the canton chief arrived at Bona, a heated exchange took place between him and Yisu, who was an influential member of the village. Yisu declared that the village was not going to provide the requested men, and M'PaAdama returned empty-handed.[2] The next day, "the whistles" were heard in Datomo and in the villages of neighboring cantons.

The whistles appear throughout the story of anticolonial mobilization in the area within the bend of the Muhun River and in the Gurunsi zone to the east of the river. People can "talk" with these whistles. The whistles transpose the tones of speech (elsewhere, this is done with drums and xylophones) and the people also play haunting tunes with them. They are accessories to the age sets and masquerades, which were shared among all ethnicities between the Muhun and Komoe Rivers. Before these populations were pacified, the whistles were closely associated with fighting and defense. We give more detail about the whistles later in this chapter.

M'PaAdama maintained that as soon as he heard the whistles he set out immediately for Bona on horseback. But he had a fall and returned to Datomo with a broken arm. Under the guidance of his assistant, he sent to Dedougou the contingent of candidates from the other villages that he had gathered in Datomo, but in the excitement that filled the air, many of these men escaped on the road before reaching Dedougou. The chief of the village of Safane, Suleyman Sere (one of the victims of the marabout affair), who—like everyone else in the area—was following these developments, left quickly for Dedougou to inform the administrator. He arrived in the residence on the night of November 17. At 9:00 P.M., the commandant of the cercle, Maguet, learned from Suleyman Sere what had happened in Bona and he entered in the cercle diary the first colonial record of the opposition in Bona.

That very night, Commandant Maguet dispatched a guard to Bona, with five horsemen to support him. This party arrived in the village the next morning. It was market day in Bona and a woman was dispensing beer in a shed at the entrance of the village; a few men of the village were drinking. The guard started blustering at these men, but at once whistles sounded everywhere. Village men came from all around, armed with bows and arrows. The guard and his men hastily withdrew (Blegna 1990, 61). They spent the rest of the day in the vicinity of the village, trying to find someone less hostile who would talk to them. At one point, the guard was able to get close to the compound of the colonial chief of the village, but other villagers spotted him before he had a chance to speak to the chief, and he was attacked again. He and his men were assaulted with bullets and arrows and chased until they were far from the village. They were not harmed, but an arrow lodged in the belt of one of the auxiliaries, and one of the horses was wounded.

On the evening of the same day, November 18, Maguet, in Dedougou, received a letter sent by Combes, the resident of Boromo. The intelligence received in Boromo confirmed the accounts that were given to him the day before, which also showed that the news was circulating fast. The chief of Safane also sent a report. By now, the agitation had spread to several villages besides Bona, and whistles were sounding in all corners. Armed villagers were declaring that they would kill the guards and soldiers. That night, Commandant Maguet left Dedougou around 10:00 P.M., taking with him the only other Frenchman at the headquarters, the doctor Cremer, and twelve guards, who constituted all the force he had available. He arrived in Safane the next morning to talk again to the chief there and then move on to Bona, which he reached around 9:00 A.M.

Such was the beginning of the Volta-Bani War (a story to be continued in chapter 6). In the rest of this chapter, we shift our focus to what, in those crucial days, was happening in Bona and its neighboring villages. A number of linked questions need to be clarified about this brief period, because taken together they determine a large part of what can be said about the nature of the anticolonial movement in Dedougou. What did the principal actors of the opposition want to achieve? Was the Bona refusal simply an altercation that got out of hand—an angry exchange that took an unexpected turn, as it were behind the backs of its principal agents? Or was it instead the setting into motion of a prearranged plan, a staged scene that the villagers used to declare their prior decision to fight the colonial government? If there was an early organization, was it based on broad popular consensus or was it the work of a small group of conspirators? There are, of course, other plausible scenarios in addition to those starkly phrased alternatives. Together, they guide our interpretation of the events.

The oral tradition in the region maintains that Yisu Kote had a personal stake in opposing the recruitment. Domba Blegna (1990, 59) reports that Yisu's last-born son was among the candidates who were to be sent to Dedougou. In Bona in 1998, however, we were told that the person at risk was Yisu's younger (classificatory) brother M'beme, from Tunu. This M'beme became later one of the "chief executive" agents of the movement.[3] Tunu and Bona were the only two villages of the canton that openly defied recruitment. The idea that Yisu had something to gain personally in starting the conflict with the French does underscore his central role in the genesis of the anticolonial movement; it gives coherence to the local narrative understanding by providing the motive according to a widely shared model of human action. But it is clear from what happened when the guard and his men arrived in Bona—and further confirmed from what followed when Maguet himself arrived two days later with his contingent of armed men—that the incident was not Yisu alone refusing to send a relative.

The evidence shows that among the residents of many neighboring villages, both before and after this Bona incident, there was consultation, argument and counterargument, and some sort of agreement about opposing the French. There was deliberate participation in a movement and the framework of an organization. There was also an official declaration of war against the French, although the colonial officials dismissed this as one more exotic curiosity of their enemy. The problem for later scholarship is that the information on all these happenings derives from subsequent recollections, which are made doubly unreliable because they are conveyed to us in partial and abridged colonial depositions and reports. It is especially difficult to arrive at a solid day-to-day chronology of what happened; without such a chronology, some interpretive moves cannot be solidly anchored. For example, it is uncertain which village meetings resulted from the confrontation with the chief of Datomo and which came before and prepared the way for it.

The accuracy of what we know about the preparatory stages of a formal anticolonial organization in the month of November can be increased by carefully sifting through the dispersed and partial bits of information provided by the historical record. We summarize the result of this effort in the next few paragraphs, after which we return to a more narrative vein.

Widespread rumors asserting that the French were going to leave the country began circulating among the villagers in the rainy season of the preceding year, 1914. As we already noted, such rumors emerged periodically, almost everywhere, before as well as after the anticolonial war. But in 1914 in the cercle of Dedougou, the rumors became more insistent—almost obsessive—as the countryside was being stripped of much of the colonial military presence. Some people in the region today maintain that from January 1915 on, the rumors were not only about the departure of the French, but more specifically about an impending war to drive them out. This information does not indicate that the villagers put together an organization for armed resistance so far ahead of time, but it does suggest that the news of resistance against the French elsewhere in the colony had already inspired in the cercle the idea of not only waiting for the French to leave but of actively organizing opposition.

References beyond mere rumors to real meetings begin in August 1915, the time in the rainy season when there is a slack period in the agricultural calendar. The grain is ripening in the fields and until the harvest there is not much to do on the farms. In the savanna belt, conventionally, this was the time when attacks were planned and preparations made for war in the approaching dry season. Normally, both the French and the local people abided by this schedule for practical reasons.

The testimony given by a group of men from Bona when they became prisoners in June 1916 provides the first somewhat precise indication of the initial anticolonial meeting. According to it, the movement was planned two months before the harvest—that is, some time in September or early October 1915.[4] The fact that this deposition was recorded in the diary of the cercle of Dedougou increases the reliability of the information. Although the diary must be treated with circumspection, its possible bias adds in this case to our confidence. A critical reading of the diary makes it clear that administrator Maguet intended it in part as proof of his conviction that the insurrection was due solely to the conscription campaign. It is full of almost redundant brief quotes simply repeating this assertion. This deposition, on the contrary, by claiming a meeting in September, implies that the preparations for the movement began before the conscription campaign. Its inclusion in the diary could even be an oversight, and the fact that the deposition was made collectively by a group of actors who were central to the anticolonial organization compels our attention.

Other, more frequent references to village meetings concern the early part of November 1915. By that time, the conscription campaign had already started. Most villages were quietly—grudgingly—surrendering the number of requisitioned men, and Bona, though lagging behind, had not yet defied the colonial authority. Picanon's report states that the colonial chiefs of Datomo and Tunu became aware of anti-French preparations in their cantons around November 10, the week before Bona made its refusal public. At that time, secret meetings took place in Bona, and representatives from other villages participated.[5]

Dedougou's diary entry fixes November 17 as the date of one crucial meeting that took place in Bona. "The rebellion was decided in a meeting participated in by the chiefs of the kameles [fighting-age men] of the villages, at the invitation of Yisu, chief of Bona. The guard and cavalrymen sent by the administrator ahead of him arrived in the village the day after this meeting." Various descriptions of this meeting have been transmitted in the oral tradition, and we will return to them shortly. Here we want to point out that the above quotation—like all others of its kind—is not truly a translation of statements made in Marka or Jula, but the commandant's abridged paraphrase. It includes important inaccuracies, such as calling Yisu "chief of Bona," thus illustrating the confusion of the French about the social organization of the villages and of the anticolonial movement. Yisu carried no such title.

One final reference that we will provide here is to a gathering at which not only the few Marka villages close to Bona participated but a much larger set, including many Bwa villages to the south of the canton of Datomo. It was held on the site of an important regional shrine near the village of Dahuan (Danguna) at 3:00 in the morning. The ostensible purpose of the gathering was to celebrate what is the most senior of the suru shrines in this region (see chap. 1, p. 41). This is how Gnankambary (1970, 64–65) recreates the speech of the senior man who took the floor:

> Our forefathers who rest under this soil advised us to follow in their traces in bravery, dignity, and honor. The whites came to our country. We let them, thinking that they would behave like the Fulbe—that is, without interfering in our business. Instead, they have become the masters, thanks to the complicity of some blacks who came with them no one knows from where. Now everything in this country belongs to them: our possessions, our women, our children, even our selves. What do we have left? They ridicule and even prohibit our customs and the sacred things inherited from our ancestors, our face marks, so that we can't recognize our children, and especially they take us to distant countries where many of us die and have to be buried outside the family graves. There is a lot to say. I cannot say it all. You all know the situation. Time is short. According to all the consultations I have made, our forefathers ask us to get rid of these harmful guests.

This meeting ended with important decisions: an organization was created and the provision of arms discussed. The Bwa villages decided to group their blacksmiths together to smelt iron and produce weapons.

Gnankambary's phrasing may be taken to imply that this meeting took place before the campaign for conscription, while from Gnankambary's second mention of a meeting (1970, 67) one could conclude that there were two meetings in that same place, the first one being before Maguet was defeated in Bona and the second in late November. We think that this is simply an editorial confusion. The Danguna meeting described by Gnankambary took place after the second battle of Bona, in the last week of November 1915.

To distill a plausible story from these references, one has to keep in mind the basic properties of village political life (for our first discussion of this, see chap. 1). In these village assemblies, a way to arrive at a binding decision did not exist. The gatherings provided opportunities for consultation and debate, but only conviction could lead the men representing the different houses to reach consensus. The elders themselves had to watch for dissenting opinions within their own constituencies, because even the houses that they led were heterogeneous and liable to fissure. Many assemblies ended in no formal decision at all, but with only a general sentiment of agreement or disagreement. No mechanism of sanction existed to compel dissenters, save for outright threat of violence. Public punishments in the village followed the lines of age-ranked groups and could only be effective when the group of seniors was unanimous. Such unity was rare, except when there was something collectively at stake against junior age sets.

One has to appreciate the skills that are necessary, in this kind of political landscape, to build support for a risky operation such as a war. That a sizable number of meetings was held indicates that the proponents of war against the French took the tack of making diplomatic effort, with an emphasis on persuasion, within as well as among the villages. They successfully secured the collaboration of senior men who held important ritual offices and who were qualified to convene such assemblies: the masa and the perenkie of each community (see p. 48). Then they appealed to the ward or village patriotism of the young men of fighting age. There was a campaign to shape public opinion through rumor, informal meetings, and networking within kinship sets and shrine constituencies.

Our conclusions from this material are the following: a small group of men started to campaign for war in the slow period of the farming season of 1915 (August-September), but until mid-November commitment to an all-out war was very limited in their communities. Their main argument was that the French were now very weak and that an organized opposition was certain to be successful. They expressed this with oracle consultations and allusions to the nineteenth-century glories that had established the reputations of the houses to which some of the war partisans belonged. The beginning of the recruitment campaign gave these partisans new arguments. General opinion started to turn their way. A core group consisting of a few determined men emerged as leaders. They hailed from a few neighboring villages and were knit together by kinship, affinal ties, and friendship. Opposition to them never died, but it did turn quiet, and more and more people became quiescent and willing to leave things to the initiative of the leaders and their committed followers.

The advocates of war brought things to a head when they made their move against the canton chief of Datomo in Bona on November 16. This led to the November 18 appearance of the guard and his men sent by Maguet and to the arrival of Maguet with his larger contingent on the morning of November 19. These confrontations went well for the war partisans, who were now numerous in the cantons of Datomo and Tunu. They were able to prove their courage, display their ability, and confirm their claims that the French were vulnerable. By the time Maguet showed up again two days later (November 21) with a stronger force, the opposing villagers had enough men to win a true battle. This gained them many more supporters, and with the increased confidence they were able to take a more heavy-handed approach in compelling hesitant communities to join them. A partial hegemony was achieved in the region, which in itself was confirmation of the claims of strength that they had been making from the start.

The meetings following the military success in Bona resulted in public decisions and a more formal organization. The agreement took the form of public oaths, creating a larger village alliance. This alliance did not remain constant but was made and remade throughout the period of the war as the fortunes of the anticolonial movement went up and down. Ultimately, the conscription campaign was a minor element in the genesis of this development, but it played a critical role in bringing about the incident that moved the organization from the stage of advocated plan to that of action.

THE LEAGUE OF BONA

Bona stands out among the small number of villages that harbored the anticolonial movement. The war is known in the Marka area and beyond as Bona-kele—the War of Bona. People of Bona precipitated the events by confronting first the canton chief of Datomo and then the guards sent by Maguet. The meeting of November 17 was held in this village. This meeting was convened by the masa of Bona in the dark hours of the morning—as was usual for hidden business—in a little wood called Suba, which is the site of a suru shrine. The place lies about one kilometer south of the village, on the far side of a marshy pond that becomes part of a small river in the rainy season. The assembly, consisting of representatives of eleven villages, promised to support Bona in its defense against the expected colonial response. Siaka Sombie (1975, 6) describes the meeting on the basis of oral accounts.

"We will rise against the white man and we will fight him." After that, Yisu took a chicken and sacrificed over the dio of Bona. Then he took some dirt of the dio, mixed it in water, and gave this liquid to drink to the village chiefs, to the perenkies, and the kambeles who were present. With this act they all promised to fight the enemy without respite, without taking account of their losses or of the success of the white man, until the final victory.

The *dio* in this quote is the generic word for shrine in the Manding language *(jo)*. The shrine in this description is the suru of the village. As we have seen, the suru are vegetation and fertility shrines; they are involved in most joint matters of the village, and their wooded sites outside of the villages were chosen for late-night gatherings that ended in an oracular sacrifice. What gave distinction to Bona was not this suru but another shrine. Like many other communities, Bona had a ritual practice complex that was its own exclusive heritage. It focused on a shrine called Danso (the house of creation), which is housed in a small structure in the middle of the village (see fig. 4).[6] In 1915, this became the central shrine of the anticolonial movement. Different regions that participated in the movement sent animals to be slaughtered over its altar. Recognizing its significance, the French targeted this shrine especially and destroyed it twice in the course of the repression campaign in 1916. This Danso, which is under the authority of the masa of the village, is often confused with yet a third shrine that also gave distinction to the village of Bona; the latter, however, was a private shrine housed in Yisu Kote's compound.

As already explained, Yisu was the person who stood up to the canton chief of Datomo; however, his impact went beyond this incident and determined much of the overall shape of the movement. The possession of a famous personal shrine added a distinctive quality to Yisu. Yisu's grandfather Dwan had been a war leader of great renown in the nineteenth-century wars against the Karantao of Wahabu. The shrine had belonged to Dwan, and Yisu inherited it from his father.

Yisu's shrine was of the type generically called *kwo* by the Marka of this region. Important senior men in this area possess personal shrines of this type, which are transmitted at death to a brother or a son. A kwo shrine is the concern of a restricted group. Unlike shrines that receive public attention, such as the village Danso of Bona or the vegetation shrines of the suru type, they are kept in residences. The kwo is a portable object. Usually it assumes the form of an animal tail. It is used either alone or as part of an assortment of objects— including bones, woods, and roots—all sewn up together in a hide. As the custodian of this shrine, the head of the domestic unit periodically kills chickens

Fig. 4. The house of the Danso shrine in Bona, June 1998.

and goats over it to enhance the health and prosperity of the members of his group and to protect them from witchcraft. The reputations of kwo shrines, like those of other ritual objects, vary according to their remembered pasts; that is, depending on the fortunes of the people who held them. The historical significance of Yisu's shrine was that it was linked to the fame of Dwan.

Other than being the possessor of this object, Yisu did not occupy a position in the formal community structure of the village. This point is obscured by frequent references to him as "the chief of Bona" and "the fetishist of Bona." Bona had a ritual head, the masa, which is an institution similar to that found in many other communities of Mande speech (chap. 1). The masa of Bona is selected in alternation from the wards of Kimaabe and Dawabe, and in 1915 the masa was an elder named Pasuuru, from the ward of Kimaabe.[7] Once the masa is chosen, he selects a perenkie from the opposite ward. Each of the eight subsections *(soku)* of the village sends a representative to a council that assists the perenkie to watch over the territory, arbitrate in intravillage conflicts, organize trade expeditions, supervise the market, and collect the tolls imposed on foreign traders. This council made the war and peace decisions that were presented for discussion to the villagers. The perenkie, who as noted earlier headed the assembly of fighting-age men,[8] remained in office until the death of the masa who appointed him.

In 1915, the perenkie of Bona was Yike. Yisu and Yike were close to each other, a friendship that acquired critical importance in getting the anticolonial organization started. Yisu was a classificatory brother and also the senior of Yike. The two men planned and carried out most of their activities together. Yisu seems to have had the more forceful personality of the two, and Yike fell under his spell and acted as facilitator of Yisu's relations with village authorities. Yike was the channel between the partisans of Yisu and the masa of the village, who became supportive of the movement from the very beginning.

The name of the masa never appeared in French documents, and no accusations were brought against him at the end of the repression. It is as if the internal organization of the villages—including the position of the masa—remained a mystery to the colonial officials, despite their diverse sources of information and keen interest in the subject. The villagers shielded the masa from the day-to-day organizational activities and protected him from prosecution.[9] The chief appointed in Bona by the colonial administration was Numake Kote. This man had a less perceptible role in the coming events. He went along with the anticolonial movement without distinguishing himself in it, and when he was made prisoner by the French eight months later, he maintained that he had participated because he was pressured.[10]

Several people made prisoner by the French in June and July declared in their depositions that Yisu had started and single-handedly promoted the idea of fighting the colonial government. As would be expected under the circumstances, Yisu's own deposition is more ambiguous, but on the whole it is not far from providing some corroboration. To assess the value of these declarations, we need to return to the dynamics of all these meetings. It seems fairly evident that the desire to fight was not unanimous—not even in Bona itself—and that it took an iron will on the part of the small group of supporters to turn public opinion in their favor. The adherence of Yike and the agreement of the masa of Bona were crucial in this development. All invitations to other villages came in the name of the masa—even if Yisu had planned the occasions—because Yisu lacked the authority to issue such a summons.

It is also clear that, from the very beginning, Yisu and Yike had a larger circle of close associates. Not all of them were from Bona. Many of them lived in neighboring villages that were the historical allies of Bona. Among them was Yisu's cousin, M'Bien Nienzien, the head of the kambele of Tunu. His participation in the early stage of the movement was vital because Bona was a small village. Yisu was able to challenge the canton chief of Datomo only because he knew that he could rely on the larger fighting force of Tunu controlled by M'Bien.[11] The dignitaries of Datomo were also part of the initial planning. The consultations were concealed from the canton chief of Datomo, but later evidence shows that he was aware of the deception.

We will probably never know the precise role Yisu played among these men dedicated to building a coalition to oppose the French. It is unclear whether he brought them together and set their agenda or joined them afterwards. The group of people around him came from the triumvirate of villages of Bona, Tunu, and Datomo. These people were a closely-knit group, and all were part of the military organizations, the kambele structure, of their villages. They orchestrated the meetings with the elders and they generated enthusiasm among the fighting-age men. Their work ensured the adherence to the cause of the historical allies of the Bona league (see chap. 1, pp. 39–41, for the league). Despite disagreements in the early meetings in mid-November, enough support for their ideas transpired to conclude them with the vague joint directive that "Yisu should blow the whistle."

The whistle, carved of wood, with three holes, is the symbolic and communicative instrument of the kambele organization. Only people who carry a title in this organization have the right to blow it, and the sound of the whistle can be a clarion call for battle. Its functional equivalent is the war drum, the three- or four-foot-tall instrument carved out of a tree trunk that is part of the regalia of important houses in many communities of the west Volta. The whistle is more portable than these drums. It was perfectly suited for the intense work of diplomacy that Yisu intended, heading delegations or sending his representatives to almost all the Marka villages in the region.

Another status marker in the kambele organization is the cord woven from the fiber of the cultivated plant *Hibiscus cannabinus* and called *dafu*. Its symbolism derives from the practice of tying the captives taken in war, and today people in the region associate it with the handcuffs of policemen. To mark warrior status, the cord was tied on the head with a knot, producing two ends that resembled two little horns. During the anticolonial war, the wearing of the cord spread beyond the Marka cultural space and became generalized, from Koudougou to San. In this diffusion, a shift of interpretation turned it into a sign of acknowledgement of the "shrine of Bona" that committed people to the anticolonial cause. Among the Marka around Bona, however, only fighters who had killed a man were entitled to display it. Therefore, the young men who donned the whistle and the cord cut a frightening figure in the village assemblies. (See further discussion in chap. 10.)

The meaning of "Yisu should blow the whistle" was that the decision was made in one of these assemblies to authorize Yisu to stand up to the conscription agent as a rallying call for general opposition. There was a vague promise of solidarity when the consequences were to be faced, but the signal first had to be nothing less than a brave act putting Yisu under extreme risk. He took this step and moved the entire situation onto an explosive plane. After Yisu's challenge, everyone knew that a response from the commandant in Dedougou was certain. Yisu and his supporters had not miscalculated. The momentum created in the previous meetings was such that when, on November 17 (following the scene with the canton chief), Yisu gathered the members of the Bona league together to discuss responses to the expected reaction, the dissenting voices were quickly silenced. The assembly took the solemn oath described in the quote above. This unity made possible the first successes of Bona (described in chap. 6). These successes in turn led to broader assemblies and wider alliances that set on track the anticolonial movement.

A larger meeting convened in Danguna in the last week of November, and the participants, taking one further step, designed a military organization. They divided the territory occupied by Bwa and Marka villages within the bend of the Muhun River into four sections. The southern villages were put under the command of Siaka, of Datomo, the center and the west under Yisu, the east under Domba, of Banu, and the north under M'beme and Yonade, of Tunu.[12] This organization presupposes the extension of the conflict. In other words, before the confrontation had even started fully, these Marka leaders envisioned and planned a large-scale conflict that would include non-Marka communities. The regional, multiethnic nature of the war was anticipated. The "command" positions in this plan were different from officers' rankings in contemporary armies, because the anticolonial movement was based on the voluntary participation of autonomous units. The discipline in the battlefields stemmed not from the compulsion to obey but from conviction. The organization put in place in the Danguna meeting remained in force even in the bloodiest moments and provided the blueprint for the military strategy of the anticolonial forces until June 1916.

WAR AGAINST THE CRUEL: TWO NARRATIVES

What above we called "a narrative self-understanding of the movement" are two stories about the war's beginnings that are repeated, with slight variations, in many sources. These stories are laced with the emblematic themes of colonialism: forced labor, road construction, cruel guards, women at work, and threats to women's fertility and sexuality. Although only one of these stories finds confirmation in a record, we presume that they take their origin in actual incidents.

We believe that these narratives are not only about two peripheral incidents or colonial hardships, but that they communicate a deeper meaning. That meaning remains elusive because they come down to us as pale shadows, without context, through multiple layers of transmission. We assume that their performative achievement can be discovered with an exegesis that situates them within the narrative corpus of the region. The attempt is worth the effort, because the anticolonial partisans did not leave behind lengthy explanations of their thoughts. If it is possible to find an expression of the telos of their movement—its plotted historicity for them as participants—these stories are one of the places to start looking.

The first story is set in a road-repair site between Dedougou and Cheriba, some time around the beginning of the anticolonial war. Nuna and Marka speakers live in this area and they provide the requisitioned labor. The principal actors are Haillot and a native officer, Daye, who visit the site, while the guard M'Pe directs the work. The guard has forced a new mother to join the work crew. The woman comes with her newborn baby strapped to her back. In the course of the day, under the hot sun the baby dies. The men stop the work. They gather around the supervisors, including Haillot, engage in an angry quarrel with them, and manhandle them. Then they return to their villages swearing that they will never work on the road site again (Gnankambary 1970, 65).

So far this appears to be a routine story about colonial oppression, but it acquires mythical proportions in the more elaborate version conveyed by Jean Hébert (1970, 14). It seems that Father Hébert is reporting from a local source, because he gives the protagonist's name as Musa Hayo, as if it is not the same Haillot he mentions a few pages later.[13] Some details in this version heighten the story's dramatic effect. The child dies on the way, before the mother even reaches the work site. The father is with the other workers. When he learns of the death of his child, he says: "If they murder my children, why should I be afraid of anything else?" The women fan the flames by tearfully invoking the great men of the old days who would never have allowed such a thing to happen. Most significantly, the ending is changed. The evening of the child's death, the leaders of the workers have a meeting in which they decide to kill the guard, even if it costs their lives. Hébert says that Yisu of Bona, Kasun of Soan, and Siaka of Datomo—leaders of the anticolonial movement—attend this meeting. They trap M'Pa and kill him. After this event, the workers disperse and the villages start preparing for the anticolonial war.

Hébert's longer narrative raises questions. Although the different ending finds its reason in narrative logic (the first version has weak resolution, and the new ending completes the form, adding performative power) had the guard actually been killed, it would be surprising not to find a record of it in the documents from Dedougou; and it is also unlikely that the three important leaders of the anticolonial movement attended the meeting where the decision was taken. A likely explanation is that Hébert, who does not mention the second of our narratives (the one below, about the guard Alamasson Diara), has heard a version that mixed together motifs from both tales.

The second story features the notorious Alamasson, whom we first encountered in chapter 4. It takes place at a different road-repair site, where the Dedougou-Bobo-Dioulasso road runs near the village of Pundu. (The site of the first story is eleven kilometers north of Bona; that of the second is fifteen kilometers west of it.) Alamasson directs the work with a gun and a whip. Again the story involves a woman worker, but this one is pregnant. She starts her labor pains, but when she asks Alamasson's permission to return to the village, he sends her back to work with blows and insults. The woman is forced to give birth on the side of the road, where male workers can see her. The enraged men decide in a meeting that night to kill Alamasson. Alamasson's assistant is warned by a village girlfriend and disappears. The workers catch Alamasson and disarm him. "If you kill me," he says, "the world will be troubled." "We know that," the workers reply, "but that will be after you." They lay him on the road and, while he is still alive, cut off his limbs. Leaving his bloody trunk in the middle of the road, they form two delegations and divide his limbs and clothes between them, going in different directions to make the rounds of important Bwa and Marka villages. "From now on, force is finished," they announce. "We killed the guard who was watching us. Here are his limbs and his clothes. We ask your help. Let us arm ourselves and defend the land of our forefathers" (Gnankambary 1970, 66). This incident left a trace in an entry in Maguet's journal: "Yesterday November 23, the Bobo of Fakena, at the instigation of the Marka of La, killed the first class guard A. Diarra and the two staff who were with him, between Pundu and Koanko."[14]

Cire Ba (1971, 106–7) adds a detail in his version, which will now be familiar: "One evening after returning from work, the women of Fakena and Buan took off their wrap-around cloths and threw them on the men, and asked to have their pants." The gloss the author puts on this: "You are incapable of defending us, we are going to take your place!" The elders do not act conciliatory as usual, but start regretting their youth. "It is as if they were saying to the young, 'This bow that our arms can no longer bend—we are giving it to you to take revenge.'" Cire Ba also proposes that the killing of Alamasson was a kind of sacrifice to the soil, which had been "profaned by the ungodly." This is an unacknowledged quote from Nazi Boni (1962, 223), but Cire-Ba modifies its original meaning with the parenthetic explanation: "He [Alamasson] had slept with a woman behind a bush, in view of her husband."

To read either story simply as a description of response to oppression is to leave out what is, in our opinion, their central point. Before explaining this with a comparison to earlier and different stories that have a similar thematic pattern, we will discuss briefly why the "despair in oppression" reading is so prevalent. The idea that the anticolonial war resulted from rage caused by suffocating oppression, that it was a desperate assertion of the self, is very common. It goes along with the assumption that the anticolonial partisans knew they were going to lose the conflict, or should have known that they would. The argument comes in two varieties. European commentators hold that the technological superiority of the French was overwhelming and that it would be impossible to entertain the illusion that the locals could win a war against them. African intellectuals, however, present a different view, and theirs is the one we want to take up here. These authors interestingly suggest that the anticolonial movement was doomed because of a wrong that its partisans had committed. It was not simply an error of judgment, but a transgression, or neglect of a transcending power. As Nazi Boni expresses in his novel (1962, 231):

> A worry held the country in its grip. Multiple prophesies all pointed the same way and confirmed each other. Cranes flew over most villages and caused great commotion. The Bwaba consider this sign as forewarning of a particular misfortune: The total destruction of the country in a war and its certain domination by a foreign "Force." No propitiatory sacrifice was considered sufficiently strong to avert this fate. Panic became agonizing because people had a bad conscience. We have committed a crime, they thought, that neither the gods, nor the ancestors, nor "God-the-great" forgives.

The crime here was the killing of the chief of Wakuy, who is supposed to have asked for clemency, and of the messenger he had sent to communicate it (the incident is related in chap. 6). The reason for the unfavorable prediction differs in the various accounts; it is generally too narrow to be accepted as general explanation. But the structure of the argument always remains the same.

Another example of the transgression motif, conceived in a more popular

idiom, can be found in a recent booklet written in Jula for the adult-literacy program in Bobo-Dioulasso. According to that account, before the war anticolonial
partisans went to consult a Muslim cleric to find out what the outcome of the
struggle would be. He gave them an amulet to place on a dead shea tree. When
the villagers carried out the cleric's directives, the next day they saw that the tree
had grown leaves. They returned to the cleric and he told them to wait one more
day. The next day the tree produced fruit. They went to the cleric again, and he
told them to make two piles of the fruit, the ripe on one side and the unripe on
the other. If the unripe fruit was more abundant than the ripe, that would mean
that success in the war was assured. They found that the unripe was less abundant. Then the cleric said that there was one more thing they could do: if they
sacrificed a human being, the outcome of the war would be favorable to them.
A man in the village volunteered as the victim, on condition that his young son
not be cheated of his share of the spoils of the war. They promised him this and
proceeded with the sacrifice. After the war started, the son and his mother encountered a group of men who were butchering an ox that they had gotten in
the battle. The son asked for his share, but the men refused to give it to him, and
they insulted him. The mother cursed the men and prayed that they should lose
the war. (Bobo Julaso ni Dedugu Serepeya 1995, 19–25).[15]

Young village farmers who possessed a copy of this booklet and whom we
talked to in 1998 were offended by this passage and denied with vehemence that
a human sacrifice had occurred. The episode, however, does seem to derive from
the oral tradition, although it is prototypical and most probably apocryphal. Its
apocryphal character is in fact the central point that we want to establish. The
"foreordained doom" explanation is a retrospective reflection on the anticolonial
movement. These stories—whether presented with an undertone of tragedy, as
in Boni's highly literary French prose, or more as a folktale, as in the Jula text—
are very different in tone and in narrative content from the road-site protest narratives with which we began. There is antinomy between them, not only in style
but also in intent. The second set explains the failure of the movement *now that
it is known,* by referring to an internal moral/ritual order. The first set of narratives
does something quite different—something that can be clarified by comparison
with political narratives that come from precolonial times.

The stories we present for comparison are normally part of biographic accounts. Like the tales of the guards M'Pe and Alamasson, they give a central
place to women who are pregnant or who have just given birth. Fertility is
threatened by harming these women, and violent retribution on the perpetra-
tors follows. This "syntagmatic structure" remains constant behind different

plot lines. The life story of Seku Watara of Tenegera, who is considered ancestor to Pintyeba and Moro-fin (see chaps. 3 and 4), recounts how his enemy Lasiri Gambele of Kong had his soldiers kill pregnant women. They did this only
because they liked to bet on the sex of the foetus. Seku, who was a wealthy
merchant, eventually built a coalition and attacked this powerful man. He
killed him and buried his severed head in the marketplace of Kong, indicating
the location with a portal so that people could step on it. This was the beginning of the political rise of Seku Watara (Kodjo 1986, 312; Bernus 1960, 248).
In another episode, Seku uses medicine to help the wife of a rich king deliver
her baby. The king rewards him with gold, with which he is able to obtain soldiers and weapons (Kodjo 1986, 325). The contrast between the two protagonists Lasiri Gambele and Seku is starkly established. The first prevents
reproduction and is killed, the second enhances fertility and is triumphant.

A similar story is told about Molo Sanon, the eponymous ancestor of some
of the Zara houses of Sia (Bobo-Dioulasso). Molo was a merchant. People of
the village of Kado first pillaged his donkeys loaded with salt bars and, a second time, killed his pregnant wife to see if the baby was male or female. Molo
returned with rage in his heart. He paid Famagan Watara in gold to help him
punish the people of Kado (Cire Ba 1971, 43). For Molo this was the beginning of a long and successful career as a war leader. The killing of pregnant
women is today also encountered in other stories linked to different heroes in
the villages of the Volta region.[16]

In these stories we see that the killing of pregnant women establishes that
the enemy deserves the hero's wrath. The act of cruelty functions in the narrative to release the male hero from constraint. He is justified in revenge, and this
decision transforms him. The enemies are quickly and easily eliminated. Before
the revenge, the hero was a merchant; after the violence he becomes a celebrated war leader. A new vocation opens up, taking him to a glorious destiny.
These narratives are about a triumphant beginning. The stories about the
guards M'Pa and Alamasson possess the same finality. They, too, are about
threats to fertility; the crimes against the women devastate the men, but also
embolden them, and a new political project is born from the experience. The
stories of the guards were probably no more about the indignities of the colonial period than the Seku and Molo stories were about the bad habits of the
villagers. The plots expressed the self-reading and self-justification of a new
movement that was looking confidently ahead.

Other evidence supports this understanding. The mood in the beginning
of the anticolonial movement, according to what is conveyed in contemporary

Fig. 5. Portrait of Gnâtéen Sèni, leader of the ambush against Alamasson, drawn by an unknown colonial employee. (Courtesy of L. Seni)

documents such as the cercle diaries, was not at all one of gloom and anxiety. The predictions made in the villages at that time were not the destruction of the country. French officials, who in fact were the ones experiencing distress and fear, recorded many references to such points. The countless oracular consultations made in the early phase of the war at a large variety of shrines all predicted unqualified success. The official diaries of Dedougou and Koudougou for November and December mention many late-night parties of dance and song, where sorghum beer flowed and early-morning sacrifices confirmed victory. There is absolute contrast between these and the episode of the shea tree and the portent of the cranes in Boni's novel. The "foreordained doom" view is not contemporary with the anticolonial movement itself, and it has been an obstacle to understanding the beginnings of the movement and its protagonists' thoughts. It is a retrospective attempt at explanation, whereas the narratives that were born with the movement were justificatory and enabling.

The performative burden of the Alamasson narratives given above comes into sharper focus when we compare them with a very different recension from a private source that we are lucky to have. The interest of this last one is that it was told by the son of the man who planned the execution of Alamasson, Gnâtéen of Fakena, and is published by the grandson of the narrator (see fig. 5).[17] It reflects a family tradition, and accordingly reveals concerns very different from the versions we have discussed so far. These memories tell us that Gnâtéen killed Alamasson because the guard was lusting after his young and beautiful wife. The sexual rapacity of Alamasson, which is hinted among the early printed versions only in parenthesis, in Cire Ba's, takes center stage here. One evening, Gnâtéen learns when he returns from the farm that Alamasson took his wife Wofe under the pretext of work. He decides to punish him for that, and with a few of his friends ambush Alamasson around midnight on the Bobo-Dedougou road, near Pundu. The author, L. Seni, knows, from what he has been told, the large baobab tree under which the event happened. The tree still stands at the side of the road.

> They took his uniform and his sword, they cut his penis and his hands, they left his mutilated body there, and they returned to Fakena. When they presented the booty, horse, sword, uniform, penis, and hands of the dreaded guard, the war drum pounded to salute them. The next day there was a great celebration in all the villages of the region when the drums spread the news of the death of the bloodthirsty guard. (Seni 1985, 25)

There is no question of a pregnant woman or the roadside rebellion, and although the story is told against the backdrop of an account of the anticolonial war, its relation to this social event remains secondary. The plot revolves around the sexual rivalry of two men, and the benefit to the community is incidental.

The difference between this family tradition and widespread variants that turn on the woman and her baby is one of narrative finality. In an interpretive essay on the Volta-Bani War, Izard contrasts the "little wars" carried out between the villages of a limited area and the wars carried out against a more imposing opponent by broad alliances achieved by reactivating dormant links (Izard 1999). This contrast becomes helpful in interpreting the different versions of the Alamasson story when we recall that the most common trigger of the "little war" between villages was the abduction (or seduction) of women. Competition over women is a correlate of the "little war." Gnâtéen's version of sexual rivalry concerns a limited space. The narratives built on the motif of threats to the mother and baby are those of the "intercommunity territory," the reactivation of submerged ties, and the grand war against a common enemy. They express and effect the birth of a counterhegemonic project, which came into existence in this instance at the time of the first successes of the anticolonial movement, and they circulated as the discursive counterpart of these successes.

The stories of the killing of the guards are often presented as the origin of the anticolonial movement. From the point of view of the time line this is not accurate. The two incidents on the road sites occurred after the Bona battles, that is weeks after the meetings where resistance to the colonial government was discussed. Placing these stories at the inception of the anticolonial movement is accurate in another respect, however, because their performative mission was part of its initial self-awareness and militancy. This is why we insert their discussion at this point, before turning in the next chapter to the battles of Bona, where the war actually began.

CHAPTER 6

The First Victories of the Anticolonial Party

MAGUET AND HIS GUARDS had arrived in Safane in order to punish Bona for insubordination to the canton chief. Having moved on to Bona, he found that the village put up resistance against him. The first phase of the conflict thus began in late November 1915 and lasted until the end of January 1916 (the period covered in this chapter).

Two engagements occurred in Bona, one day apart. They established for the two sides, and for the rest of the population not yet involved, that what had started was not a simple case of disobedience. After these engagements, the anticolonial movement spread quickly, as the leadership of the Bona-Datomo-Tunu area stepped up its propaganda and diplomacy campaign. Attacks were organized against colonial chiefs, and hesitant villages or those that remained openly loyal to the colonial administration were intimidated. Villages began to crack as their different wards aligned themselves with opposite sides. The second major confrontation happened a week after the Bona battles, when Commandant Henri Maubert of Bobo-Dioulasso went to Nienegue country to rescue the chief of Bondokuy. He was trapped in the village, and while he inflicted a large number of casualties, his company just barely escaped total annihilation.

In response to these two failures, the government gathered in Dedougou a special expeditionary force. A battle against this force is the third major confrontation of this phase. It, too, resulted in defeat for the colonial army. Between these clashes, the anticolonial forces undertook two important attacks to punish the colonial chiefs who supported the French action. Thus December

1915 ended with euphoria on the anticolonial side, and the rapid expansion of the movement (see map 1). The administration in Dedougou was paralyzed with panic, and the government-general in Dakar set out to build a larger column by concentrating most of the military resources available in French West Africa in that cercle.

THE TWO BATTLES OF BONA

When Administrator Maguet arrived in Safane on November 19, 1915, he thought he was handling a common case of insubordination triggered by the requisition of conscripts. The twelve guards that he had brought with him, he hoped, would be sufficient to scare the population of Bona to deliver the draft candidates; perhaps also he had in mind a light fine or a pardon, as in the successful negotiation he had had earlier in the year in the village of Sami. From Safane, Maguet dispatched emissaries to Bona, but they returned to say the villagers had fired upon them. He then sent the chief of Safane with a group of the chief's own men to Bona. After their departure, the villagers persuaded Maguet that he was putting the chief at great risk and that he should go to Bona himself. In addition to the guards he had ten local men, whom he placed under the command of a former soldier of the colonial army. These auxiliary soldiers served as scouts and guarded the equipment and supplies of the company.

Maguet arrived outside Bona with his company around 9:00 A.M. He found the chief of Safane waiting there for him. Shortly afterwards, the guard who had been sent the night before from Dedougou with five other men arrived from Yankaso, where they had spent the night. Thus Maguet had under his command more than forty people. The village of Bona had prepared for his arrival. The villagers had fitted the outer walls of the village with loopholes, through which they could fire their weapons (guns and bows and arrows) and repaired the walls around the terraces. In the village were many fighting-age men from surrounding villages allied to Bona.

Bona had the shape of a rectangle stretching north-south (see map 4). The defense was concentrated behind the western wall, facing the road from Safane—the way Maguet's company approached the village. Upon his arrival, Maguet divided his men into two squads and positioned them on two points of slight elevation against the northwest and the southwest corners of the wall. Whistles were blowing in the village, and from their positions the colonial troops could see people running in the narrow streets to go from house to

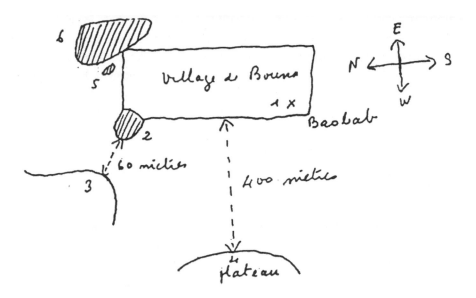

Map 4. The village of Bona as drawn by Maguet. From Haut-Sénégal Niger, Cercle de Koury, "Compte-rendu de la révolte en pays marka et bobo (depuis le commencement de l'affaire de Bona jusqu'à l'affaire de Yankasso, 17 novembre–23 décembre) 1. Baobab tree; 2, 5, 6. compounds; 3, 4. plateau."

house. Hoping to draw the villagers out into the open, Maguet feigned a retreat. When this maneuver failed, he sent some of his troops closer to the village, while the rest aimed their fire inside the loopholes and at defenders seen in the streets. The guards suddenly broke into a spontaneous assault, but strong fire from the village stopped them and they were called back to their positions by Maguet. As the firing continued, the villagers made a charge outside. They suffered casualties under the sustained fire of guards hidden from view and withdrew behind the walls. The defenders flocked to a strong point in the northwest corner of the village, which according to Maguet's report was the compound of the hunter Yusiri (this might be Yisu). This house seemed to be the center of the resistance.

At 2:00 P.M., Maguet learned that reinforcements to the defenders were about to arrive from many other villages. He ordered a general assault against the northwest corner of Bona. Despite heavy return fire from the villagers, his troops managed to clear the wall and occupy several houses. But the advance could not be sustained and he ordered a retreat. At the same time, the first reinforcements to the defenders—men with guns and bows and arrows—were sighted. They were moving forward carefully, in scattered ranks, from the northeast and the south. When the defenders of Bona saw the reinforcements, they, too, came out for an assault. Skillfully using the terrain, the newly arriving men tried to encircle Maguet's troops. At 4:30 P.M., Maguet, thinking of his limited supply of ammunition, the enemy's overwhelming superiority in numbers, and the approaching evening, decided to retreat. The small company was pursued for about six kilometers and had to fire all the time on the enemy. The pursuit ended only when Maguet's men reached the first houses of the village of Bara. Maguet's men made it back to Safane around sunset. They had spent 940 cartridges and had only 70 left. Maguet estimated that they had killed about fifty people and wounded many more, mostly among the reinforcement troops who had tried to encircle them and those who had pursued them during their retreat. Among his own men, he had four wounded, none dead.

The company spent the night in Safane. The next morning, it was confirmed that there was a general mobilization against the colonial forces. Maguet sent messages to his administrative assistant, Lowitz, who had returned to Dedougou from a mission the night before, and to Combes, the resident of Boromo. He asked them both to bring all available guards and ammunition. Lowitz was also instructed to bring the guards who had recently been dismissed on extortion charges and all the discharged tirailleurs that could be found in the cercle. Maguet also wrote to Lieutenant Taxil, who was on duty in the cercle with the conscription campaign, to join him with his twenty soldiers.[1]

Three French officials — Combes, Lowitz, and Sergeant Dougaud — arrived in Safane on the evening of November 20 with all the men they could find. The tirailleurs, guards, and other auxiliary fighters thus brought together in the enlarged company now numbered more than two hundred. Fifty of these were armed with sophisticated Lebel rifles; the rest, auxiliaries, had single-shot muskets, bows and arrows, or spears. Among them were fifty horsemen.[2]

According to the intelligence reports received by Maguet, the insurgents had mixed feelings about the outcome of the first battle. Almost all of the villages of the cantons of Tunu, Datomo, Koury, Bagasi, and Pompoï sympathized with Bona's defenders, but some of the battle's participants — such as the village of Tunu — had had a change of heart. The leaders from Bona were pursuing an energetic campaign of persuasion and intimidation to dispel the fear and hesitation and to maintain the momentum of growth of the opposition. The small village of Pakoro, which had given water and food to Maguet's retreating company the day before, had been sacked. Representatives of the anticolonial camp had visited all of the Marka and Bwa villages within the bend of the Muhun River, and large villages such as Datomo and La had said they would send fighters to Bona.

The few villages in the immediate vicinity of Safane were the only ones to send delegations expressing loyalty to Maguet, but even there Maguet sensed indecision and doubt. Instead of returning to Dedougou, Maguet decided to try another attack on Bona in the hope that a victory with his now larger company could turn things around and convince many villages to calm down.

To increase his chances of success, he decided that he had to act swiftly — to hit Bona before even larger numbers of anticolonial volunteers massed there. He wanted to set out that night so that he could start his attack on Bona with the rising sun, before reinforcements for the defense arrived from more distant villages. However, learning that the countryside was teeming with partisans converging toward Safane, he found it prudent to wait until the morning. At daybreak, November 21, the colonial company set out for Bona, and again Maguet sent ahead of him a series of messengers, hoping for conciliation. His message promised to forgive the rebels if they met him outside of the village to offer submission in good faith. The villagers met the messengers with bullets and arrows, shouting insults, and the emissaries quickly rode back. At 9:00, Maguet's company arrived in front of Bona and took position. The defenders had modified their tactics since the previous day's encounter. The streets of the village were empty and absolutely silent. The village appeared deserted. This unexpected sight disconcerted Maguet, but his informants insisted that at least one thousand defenders were in the village — twice as many as the previous day. As a small contingent of the company cautiously moved closer to the houses of the village in a last attempt to start dialogue, a burst of gunfire broke out from behind the walls, killing one of the auxiliary soldiers and wounding another. The company then regrouped, and Lieutenant Taxil launched a general assault. A fierce and bloody battle followed, lasting several hours.

Two hours into the fighting, the colonial troops managed to take a few houses and establish a foothold in the village. Then a gruesome phase of the battle started, fought at close range, as each room was ceded individually. The colonial soldiers slowly advanced, room by room, through the maze of communicating houses and terraces. According to Maguet's account of the battle, at 3:00 P.M., colonial troops controlled about half of the houses in the village and smoke was rising from the beams set on fire by Maguet's demolition team. At the same time, the French learned that new reinforcements for the defenders were on the way. Aware that if his forces stayed in the village they risked being surrounded, Maguet ordered a withdrawal. His troops then faced another challenge: a battle in open country against the new arrivals. The anticolonial forces suffered high casualties, but fought on with determination. It was clear that they were especially targeting the five Frenchmen of the company. Several anticolonial volunteers made suicidal charges to come closer to one of the Frenchmen.

When Maguet estimated that reinforcements to the defenders had reached one thousand—with many more on the way—he realized that he had lost the battle. He decided again to withdraw to Safane. He had little ammunition left. The porters carrying the baggage of the column had run away, as had the auxiliary soldiers charged with their protection. The medical post had been invaded, but the troops managed to rescue the bodies of their dead, the wounded, and the small supply of ammunition that was left, although they were forced to abandon other equipment. The remains of the column slowly retreated. For seven kilometers, it had to defend itself painfully against relentless attacks by fresh waves of anticolonial assailants.

The broken column arrived in Safane shortly after sunset. Seven of its members had been killed and several were seriously wounded. Among the latter were four of the five European officials of the company—including the physician Cremer, who was therefore unable to care for the wounded. Administrator Maguet was the only European to come out unscathed. During the combat, the colonial forces had spent seven thousand cartridges. Maguet wrote that they had counted more than four hundred enemy bodies, more than half of them killed within the village. Still, the enemy was massing around Safane, and fearing an attack there the remains of the column set out for Dedougou by night after a rest of only two hours.

Back in Dedougou, Maguet wrote in his report that among those killed in the fighting were important leaders among the defenders, including "the chief of the fetish." Hébert, in his long article that later became one of the principle sources for secondary accounts, closely followed Maguet's description (1970, 23). He seems to have taken Maguet's note to mean that Yisu Kote was among those killed. It is clear, however, that Yisu was not killed in this battle. He continued to play a prominent role in the organization of the movement.

In his first deposition, Yisu is reported to have said that Yike, his close associate and perenkie of the village, was killed in the battle of Bona. This may be what was meant by Maguet's reference to "the chief of the fetish." But in Bona we were told that Yike was not killed in that battle, that he, too, was made prisoner in the following June, that he served a long prison sentence, that he returned to Kieru, where his family was relocated, and that he died around 1930. In the colonial records, however, we found no record of Yike's captivity. Maguet noted that in the second battle of Bona, Siaka of Datomo, M'Bien Nienzien of Tunu, and Tarahe of La emerged as the most important military commanders of the anticolonial side. In Bona, the elders we interviewed named

Lasina Nyanu from Datomo as another important figure in the first set of leaders to emerge from these battles.

Immediately following the Bona battles, the conscripts who had been gathered in Dedougou and were waiting for their transfer ran away. The prisoners in the jail of the headquarters also escaped. The villages entered a period of turbulence. Meetings were held to decide whether to join the anticolonial camp or remain on the side of the administration. Maguet sent messengers to all of the villages in the central part of the cercle, asking the people to send delegations confirming their loyalty to the colonial administration. Many hesitated to do so, and the refusals were reflected in the staggering estimates of the number of rebel villages that the frightened administrator was composing. The Bona-Datomo leadership was continuing its propaganda with dexterity. The large amount of colonial material that the defenders had captured in Bona—personal effects of the Europeans, cooking utensils, and medical kits—was paraded in villages. Yisu Kote personally undertook many visits, headed delegations, and took messages to the masas, the perenkies, and other authorities of the villages, inviting them to meetings to hear the case for joining the war. In the villages of the bend of the Muhun, an image of him going from village to village, blowing the whistle, haranguing the population, and hurling insults and threats to those who hesitated, has now acquired mythic proportions. It is also said that he crossed the Muhun River to the west and visited the village of Sanaba. One wonders if this image is not an amalgam of several propagandists and ambassadors sent out from Bona and Datomo.

Those who decided to join the anticolonial camp began settling accounts with the local agents of the administration, and—as they became bolder—they started attacking communities that refused to join. Some spontaneous incidents seem to have taken place independently of the anticolonial leadership. The insubordination against Haillot in the road construction site and the killing of Alamasson belong in this period. Nazi Boni says in his novel (1962, 222–23): "The wisdom of Bwamu recommends to sweep the house before the surroundings. The purification started, then, with the enemy within, the 'traitors and black mercenaries.'"

Purification occasionally took ritual form. In Badema (cercle of Bobo-Dioulasso) a group of traitors was punished by having torches applied to their sexual parts; the eight men in the group were killed, the women being released to heal from their wounds.[3] Such a sanction by fire is normally reserved for crimes against the earth, most typically those who have had sex in the wild. In this case, it was part of the general cleansing of the community. The more common way of declaring oneself for the anticolonial movement was to attack the hated collectors of market tax. People discharged from the colonial army or service also became targets. Many canton chiefs had to flee their villages to avoid certain death, including the chiefs of Tunu, Datomo, Koso, Warkoy, Sodien, and Kona. The Jula traders who were associated with the whites and suspected of acting as their spies were attacked, dispossessed, and in some instances massacred (Boni 1962, 223). A few colonial guards who escaped the fate of Alamasson on November 23 (including his assistant Bandiugu) took refuge in the compound of the chief of Warkoy (Sombie 1975, 12). The compound was surrounded. With the help of guides sent to them by Maguet, the guards managed to escape together with the family of the chief during the night of November 25.

Against this swelling tide, the small contingent of colonial administrators and employees in Dedougou felt helpless, nursing their wounds as they waited desperately for reinforcements to be sent by the lieutenant governor. People in the villages were aware that the guards in Dedougou did not have much ammunition left, and Maguet feared an attack against Dedougou. He chose the prison building in the town as his stronghold and put the guards and soldiers to work to reinforce this building. The irony of the whites and their personnel now enclosing themselves in the prison building was not lost on the population. Maguet also established small posts in Bara, Pie, Koana, and Sokongo as a first line of defense. There was an attempt on the part of the anticolonial partisans to walk to Dedougou, but they were stopped at skirmishes in these posts. In the villages, the hearts of most people were for the opposition. Even in the wards of Dedougou itself, opinion was favorable to the anticolonial partisans.

THE SIEGE OF BONDOKUY

In this atmosphere of heightened excitement, the next major engagement came after a miscalculated response by the administrator of Bobo-Dioulasso. Bondokuy is a large Bwa village in the south of the cercle of Dedougou, near the border with the cercle of Bobo-Dioulasso, located seventy-eight kilometers from Dedougou and a hundred kilometers from Bobo-Dioulasso.

The chief of the canton of Bondokuy, Sibiri Kulibali, who was from one of the established old families of the village of the same name, lived there. After the second Bona battle, the residents of the ward of Dampan invaded the Roman Catholic mission that had been established in 1913 in the ward of Tankuy. The French missionaries had left in June when they were called up for the army, and the mission compound was guarded only by a newly converted villager and his family (Prost 1971, 106; Hébert 1970, 24). The invaders did not harm these people, but looted the mission, damaged its buildings, killed the pigs that were being raised, and destroyed its vegetable garden. Then they cut the telegraph line between Dedougou and Bobo-Dioulasso. Beniamu, who was presented in official reports as the head of the ward, incited this action in Dampan.[4] When Sibiri attempted to oppose these acts, the invaders attacked him (Sibiri's father was already a notorious person; when the French first arrived in the region, in 1897, he had allied himself with them and they made him canton chief, one of the most disliked in the region).

Sibiri took refuge from his pursuers in his fortified compound and tried to send messengers to the commandant in Dedougou. The anticolonials' blockade surrounding the compound prevented his couriers from reaching Dedougou, but one of them managed to wend his way to Bobo-Dioulasso. Therefore Commandant Maubert learned of the situation before the news reached Dedougou. He sent a telegram to Bamako on the morning of November 24 asking the head of the colony, Lieutenant Governor Digué, to authorize rescue of the chief of Bondokuy in the neighboring cercle. He also informed his colleague in Dedougou. Maguet responded immediately by telegram, advising Maubert against the rescue mission (since the lines had at some point been cut, it is not clear if Maubert received the telegram).

Digué authorized Maubert to go to Bondokuy if he could gather 35 guards. Maubert could find only 24, but disregarding this order he set out from Bobo-Dioulasso in the predawn hours of November 25, taking with him an additional 47 auxiliary horsemen equipped with advanced rifles and 140 auxiliary infantry armed with muskets.[5] He had 4,500 cartridges and 20 kilograms of locally produced gunpowder. Another 15 guards who were on various missions and 28 additional auxiliary horsemen were told to join the company later. The company spent that night in Satiri, and the next day, Dr. Rousseau, who had been on his way to Dedougou but had been called back by Maubert because the roads were insecure, joined the company in Katoba.

As the column made its way toward Bondokuy, it encountered signs full of portent. It found the large Bwa village of Sara almost deserted. This village had a legendary reputation for military prowess: in the final decades of the nineteenth century, it had led a strong confederation (chaps. 1 and 8). Maubert spent the day in the village and made the local chief promise to try to convince the inhabitants to return home. In the evening, a few more guards from Bobo-Dioulasso joined the column. That night, the chief of Wakuy, Beopa Bihun, sent fifty archers to the column. They would play a fateful role in Maubert's coming retreat, but Bihun still paid dearly for giving Maubert this support.

On the morning of November 27, an hour after Maubert's men left Sara, an archer attacked the column and wounded a horseman. The archer was caught and discovered to be a resident of Sara. When the column arrived in the Tankuy ward of Bondokuy—a large, reinforced settlement far from the other wards of the village—the inhabitants received the soldiers well. The company moved to the colonial compound, where the chief, Sibiri, explained to Maubert that there were several concentrations of anticolonial partisans, the most important of them in the ward of Dampan, some two kilometers away. Maubert left Dr. Rousseau with fifty auxiliary soldiers and the men of Sibiri to protect the compound and took the bulk of his forces to Dampan.

We pause here to ponder what drove Maubert to undertake this risky adventure. There can be little doubt that after the Bona battles he had received intelligence on the dangers of the situation, and—notwithstanding that he had disregarded the instructions of his superior as to the number of guards—the size of the column he assembled shows he expected serious resistance. Embarking on this self-assigned mission, Maubert could demonstrate his superior abilities, teach the rebels a lesson, and humiliate Maguet by succeeding where he had failed. We should note that the disastrous outcome of this foolhardiness did not moderate Maubert's impulsive ways in the subsequent months. His campaigns in the ten-month history of the war stand out as some of the most murderous—not only in enemy deaths but also in those among his own troops. Yet there was something in his brazen courage and his utmost disregard for his own safety that worked in his favor. In Maubert, the anticolonial heroes found a match: a man in action oblivious to sense and reason remained.

The leading figure of the resistance of Bondokuy was Beniamu, of Dampan.[6] As Maubert's forces approached Dampan, they encountered the conventional style of local warfare: the defendants came out of the walls of the settlement to meet the enemy and, after some intense fighting in the open, retreated behind the walls and took position there. Maubert stopped his column at about 250 meters from the first houses of the ward. He realized that the walls were solid and that the defense had been well prepared. He decided to ask for more men from Sibiri before launching an assault.

While Maubert was evaluating the situation in front of Dampan, back in Tankuy (see map 5) a major surprise attack had taken place against the colonial compound. Hearing the shots and other sounds of fighting from a distance, Maubert realized what had happened and hurried back to the compound with

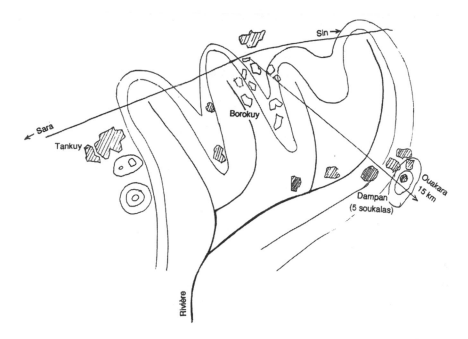

Map 5. Bondokuy. From the Molard report (SHAT 5 H 196).

his men to try to save the company and the equipment left there. On arrival, they found the auxiliaries and Sibiri's men at the point of being overrun. The column gave battle for nine hours — first to repel the attackers of the compound and then to take the three nearby settlements from which this attack had been organized. The anticolonial forces suffered — as they had in Bona — a disproportionate number of casualties, but the colonial column also had many killed and wounded.

The most important outcome of the day-long battle was that the anticolonial leaders, having taken the initiative, had forced Maubert to recognize that he was simply responding to their tactics. When guards and horsemen freshly arrived from Bobo-Dioulasso were intercepted by anticolonial partisans shortly before they reached the column, they survived only thanks to a squad that Maubert sent to help them. A few other guards and auxiliaries who were further behind, however, fell into the hands of the anticolonial forces and were killed near Sara; their bodies were cut into pieces and their heads were placed on pickets along the Bobo-Dioulasso–Dedougou road. The anticolonial movement was becoming more confident; reaching a state of feverish consciousness, with such markers it was claiming space.

As night fell, Sibiri and Maubert concluded that the colonial compound would be impossible to defend against a similar assault the next day. The column moved to Sibiri's fortified compound. The night passed without incident, but the anticolonial side was receiving reinforcements from other villages, and it became clear that massive forces were arraigned against the column. It was also clear that the column was in no position to provide help to any friends outside Sibiri's compound. On the morning of November 28, the inhabitants of Mukuna—who felt that they were likely targets of the anticolonials—took refuge in Sibiri's compound. This made the crowding worse.

The anticolonial forces began their attack at around 10:00 A.M. The assault took the form of a run by a packed mass of assailants. Despite heavy firing from the column, the run was not stopped until it was only two hundred meters from the compound, and this was followed by two hours of close-range combat. Eventually the attack became weaker and the partisans were driven back to Dampan. On the bloodstained grass of the area surrounding Sibiri's compound lay many bodies. The assailants had suffered very heavy losses. But the colonial column had used up more than three-fourths of the cartridges that it had brought for the 74 and 86 Lebel guns and all of its loose gunpowder for the muskets. They were still besieged, and the anticolonial side continued to receive reinforcements. Sibiri's men could manufacture only one kilogram of gunpowder per day.

The news that a white man was with the hefty column trapped in Bondokuy became the event that tipped the anticolonial movement over a critical line. In terms of morale, it more than counteracted the other news that the first contingents of the suppression column that the government-general was building up in Dedougou had started to arrive. The first of these contingents was that of Captain Henri Labouret, who arrived in Dedougou from Gaoua with forty-four tirailleurs on November 28. The following day, Digué, the interim lieutenant governor of the colony of Haut-Sénégal-Niger, arrived from Bamako accompanied by Brévié, the head of the political office (and future governor-general of the AOF); they were to remain in Dedougou for about a month, until January 1. On November 30, a cannon and twenty more tirailleurs arrived from Ouagadougou. The dampening effect of these arrivals on anticolonial adhesion was noticeable, but temporary. For the anticolonial partisans, this was the most hopeful and successful period of the entire war.

Maguet regularly measured the strength of the movement by dispatching messengers to the villages and asking them to send representatives to Dedougou to renew their pledges of loyalty. After the first colonial reinforcements arrived, the number of villages that reaffirmed their loyalty to the French began to increase, but as the news spread that Maubert's column was still held up in Bondokuy, the number of village delegations that came to Dedougou plummeted again. The emboldened anticolonial movement had now a broader geographic range. On November 30, a group that had gathered in Pundu — only thirty kilometers south of Dedougou — attacked Kari, which was even closer to Dedougou and had remained loyal to the administration. The colonial officers in Dedougou decided to make a show of force so as not to remain totally passive and also to give indirect support to Maubert by diverting the attention of anticolonial forces from Bondokuy. On December 1, a column with all tirailleurs and guards available in Dedougou at that time, including a cavalry unit provided by Idrisa Sidibe, chief of Barani, headed for Kari under the direction of Labouret, Maguet, and Digué. A bloody, three-hour battle between the anticolonial forces besieging Kari and the colonial column took place just outside of the village. It ended when the colonial troops could no longer sustain the force of the attack and retreated. After their departure, the anticolonial forces, which had suffered very heavy losses, also decided to lift their siege of Kari and withdraw to their base in Pundu. From a strictly military perspective, the battle was inconclusive, but in the days that followed, after the initial shock passed, this withdrawal of the column in the presence of the governor of the colony became, in the hands of the anticolonial propaganda effort, another victory.

Meanwhile, in Bondokuy the ferocity of the assault of the first days had diminished. According to the account provided by Nazi Boni (1962, 225), the main reason for this was a dispute between the Bwa fighters of the surrounding villages and the Marka fighters who had come to provide assistance. Underlying the tension was the terrible casualty rate of the first two days. There was growing suspicion between hosts and guests that the protective charms given to the fighters (probably those brought by the Marka) had been ineffective. At some point, a section of the Marka forces seems to have withdrawn, to the great relief of the besieged. Nonetheless, by night the drums of Tankuy intoned stronger than ever, insulting the white man and his friends, predicting the exhaustion of all their ammunition and promising to catch them alive and "slaughter them with dulled knives" (Boni 1962, 225). On November 30, a more rigorous attack on Sibiri's compound took place, and the colonial defenders, by then they were relying mostly on arrows, were barely able to repel it. Maubert had restricted the use of muskets and rifles to sharpshooters, and they were being kept on reserve as a last resort. In that day's counterattack, the anticolonial camp lost Dawe Boho, "the chief of the rebellion of Bondokuy."[7] Sumu Boho, the second leading figure of the anticolonial organization in the

Bondokuy area, also fell in the battles during this siege (Boni 1962, 225; Hébert 1970, 30).

Maubert's hope was that a rescue mission would arrive from Dedougou. When he learned on the night of November 30 that a company was preparing to leave Dedougou, his hopes were raised and he wanted to send a messenger to tell them of his desperate ammunition situation. His messengers were unable to break through the road blockade. Maubert then entrusted his mission to Lamusa, a classificatory brother of Sibiri and a fighter of great renown. Boni's fictional account (1962, 226) gives us a glimpse of the choices that were tearing apart the Bwa communities:

> Lamoussa, the skilled horseman! Lamoussa, the brave of the brave! Lamoussa whom the Bwawa admired for his outspokenness, his tall stature, and his courage! Ah! What a bitter regret only to think that he could have left himself to be dragged behind the scoundrel of Sibiri, caught up in this chain of renegades! Yes, the prestigious Lamoussa Coulibaly, in loyalty to his family was won to this new cause. Well! Too bad. He was going to meet the lot of the renegades.

Lamusa managed to pierce the blockade and deliver the message, but the expedition prepared in Dedougou was headed not for Bondokuy but for nearby Kari. The colonial army gathering in Dedougou was still too weak to go as far as Bondokuy. Vulnerable to attack, it would likely be annihilated on the road. Even if this army could reach Bondokuy, a lengthy mission such as this would make Dedougou an easy prey to the anticolonial forces massed around Pundu. The absolute priority of the French officials was to keep the headquarters of Dedougou from falling into anticolonial hands.

No fighting took place on December 1 because it was a Wednesday; in the custom of the Bwaba, this is the day of cessation of hostilities to allow the antagonists to bury their dead. Maubert, who in any case had little choice in the matter, respected the unilateral truce. The anticolonial forces continued their attacks on December 2, 3, and 4, although on December 2 a very large group of anticolonial fighters left the Bondokuy battle zone and went to Dafina and Pundu when they heard that a company with thirty tirailleurs under Captain Ferron was about to arrive from Bandiagara.[8] Despite this partial withdrawal, the assailants in Bondokuy were now able to control the marsh contiguous to Sibiri's compound; Maubert's men had found it increasingly difficult to repel the waves of attack and to keep the enemy at a safe distance. The siege was prolonged now only because the assailants knew that no rescue mission would come soon for Maubert. Wanting to avoid the heavy losses that might be expected in taking a reinforced compound by room-to-room combat, they were delaying the final assault until the enemy totally ran out of ammunition. They also wanted to capture the enemy alive, which had been one of their aims from the very beginning. This likely fate was communicated to the besieged in drum language and in song and dance every night. It was cause for unrestrained celebration in the anticolonial camps: the new harvest was almost in and grain and beer were plentiful in the villages. With the mystical atmosphere and a new sense of power, and with the excitement of initial successes, drunken revelries reached orgiastic proportions.

The hopelessness of their situation was as clear to Maubert and his associates as it was to their opponents. Realizing that not only a rescue mission but even the dispatch of a small contingent of well-trained soldiers as reinforcement with fresh ammunition from Dedougou was for now out of the question, Maubert took a decision that showed his uncommon intuition. Before his ammunition was totally exhausted, he and his men would try to break the siege and escape with the convoy of people under his charge. Maubert made this decision on December 4, but told no one about it—not even his closest associates—because he knew that the anticolonial leaders followed what happened in his entourage with a tight network of spies. He suspected a number of informants among the large group of refugees from Mukuna who had sought asylum in the compound. An example was the Fulbe man from the ward of Tankuy who visited him pretending to be his friend but who had a son fighting in the ranks of the insurgents.[9]

At 2:00 A.M. on December 5, Maubert announced his decision, first to Dr. Rousseau, then to his second in command Makan Traore, the interpreter Diaman, and Sibiri. The convoy was prepared with great haste. Maubert's plan was to split the large group of a few hundred into two. Maubert and the guards, carrying most of the remaining ammunition, would take the main road. They would thus draw the main fighting force of anticolonial partisans behind them and would try to make it past the dangerous zone to Bobo-Dioulasso. Sibiri, with his family, the auxiliary soldiers, and all the women and children of the population who had taken refuge with them, after coming out of the compound with the main force would separate from them somewhere past Sara and less conspicuously take a different road in an attempt to reach Bosora. The marching column would be protected in front by twenty horsemen armed with lances and two Lebel rifles. Following them at a hundred meters would be Maubert, commanding ten guards in the front and sixteen guards on the two sides, and then the bulk of the convoy, refugees and auxiliary soldiers who had no gunpowder left for their muskets. These would be followed by the archers, then in the rear, nine guards, who were each given twenty-four cartridges. The entire convoy stretched several hundred meters.

The convoy set out from Sibiri's compound in the dark at 4:30 A.M. The Tankuy lookouts spotted the column's movement but thought that Maubert was engaging in some kind of encircling movement to try a new tactic in the morning. They remained behind their walls, trying to figure out what the maneuver was. Only after the convoy had almost entirely passed did the Tankuy fighters understand their mistake. Then the war cries rose, the drums started to beat, and the fighters of Tankuy emerged and started showering bullets on the column. The rearguard was at one point almost surrounded, but the column managed to clear its way and walk at a fast pace, pursued by a large crowd of enemy soldiers. At 7:00 A.M. the horsemen in the front encountered the first armed fighters from Sara, and the column came within view of that village half an hour later.

Two or three thousand fighters had massed outside Sara, blocking the road to Bobo-Dioulasso. The leaders directing the attack of Sara were Diumugu and Lamisa (the latter would be the last rebel to be executed in Bobo-Dioulasso for having killed the guards who were trying to reach Maubert in Bondokuy; see chap. 8). The Sara fighters attacked the colonial column as soon as they sighted it. Maubert dismounted and ordered a volley of shots to stop the momentum of the enemy charge. To hinder the work of enemy archers, he led the column within the tall grasses on the left side of the road. The column thus painfully continued its progress for about three kilometers, under constant heavy attack and protected by only eleven firing guns. When it came within a few hundred meters of the main road leading to Bobo-Dioulasso, its pursuers made a major effort to prevent Maubert's men from reaching it. During the battle, a few guards from the column took control of a small hill dominating the crossroads, and the column was able to pass. Maubert mentions that among the leaders of the Sara opposition, Numuke (who was the uncle of the chief, Bandiuru), and Tumme (a man who had been a domestic servant in Bobo-Dioulasso) were wounded or perhaps killed on this spot. According to Boni (1962, 227), one reason why the column was able to pierce the blockade around Sara is because the anticolonial fighters, determined at all cost to take some of its leading figures alive, were shooting with restraint.

Then an unexpected development led to a great number of casualties for the column. The troops had passed the worst of the blockade and were emerging onto the main road when the archers of Wakuy, who had so far protected the column, all changed sides. "They were impressed by the number and determination of their fellow countrymen and revolted by the carnage to which they were subjected," writes Boni. The Wakuy men aimed their arrows at the backs of the convoy members who were running to reach the road ahead of them. By the time the rearguard understood what was happening and arrived at the scene with a few fresh packages of cartridges that Maubert had sent them from the front, the archers had silently killed about forty people, most of them refugee civilians, which group at this point was still with the main column.

The anticolonial partisans, despite their heavy losses, pursued the column on the main road for five kilometers, to near the village of Kadoba. From Bondokuy, the pursuit had lasted forty-three kilometers. The column was now in somewhat neutral territory. The firing had stopped, but it hurried forward and arrived in Satiri early in the afternoon. There Maubert encountered a French lieutenant, Pal, with a small number of soldiers carrying cartridges and gunpowder intended for the column. The end of the column entered Satiri around 4:00 P.M. After only a few hours of rest, Maubert and his men proceeded to Bobo-Dioulasso. The next day, he learned that the convoy that had taken the road to Bosora and Lahiraso had reached safety with fewer than ten people killed.

In the nine days under siege, Maubert's column had confronted partisans from villages representing all ethnic groups of the area. In the siege of Bondokuy partisans from La, Fakena, Sokongo, Kera, Wakara, Wakuy, Buan, Tia, Sara, Koso, Dora, Si, Bankuna, Lora, and Kamana had participated (Capron 1973, 101; Sombie 1975, 14). In the fighting around Sara, volunteers from many other places were involved. Despite the numerical superiority of the enemy, the column had suffered few deaths of guards and auxiliary soldiers. The column had inflicted tremendous losses on the assailants. Maubert's sources indicated that during the retreat about one thousand men had been killed in the intense engagements in the vicinity of Sara. An estimated one thousand more were killed during the eight-day siege preceding that, more than half of them during the massive assault on the compound of Sibiri during the first day. Maubert's boldness had deprived the anticolonial camp of a victory that had seemed to be almost within reach. For the unrealized goal—destruction of the column—the partisans had endured these staggering losses.

Despite this extremely skewed distribution of casualties between the two parties, the population considered the outcome of the entire episode unfavorable to the colonial party. In the course of the siege, the majority of the population of the zone between the two cercles of Dedougou and Bobo-Dioulasso had mobilized against the French. The siege, like the two Bona battles shortly before, was taken to have confirmed the assertion of the anticolonial leadership:

It was proven that the white man was afraid of death and that if divinity he had been, he was now deposed by the Great-god. For the Bwaba who were furious at the deadly meddling of the White Man in their affairs, the battle of Bondokuy was only a prelude, a simple stretching exercise. They were going to hurry to bring in the harvest of millet, and then, after that, the world would see. (Boni 1962, 227)

The siege of Bondokuy became the turning point in the extension of the war. The entire Bwa/Nienegue area in the northern part of the cercle of Bobo-Dioulasso, which up to that time had remained hesitant, went over to the anti-colonial side. This included large Bwa villages such as Maro and Boho, which subsequently played important leadership roles in the anticolonial movement (see chap. 8). Further west, during the same ten days Sambla and Tussia villages and then the surroundings of Fo awakened to the possibility of a successful anticolonial coalition.

HEADING FOR THE GREAT CLASH

A new cadre of anticolonial leadership had by now emerged, replacing the dis-credited and chased-away canton chiefs appointed by the administration. French officials referred to them as "the chiefs of the kamele." The French noted that these people were organizers but not necessarily commanders during the battle; each village had its own war leader.[10] The perenkie (or head of the kamele) connected the villages to the leadership group in Bona and provided the basis for a loose territorial organization. The population supporting the movement was heady with perpetual celebration. Chicken oracles, performed one after another at important shrines everywhere, all gave good omens. Lieu-tenant Governor Digué, who spent these days in Dedougou, somberly noted that people were "in the mind-numbing excitation of sorghum beer and inca-pable of the slightest reflection."[11]

But the people were in fact far from incapable of reflection: in their hours of sobriety they were busily arming themselves. They were manufacturing gun-powder and arrow poison (both enormously time-consuming activities), pur-chasing arrows and muskets, strengthening the walls of their villages, and fitting the walls with loopholes and parapets.[12] Bwa villages brought blacksmiths to-gether in secret places and had shelters built for them, supplying them with food so that they could spend all their time smelting iron and manufacturing arrow heads and gun parts. One of the most important production places was a large smelting furnace, now abandoned, located in what today is the classified forest of Maro, near Bekuy. Elderly villagers living nearby told an archeologist that, although this area had been a significant metallurgical center for more than a century, smelting activity there had never in living memory been as high as during this year of anticolonial war (Coulibaly 1997, 464). Telegraph lines were cut down and the metal recycled for weaponry. The wire was cut into small pieces and forge-welded to produce arrow tips; bolts were divided into segments to be used as gun projectiles; and sulfur, found in the insulators, became an ingredient in gunpowder. Craftsmen were also capable of producing a good powder using only local saltpeter and charcoal dust, without adding the precious sulfur.[13] The manufacture of weapons was especially important in the Nienegue region (in the north of the cercle of Bobo-Dioulasso), where Maubert had pursued a vigorous disarmament campaign in the preceding months.

Reports that the population was arming itself in late November and early December were written not only in Dedougou; they can be found also in the diary of the post of Koudougou, which was attached to the cercle of Ouagadougou. On November 26, people arrived there from Boromo, wanting to purchase horses. In many villages, the diary records, sacrifices were made at important shrines. Blacksmiths were producing arrows in large quantities. The prices were 450 arrow tips for an ox, 20 arrow tips for a stone bracelet. One blacksmith was making and selling bows at 230 cowries each. This commerce occasioned much travel. While partisans from the cercle of Dedougou were arriving in Koudougou as propagandists and organizers, villages from around Koudougou were sending their people to the west, especially to the villages that housed important Muslim families, in order to purchase war charms. Although all the Muslim houses openly supported the French repression (see chap. 4) and some of them actively participated in its military action, their elders (those who had not been jailed during the marabout affair) continued to supply war charms to the anticolonial fighters from the Marka and Bwa villages and from the Gurunsi area, in the east.

The territorial organization of the Bona-Datomo leadership divided the war zone into sections, with one or two villages in each selected as gathering points. The arrangement made possible the massing of fighters at short notice. Two major centers south of Dedougou kept the movement of the French in check. The first was Pundu, in the west, with Dafina, Acana, and La as secondary centers. The second was in Sodien, in the east, with Bara-Yankaso, Bona, Tunu, Kongoba, and Konkoliko as secondary concentrations. As it became evident that the Frenchmen in Dedougou could not initiate military action in the area, the anticolonial forces concentrated in these points started pushing north, closer to Dedougou. On December 13, anticolonial partisans in Warkoy, the site of an important marketplace, had killed the collector of market taxes and his assistant. The next day, partisans in Pundu had attacked Kari again, and although they were unable to take it, this village loyal to the French remained in precarious position for the following month. Its security became the barometer of the shifting relative strengths of the colonial party and the anticolonial side, as the former rose when new contingents and supplies arrived in Dedougou, then sank again when the anticolonial side won the adherence of new villages.

A series of events around Nunu was part of the same northward push. On December 13, the anticolonial fighters of Yankaso had sent a reconnaissance mission toward Karo, only twenty kilometers from Dedougou, which Maguet had transformed into a defensive post staffed by two hundred local archers. When denied the right to pass through Nunu territory, the Yankaso troops threatened this village, whose chief called Maguet for help. Maguet relocated the archers from Karo to Nunu and sent a hundred men with muskets and another hundred mounted men, provided by Idrisa, chief of Barani, to help defend the village. At midday, the forces from Yankaso-Sodien arrived at Nunu to attack the village, but they were too few in number and, confronted with Idrisa's cavalry, they withdrew to a hilly area in the south to await reinforcements. Idrisa was able to enter Nunu and raise the morale of its inhabitants. Having received new contingents, the anticolonial partisans attacked Nunu again on December 16. Domba of Banu directed the military action, employing men from Cheriba, Yankaso, Tiga, Tionkuy, Toena, and Ula.[14] On December 17, only two of the three wards of Nunu continued to defend themselves. By the next day only one enclave in one ward continued resistance. The prospects for the remaining resisters looked bad, but both sides had run out of ammunition. Profiting from a pause in the fighting, the archers and gunmen sent by Maguet and the horsemen withdrew to Karo. Maguet sent reinforcement to Karo and, to protect Dedougou, increased the number of horsemen in its surroundings.[15]

Meanwhile, December 17, the main battalion assigned to the task of suppressing the anticolonial movement—450 tirailleurs and three 80-mm mountain guns—had arrived in Dedougou under Captain Modeste. Major Simonin, who was to take command of these forces, had arrived two days before, and Maguet wanted the new column to set out immediately. Modeste, however, was much less alarmed by the progress of the anticolonial forces and more confidant about the impact that the column would have. He put off the action for a few days, saying that he was not personally ready for it. On December 19, Maguet convinced Modeste to send at least Labouret's company ahead to relieve the last few compounds that were holding out in Nunu. The news that the tirailleurs were marching convinced the anticolonial partisans to stop their action in Nunu; they destroyed the houses of the sections they had occupied, burned the timber, took all the livestock and other transportable goods of value that they had found, and withdrew to Yankaso.

Meanwhile, as the French prepared, the territories between the immediate surroundings of Dedougou and Bobo-Dioulasso had fallen totally under anticolonial control. To the west, in Wakuy, on December 20 the partisans attacked the compound of the chief Beopa Bihun, who had provided archers to Maubert. Part of the population of Wakuy joined them and "a battle of unheard violence started" (Boni 1962, 229–30). Without hope of outside assistance, Beopa's followers defended themselves for thirteen days, when they exhausted their ammunition. On January 2 the compound fell, and Beopa and about two hundred of his followers were killed as they defended themselves with knives and swords. Beopa's son Kamma escaped this fate because he had left the village before the attack started. Remaining in the vicinity, he watched the protracted struggle from a distance. After the fall of the compound, he reached Bobo-Dioulasso and later returned to the region heading a company of auxiliaries to take part in the repression.

To prepare the ground for the coming confrontation, the French ran a disinformation campaign. Labouret writes in his diary that he announced false news, giving it the appearance of confidentiality, which was immediately known in all the villages and reached the ears of anticolonial fighters. The latter, on their side, responded with ruses of their own: they sent a man to Karo announcing that the rebels had taken prisoner the people of Nunu, which was untrue, but it allowed the scout to see if new colonial soldiers had arrived in Karo.[16] Both sides were preparing for the "great shock." It came within the month of December, before the French could celebrate Christmas.

YANKASO

The colonial army that had gathered in Dedougou toward the end of 1915 was one of the largest ever assembled by the French in West Africa. After Captain Labouret and his forty-four soldiers arrived on November 28, four French officers came from Ouagadougou with a cannon and twenty soldiers on November 30. Captain Ferron's company with fifty soldiers came from Bandiagara on December 2, and forty-four more soldiers under a Sergeant Paille came from Segou on December 3. The bulk of what became the column arrived on December 17, with three more cannons under Second Lieutenants Cartier and Breton.

To lead the repression operation, the governor-general in Dakar had appointed Colonel Molard, commander of the armed forces of Haut-Senegal-Niger. Since an officer of the grade of colonel rarely participated in the field operations of a column, the command of the troops was left to Captain Modeste, who knew the Dedougou region well. The self-confident Modeste declared to Maguet, "I know the natives of this land perfectly well from the campaign I conducted eighteen years ago when I obtained results with eleven tirailleurs."[17] However, the repeated successes of the anticolonial movement led to a change in field command, which was given to Major Simonin, and Modeste became his assistant. Simonin had more experience in suppressing opposition in other parts of West Africa and in 1898 had served as cercle administrator in Bobo-Dioulasso.

When Simonin arrived in Dedougou, Maguet wrote that the insurgents in the cercle controlled 112 villages and could possibly raise thirty thousand fighters, five to six thousand of them equipped with firearms. These men were now dispersed, but could come together to form one large army in less than a day. In these and subsequent notes Maguet appears well informed, both about the organization of the anticolonial movement and their war strategy. He knew that the plan of the insurgents was to wait for the French army in their fortified villages. However, he mistakenly thought at this point that because the French had brought so many pieces of artillery, the anticolonial partisans would be scared to concentrate in the villages and would take to the bush for a kind of guerilla warfare.[18]

The French had achieved their concentration of troops at some cost because the government in Dakar was facing hard choices. Other spots in Haut-Sénégal-Niger demanded the government's attention, and Captain Labouret had himself left behind in Gaoua an uncertain political situation. More alarmingly, the Tuareg of Hombori, Mididagen, Iguadaren, and elsewhere—together with their Bella, Daga, and Fulbe clients—declared in December that they no longer recognized French suzerainty and attacked Songhai agricultural settlements loyal to the French.[19] Thomas, the administrator of Dori, was sending insistent distress signals and requests for soldiers to his superiors. The governor-general, who considered the movement in Maguet's cercle to be a greater threat to the colony in general, decided to ignore these requests and concentrate the little military power he had in Dedougou.[20]

The column of Dedougou, as the force under Simonin came to be known in colonial documents, set out on December 21. The highest civilian authority of the colony, Lieutenant Governor Digué, who was still in Dedougou, participated in it. The column was directed by seven high-ranking French officers and included two doctors, sixteen second lieutenants and sergeants, 660 tirailleurs, 40 guards, 100 cavalrymen, and 630 porters. The artillery unit had four 80-mm mountain guns with four hundred shells and another fifty shells in reserve for after the main battle.[21] Dedougou was left under the protection of only 50 tirailleurs commanded by a French sergeant.

This show of force, it was thought, would be sufficient to bring the turbulent populations back to order. Simonin and Modeste evidently shared this belief, but not Maguet, who was at his wits' end trying to persuade them of the danger of the situation. Because of the confidence of the government in Dakar, no particular military strategy was devised. The commanding officers in the field were allowed complete liberty of action.

The column moved out of Dedougou in two parts. Captain Labouret's company had already been sent ahead, on December 19, to save what was left of Nunu. After marching less than fifteen kilometers, these soldiers came to Kunandia, where they spent the first night. The following day they advanced another ten kilometers and stopped at Karo, where they waited for the rest of the column. Also, in what was planned as a strategic move, a company of auxiliaries was sent on a slightly more westerly course to prevent help from the western anticolonial forces reaching the targeted ones in Sodien-Yankaso and to make the latter feel insecure. The plan did not work, however: the anticolonial forces on the western front under the leadership of La, Koana, and Dafina responded by again laying siege to Kari, thus tying up this company of auxiliaries and preventing them from accomplishing their mission.[22]

The two other companies of the Dedougou column, including Governor Digué, joined Labouret in Karo on December 21, and the three companies left Karo together on the morning of December 22. They arrived in Nunu the same day. The officers expected opposition, but found the village evacuated by the anticolonial forces. Only the chief's enclave was occupied by the last resisters to the anticolonials. The soldiers destroyed the one ward that had collaborated with the enemy and the column set camp for the night.

The anticolonial leadership decided to meet the column of Dedougou in a conventional battle, to be conducted from a fortified village, not on an open field and not in a guerilla action from the bush. This crucial decision set the fundamental strategy for the rest of the anticolonial campaign; unfortunately, we do not know how it was reached, what alternatives were considered, how the debate was conducted, and whose opinion prevailed. Was this the decision of Domba of Banu? We do not know. During the night spent in Nunu, the colonial soldiers could hear war drums and gun shots coming from Yankaso, a large village only nine kilometers away, setting the mood for the encounter that was soon to follow.

The French officers learned that the anticolonial fighters had massed about ten thousand soldiers at Yankaso, which they had chosen as the battle site. The anticolonial soldiers included the Marka of the villages of the region and many Nuna speakers from the cantons of Cheriba and Tise to the east. The place was chosen sagaciously. Since the colonial column was heading south toward Bona, the anticolonial leaders had accurately predicted that it would not take the shortest road, which went through the hilly region of Sodien, but the road through Nunu and Yankaso, which though slightly longer involved fewer hills. Yankaso proved to be the prescient choice for other, less obvious, tactical reasons as well, but the French command was not yet alerted to that.

Before we reach our description of the Yankaso battle, it will be useful to remember that the colonial army, though led by the French officers, was made up of soldiers from other parts of West Africa and locally recruited guards. Trained technically in the manner of European infantry, these people nevertheless shared with the anticolonial forces some of the basic premises of the common West African civilization. It is important to keep this point in mind in order to understand some of the cultural dynamics of the battle situation: they account for a large part of the outcome. The leadership of the anticolonial movement had evidently given considerable thought to developing the tactics that had been successfully tried in the second Bona battle. This is obvious in their ability to coordinate the movement of thousands of volunteer fighters who were coming from communities spread across a vast area and to solve the basic supply problems that could turn into a nightmare if not handled with foresight.

Another important factor was the absolute discipline of the anticolonial volunteer fighters, which contrasted sharply with the lack of discipline in the colonial column. The French officers blamed much of what went wrong in Yankaso on the failure of their soldiers to follow orders, and attributed this shortcoming to the soldiers' lack of experience. But more than lack of experience shaped this collective behavior: there was also an intangible element. The anticolonial leadership had managed to communicate its definition of the confrontation to the attacking soldiers, obtaining the advantage of imposing its premise of seniority over them. This factor was grasped by the experienced

French officers, and in despair they observed its effect in the behavior of their soldiers. Their insight was subsequently articulated only obliquely as "lack of discipline." This factor will become clearer as we describe the unfolding battle.

At sunrise on December 23, the column left Nunu in square formation and arrived near Yankaso early in the morning. The road to the village goes through a narrow pass, but the cavalry secured this place and the column went through without incident. Yankaso possesses a ward, Tiena, that stands by itself about two kilometers east of the main settlement. The cavalry units sent to check on that ward received a shower of arrows, but the rest of the column came within four hundred meters of the main village without encountering any resistance.

Like most villages in this region, Yankaso was built on the bank of a watercourse. Thus, in this slightly hilly region the village was situated in a shallow depression with a diameter of about two kilometers, surrounded by a crest of mounds. The main village was located in the middle of this depression, near the river, which in this season was reduced to a marshy pool of water. The settlement was divided into two sections separated by what looked like a wide street.

When the column arrived, few people were visible in the village. A few gunshots were fired, but the place gave the impression of being deserted. No one was waiting outside the walls, and there was none of the usual ritual cursing, drumming, and whistle blowing. The assault followed the classic French plan against fortified villages. First the artillery opened two breeches in the northern end of the walls, then two companies were sent in on a charge. As they neared the village, however, heavy gunfire started from all the loopholes in the walls and from all of the houses' terraces, killing and injuring many of the assailants and breaking the momentum of the charge. Three sections of Labouret's company managed to reach one of the protruding points that they had targeted and started occupying a few houses, but they lost many men in the process. The first company was pushed on a charge a few more times, but its young soldiers had clearly lost their nerve. Their charges were not strenuous, and the company was driven back. Among the wounded were Frenchmen, including the company's commander, Breton. Captain Ferron took charge of these men and tried to take them around the west corner of the village, but the company met even stronger fire.

The artillery now renewed its shelling in the hope of rekindling the totally blocked assault effort. This did not reduce the intensity of the fire of the defense. The second in command, Modeste, noticed at this time that soldiers were no longer obeying orders. They were hiding behind each other and many were trying to avoid the fighting by insisting on carrying the wounded behind the lines. He tried to jostle them with a rifle, to drive them back to their places and send them again to the front. They walked halfheartedly up to the wall, but retreated under heavy fire, accomplishing little.

A new phase of the battle began when Captain Ferron noticed that hundreds of enemy fighters were arriving from the direction of Sodien. Walking in silence, these men were in lines, with several yards between each man—a discipline that the colonial army drilled its soldiers in. Ferron had to turn his company west to stop them. The column then executed a partial withdrawal, another round of shelling, and another charge. The fire it encountered was as intense as before. In fact, so many of the column's members were wounded or killed now that the person loading the artillery was a French mechanic.

The situation was rapidly deteriorating for the French. On all sides around the plain anticolonial partisans were walking down the ridges in lines, not uttering a sound. On the west side, there was nothing to stop them. A section of the second company that was kept in reserve slowed them down for only a few moments. An artillery shell, dropped in the midst of the arriving partisans, held them a little, but the forerunners of that group were already on a small spur only 250 meters from the battery. A group of mounted guards and a reserve platoon dislodged them from that spot only with difficulty. The partisan reinforcements continued to walk in great order up to the walls of the village and to enter it, despite the large numbers of them who fell. On the right flank of the column, anticolonial fighters with rifles had formed an uninterrupted arc, four hundred meters long. In the east, on the side of Tiena, many were walking fast and closing in on the left flank of the column. Firing a few shells, the battery managed to stop this encircling operation when it was barely five hundred meters away. Some of the reinforcements withdrew toward Tiena; others entered the village.

It was not yet noon when the French officers had to reassess the situation. In the best scenario, it was not yet ruled out that, if the assault continued, the village could be taken by sunset. This would involve losses at least as large as the ones sustained so far. And then what would they do? One difficulty was the shortage of water. It would be necessary for the column to return immediately and to do this in the dark through hostile territory. Bringing sufficient water from Nunu behind their ranks was nearly impossible. Sending just the wounded to Nunu was also not feasible. There were already more than one hundred wounded, and the porters of the medical unit would not be able to carry them all. An important detachment would also have to be sent to protect them. Assuming that the column took the village, if it spent the night there it would have to reach the pond behind for water, which would require battling hundreds more partisans, whose forces were growing in number by the hour. And then, the moment the column left the village to get to the pond, the anticolonial forces would certainly reoccupy the houses. The colonial forces would have water, but they would find the village filled again with enemy, between them and the road of return to Dedougou. Ammunition was also in short supply. The artillery unit had already spent more than three-quarters of the shells earmarked for the first major battle. That the village could be taken without artillery was not at all certain.

After reviewing these factors, Simonin decided to retreat. The wounded were mounted on the horses of the cavalry, and even the lieutenant governor and his retinue had to undertake the return trip on foot in order to free up horses for the wounded. Some equipment was burned. Horsemen were sent to the ridges to secure a passage, and the column slowly started its return. At Nunu, they paused briefly to drink water. Then the column continued on to Karo, where it spent the night. It is a measure of how much the experience had taught the French officers that they considered it a partial success not to have been attacked in Karo during that night. Around noon on December 24, the column entered Dedougou. The report said there were 122 casualties, including 10 killed, and 3 Europeans were among the wounded. In the following days, another 22 of the wounded—including a Frenchman—died.

Yankaso was a resounding defeat for the French. The strongest column ever put together, with a strong artillery unit, had abandoned the battlefield in the middle of the day. The bitterness of the civilian administrators toward the officers already shows in the way that Lieutenant Governor Digué described what he had experienced—"a retreat that resembled a rout, since despite the exhortations of the governor the column could not protect the village of Nunu, located at six kilometers from Yankaso, which was easy to defend and which had remained loyal to us."[23]

Reviewing the reports of the battle, the higher command had to come to terms with the fact that the anticolonial army not only had a vastly superior number of men who could use their knowledge of the terrain to great advantage, but that it also was led by people who had proved to have greater military acumen than the commanding officers of the column. To think that a place like Yankaso could be taken by assault in a few hours was an error, and to accept battle in this location was a military blunder. Simonin left Dedougou in semidisgrace to return to his regular position in San. But it was questionable now whether the column could defend itself against attack, even from behind a reinforced stronghold. Superior firepower and the artillery were no longer sufficient to prevail. The conclusion of the Simonin report stated: "The situation is very serious. The need for reinforcements is very urgent at the cost of whatever sacrifices, if we don't want to find ourselves soon in a position to have to restart with the entire conquest of the Soudan."[24]

A FALLEN DIVINITY

The officers in charge of the column insisted that the reason Yankaso was not taken in the early morning assaults—before the reinforcements to the defense started pouring in from the hillcrests—was because the column's mostly young and inexperienced soldiers "lacked cohesion [and] enthusiasm, [and were] hesitant." When the head of their platoon fell, they went into disorder.[25] While their lack of experience may have had something to do with the attitude of these soldiers, one also observes that what they displayed was a common reaction in attacks against strongholds of great reputation in the western Sudan. Examples can be found from the battles in which the French were involved at the end of the nineteenth century, during the initial occupation of the Volta and Bani region. The full impact of the claims of the anticolonial movement on the minds of the population, including the soldiers of the colonial army, followed from the meaning people ascribe to worldly success.

In the latter part of the nineteenth century, there were several towns with long-standing reputations for invincibility. Attacking such a town or village was dangerous, not only because of what we would perceive as technical reasons—weapons, defensive structures, and the bravery of the fighters—but primarily because of the spiritual forces that its inhabitants were able to rally to their cause. The military successes were manifestations of these mystical factors. When a town could establish its reputation as impregnable and inspire fear in assailants, the assumption helped bring about more successes. The self-perpetuating cycle could only be broken by a reversal of fortune, but any army trying to challenge a famous town had to struggle against considerable odds. Therefore, communicating a strong image of the town by discursive means, including the mystery of ritual activity, was an important part of defense and aggression. This was one of the fronts on which the anticolonial defenders of Yankaso won their battle.

The village or town defending itself had the advantage because the most important protective forces were grounded in the locality. Those who came from elsewhere were at risk. When a group came from afar for a showdown, the action could succeed only if the leaders of the attack possessed the strength to supersede the mystical forces of the locality. When Samori's forces sacked Kong in 1897, for example, it was said that his spirits were stronger than those of the marabouts of Kong. This was one important reason why reinforced settlements were rarely subject to large-scale attacks in the nineteenth century. The French had acquired a somewhat mystical aura because of their successes during the initial occupation of the region. But following the second Bona battle and the Bondokuy siege of Maubert, the anticolonial party and propaganda had successfully eroded this image. The French no longer enjoyed the advantage of their previous reputation.

The hesitation of the young soldiers of the Dedougou column when they attacked Yankaso can be compared with the case of the October 1890 attack on Kinian, situated in what is now eastern Mali. The army attacking Kinian was a union of the forces of Tieba of Sikasso and those brought by Bodian (a man the French had appointed *faama* in Segou), and Captain F. J. H. Quiquandon, as French resident, supported and personally participated in this action. At the time of this attack, Tieba was at the peak of his reputation, enhanced by his successful resistance in Sikasso to the obstinate, sixteen-month attack of Samori. The Kinian attack shows that the reputation Tieba had achieved in defending his own Sikasso was insufficient to give him the advantage when he was attacking a town such as Kinian.

The Kinian assault had started, like that of Yankaso, with the artillery pounding the walls of the city and opening a breach twenty meters wide (Quiquandon 1891, 262:4679ff). Hundreds of men from the attacking army then rushed toward the town. The momentum of the charge suddenly stopped when Kurumina, the other famous faama who was the leader of the town, came to the breach to encourage his own soldiers. The assailants would stop at about thirty meters from the walls, discharge their guns, and start dancing, and waving their ritual tails without going forward. Quiquandon sent a few more shells and then ordered another charge, but the result was the same. He wrote in his account that "there was a barrier of superstition and fear that had to be reversed in the soldiers, a spell that had to be broken." The explanation given to him later was: "A village with a faama cannot be taken like this. You never know what there is in a village like this. Kurumina has strong charms." The town finally fell, but only after five months of uninterrupted siege, and not before Kurumina left it with a following of about two hundred armed men.

Slightly more than seven years after the Kinian war, the French attacked Sikasso, with the largest column formed in this initial period of the conquest of the western Sudan. By then Tieba had died, and the assault was directed against the leadership of his brother Babemba. Although the fourteen hundred colonial soldiers were outnumbered one to ten by the defenders, they had the advantage of a battery unit of four cannons and were all equipped with advanced rifles. Even so, we find that the soldiers of the colonial column displayed then the same "hesitation" as in Yankaso. After days of bombardment, in the morning of the day of the great assault on May 1, 1898, the three companies of the column entered the town through three breaches that had been opened in the outer wall. By 1:00 P.M., a mountain gun had been carried all the way inside and positioned in front of the interior castle, where Babemba was thought to be. Defense at this point had almost ceased to exist. Nonetheless, the morale of the African colonial soldiers had also fallen, and at this spot they became possessed by fear. No one wanted to step across the new breach into Babemba's compound. The French captain went ahead with a few volunteers to encourage to his soldiers, but no one followed him. He had to return.

The soldiers stayed there until one hundred more soldiers were sent to join them. The castle was pounded by the cannon for another hour and a half, and the commander of the column, Pineau, had to conduct this last assault in person at the sound of the clarion. According to local tradition, one of the important leaders in the entourage of Babemba had defected to the French, and the taking of the fortress had been possible only because of that. A researcher who recently sifted through the various accounts of this event and also looked at the aftermath of the battle concludes that there is evidence to support this assertion (Rondeau 1980, 304). The popular perception and the probable reality of the defection are both relevant to our point.

Large reinforced centers in the western Sudan could not be taken by storm, they were defeated only after prolonged and stubborn sieges, once the confidence of the defenders was sapped, and following defections or betrayal in the inner circle of the stronghold's leaders. Treachery is invariably the most salient explanation for the fall of such centers. The moral core of the defense had to be broken in order to weaken the spiritual forces protecting the defenders.

The result of the fall of Sikasso—and shortly afterwards the capture of Samori without even a battle—enhanced the reputation of the French beyond all bounds in the West African savanna. This did not stop the organized village coalitions of the Volta region from responding with rigorous resistance, but the commanders of French columns enjoyed at least the confidence of their soldiers. It was this advantage that, by their failure to win the Bona battles, at Bondokuy, and finally at Yankaso, the French lost in the initial months of the Volta-Bani War.

Yankaso became the crowning argument in the anticolonial leadership's struggle to win the populations of the Volta region. The commander who transmitted Simonin's report pointed out bitingly, "In the old French Soudan, military operations undertaken by a column of six hundred soldiers equipped with artillery and munitions, in a battlefield that is only forty kilometers away from its base, did not seem to end up being surrounded by natives armed with bows and flint guns."[26] The anticolonial army had matched the words of its promoters with its deeds. The "force" of the white man was finished. This became the battle cry of the partisans, resounding in the villages and in the camps of the anticolonial fighters. It summed up a new awareness, the complex reasoning behind which novelist Boni — in his inimitable French style — translated into European imagery by saying that the white man was now a "fallen divinity."[27]

After the column returned to its Dedougou base, Domba, the leader of anticolonial forces in the Safane-Yankaso region, declared that "the whites would not be able to return to the country." The delegations from Bona, Tunu, and Datomo took the thought further: "After Yankaso everyone shouted victory, they said that all the whites had been killed, that there were no more cercle guards, no more tirailleurs, and that the Marka were the strongest. Yisu sent emissaries to the other side of the Volta, toward Sanaba, to bring back declarations of submission and gifts, and spread rumors that he had won over the White Man and that the Marka were the strongest."[28] While these claims were exaggerated, little could be offered as counterargument to the people making them. Dedougou was isolated, and Maguet had difficulties even communicating with the nearby villages. His messengers to the villages were caught and killed before they could deliver their messages. In January 1916, the zone west of the Muhun River in the northern part of the cercle of Bobo-Dioulasso and the Gurunsi region of the cercle of Ouagadougou joined the anticolonial movement. Even in the cercles of San and Koutiala, some villages entered into the orbit of the leadership of the Bona, Tunu, and Datomo area.

Of course, the French had not given up. The government-general had acquired a more realistic sense of the scale of the movement they were facing and was busy moving all its available military units to the cercle of Dedougou. It was now decided that Molard, the overall military commander for Haut-Sénégal-Niger, would come from Kati personally to take command of the new column that was gathering in Dedougou. Meanwhile, Maguet and the other cercle administrators were instructed to keep a strictly defensive posture. Since further attacks against villages could result in more French defeats, they were forbidden from undertaking provocative actions. In Dedougou, the Ferron company moved to Kari to use it as a temporary base. The other defensive posts, established with small contingents at a distance of twenty to thirty kilometers south of Dedougou, were communicating with each other through the cavalry patrols of Idrisa of Barani. They engaged only in small occasional raids, to divert the anticolonial forces and test their level of readiness.

In the cercle of Bobo-Dioulasso, Maubert had recovered from his shock and was becoming restless again, but he was told to keep a low profile and organize defensive posts around the city. Nonetheless, in the month of January he led six small expeditions with auxiliary soldiers provided by friendly chiefs and supervised by the small number of guards of the cercle. In the Koudougou residency of the cercle of Ouagadougou, the defense depended on the auxiliaries provided by the Mose chief.

The strength of the anticolonial movement had now reached such proportions that even the buildup of a massive new column in Dedougou, with troops and munitions from all over French West Africa, did not excessively worry its leadership and partisans. The French had corresponding doubts as they went about their preparations. The whites had lost their assurance, and people in the colonial camp no longer trusted that the artillery could give them the clear advantage that they had previously taken for granted.

CHAPTER 7

Terror as Strategy

The War in the Cercle of Dedougou

THE DEFEATS SUFFERED BY THE COMMANDANTS of the cercles of Dedougou and of Bobo-Dioulasso in November and December 1915, followed by the retreat of the Simonin column from Yankaso, gave rise to a sense of urgency that pervaded all levels of the colonial administration. The few Europeans—administrators, the military, and missionaries—still in the region took refuge in Dedougou, isolated in a region at war. On December 26, the commander in chief of French West Africa, General Pineau, ordered Colonel Molard, the military commander of Haut-Sénégal-Niger, to replace Simonin and organize a new column with the available troops in French West Africa. In the meantime, the companies that had made up the Simonin column conducted reconnaissance patrols and hit-and-run attacks supported by cannons to keep the movement away from Dedougou. These sorties resulted only in boosting the morale of the anticolonial villagers, helping them to overcome their fear of fighting against cannons.

The cannon had been the great instrument of French military success in Africa, but even Louis Digué, the lieutenant governor of Haut-Sénégal-Niger, worried that this time around it might not be sufficient to win victory. Back in Bamako, Digué, unable to recover from the debacle of Yankaso, expressed to Marie François Clozel, his predecessor and new governor-general of French West Africa, his skepticism about the chances of success of the Molard column. Three battles as intense as that of Yankaso, he thought, would be enough to exhaust the column's supply of artillery shells and annihilate the entire force. Digué insisted on the need for "modern means of destruction such as incendiary shells, aerial

173

mines, and above all an airplane that would make a strong impression on the rebels and cause such heavy damage that they would abandon their villages without waiting for the assault."[1]

Digué's attitude was symptomatic of the spirit found by Molard when he arrived in Dedougou in February 1916. Molard reported

> panic . . . gaining in almost everyone, military as well as civilian, provoking a kind of paralysis among those who witnessed the explosion of hate directed at us. . . . An atmosphere of malaise — and this is an understatement — prevails in the headquarters. The entire Volta bend, with the exception of a few villages, is in revolt. . . . The revolt has spread as far as the cercles of Koutiala and San; to the East [it spread] to the Samo of [the cercle] of Dedougou and to the Gurunsi of Koudougou. To the south, it includes the whole northern region of the cercle of Bobo-Dioulasso. . . . We estimate that the rebels are able to gather at a notice of less than a day 30,000 men, including 5,000 to 6,000 armed with guns and the others with bows and arrows. . . . We fear for the post [Dedougou] itself; one of the wards of Dedougou is less than reliable.[2]

THE MOLARD COLUMN: CONSTITUTION, ARMAMENT, AND STRATEGY

By February 1916, the armed forces that converged on Dedougou represented the biggest military column assembled in the history of French West Africa — in both manpower and firepower.[3] It consisted of five companies of regular soldiers (tirailleurs) under the command of French officers,[4] adding up to about 1,500 (although some of the tirailleurs were hurriedly trained and little-prepared for battle). The irregulars who joined the column included a goum of 120 horsemen, 200 guards, and about 2,000 auxiliary soldiers, mostly recruited by Idrisa Sidibe from Barani. The column was also reinforced by an artillery platoon of six 80-mm mountain cannons and one machine-gun section (a second machine-gun section was dispatched by Dakar in the second part of the Molard campaign). A machine-gun section could include as many as 20 tirailleurs and between 5 and 10 French and African officers. There were about 85 French officers and soldiers in the column. Three French doctors headed a medical team, and Roman Catholic missionaries were enrolled for tasks such as food supply, medical assistance, and translation. Father Dubernet (from the mission established in the Samo village of Toma) was responsible for the food supply (de Benoist 1987, 240; Prost 1971, 106). Hundreds of porters and pack animals were used, and crowds of hangers-on followed the column to loot defeated villages.

Putting together this force required enormous effort, and tremendous logistic difficulties had to be overcome. An example is the Lucas company. With 350 men and a machine-gun platoon, they had set out from Dakar by steamboat. At Conakry, Guinea, the men boarded a train to Kurusa on the Niger River. At this landing, a flotilla of small boats took the company first to Kati, near Bamako, and then north to Mopti. The company had to travel 290 kilometers more to reach Dedougou, which it did on foot, split into two groups traveling separately in order to ensure that enough food could be found on the way.

The Molard column still proved insufficient to suppress the movement, and in April 1916 a second column was formed in the cercle of San under Commandant Simonin (chap. 9). A comparison of these two columns with those that, less than twenty years before, spearheaded the colonial conquest of most of today's Burkina Faso gives a sense of the relative enormity of the effort in 1916. The Voulet-Chanoine column set up in 1896 to conquer Mose country had two officers, twenty-three soldiers, ten regular cavalry *(spahis),* 180 auxiliary troops, and a cavalry of forty auxiliaries provided by Widi Sidibe of Barani (Idrisa Sidibe's father) and Aguibu of Bandiagara. The column set up in 1897 by Destenave to effectively occupy the Volta region, and whose size and armament were intended to definitively impress local populations, included 14 officers, 384 auxiliaries, 28 Fulbe cavalry, and two 80-mm cannons. These early units had little in common with the Molard column, not only in their size but also in their constitution. They had few regular troops and relied mostly on auxiliaries. One thing both cases did have in common, however, was that the cavalry was provided by allied Fulbe leaders from Bandiagara and Barani.

The armament the French columns used in 1915–16 was similar to that employed in the late nineteenth century. The 80-mm mountain gun had proved to be an exceptionally well adapted weapon for operations in West Africa because of its ease of transport (Echenberg 1971, 269). Its effective range was only twenty-five hundred meters, but this was sufficient for attacking enemies who did not possess artillery. It weighed only three hundred kilograms and could be disassembled and carried by three mules (see fig. 6).[5] The cannon's drawback for the understaffed French army was that an artillery platoon required a disproportionately large number of French military—at least one French officer and four French gunners, assisted by an African officer and five African gunners and porters—because the functions of gunners (aiming, triggering, and cleaning the barrel) were not entrusted to African soldiers.[6]

Fig. 6. A disassembled mountain cannon being carried across a ford by mules. A. G. Furst, *L'Artillerie coloniale* (Paris: Chapelot, 1917).

The number of cannons in French West Africa in 1915 was very small. In November 1915 there were only six 80-mm cannons in Kati, one of the main centers of military operations for French West Africa. Ammunition for the cannons was in restricted supply because of the war in Europe, but given the urgency of the situation in the Volta-Bani region, Molard obtained all the ammunition he requested. Regular supply to Dedougou represented, however, a major logistical problem that was never successfully solved. Molard made extensive use of melinite (lyddite) shells, a new explosive patented in 1886.[7] The shell fragments or the force of the blow killed anyone within twenty-five meters of where it landed.

An important new weapon used by Molard was the machine gun. Although hand-cranked, multibarreled machine guns were not new (they had been used in the American Civil War), their size and weight made them not very useful for the very mobile columns in Africa. The first truly automatic machine gun, the Maxim, had been adopted widely by Britain, Germany, and the U.S. Navy only after the turn of the century,[8] and it did not dominate the battlefield until World War I. A recent study of the conquest of Sokoto (1897–1902) shows that the British military superiority in that war was due not to the use of machine guns, as historians have assumed, but to cannons (Marjomaa 1998), as was the case for the French in the west Volta. The French introduced a modern machine gun to West Africa only in 1915. It rapidly became the colonial infantry's weapon of choice,[9] but proved to be most effective in open-field engagements against the Tuareg, who made sudden cavalry charges; in such battles, the issue was decided in the few seconds that followed the sighting of the enemy.[10] In the Volta-Bani region, assaults of compact villages protected by defensive walls made the machine gun less critical for success. Yet as we will see, Molard found a use for it — shooting villagers who fled from one block of houses into another or to the surrounding bush.[11]

Although special platoons were in charge of the cannons and machine guns, the rifle remained the personal weapon of the tirailleur. Various models of breech-loading rifles were used by the tirailleurs of the Molard column, and officers availed themselves of the most sophisticated magazine rifles. The anticolonial combatants relied heavily on muzzle-loaded firearms, but they also used the popular Gras rifle, or replicas of it made by blacksmiths. The Gras, a single-shot breech-loading rifle, has remained until today one of the most popular guns in West African villages.

Two men who participated in the column, Doctor Jean Cremer and Captain Henri Labouret, deserve particular notice as they later became known for their ethnographic work. Cremer was a doctor with Assistance Médicale Indigène (Indigenous medical assistance), a health service set up in most French colonies. He had arrived in the Volta region in 1910 and died ten years later in Ouahigouya while serving as a member of a recruiting commission. Some of his field notes were posthumously edited and published by his fellow administrator-ethnographers Delafosse and Labouret.[12] Labouret was the first official to arrive in Dedougou (Nov. 28), because his military brigade was the only one left in the Volta region after the general pullout of 1914. He had served in the violent "pacification" of Ivory Coast. He was then appointed administrator to the Lobi cercle, known to be one of the most volatile in French West Africa (the headquarters in Diebougou, then in Gaoua), a post he kept for an exceptionally long tenure (1914–24).[13] Later Labouret published many articles, a major ethnographic work on the Lobi (1931), and an ethnographic and linguistic book on the Manding (1934), which made him one of the most famous French administrator-ethnographers. He replaced Maurice Delafosse as professor at the Colonial School in Paris, a training center for colonial administrators.

Molard — unlike Pineau, Simonin, and Clozel — had no prior knowledge of the people of the Volta-Bani region.[14] The initial strategy had no pretense of subtlety. It basically called for the destruction of the main centers of resistance, whose names were provided by administrator Maguet. Before leaving Kati for Dedougou, Molard received the following telegraphed instructions from Pineau:

> Unnecessary to take all villages in state of rebellion only hit centers con- trolled by influential leaders whose submission will bring that of neighboring region. . . . Rebels insufficiently armed and little disciplined are not capable of organizing serious offensive. . . . Will send you all ammunition you will re- quire but keep in mind low ammunition stocks in colony and avoid unneces- sary consumption.[15]

This approach failed to take into account the more than fifteen years of colonial presence during which the local people had become familiar with French ad- ministrative and military practices.

As it turned out, despite the systematic destruction of villages, the column met strong and unabated resistance everywhere. In the first months of his campaign, Molard received no submissions and was not able to capture any leaders. Anti- colonial combatants successfully escaped the attacked villages to take up a new position in the next military center. While the anticolonial combatants moved from one fortified village to another, leading the column on to the next engage- ment, the inhabitants of the destroyed villages reoccupied the ruins and rebuilt their homes and defensive works. The French were unprepared for this protracted conflict and for the regular and enormous supplies of ammunition that it required.

We find the following assessment in Molard's report of the situation he found the day he first arrived in Dedougou (Feb. 10) (the passage was actually written at a later date with the benefit of hindsight, probably to forestall the blame for the ineffectiveness of his first campaign):

> The numerical strength of the column seems to me insufficient, and it can only be compensated by an intense consumption of ammunition and artillery. It will not be enough to have a large success at a given point, but we will need to subjugate the insurgent populations by occupying the territory . . . which will necessitate without doubt a series of uninterrupted engagements, the es- tablishment of posts, all efforts that will rapidly weaken the main column.[16]

The effective occupation of the region by establishing posts—which Mo- lard claims was his goal from the beginning—was implemented only in the later phase of the war, after the column had laid waste the entire region. This two-phase strategy — first the destruction of the villages with artillery, then occupation and pacification — replicated the experience of the initial conquest of the Niger bend area at the turn of the century. The pacification phase was modeled on the idea of the "oil stain" (see chap. 3).

With no significant support in the region, Molard was compelled to use the remote town of San as a rear base, as the Volta column had done under the command of Caudrelier in 1897. The two columns encountered many similar logistical problems.[17] Molard, despite the size of his column, was not able to deploy troops to ensure communications with San. In fact, as Molard was engaged in the cercle of Dedougou, the war gained momentum in the region of San. Reinforcements and supplies of food, medicine, and ammunition to the column, as well as communication between Molard and his superiors, proved extremely difficult. The insurgents had cut all the telegraph lines between the towns of Dedougou and Bobo-Dioulasso, Dedougou and Ouagadougou, Dedougou and San, San and Bandiagara, and San and Koutiala. Foot couriers had to go through Ouahigouya and Jenne, thus traveling a distance of about 575 kilometers, instead of the normal 220. Even if the dispatch was not intercepted, it took them between ten and twenty days to reach the lieutenant governor in Bamako.[18]

The war led by Molard included three different campaigns. First, from February 13 to March 23, Molard operated in a radius of about fifty-five kilometers around Dedougou. At the end of this first campaign, the French lost control of the region between the Bani and Nazinon (Red Volta) Rivers, and the war reached its greatest extension. From April 13 to June 23, Molard campaigned to the east and south of Dedougou, and in the north of the cercle of Bobo-Dioulasso, covering the Marka, Nuna, and Nienegue regions of the cercle.[19] Finally, from June 23 to July 24, Molard led part of his troops west of the Black Volta (Muhun) River into the region bordering the cercle of San (see chap. 9).

RESPONDING TO LOCAL MILITARY STRATEGY: MOLARD'S FIRST CAMPAIGN

Administrator Maguet was of the opinion that it would be easier to defeat a Bwa rather than a Marka village. Because the French desperately needed to turn the tide of defeats and inconclusive engagements with an unambiguous success, he proposed that the new column should first target the insurgents who were predominantly Bwa. Their defeat could provoke a flood of submissions. This view was based on the immediate experiences of the past two months, but it was not informed by the occupation history of the turn of the century, when Bwa confederations had offered the most bitter resistance, while most Marka villages had remained passive. While Maguet pressed for immediate action against nearby Bwa centers of concentration, Molard found it more prudent to wait until the formation of the column in Dedougou was completed.

A brief historical overview will help elucidate the anticolonials' military strategy. Maguet's assumption that the Bwa people lacked experience in fighting organized armies was based on the incomplete observation that small-scale raids among villages constituted the most common form of local conflict. He was mistaken in this assumption (see chaps. 1 and 2). In the nineteenth century, important military centers had formed shifting alliances with the villages around Dedougou. The Marka called villages that had military importance *kèlècè-ben-yoro,* "the meeting place of warriors" (Koulibaly 1970, 45). In the region south of Dedougou, where Molard set out to campaign first, the main centers had been Kari, Dedougou, and Pasakongo, allied to nearby Masala, Pundu, and Sokongo (Cremer 1924b, 23–24, 131–36, 144–46; Capron 1973, 85; Kote 1982, 89). A deep-seated rivalry existed between Dedougou and Pasakongo, but many villages—such as Kari and Pasakongo—were linked to each other through matrimonial exchanges. When faced with a major external threat, these centers—even if otherwise at odds with each other—were able to form broader ad hoc alliances. Thus, in the nineteenth century, Dedougou, Kari, and Sokongo responded to the call of Pasakongo and Masala to resist the army of Mahamudu Karantao of Wahabu. When the Karantao defeated Masala, the Bwa retreated successively to Dedougou, Kari, Pundu, and Sokongo as each one of these centers—with the exception of Dedougou, which went over to the Karantao side—was defeated.

The basic strategy at that time was to mass a large number of fighters from all the villages of the coalition in one fortified village and wait there for the enemy. By defending such a site, the alliance could cause an assailant much more damage than it would suffer itself. When allied fighters endured a trying siege and exhausted their supplies, they escaped into another fortified village that had in anticipation been prepared beforehand. A series of such encounters could run down even the most formidable enemy. Coalitions of Bwa villages used this same strategy against the invading French columns between 1897 and 1900, and although the cannons shortened the length of time a fortified site could hold out, the results were still impressive. This strategy was now adopted against the Molard column.

The campaign started on February 13, after most units assigned to the Molard column arrived in Dedougou. Of the two massive concentrations of anti-colonial fighters, the formidable Marka dominated that of Damien, in the east, whereas the one in Pundu, in the west, consisted of mostly Bwa villages. The column set Pundu as its target (see map 6). After spending the night at the post of Kari, it arrived in front of Pundu early in the morning on February 14. The village consisted of five compact wards lying a few hundred meters from each other (see map 7). The defenders concentrated themselves in two of these wards. The column attacked successively each ward of the village. Firing 165 cannon rounds, the French opened breaches in the thick walls of the first ward. One platoon entered through these openings, but the one that followed it met with heavy fire and a broadside of arrows. The colonial soldiers hesitated, huddled, and sought cover, while firing in all directions. As in Yankaso, Captain Labouret had to intervene with his more experienced soldiers who had fought in the rough Lobi country. With his help, the first ward was taken. The defenders resisted for five hours, ceding the rooms one by one, house by house. At midmorning, reinforcements came to them from Warkoy, Sokongo, Keka, Dafina, Moana, and Fakuy (Sombie 1975, 22). At midday, the second ward was taken by Molard. That night, the anticolonial combatants fled the ruins of the village, leaving behind their possessions and old people, women, and children. The next day, auxiliaries pillaged the village and burned it. Four members of the column had died, seventeen were wounded. Sombie writes that the defenders lost about fifty fighters (1975, 22), but the final count was probably at least twice as high.

This battle established the pattern for most of the subsequent engagements. During the preliminary shelling, the mounted auxiliaries were placed outside the village to prevent the escape of the residents and to fend off any attempt at attack or encirclement by neighboring villages. The auxiliaries performed these tasks poorly. In Pundu, they were surprised by the attacks coming from outside and suffered heavy casualties. Molard reported that this experience instilled a deep-seated fear among horsemen that made them unreliable in the following engagements. Once the village was invaded, machine guns were used to prevent movement from one compact housing block to another. After the resistance ended, auxiliaries and local followers were permitted to loot and destroy the village as a reward for participating in the column.

One of the great difficulties encountered by the French was the village architecture, which was a fortress from the outside and a maze once inside. With the experience he gained in the first engagements of the column, Molard gave the following instructions for village assaults:

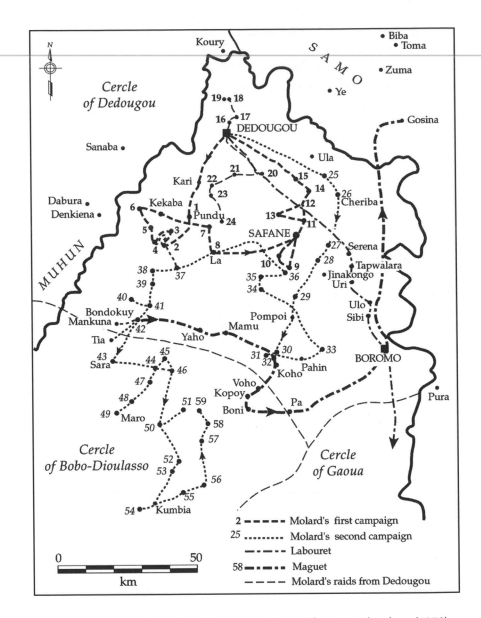

Map 6. Repression in the cercle of Dedougou. Adapted from Gnankambary (1970).

Key to Map 6 and Chronology of Major Engagements

Molard's First Campaign (1916)

1. Pundu	(Feb. 14)	12. Yankaso ⎱	(Mar. 2)	
2. Warkoy	(Feb. 16)	13. Sodien ⎰		
3. Bekuy ⎫		14. Makongo	(Mar. 2–6)	
4. Dankuy ⎪	(Feb. 16–18)	15. Tiekuy ⎱	(Mar. 7)	
5. Kwena ⎬		16. Pasakongo ⎰		
6. Monkuy ⎪		17. Masala ⎫		
Kamako* ⎭		18. Bokuy ⎬	(Mar. 11–13)	
7. Sokongo	(Feb. 18)	19. Bana		
8. La	(Feb. 20–21)	20. Ulani ⎫		
9. Bona	(Feb. 24–25)	21. Fakuna ⎪		
10. Bara	(Feb. 26–27)	22. Worokuy ⎬	(Mar. 17–19)	
11. Banu	(Feb. 28–Mar. 1)	23. Wakuy ⎪		
		24. Pie ⎭		

Molard's Second Campaign (1916)

25. Tiga	(Apr. 14–15)	40. Kamana ⎱	(May 22)
26. Chcriba	(Apr. 17)	Labu* ⎰	
27. Kokun	(Apr. 21)	41. Sin	(May 23)
28. Da	(Apr. 22)	42. Bondokuy	(May 24)
29. Datomo	(Apr. 26)	43. Sara	(May 27)
30. Bagasi ⎱		44. Popiho ⎫	
31. Dusi ⎬	(May 2)	45. Kura ⎪	
32. Sipoy ⎰		46. Wakuy ⎪	
33. Vi	(May 6)	47. Dimikuy ⎬	(May 30–June 2)
34. Konkoliko	(May 10)	48. Yabe ⎪	
35. Tunu ⎱		49. Maro ⎪	
36. Kongoba ⎬	(May 11)	Dio* ⎭	
9. Bona ⎰		50. Boyere	(June 3)
8. La	(May 16)	51. Dohun	(June 5)
37. Fakena	(May 18)	52. Kari ⎫	
2. Warkoy ⎱		53. Dankari ⎪	
4. Dankuy ⎬	(May 18–21)	54. Kongolikan ⎬	(June 6–11)
3. Bekuy ⎪		55. Sebedugu ⎪	
6. Monkuy ⎰		56. Pe ⎭	
38. Koso ⎱	(May 21)	57. Koho ⎱	(June 12)
39. Kera ⎰		58. Hunde ⎰	
		59. Karaba	(June 14)

* Village that could not be located on the map.

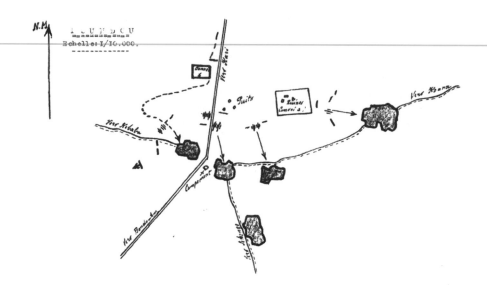

Map 7. Pundu. From the Molard report (SHAT 5 H 196).

Stop the vanguard at 400 to 500 meters before the first ward, with a section
or two facing the ward and the others remaining in reserve about 100 meters
behind. . . . Available men cut dry grass to burn the village. . . . Send to the
side that is to be attacked a patrol with a corporal and three men walking at
a distance of six to eight meters from each other, to check if the ward is occupied or not. If the patrol receives neither fire nor arrows, they enter the
ward structure. They are immediately to be followed by a half section carrying the dry grass, then a second, and they set the fire. If the patrol does receive projectiles, they withdraw, jogging at a trot. Then the artillery goes into
action. It has to be used exclusively to open one or two breaches for the infantry to penetrate the attacked side. As soon as the breaches are wide
enough, a squad or half a company at most, deployed with four or five steps
between each man, moves forward. The artillery raises its aim [firing over
the heads of the attackers] to prevent the defenders from returning to the
breach. It stops when the squad penetrates the ward and tries to advance from
house to house by drilling the partition walls. Formal interdiction of walking
in the streets and climbing on the terraced roofs. As soon as a group has entered the breach, another one goes there with the bundles of dry grass and
sets the fire. The progress is made thus slowly until the occupation is completed. Then the same is repeated for the next ward, and so on. . . . Burn carefully all the timber, which is necessary for rebuilding and difficult to find.

After the fire, have the porters knock down the walls under the supervision of the soldiers, and use as rams the beams you find on the spot.[20]

Planning to hasten the demise of the movement, Molard attempted some psychological warfare. He took people from Masala and Pasakongo to Pundu, to "show them the terrifying effects of our artillery" (the people of Pasakongo had harassed Dedougou since the beginning of the war).[21] But Molard's plan backfired. Two days after the capture of Pundu, both Masala and Pasakongo—which had up to then remained divided—openly joined the anticolonial side. Another Molard stratagem met a similar fate. In the aftermath of the battle, he sent women captured in Pundu to as many villages as possible with the mission of telling everyone what they had seen. He wanted them to explain that the French were willing to treat with leniency all villages that surrendered. The women did visit many villages, but they announced instead that the French were about to surrender and urged the men to continue the fight. Not only were the French officers too pedestrian to outplay the Bwa and Marka leaders in the game of propaganda, but they had not yet come to terms with the resolve of the enemy they were facing and the enemy's aptitude for turning any situation to their advantage.

At the start, Maguet's and Molard's plan to confuse the enemy and hearten their troops with easy victories seemed to be working. Molard's next stop, Warkoy, was a large village, and the anticolonial leadership, thinking that the column would first target the strong Marka centers of resistance in the east, was not expecting Molard's visit in this part of the country. Molard shelled the village, provoking the escape of its inhabitants, and razed and burned it the same day.

In the days following (Feb. 16–18), the column marched in a loop between the Dedougou-Bobo-Dioulasso road and the Muhun River, razing deserted Bwa villages (see map 6 and key). The unprepared inhabitants had fled their villages before the arrival of the column, seeking refuge across the river in the villages of Sanaba, Denkiena, and Dabura (see chap. 9 for the significance of Sanaba). The column moved rapidly. As soon as the demolition of a village was completed, the column headed for the village that was next on the list compiled by Maguet.

The column returned to the surroundings of Warkoy and attacked the Bwa village of Sokongo, a large village that consisted of twelve distinct wards (see map 8). The great number of Bwa and Marka fighters gathered in the village forced the column into its second major battle after Pundu. They easily drove back an attack of the cavalry. Idrisa's men, who made up 100 of the 120 goumiers in the

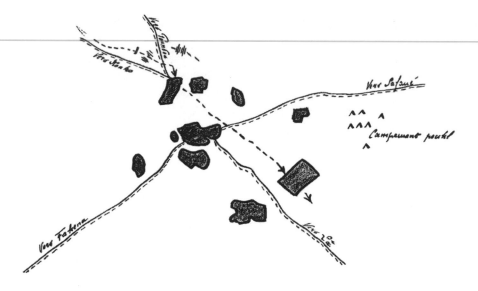

Map 8. Sokongo. From the Molard report (SHAT 5 H 196).

column, were poorly armed, rode their own horses (which they tried to protect), and were much impressed by the Bwa and Marka fighters. In later battles they even refused to obey orders. The goum being ineffective, Molard started to shell the village, which resisted all day and night. As in the siege of Bondokuy described in chapter 6, there was a breach between the Marka reinforcements and the local Bwa fighters during this battle, the former abandoning the latter saying that they did not know how to defend themselves. These disputes show that the joint action was not undertaken without strife. The defenders of Sokongo fled the village before daybreak, and the column destroyed and burned the village in the morning.

Next Molard attacked La (map 9), which was under the leadership of Tarahe. La, one of the first villages to respond to Bona's call, was Bwa in majority but had an important contingent of Marka, a strong military history, and many connections to the villages to the east (see chap. 1, p. 47). Its fighters had participated in the battle of Sokongo, and among its defenders were people from Bona, Nana, Ble, Tunu, Yanhoro, Konkoliko, Wona, Yona, and Banu (Sombie, 1975, 23). The Marka leadership wanted at all cost to halt the eastward advance of the column, and La offered the strongest resistance that Molard faced in his six-month campaign.

The defenders met the enemy in the classical style of precolonial warfare—with gunfire outside the village walls while shouting insults and dancing to the beat of drums and whistles. They had drunk large quantities of sorghum beer,

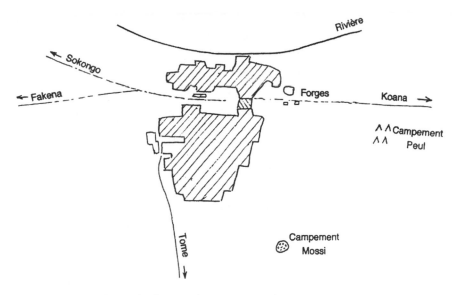

Map 9. La. From the Molard report (SHAT 5 H 196).

probably starting during sacrificial rituals the night before. Molard described the scene as filled with "dreadful screams and epileptic dances." He ordered the machine guns to open fire, and the defenders quickly withdrew inside the village. "To this period of tumult," Molard wrote, "succeeded the most complete silence." Proceeding as usual, the battery started its shelling. Molard noted that the sudden silence—coming after the invectives and also after the shelling of the walls—was effective in disconcerting the colonial troops trying to penetrate the village. At midday, a large number of people escaped from the village, despite Molard's efforts to stop them: "I was not able, in spite of my orders, my imprecations, and even my insults . . . to have the goum charge that mass of women and children protected by a few archers." Several hundred men coming from the neighboring village of Koana tried to ambush the column from behind, but they were driven back after they managed to take seven or eight horses.

Fighting stopped at dark after part of the village was occupied by the column. The colonial soldiers passed a painful night. The only well they controlled did not have enough water, and the soldiers who had fought all day had not been able to prepare their meals. During the night, most defenders stealthily evacuated the village, after having contaminated the wells and destroyed all the food they were unable to take with them. To create the impression that the village was still occupied, a few self-sacrificing volunteers remained behind and continued to shoot their guns at regular intervals. In the morning, the column resumed its attack on a grand scale until it discovered that only a few people remained in the village. Nonetheless, it was able to control the entire village only in the afternoon. It spent the remainder of the day and the next day demolishing La. A detachment under the command of Captain Cadence joined the column, bringing new artillery shells to Molard, who had very few left.

The main lines of defense of the Marka, which had been perfected since Pundu, emerged fully in the battle of La and remained constant in subsequent months: evacuation of the nonfighting population of the village before the battle or in its first phase; fierce resistance in the daytime and retreat in the dark of the night, leaving no supplies for the enemy. During the battle, sharpshooters made a special effort to hit the European officers.

The capture of La after a day and a half of battle cost the French three lives, including that of a French sergeant, and twenty wounded. Molard's assistant commanding officer, Commandant Ozil, and a second French sergeant were seriously injured. The column had spent the largest number of ammunition in any combat of the Volta-Bani War.[22] The dead French sergeant and the soldiers were buried secretly on site. The lack of drinkable water forced Molard to leave immediately after the destruction of La on February 22. Marching his hungry and thirsty soldiers along bush paths in order to avoid villages, Molard decided to regroup in the allied village of Safane, which had remained isolated, in hostile country, since the battle of Yankaso in late December.

The day after the column left, the inhabitants of La returned to their ruined village. They found the buried bodies of the French sergeant and the two soldiers and exhumed them. In times of peace, suspicious death (indicating a transgression on the part of the deceased) leads to the denial of a proper burial because the earth is desecrated by an impure body. The burial of an enemy in the village was considered an act of estrangement from one's own territory.[23] The exhumation of the enemy corpses was a celebration, a vengeance, and a way of regaining mastery of the world. La's inhabitants cut off the sergeant's head and feet and paraded them through the villages. News of the dead enemies found in the village transformed the battle of La into a victory. The inhabitants of the village also immediately started to rebuild their fortified houses.

Using Safane as a base in the heart of insurgent Marka country, Molard attacked Bona on February 24. The women, children, and valuable supplies had been evacuated, but Bona was poorly defended because most of its fighting population had gone to Banu (Sombie 1975, 23).[24] Although people from all the villages of the region came to defend Bona, the village was taken and burned, and the Danso shrine was destroyed. This was not, however, followed by the submis-

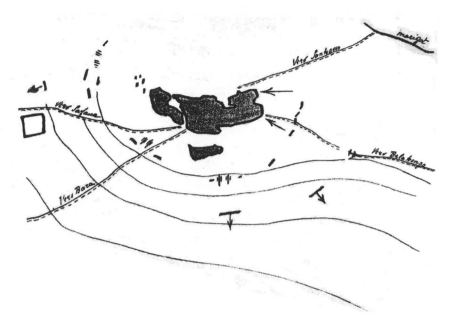

Map 10. Banu. From the Molard report (SHAT 5 H 196).

sion of leaders, as Molard and Maguet expected — in part because the column left it immediately, but also because it had no significant military consequences.

On the way back to Safane, Molard's troops had to fight another major battle, in Bara, but they were able to take a considerable amount of booty in spite of the goumiers' refusal to obey.[25]

On February 28 and March 1, Molard attacked Banu (map 10), which had ritual precedence in the region and was the home of Domba, one of the major leaders of the anticolonial movement (see chap. 1, p. 39). After a day and a night of combat, the defenders escaped the village before morning. Banu lost a great number of men in this battle because many fighters chose to die in the village rather than escape to the bush. The defeat of Banu made a big impression in the region, and of all the battles around Safane it is the best remembered today. Contingents from Yankaso, Cheriba, Tiga, Makongo, Bilakongo, Sion, and Bona had gathered in Banu (Sombie 1975, 23). Here for the first time, Molard tried to partially surround a village, but he observed that it presented enormous risks for tirailleurs, who shot wildly.

As in La, Banu was the scene for unsettling acts of courage. Immediately following the explosion of a cannon shell, villagers stood in the breach of the wall, firing at the soldiers and trying to patch the opening with heavy beams.

The defenders also tried a new trick: they staged a retreat to draw colonial soldiers into a trap, and the tactic met with some success. The second day of the battle, a large contingent of reinforcements arrived from Yankaso and tried to encircle the column; the maneuver turned against them and a very large number of them were massacred—many more than during the attack of Yankaso itself, which took place the next day.

Because of the defeat of the Simonin column, Yankaso had become an important symbol for both sides. Against Molard the defenders here refined their earlier tactical innovation: approximately one hundred fighters emerged from the village to attack the column in the open and then retreated in previously arranged ways, drawing the pursuing soldiers toward hidden fighters, who then shot at them. This ploy cost Molard several casualties but did not change the outcome. After a hard-fought, twenty-hour battle, the village was taken and destroyed. Five colonial soldiers lost their lives and ten bodies were found in the village,[26] a surprisingly small number considering the huge amount of ammunition fired by the column (137 shells and 6,897 cartridges). This low death rate is a tribute to the ingenuity of Marka defense, which was not only well prepared but, more importantly, proceeded as planned. The untiring efforts of the blacksmiths were evident in Yankaso; the bullets fired by the Marka and Bwa fighters were made of shrapnel from used cannon shells.

After demolishing the deserted villages of Sodien and Makongo, Molard attacked Tiekuy, which was the gathering point for all Marka forces of the region and which had killed a few days before many members of a detachment carrying mail. In Tiekuy (map 11), Molard found a "desperate resistance." One of the two main wards was inhabited by Poulo-fings (dependent Fulbe, living with the villagers), and they defended themselves bitterly.

A forced interruption in the campaign of the Molard column now gave new life to the anticolonial movement. On March 9, Molard decided to return to Dedougou because his troops were running out of ammunition and needed rest (on his way back, he set up a post in the abandoned village of Karo, to control the Dedougou-Boromo road and the southeast region of Dedougou). From Dedougou, he sent a detachment of two companies to San to bring back munitions and supplies. As the anticolonial forces controlled the entire region between Dedougou and San, this detachment had to be of a considerable size (240 soldiers and 8 French officers) and also took a cannon.[27] On the instructions of the lieutenant governor, the detachment spent more than a month in San before returning to Dedougou in order to slow down the extension of the movement in that part of the colony (chap. 9). In Dedougou, Molard anxiously waited.

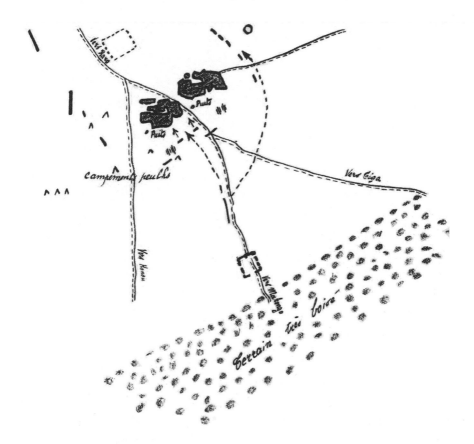

Map 11. Tiekuy. From the Molard report (SHAT 5 H 196).

In the first week, Molard's men made two more short expeditions near their base in Dedougou before the column ceased all operations. On March 11, Molard sent the four companies to attack Pasakongo (map 12) and Masala, which were only a few kilometers northeast of Dedougou, and raze other villages in the vicinity (see map 6 and key). On the 17th, Molard himself headed his three companies on an expedition south, where he destroyed many abandoned villages (see map 6 and key). The only battle took place in Pie, where the combatants of these villages had gathered. On his way back to Dedougou, Molard sent Haillot with the cavalry to burn other abandoned villages. After that, the column's activities came to a halt, because Molard, who had no more cannon ammunition, decided to rest in Dedougou rather than face a possible defeat.

In this extremely violent campaign, lasting more than a month (February 14 to March 22) including the last forays out of Dedougou, Molard destroyed many

Map 12. Pasakongo. From the Molard report (SHAT 5 H 196).

military centers without obtaining tangible military or political results. At least thirty villages were demolished and burned and eleven major battles were fought; 751 artillery shells and about 55,000 cartridges were spent. On the colonial side, 19 men were killed and 160 wounded; on the anticolonial side, the losses were possibly as many as 3,000 men. But the expected widespread defections and submissions had not come, and no anticolonial leader had surrendered to the French. The number of villages rallying to the anticolonial side was growing, including even some villages that had been spared by Molard, such as Kekaba, which had received the column with welcoming dances.[28]

On the day the column returned to Dedougou from its first campaign, a company under Captain Amalric, based in Guinea, had arrived in Dedougou to reinforce Molard. It included 10 French officers, 211 soldiers, 40 auxiliaries, and 300 porters. The company had left 40 soldiers and a French officer in Bobo-Dioulasso to help defend the city (chap. 8). The Amalric company included young recruits who had never fired a gun. Two hundred armed Mose people who had been expelled from Bwa villages such as Sara and Bondokuy and had sought refuge in Bobo-Dioulasso followed the company.[29]

The experience of the Amalric company during the seven days it took to travel the hundred kilometers between Bobo-Dioulasso and Dedougou reflects the state of countryside at that time. From Sara to Warkoy, groups of a few hundred men repeatedly ambushed the company. Amalric, who had received orders to avoid villages, followed bush paths, even at night. In the heat of the dry season, this march was extremely strenuous. After the company passed Bondokuy, the porters, who had run out of water, mutinied. Amalric distributed their loads among the Mose and left the porters behind. The porters were then assaulted by the anticolonials of the area. Between Bondokuy and Warkoy, the company, led by Fulbe guides from the area of Bondokuy, was forced to attack the village of Kera in order to find water. Amalric tried to avoid Warkoy, which Molard had destroyed on February 16, but people from the village still attacked the company. From that point until Dedougou, Amalric found only deserted villages. To compensate for the poor military training of its soldiers, the company fired 17,620 cartridges, an enormous number for troops trying to avoid engagement.[30] The Marka propaganda machine dubbed Amalric "the white man trying to find his way."[31]

After the return of the Molard column to Dedougou, Labouret's company now had to return to Gaoua because of grave stirrings in that cercle, encouraged as much by the absence of Labouret as by the news of the events in the cercles of Bobo-Dioulasso and Dedougou. On his way to Lobi country, Labouret marched through Nuna and Winye (Ko) villages and stopped in Boromo, the headquarter of a subdivision of the cercle of Dedougou and home of the Karantao, which colonial troops had not visited since the start of the war. A few kilometers east, across the river, Nuna and other Gurunsi villages were fighting against a small French column that had set out from Koudougou on March 10 (chap. 10). The Labouret company found itself involved in minor engagements against some villages (see map 6). Labouret was trying to avoid combat, marching past villages in hollow square formation while firing at assailants. Around Uri and Ulo, anticolonial combatants, wearing the woven cord, motivated by griots and under the direction of Marka leaders from the village of Da, attacked the company but failed to stop it. The events in Gaoua prevented Labouret from returning to Dedougou until May.[32]

Combes, the resident of Boromo, who in November had joined Maguet for the Bona battles, returned to his post in the company of Labouret. In the meantime, Suleyman Karantao, a young son of Moktar, leading a force of almost four hundred young men, had on his own organized the defense of the Boromo-Wahabu region against Bwa, Winye, and Marka anticolonial forces. During the marabout affair of the preceding year, this Suleyman Karantao had been tortured by Haillot (as had some of his relatives and friends, including two of his brothers who had died under the torture).[33] The administrators in Dedougou, and their sympathizers, attributed Karantao support for the French during the repression to the fear inspired by Maguet's crackdown the previous year. It is clear, however, that Suleyman's combativeness was far too intense to be understood in such a manner. Fear of punishment can explain passivity but not this much enthusiasm. The Karantao remained allies of the administration despite the crackdown and not because of it; they preferred to support the French — awful though they might be — rather than see their local enemies victorious.

At the end of Molard's campaign, and despite the arrival of the Amalric company, the morale of the anticolonial coalition was high. The anticolonial population considered the forced inaction of the column a success. In the traditional exchanges of invectives prior to the battles, the defendants had shouted to Molard's troops that the column would soon run out of ammunition, and that is precisely what had happened. The return of the column to Dedougou had made the position of the minority population siding with the French yet more difficult. The rumors spread that the shells fired by French troops did not kill and that one could escape besieged villages at will.[34] The taking of empty villages after long and violent assaults was interpreted not as an achievement but as a failure of the Molard column. Combatants who had fled Pasakongo after Molard's attack spread the news in the villages south of Dedougou that "the stench of white corpses was so strong in their villages that their houses had become uninhabitable." The locals told them in return that the column had gone back north to Dedougou because it had lost all its chiefs and had run out of ammunition and was now completely exhausted.[35]

These rumors combined self-fulfilling prophecy and disingenuousness, but above all it expressed the iron will to continue the war until victory, as the promise had been made over ancestor, village, and personal shrines. Villages had joined the anticolonial movement because they believed "force" (*fanga,* in Jula) had now shifted to their side. The column's bloody but ineffective military campaign had not altered their view so far. In fact, the local perception was still that the French were losing the war.

During the first Molard campaign, the anticolonial side came up with the most innovative military tactics, whereas the French simply followed Maguet's initial plan of systematically destroying rebel villages and giving battle when there was resistance. Our knowledge of the defensive organization of the anticolonial fighters comes mostly from Molard's evaluations, which at times reveal great respect for the resourcefulness of his enemies. In the cercle of Dedougou, anticolonial forces refused to give battle in the open field. The initial confrontation outside the walls of a village, in the din of drums, whistles, insults, gunshots, and arrows, was solely designed to produce a psychological effect. The battle was always given behind thick walls prepared for that purpose: "The potential defensive value [of villages] has been judiciously increased by the opening of a large number of loopholes, allowing up to three levels of fire . . . by the placement in the open field of small stakes carved of hard wood in the shape of arrowheads . . . hidden in holes covered by twigs and dry leaves."[36] Most of these measures came from war conventions of the past, but they were being adapted to take into account the superior firepower of the colonial troops—especially cannons. The most successful adjustment was the procedure of holding the position within the reinforced villages for only one day, moving from block to block and yielding slowly to the invasion of the troops, then withdrawing in the dark of night. Thus, the column was forced to expend the maximum number of shells and cartridges and put its soldiers at greater risk, whereas the defenders' losses were reduced, relative to the crushing superiority of enemy firepower.

In the conventional warfare of the savanna, a fortified village would defend itself until the end. The final house-to-house occupation being extremely deadly for the assailants, it was not uncommon for them to withdraw at that point. Although the French artillery made such an outcome unlikely, by defending the villages for only one day and evacuating them at night before final capture, the Marka leaders inflicted maximum damage on the enemy and left behind little of value, while cutting down their own losses. This strategy in turn necessitated tremendous effort for reinforcing, repairing, and rebuilding the houses and defensive works, requiring the contribution of the nonfighting sectors of the villages on a much greater scale than before. The intensive construction work that went on in the dry season of 1916—at a time of water scarcity and in addition to labor-consuming activities such as the preparation of gunpowder and arrow poison—must have necessitated an extraordinarily feverish work schedule for women and children.

Molard described how the nighttime withdrawal of the combatants was a tactical move and not a panic-driven stampede. It was thought out well in advance and executed by men in widely spaced formations, similar to moves carried out by the tirailleur themselves but with even greater intelligence and discipline:

When a *sukala* [ward] is going to be invaded by the whites, they go to the next sukala or, depending on the situation, to the bush, by groups of ten men at most, succeeding each other at intervals of few minutes. Within each group, the men leave between them a distance of seven to eight meters as they run

from cover to cover. . . . How many times did I point out to my officers and
tirailleurs this march under fire, as a model carried out in an impeccable way.
These dispersed groups fall regularly under the fire of machine guns or of the
infantry sections arranged for that purpose, yet they present only an elusive
target, very difficult to reach, as they often place themselves so as to move at
a right angle to the direction of the shots fired at them.[37]

Because the wards of a village were often scattered, colonial troops could
not encircle a village. This was not, however, the only problem for a full siege.
In the first days of the campaign, Molard tried to place troops beyond the village, on the side opposite the attack, in order to inflict greater casualties to people
trying to escape. But this tactic resulted in a cross fire that was more dangerous
to the column than to people running away. Molard blamed this on the lack of
training of his young tirailleurs. The machine guns somewhat compensated for
their failure:

With the tirailleur shooting at anything in sight, in any direction, without
worrying about what is in front of him, it is impossible to encircle a village,
whatever the number of troops in the column. The machine guns placed on
the flanks, cross firing on the uncontrolled zone, made that encirclement possible. Their fire had a considerable effect on enemy morale, and many escapes
have been checked by their mere threat.[38]

The posts Molard established in Kari, Teona, Karo, Kunandia, Siu, and
Bekuy were temporary and therefore had little strategic utility. A group of warriors based in Da even attacked the post of Siu. Nonetheless, sorties from these
colonial posts inflicted a high number of casualties. In two months, the detachment based in Bekuy alone killed 382 people. This violence, however, did not
check the movement's hold in the region.

In late April, the lieutenant governor summarized the situation: "After a
month and a half, the destruction of twenty-five villages, and causing depriva-
tion to about 30,000 people, we are still waiting for the first submissions. This
furious determination *(acharnement)* to resist is unheard of in the history of the
Soudan."[39] When Maguet returned to Dedougou, he wrote in his journal: "Instead of the 112 insurgent villages at the time of the Yankaso attack, we now
have 500 insurgent villages, or about 250,000 to 300,000 rebels [for the cercle
of Dedougou]."[40] In the northern part of the cercle of Bobo-Dioulasso, about
90,000 fighters had joined the anticolonial war. In the cercles of San, Koutiala,

and Bandiagara, "the situation seemed very serious" and in the Kipirsi (the Gurunsi region of the cercle of Ouagadougou) "the situation was not bright."[41]

WIPING VILLAGES OFF THE MAP: MOLARD'S SECOND CAMPAIGN

The supplies Molard was waiting for—food, artillery shells, cartridges, and medicine—arrived in San on March 24. They were brought by a company under the command of Captain Stefanini that had left Saint Louis, in Senegal, forty-five days before.[42] But the Stefanini company was delayed in San for one more week, along with the Carpentier and Breton companies that had come from Dedougou, to help the one hundred soldiers, guards, and auxiliaries who defended San. The three companies finally left San on April 1 and arrived in Dedougou a week later. With them was Chief Inspector Jules Vidal, whose mission was to inquire into the origins of the insurrection and who later wrote an influential report.

For its second campaign (April 13–June 13), the Molard column comprised seven companies (those of Breton, Carpentier, Stefanini, Lucas, Amalric, Ferron, and Cadence), new ammunition, four cannons, and two machine-gun sections. The continuing extension of the anticolonial movement despite all the destruction and bloodshed made it essential that Molard gain a resounding victory. On April 23, in the cercle of San, a second column was constituted under the command of Simonin. The Molard and Simonin columns operated simultaneously but independently since communication between them was extremely difficult.

In this second campaign, Molard abandoned Maguet's plan of first hitting Bwa villages and went southeast to attack the major anticolonial centers inhabited by Marka, Nuna, and Ko people. Only after these were destroyed did the column turn west to battle Bwa villages, extending its campaign far south until it reached the Nienegue villages in the northern part of the cercle of Bobo-Dioulasso (see map 6). Molard attacked villages that he had destroyed in the first campaign but that had been reoccupied and partly rebuilt. In response, the Marka intensified guerrilla tactics: barricades, pits, and poisoned stakes were placed on major roads and around villages, and small groups attacked the column as it moved from one village to another.

The first important battle took place on April 14 in Tiga (map 13), a village of two thousand inhabitants that resisted for a day and a half. The defensive strategy was the same as in the first campaign: "We find among the Nourounas [Nuna] the tactic employed by the Marka. This tactic did not change much, or

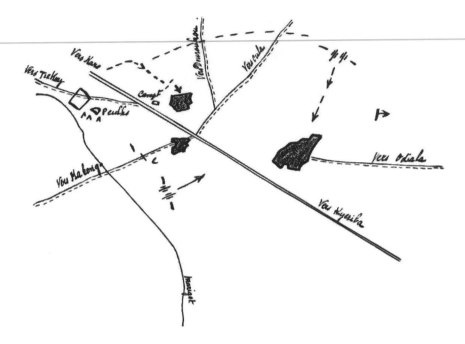

Map 13. Tiga. From the Molard report (SHAT 5 H 196).

changed very little, from one race to the other, from one tribe to another; this seems to indicate that everyone obeys to a given decision."[43]

From Tiga, two companies were sent to demolish the abandoned villages of Ula and Duruku, and to control that region, a post was set up in the village of Bladi, between Dedougou and Ula. Then Molard attacked the large Marka and Nuna village of Cheriba (see map 14), home of the great war leader Wani. Cheriba was a commercial town of four thousand residents, but most people had left their homes prior to the battle as Cheriba was being transformed into the region's main war center (on Cheriba history, see chap. 1, p. 47).

After defeating Cheriba and burning several deserted villages east of the Yankaso-Safane line, the column arrived in Da, which was a major ritual center for non-Muslim Marka but also had an important Muslim sector that had been among the leaders of the alliance against the Karantao in the nineteenth century (see map 15, also pp. 54, 58). According to Gnankambary, combatants from all the villages of the region had come to Da, ready to die in the name of its shrine (Gnankambary 1970, 80). Consequently, the battle of Da uncharacteristically lasted several days, with constant reinforcements coming to help the defenders. It was one of the deadliest engagements since the beginning of the war. While

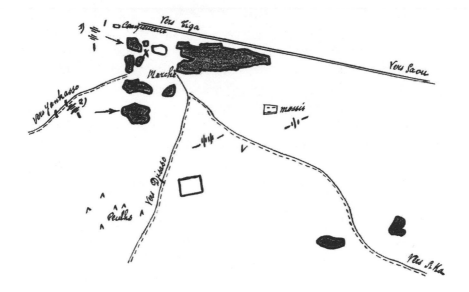

Map 14. Cheriba. From the Molard report (SHAT 5 H 196).

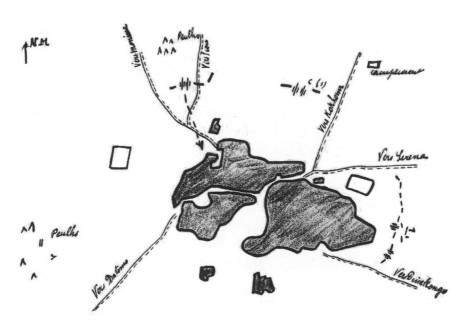

Map 15. Da. From the Molard report (SHAT 5 H 196).

the column fired "only" seventy cannon shells, it expended almost twice as many cartridges (7,708) as in Cheriba. Eight colonial soldiers were killed, and a French sergeant died from his injuries a few days later in Dedougou. The Marka left behind forty bodies. Following the defeat of Da, Molard sent detachments to burn down other villages in the region abandoned by their inhabitants — among them, Jinakongo, the great ally of Da during the Karantao wars.

The collapse of Da and Cheriba had profound consequences for the continuation of the war in this region. Winye (Ko) villages such as Uri, Ulo, and Sibi that had perpetuated the historical alliance with Da and Jinakongo surrendered after the fall of these two important centers. The destruction of villages by the Molard column in this area resounded across the Muhun River into the Gurunsi region. The Marka leaders who hailed from the surroundings of Da and Cheriba and had gone there to help organize the anticolonial movement decided to return to their villages (chap. 10).

The column now proceeded southward to Datomo, razing many villages without encountering opposition. Datomo was the village of Siaka, one of the great Marka leaders who had been a major influence in the spread of the movement to the northern part of the cercle of Bobo-Dioulasso (chap. 8). No combat took place in Datomo because it had been deserted, but in a show of conceit and arrogance, colonial troops paraded and performed drills and then shelled the village (Gnankambary 1970, 81). Detachments from the main column sacked and demolished Pompoi and many small villages, but they were still being harassed by small groups of guerrillas. From Pompoi, a detachment under the command of Cadence left for Koudougou (chap. 10), while Amalric left with a few men for Sansanne-Mango as the new military commander of Togo, in the part of the German colony that had recently come under French control.

Reflecting the changed nature of the conflict, the style of defense had been transformed. It had become less cautious, less foresighted. This was the beginning of the period of suicidal resistance that ultimately accounted for a large proportion of the anticolonial fatalities and that later came to be viewed, mistakenly, as characteristic of the war strategy from the beginning. When the column arrived at Bagasi on May 2 (map 16) it found the village well prepared for defense under the leadership of M'Bwa Yere. But the villagers had not taken precautions to reduce fatalities among nonfighters. Administrator Maguet wrote in his journal:

> There are a lot of people in the village (about 2,000). The entire village is there, with women and children, and a few outsiders (but not many). They are

certain that we will not be able to take the village. . . . A few rebels come out as a small group, but a few rounds of machine-gun fire forces them quickly back into the village, leaving a few bodies on the ground. The tirailleurs move forward rapidly and enter the village. The Bobo [Bwa] do not have the experience or the technique of the Marka. Disastrously, they try to escape before dark. A large number (137) are killed by machine-gun fire and there are many wounded. On our side, two tirailleurs are killed and six wounded.[44]

The confidence that the people of Bagasi had in the protective powers and dispositions of their village is noteworthy and perhaps partly a "failed prophecy" kind of psychological symptom, but it is also clear that Maguet's vision continued to be shaped by a contrast between "primitive" Bwa and more advanced Marka, a product of the fanciful colonial ethnohistory surmising the invasion of simpler "autochthons" by superior "Mandingues." In reality, many Marka from Da and Datomo were present in Bagasi. Maguet's description does not do justice to the extraordinary resistance of the people of Bagasi, which could be put down only with heavy artillery and gunfire— 127 shells and 16,688 cartridges, more than in any previous battle. In this encounter, troops that were formerly part of Amalric's company saw their first combat and were stricken with panic.

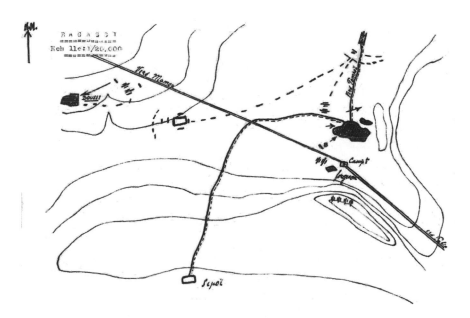

Map 16. Bagasi. From the Molard report (SHAT 5 H 196).

Using Bagasi as a base, detachments from the main column demolished and burned all the villages of the region, including nearby Dusi and Sipoy, where people from Bagasi had found refuge. Dusi had attacked the supply train that followed the main column. Destructive and predatory actions for no apparent reason other than the demonstration of power and pillage proceeded at the rate of about eight villages per day. Molard grew increasingly weary of these raids, and this experience was the beginning of a crucial change in military strategy for the French (a topic to which we return below).

The village of Vi, which was accused of having ambushed twenty-seven Fulbe herders under the instigation of Siaka of Datomo and having "sold their women for 2.5 francs a piece to the insurgent Bwa farmers," was crushed on May 6 after strong resistance, and all its food stocks were delivered to the nearby loyal Karantao of Wahabu.

The Molard column turned back north, to the area it had visited in its first campaign (see map 6). In seven days it razed another twenty-four villages in the area of Tunu, then more villages around Kongoba. Demolition was carried out from dawn till dusk, and even the heavy storms of the new rainy season did not slow it down.[45] From Kongoba, three companies were sent to Bona, which was still in ruins. But one structure had been rebuilt: the house of the Danso shrine. Soldiers and auxiliaries destroyed the shrine house a second time.

One of the most bitter episodes of vengeance took place in La, where the column went next, leveling to the ground communities on its way. When Molard entered La for the second time, he found it largely rebuilt, with loopholes in the fortified walls. He discovered the desecration of the French sergeant's tomb. In March, people from this village had also attacked Amalric's company. In revenge, soldiers tortured the inhabitants—including women and children—by assembling them and keeping them all day in the sun. Sixteen young men were lined up around the tomb of the sergeant and killed by gunfire (Gnankambary 1970, 82). Today people say that the population was tricked to return with a promise of total amnesty, and then fifty-five young men were selected and hanged. Colonial forces destroyed La again, prohibiting any rebuilding for thirty years. Gnankambary maintains that the village had more victims this time around than it did in the first attack. The lieutenant governor of the colony decreed that this village had to "disappear," its inhabitants to be deported to "a remote cercle."[46]

The column continued to the region of Warkoy, already devastated in the first campaign. On May 18 it destroyed Fakena (map 17), the village that had planned the execution of Alamasson (see chapter 5, pp. 134–39). This was fol-

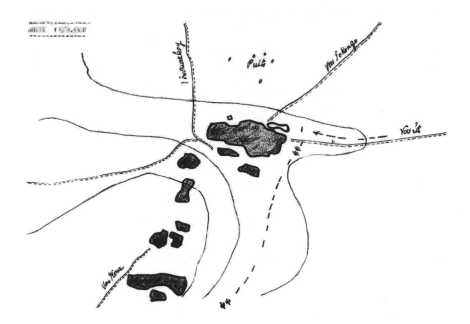

Map 17. Fakena. From the Molard report (SHAT 5 H 196).

lowed by the demolition of other villages already attacked in the first campaign, many of which had been rebuilt with defensive walls (see key to map 6).

On the eve of May 23, all the detachments that had been sent on demolition
missions were recalled to join the main column for an attack on Bondokuy, where
Maubert had been almost fatally trapped in December 1915. Approximately
eight thousand people inhabited Bondokuy, and like many other important villages it encompassed separate wards, with populations of different ethnic and
religious affiliation. The Muslim population had managed to persuade some of
the villagers to end their opposition to the administration. Molard tried to engage in negotiations with the rest, but to no avail, and he attacked Bondokuy.

The main resistance came from the ward of Tankuy (map 5), whose whistles
and drums praised the skill and power of its hunters and claimed that the village
would not be taken before nightfall—if at all. The people of Tankuy repelled
several assaults. Reinforcements came from Sara, Tia, Mankuna, and Popiho, but
they were driven back. Indeed, the village was taken only after 136 cannon shells
had been fired, and not before many of the defenders had fled by night.[47] The
other villages of the area (Mukuna, Tia, Donkuy, Diekuy, and Bokuy) were razed
without resistance.

The battle of Bondokuy marked a major step in the war. With the fall of

Bondokuy and the destruction of many villages for the second time, the French now sensed that the column had definitively broken the anticolonial movement in its birthplace. One company remained in Bondokuy to establish an important military post. The rest of the column split into two sections. The main column, under Molard, proceeded south and west through the Bwa villages of the northern part of the cercle of Bobo-Dioulasso; the companies of Breton and Labouret (the latter had returned from Gaoua), accompanied by Maguet, campaigned north and east, in the adjacent part of the cercle of Dedougou (see map 6).

Molard, marching through the area that had been subjected a few days earlier (May 5 to May 12) to a devastating expedition led by Maubert (chap. 8), attacked Sara on May 27.[48] Sara lived up to its reputation; its fighters hid in the forest and attacked Molard's troops for two days before being defeated. Despite the destruction of Bondokuy and Sara, the villages of the area continued to resist, and logistical problems again threatened to impede the movement of the column. The reserve rations of the column were almost exhausted, but Maubert came to the rescue, supplying Molard with an immense quantity of food: two hundred head of cattle and five metric tons of millet, probably the spoils of his ongoing campaigns. Supplies from San could not yet reach Dedougou because the region between the two towns remained under anticolonial control (chap. 9). The stock of cannon shells was also diminishing rapidly, and Molard feared an eventual immobilization that would be "disastrous, politically and militarily."[49] In mid-June, however, new munitions arrived in Dedougou.

At the end of May, the column was finally getting the upper hand. It destroyed Popiho, whose combatants had participated in the defense of Sara and of a number of neighboring villages, and Boyere, where the chief of the village of Biemido and the movement leaders Kari Dofini and Bangnie (see map 6 and key) were among the people killed. A company with a cannon was sent to Dohun, where fighters offered submission first as a ploy and then attacked the company with such ferocity that the company had to ask for reinforcements. After Dohun was taken, its fighters, strengthened by those of other villages in the area, hounded the company on its way back to Boyere, and on June 5 a company was sent back to Dohun to raze the village. Partisans still harassed the company from the woods outside the village. Another important gathering place, Kari (a canton headquarters, a different Kari from the village near Dedougou), was destroyed on June 6. Molard, who was sick, remained in Kari, but the following week his troops razed the deserted villages in the vicinity before the campaign came to an end (see key to map 6).

A Turning Point in French Strategy and First Submissions

An important change in military strategy occurred in the month of May, with consequences for French colonial practice that lasted far beyond the suppression of the Volta-Bani opposition. A new direction in the conduct of the war sprang from Molard's experiences during his first and second campaigns. In the initial French plan, the main purpose of the column had been to destroy systematically the villages that had not sent a delegation of submission. The military might of the column was a means to that end; it scared the villagers away so that demolition could take place. There was no clear definition of an enemy and Molard and his staff did not have a strategy to defeat it; they accepted battle at the sites that the movement's leaders had planned ahead of time. The repression of the movement was thus conceived in the tradition of the punitive expeditions of the colonial administration, acting both as retaliatory expedition and as deterrent for future movements. This attitude was evident in the first action of the column in December; when it marched out of Dedougou under Simonin it was prepared for only one major battle, with some police work to follow. Much effort was spent clearing a path for the automobile of Lieutenant Governor Digué, who accompanied the troops to assist in this exemplary spectacle of punishment.[50] As that expedition ended in a disaster for the French, it came to be realized that the suppression would take more than the demolition of one or two villages. But there had been no change in the definition of the situation.

The plan to punish villages by destroying them had nothing original, but found in Maguet an enthusiastic supporter. He periodically provided Molard with new lists of villages. In a way he was displaying a common tendency of civilian officials. Punitive expeditions ending in demolition helped cercle administrators vent their feeling of frustration and vengence because generally they did not have at their disposal the means to get back at "stubborn" villagers. However, lacking a true military strategy, the plan left Molard little room for maneuver. He could not set himself a truly military course of action because the column was tied down by demolition work.

Molard became increasingly dissatisfied with this situation, but a departure from the procedure adopted so far required, more than a simple change of tactics, an entirely new perspective on the events. It involved thinking about the campaign not as punitive expedition but as a true war against a skilled enemy with a political purpose. Molard's first sign of discordance did not go that far but more narrowly took the form of a response to a new list of twenty-six abandoned villages to be demolished that Maguet had submitted to him on May 4.[51] At that point the column was demolishing an average of eight villages a day; battles came three days to a week apart. The tirailleurs were spending most of the time on the arduous task of tearing down buildings with hand tools, with only occasional help from artillery shells, which were used sparingly. The auxiliaries and the considerable crowd of villagers who accompanied the column looked on, waiting for the next opportunity to loot. Molard felt that after the battles of Da, Pompoy, and Bagasi, the determination of the enemy was weakening and that a more focused pursuit of military targets could hasten the demise of the opposition. Every delay occasioned by the destruction of villages could bring a reawakening of ardor in the enemy, as had happened before. His letter to Maguet reveals Molard's irritation at finding himself in a position where he had to respond to the civilian commandant, with whom his differences in personality and in outlook on the war had come into increasingly sharper focus. He started his letter by noting that the demolition work slowed down the column considerably, whereas speed was essential to winning the conflict. He proposed that Maguet establish a special corps of wreckers, using prisoners of war and including some people from among the "swarm of people" [tourbe] who followed the column for pillage. Clearly he wanted to shift the burden of this work from his troops to Maguet's shoulders. The outcome of this correspondence is not clear. Demolition continued at the same rate during the following two weeks.

Molard then made a more forceful declaration in a new letter to Maguet on May 21 (at this point Maguet was still with the column). Molard laid out more explicitly his objective and assumed a more resolute tone. The blanket demolition of villages had to stop to allow the column more freedom of movement and to give the tirailleurs respite. The language was martial: "It is necessary to aim not at the villages that have been deserted before the expected arrival of the column but at those where [the rebels] have taken refuge with their possessions. . . . To strike them in their person and their food resources will be in my opinion more effective for our ultimate purpose than simply destroying villages."[52] This reaction must have provoked a fury of communication between Maguet and Lieutenant Governor Digué, Digué and Molard, and all of them and Governor-general Clozel in Dakar. Clozel sided with Molard. He wired instructions to Koulouba on May 30, and five days later he wrote again to make the point clearer: "Contrary to the measures that seem to have been favored by the interim lieutenant-governor, one should *absolutely refrain* from destroying villages."[53]

Presumably echoing Maguet's perspective on the matter, Digué objected to this new policy, arguing that "to maintain villages intact would be dangerous because the rebels with shelter and food would indubitably persist in their attitude."[54] Shortly after this exchange, Clozel was temporarily replaced by Gabriel Angoulvant, who soon sent a letter to Digué to show that the view in Dakar had not changed. In this first letter of June 16, the new acting governor-general explained that he was in "close communion of ideas" with Clozel and asked that standing crops not be destroyed. The point was further clarified in a second letter sent five days later: "The destruction of abandoned villages . . . is a futility, an injustice, and a disastrous procedure."[55] In these letters, emphasis was placed on the need to return to normal life rather than on military repression, which was expected to come quickly to an end.

That this new humanism did not spring from an angelic disposition in Angoulvant is evident from the reputation he had established earlier during his ruthless military campaign against the Baule as governor of Ivory Coast. With regard to pacification, Angoulvant represented the hawkish faction of the administration, in contrast to Ponty and Clozel, who were known to favor a more gradual approach. But it was the administrative position rather than personalities that made the difference in this instance, and the higher command was responding to the grueling experience of the Volta-Bani War and the lessons that Molard had learned in his six-month fight against an organized enemy. Angoulvant sent yet another letter in August to express that the policy had not changed and to forbid "the destruction of abandoned villages." This letter has a little ethnographic touch—an explanation that the square houses with thick walls and terrace roofs represent "a more developed social state," and that it was unfair to ask these people to live in less-civilized round huts with straw roofs.[56]

The high volume of correspondence suggests that the resistance to the change in strategy by Maguet and his superior in Bamako was significant. But the government in Dakar did not go back on its new course. On the contrary, it made the new principles of focusing on military objectives and avoiding the blanket destruction of villages part of its long-term policies. Most notably, the suppression of a new armed movement in Borgou in northern Dahomey, which lasted from December 1916 to January 1917, was based entirely on what was learned during the Volta-Bani War. In their action there, the colonial troops did not demolish villages or destroy granaries and crops unless either they were attacked or the resistance could not be put down without battle.[57]

The new policy did not mean the end of all demolition work. Defensive walls were torn down and villages that had been important anticolonial centers continued to be destroyed. On June 12, the Molard column razed what was left of the defensive structures of Koho and Hunde, even though they had been deserted, but they left the other villages in the area standing. On June 14, Molard burned down the important anticolonial center of Karaba, north of Hunde, the home of the important war leader Plenza, to punish its inhabitants for shooting arrows at auxiliaries. With this destruction, the Molard column ended its campaign in the cercle of Bobo-Dioulasso and returned to Dedougou.

Out of the forty-seven Nienegue villages that had taken up arms, thirty-seven had surrendered to Molard.[58] Yet, these people did not feel bound by the promises they made these strangers. Vidal, who accompanied the Molard column in the cercle of Bobo-Dioulasso, warned the authorities in Dakar that the "rebels [are] still active in the bush. They still hope that we will run out of ammunition. Their determination has remained unchanged."[59] This indomitable spirit of resistance manifested itself as the Molard column was returning to Dedougou on June 19. A coalition of villages that included Karaba, Hunde, Koho, Wani, Dohun, and Tiombini, many of which had been destroyed by the column, attacked and killed porters near Hunde. Even in September, a military detachment was attacked near Dosi. Although the war continued for a few months in the northern part of the cercle of Bobo-Dioulasso, when Maubert returned to the Nienegue on July 8 he was able to capture many local leaders of the movement, among them Plenza, from Karaba.

After splitting from Molard, the second section of the column, under Maguet and Breton, closely followed the border of the cercles of Dedougou and Bobo-Dioulasso, attacking villages (some of which had already been destroyed once in early May; see map 6). Boni surrendered, but sent combatants a few days later to Dohun, which was being attacked by a detachment from the Molard column. Colonial forces burned Voho as punishment for allowing the Bwa leader Ombak to escape. On May 29, the Marka inhabitants of Kopoy were forced to deliver to the French the famous leader Siaka, of Datomo, the commander of the southern flank of the movement in the organization set up in November. June 3 saw the surrender of another influential war leader, Domba, of Banu. After a six days' rest in Boromo, the company marched northward to Sibi and Ulo. Yisu Kote, the foremost leader from Bona, surrendered in June to Lieutenant Stefanini, who was in command of a post established in Tunu. According to his family and other elders in Bona, Yisu was sent to jail and died there shortly afterwards. A military post was established in Serena to suppress the opposition still coming from the important centers of Tiga and Cheriba. Within a few days, Maguet had received the submissions of the most influential Marka leaders. The Breton company left for Koudougou to reinforce the Cadence company (chap. 10), while Maguet continued north across the river to the Samo region (see maps 6 and 18).

SAMO COUNTRY

Most villages as far north as the Tougan-Bunu line, an area that includes mostly speakers of the Maka language, had joined the anticolonial ranks in January 1916. Many Samo villages that fought against the colonial administration in 1916 had earlier, at the time of the first colonial conquest, put up very strong resistance to the columns that raided and pillaged the region.[60] In 1916 the movement reached Samo country through emissaries sent from the region of Pundu, and people in this area called it the War of Pundu, rather than the War of Bona (Pare, 1984; Toe, 1994).[61] Later they also received Gurunsi fighters from the south (chap. 10). Many Samo warriors pledged to fight against the whites over a shrine, possibly of Bwa origin, represented by a fighting club. Although there is no acknowledgement of the shrines of Bona in our sources, like most other anticolonial fighters the people of this region wore the headdress made of a cord, thus situating themselves within the larger movement.[62]

Perhaps more than in other regions, Samo villages were sharply divided between wards supporting the antiadministration movement and those refusing to join the movement. Some even remember this troubled period as a civil war, rather than an anticolonial war (Pare, 1984, 156). The important village of Toma presented an extreme case of internecine conflict. It was home to Paragui Kawane, one of the main anticolonial leaders, and also to Isa Pare, one of the staunchest allies of the French in the region. Isa had been recently appointed chief by the administration. He had promised to protect the Catholic mission established in the village by the White Fathers in 1913.[63] Thus the development of the anticolonial movement was held in check by the action of powerful chiefs allied to the French, such as, in addition to Isa, Bere Jibo, in Kougny, and the chiefs of Yaba and Biba. The villages—or in some cases the wards—of these chiefs were, however, surrounded by a multitude on the anticolonial side. The role of the rivalry between Suru on the one hand and Gasan and Jere on the other, both in 1896 and in 1916, was discussed on pp. 65 and 67.

Since the beginning of the hostilities five months before, the French had not set foot in Samo country. Father Dubernet, from the mission in Toma, had taken refuge in Dedougou but then returned to Toma in late April. He traversed

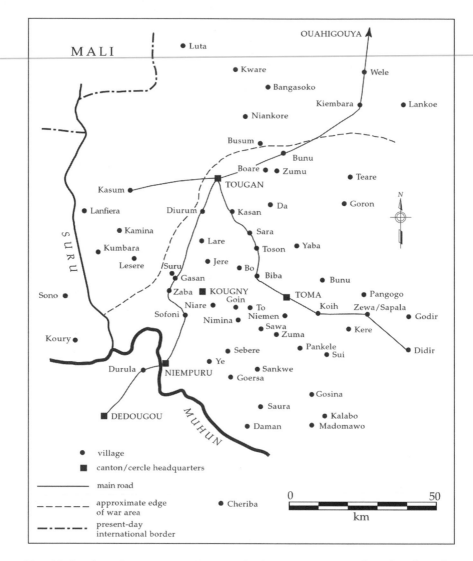

Map 18. Southern Samo country. Composed using maps in H. Pare (1984) and Sombie (1975).

the region at war on his bicycle, taking four guns with him (de Benoist 1987, 245–46). On May 6, while the Molard column was far away in the southern part of the cercle of Dedougou, a formidable force of between three and four thousand Samo, Marka, and Gurunsi warriors, armed with a large number of guns, attacked procolonial Toma, which was defended by about four hundred men. The principal Samo villages that participated in this attack were Zuma, Sapala, Toson, Da, Pankele, and Jere.

Toma was surrounded with the sounds of whistles, war horns, and gun shots.
. . . The assailants wearing headdresses made of fiber entered Toma through
the ward that was on their side. . . . "We want the head of the White Man,"
they shouted, "otherwise we will burn and raze the village of Toma!" . . . Arrows were flying from everywhere. The griot named Dane came out with his
little armpit drum and started calling out at the worthy men of Toma . . . the
warriors shouted back to answer that they were present; each one of them
recognized his own war name in the drum language.[64]

The attack was pushed back only with the help of people from Biba and Yaba.
Toma suffered at least sixty deaths in the attack.

On May 9, a small detachment of thirty tirailleurs from the Molard column
was sent to Samo country to rescue Father Dubernet and to protect the neighboring villages of Biba and Yaba. Some tirailleurs from Dedougou were also
sent to reinforce Toma. They dressed in civilian clothes and dispersed in groups
of three in order to reach the village through enemy lines. The anticolonial
troops had regrouped in the village of Zuma. They attacked Toma again a week
later, but taken by surprise by the reinforcements and the firepower of the de
fenders, they retreated again, this time for good.[65] The administration maintained a military post in Toma until early October 1916.

Maguet arrived in Samo country in June, with a unit of guards and auxiliary
soldiers, marching through the regions of Ye, Gosina, Toma, and Zuma, opening
the roads to Ouahigouya and Ouagadougou (see p. 204 and map 18). He continued north to the region of Sara and destroyed the centers of resistance of Da
and Kasan, then returned south and attacked Toson and Pankele.

The last major battle took place on June 25 in Jere, a point of concentration
for the warriors, who received Maguet's troops with customary insults and the
"awful music of horns and whistles."[66] The battle lasted an entire day. Samo
forces organized three successful counterattacks and forced the assailants to
fight for every step. At the end, the villagers dispersed into the surrounding
bush, and Maguet found fifty-two dead, among them Somasa, the most important war leader in Jere. In July, with his small company reinforced by the tirailleurs of the post of Toma, Maguet attacked Sapala (Zewa) which was
occupied by Gurunsi warriors from the region of Koudougou (chap. 10).

In the course of his Samo campaign, Maguet obtained the surrender of
Damu, who had played a central role in involving these parts in the war. The
great Samo leader Paragui Kawane was also arrested; eventually he was given a
life sentence.[67] In early June, a man known as El Hajj Uli was arrested, which

contributed to putting down the movement in the Toma region.[68] His involvement points to the presence of a Muslim element in the Samo movement, which
shows continuity with the movement in Gurunsi country (chapter 10). Maguet
returned to Dedougou on July 25 with fifteen metric tons of millet plundered
in this campaign.[69] In Dedougou, Maguet briefly met with Molard, who had
just returned from the western part of the cercle of Dedougou. Since the anticolonial movement west of the Muhun River was closely linked to events in the
region of San, this third and last campaign of the Molard column west of the
Muhun River will be taken up in chapter 9.

Molard's campaigns show most clearly the extraordinary nature of the
French effort to suppress the opposition. In its three campaigns, the Molard
column used a total of 124,341 rounds of rifle ammunition and 2,002 cannon
shells.[70] In the words of Governor-general Van Vollenhoven, the military columns had "transformed into a desert one of the richest regions of the colony."[71]
Yet in his final report, Molard was critical of the military means put at his disposal. Echoing the demand that the lieutenant governor of Haut-Sénégal-Niger
had formulated before he set out on his first campaign, Molard pointed out that
bombs dropped from an airplane on villages would have had a "considerable
moral and material effect that would have prevented much human loss, weari-
ness, and financial cost."

Although such drastic means of repression were not used by the French until
much later — not until the post World War II nationalist movements of independence, particularly in Madagascar — the military lessons of the Volta-Bani War
were immediately put into practice in the suppression of other insurgencies in
French West Africa.[72]

Chapter 8 describes a different aspect of the 1915–16 war in the cercle of
Bobo-Dioulasso, where the movement of opposition showed less of a united
front and Maubert's personality and action had a greater shaping role.

CHAPTER 8

The War in the Cercle of Bobo-Dioulasso

THE MAJORITY OF THE PEOPLE in the northeastern part of the cercle of Bobo-Dioulasso were called Nienegue in colonial documents, and sometimes Kademba in the ethnographic literature of the time. They are speakers of dialects of the Bwa language and most of them became the earliest and most steadfast participants of the anticolonial movement. Many villages were involved in the formative event of the movement, the siege of administrator Maubert in Bondokuy in November 1915. During Maubert's retreat, the village of Sara and its neighbors organized a major offensive (chap. 6). After the Frenchman was able to escape, the conviction that colonial rule could be ended became more resolute, and most other villages joined the movement.

Villages within the fan-shaped area between the Dedougou and the Ouagadougou roads (Maro, Boho, Dohun, Popiho, Niendekuy, and Diendekuy; see map 19) had sent fighters to Bondokuy. Others just beyond the boundary of the cercle, in the area of Bagasi, entered the movement under the influence of the leader Womba in early December. After the siege, messengers from Bondokuy and Sara visited other villages of the region and announced that the French had no ammunition and no troops left. This massive slide into the opposition was strengthened by the arrival of representatives from the Marka centers that had started it. Siaka of Datomo was the most effective agent spreading the movement in the Nienegue area and west of the Muhun River. The procolonial chief of Bereba later explained the effect of the early successes of the anticolonial movement on the people of this area:

213

The people of my canton had learned that there were no more tirailleurs left in Bobo, and that the whites of Dedougou had been chased away by the great chief of the dio of Bona. Emissaries from the Marka and Nienegue countries of the cercle of Dedougou came to tell them that the great fetishist of Bona was controlling all the neighboring territories. He had the power to transform ants into invincible warriors, and people had to submit to the dio. White rule over the country was finished forever. People started to become agitated, and when they learned that the commandant of Bobo had been forced to flee from Bondokuy with his guards, most people picked up arms and forced the rest to follow them.[1]

The anticolonial partisans directed their first action against local low-rank native representatives of the colonial order. The most significant was the assault

Fig. 7. Postcard showing a young Bobo man and a woman. The Fortier enterprise, which produced this card, was active between 1914 and 1922. (Private collection; a gift from Thomas Bassett.)

on the compound of the canton chief of Wakuy, Beopa, who had provided archers to Maubert (chap. 6, p. 161). A few days later, anticolonial fighters attacked the chief of the village of Pe; he and eight other people were killed.[2]

By the end of December, Maubert estimated that a population of sixty thousand people, including fifteen thousand fighting-age men, had actively joined the war against the colonial administration in the cercle. Besides the Nienegue villages, the movement had won the Bobo-speaking population of the villages situated on the flood plain of the Muhun River, Lahiraso, Badema, and Dande, and also the villages at the northernmost part of the cercle, in the canton of Fo. Siankoro (or Tiankoro) became an important center of resistance. Here the movement established a connection with the villages that had always been trouble spots for the administration (Sami, Perive, Nampela; chap. 9) in the area straddling the borders of the cercles of Dedougou, Bobo-Dioulasso, and Koutiala (the first two in today's Burkina Faso, the third in Mali). Thus in January a vast zone representing the northeast quarter of the cercle was completely absorbed in the anticolonial movement.

Simultaneously, the movement spread to a zone to the west of the city of Bobo-Dioulasso, among the Sambla speakers. In this zone, local leaders initiated the movement and remained mostly responsible for its development, in contrast to the Nienegue area and the canton of Fo, which were in constant contact with the centers of resistance further north. This relative isolation, and possibly also the prevailing ethnic model, induced the colonial administrators to think that the Sambla-Tusia opposition rose independently from that of the Marka, Bwa, and Bobo of the north. Although the lack of coordination and consultation with Marka and Bwa leaders showed in important matters such as the conduct of battle, the initiative of the Sambla leaders was directly connected to Maubert's military failure in Bondokuy and the explosion in the cercle of Dedougou. Also, the isolation was not complete; in the final stages of the resistance, some Sambla leaders joined those from the Bobo village of Lahiraso on the Muhun River flood plain for a last-ditch stand.

Sambla villagers gained a first-hand experience of the storm sweeping the Nienegue region in November, when the chief of the canton of Bwende, Si-Boro, gathered a group of men to take part in Maubert's expedition as auxiliaries. While Maubert was under siege in Bondokuy, more men from this area were gathered and sent to him as reinforcements, but on the road to Bondokuy they met the retreating commandant in the village of Satiri, not far from Bobo-Dioulasso, and they were released.[3] When these discharged recruits returned to their villages, they announced that the whites had surely been defeated, that they had no ammunition left, and that they had lost their "force."[4] The few Sambla men who distinguished themselves in stirring the anticolonial sentiment were among the recruits who had witnessed Maubert's flight from Bondokuy. They emerged as the leaders in this area and directed the local forces in the opposition. They were Sa-Dagaburu, Si-Bena, and Sa-Pe, from the village of Bwende; Sa-Kono and Si-Kugeka, from Toroso; and Si-Ju, from Surukudinga.

The action started in the village of Toroso, when a collector of market taxes, a subordinate of the canton chief Si-Boro, was killed by a mob led by Sa-Kono and Si-Kugeka. The appendages of the victim's body were cut off and his head was paraded in the village, a transition into violence that, as we have seen in the other cases, served to demonstrate a radical shift in "force." In January 1916, four other villages defied the administration with public anticolonial declarations: Bwende, Toroso, and Kongolikan, located in the hilly region, and Kunseni, which is mostly Tusia, but was included in the Sambla canton because it has an important Sambla population.

At the beginning of February, the movement thus dominated the northeast quadrant of the cercle of Bobo-Dioulasso. First, the cantons of Bereba, Wakuy, and Kari joined the movement, under the direct influence of Bondokuy and Sara, themselves part of a regional organization coordinated from the Datomo area in the cercle of Dedougou. Then, south of this zone, under the influence of Boho, the movement was gaining ground among the Bobo-speaking villages of the canton of Kotedugu, had crossed the road to Boromo and Ouagadougou, and had reached the elbow of the Buguriba River. On the left bank of the Muhun River, the movement was quickly spreading southward under the influence of Sanaba, which had been visited by Yisu Kote, and of Solenzo. The Bobo villages on the flood plain of the river, Lahiraso, Syoma, Badema, and Segere, had been transformed into anticolonial strongholds, exerting a pull on the villages immediately north of Bobo-Dioulasso. Finally, at the northernmost point of the cercle, in the canton of Fo, all the Bobo villages had passed to the anticolonial movement, and Tiebani had become a fortress. These three areas are contiguous, and although the topography and historical ties favored the circulation of ideas and people in the direction northeast-southwest, there was also lateral movement across the Muhun River (map 19).

At the same time, between the headwaters of the Muhun River and the road to Sikasso a vast area lying west of Bobo-Dioulasso was up in arms, without being visited by Marka or Bwa emissaries but spurred to action by local leaders who took their cue from the Bondokuy events. The Bwa-Bobo and the Sambla movements came close to contact around Samandeni, about thirty-five kilometers north of Bobo-Dioulasso.

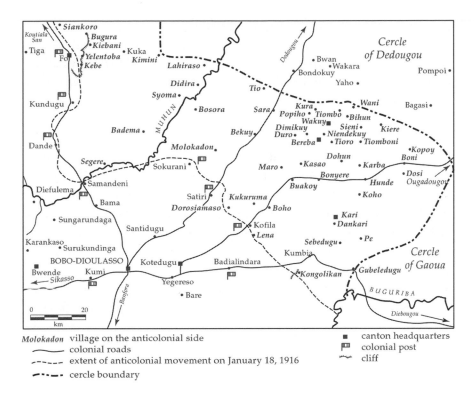

Molokadon village on the anticolonial side
⌒⌒ colonial roads
- - - - - extent of anticolonial movement on January 18, 1916
▬ ▪ ▬ ▪ ▬ cercle boundary

■ canton headquarters
🏳 colonial post
⌒ cliff

Map 19. The northeast quadrant of the cercle of Bobo-Dioulasso. Boundaries of the war zone and government post villages taken from "Croquis des territoires et état de rebellion à la date du 18 Février 1916" in Maubert's monthly political report for March 1916, ANCI 5 EE 6(3).

The westernmost stretch of the cercle bordering with Sikasso (the present-day Kenedougou province of Burkina Faso) was ignored by the colonial authorities. No repressive activity took place in this area and it is difficult to say what was happening there. The southern half of the cercle (where in 1914 Maubert had experienced the "rebellions" described in chap. 4) was also completely emptied of any colonial troops and left on its own. When the colonial forces eventually returned to this area in 1917, after the repression in the north had been accomplished, they encountered no resistance, and because of this it was officially considered not to have participated in the anticolonial movement. We have no access to the debates that happened in the villages of those places during that time.

As the shortage of troops and equipment forced the government-general of French West Africa to focus all its energies on the organization of the Molard column in Dedougou, in the cercle of Bobo-Dioulasso, like in all the others, it adopted a policy of "strict defensive and political action."[5] Administrator Maubert,

who had already caused great damage in Bondokuy, was ordered to manage the
situation with his meager means, provide what little support he could to loyal
chiefs and villages, and avoid risky situations that could lead to further military
setbacks. His compulsive disposition took very badly to these orders and he
started showering the colony headquarters with distress signals, asking for men
and materials that would enable him to take some independent action.

In January he was able only to establish a line of defensive posts *(postes d'arrêt)*.
Four of these were on the road leading north to Koutiala and San: Samandeni,
Dande, Kundugu, and Fo. Although villages on both sides of the road had joined
the movement, Maubert considered this traffic route to be the western limit of the
anticolonial movement in the cercle, and the posts were meant both to keep the
road open and to prevent the spread of the insurgency further west. He created
another set of posts northeast and east, forming roughly a quarter arc around
Bobo-Dioulasso, and at a distance of about forty kilometers from it: Sukurani,
Satiri, Kofila, and Badalindiara. On the west and facing the Sambla zone were two
posts, at Kumi and in Tiara, guarding the Sikasso road, and a third one, occupied
by archers only, in Banzon, at the far end of the Sambla insurrection area (map 20).

THE SOCIAL CONTOURS OF THE OPPOSITION

In the Sambla area, the spread of the movement followed the divisions that
were the legacy of the nineteenth century. The villages in the southern, hilly
part of the Sambla speech area focused around Bwende had historically been
hostile to the Watara house of Mori-fin. As we have seen, they spearheaded the
opposition. In contrast, the Sambla villages of the northern plain wavered, because Karankaso, the ritual center of this area, was itself divided. Its founding
lineages had historical ties to the Watara house of Mori-fin, who maintained
strong connections with the ritual chief of Karankaso, called masa (for the masa
among the Sambla, see Royer 1996; for the masa among the Marka, see chaps.
1, p. 38 and 5, pp. 129–30). The senior houses of Karankaso saw the village of
Bwende as a rival, and hesitated, whereas the ward of Koko, inhabited mostly
by more recent settlers, quickly went over to the anticolonial side.[6] The village
chief of Karankaso was Si-Dienfon, who belonged to one of the senior houses
and was the son of the first village chief named by Mori-fin. Sa-Pe invited the
people of Karankaso to either join the anticolonial side or face punishment.
The chief fled the village, and its population joined the movement.

The social status of these men was similar to that of many other leaders of the anticolonial movement. They were not village chiefs, nor were they young men looking for exploits or fame, a category of men for whom the Sambla have a special term, *tan*. Rather, the Sambla leaders were heads of families in their late thirties or early forties who possessed all the ritual and political responsibilities accorded to such men in their communities.[7] Sa-Dagaburu and Sa-Kono were the two most prominent figures, regarded with awe by many Sambla. Sa-Dagaburu was not only physically imposing but he spoke with eloquence. Sa-Dagaburu and Sa-Pe continued to resist long after the repression of the movement and the surrender of all Sambla villages. Sa-Pe was captured only on October 26, 1916.[8]

On the eastern front of the cercle also, the configuration of the movement had a direct connection to the late-nineteenth-century legacy. The anticolonial forces had set up the large village of Boho as a formidable fortress that dominated its surroundings. Under its leader Kanda, Boho was defended by fighters from many villages of the cantons of Wakuy, Kari, and Bereba. The villages of Bobo speech of this area at first hesitated to join these Bwa partisans, but they were more afraid of the forces in Boho than of Maubert, and eventually most of them, but not all, verged toward the anticolonial camp.

The Bobo villages that ended up going over to the Boho side belong to a "subethnic" group labeled Soxokire (Le Moal 1980, see map "Les Bobo"), whereas those that remained loyal to the administration belong to the cluster of twenty-odd villages who distinguish themselves as Bɛngɛ. There are differences of dialect and social practice between the people of these two clusters. The communities called Bɛngɛ, together with the people living in villages closer to Bobo-Dioulasso (whom Le Moal considers under the rubric of Syakoma), have a social organization of the classic dual-descent pattern. Matrilineages play a central role in ritual life among them and serve as the arena for holding and circulating movable wealth. In contrast, in the so-called Soxokire communities, matrilineages are much less discernible.[9]

In understanding the alignment of 1916, what is more important is that in the nineteenth century the Bɛngɛ group was allied to a set of warrior and trader Zara houses based in Sia (Bobo-Dioulasso), carrying the patronymic Sanu (this alliance perhaps also underlies the Bɛngɛ's sociocultural differences). The people called Zara are also of Bobo speech. The Zara houses of Sia (mentioned in chap. 4 with respect to Maubert's canton politics) have oral traditions that trace their origins to the Bɛngɛ area (Ciré Ba 1971, 11–20) and maintain connections—ritual, military, and political—with Bɛngɛ villages. For this reason, after the colonial occupation the French considered the forty or so Syakoma and Bɛngɛ villages around Bobo-Dioulasso that were under the hold of these Zara houses to be a principality. They organized these villages as an independent canton, Bobo-Dioulasso, kept outside the états given to Watara chiefs.

What complicated the situation is that the Zara houses in Sia were divided, and although they collaborated with each other and with Watara houses, their collaboration went under stress with the events at the end of the nineteenth century. After the occupation, in the colonial period, the office of canton chief became the focus of the competition. Despite the rivalry, the canton chiefs of Bobo-Dioulasso were able to deliver the tax, labor, and commodities that the administration requested. The canton of Bobo-Dioulasso became the least troublesome one in the cercle for French administrators.

As to the so-called Soxokire Bobo villages, whom the Bobo of the central zone call Bobo-Ule (an expression that already indicates that these labels register not ethnolinguistic affinities but political ones), they had historically been at odds with the Zara houses and in the colonial organization were not included in the Bobo canton. When the explorer Gustave Binger went through this area in May 1888, he encountered the Zara leader Zelelu in the Bɛngɛ village of Koroma and another Zara elder, Mamuru, in Bosora (Binger 1892, 396–404). Neither of them had a foothold in the Bobo-Ule villages in between, and crossing this area Binger was given a cold reception in Satiri. Zelelu and Mamuru were organizing raids against a league led by the Bwa village of Sara. One surmises that the Bobo-Ule villages were at one with the Sara league or actively allied to them. Thus in 1915–16, the boundary between the anticolonial villages and loyal villages recapitulated the lines of the conflict at the end of the nineteenth century.

Kofila, a village with a mixed Zara and Bobo-Ule population, was the home base of Zezuma and Basabati, the men that Maubert had appointed as the new canton chiefs of Kotedugu. But Kofila had gone quickly over to the anticolonial side. In order to establish his post there, Maubert had to engage in a fierce battle; his forces killed fifty-three men. Thereafter, Kofila stood as the advanced post of the government, facing the fortress of Boho, which was less than ten kilometers away on the Ouagadougou road. Kofila was attacked numerous times by anticolonial forces and remained on the defensive most of the time until May, but it stood fast and did not fall, protecting for the administration the Bɛngɛ villages behind it and the surroundings of Bobo-Dioulasso.

Among the people who energetically helped Maubert against the Nienegue villages and around Fo were the new canton chiefs that Maubert had appointed—Suro, Zezuma, and especially Basabati, as well as Mamuru Kwese, an aspiring candidate from the deposed Sangbeleluma Zara house in Sia. They raised auxiliaries from the villages and among their own men and headed them in action. Among the population of the villages that remained loyal, however, sympathy for the anticolonial movement was strong, especially so in the Bobo villages immediately north of the city, which were open to influences from the agitated region lying across the Muhun River. Maubert was uncertain even of the wards making up the Bobo-Dioulasso agglomeration. But it seems that this population was afraid of the Zara chiefs and of their colonial overlords, and no overt support for the movement materialized in this area.

In the canton of Fo, the very same historical factors were acting upon the shape of the conflict in 1916. Fo had been the spot where the famous Zelelu lived in the 1860s. The Watara leader Pintyeba was operating out of Kongoma (very near Kundugu, where Maubert established his post), while Baba Ali, leading Zara fighters, was stationed in Kwere. In Dande was the Watara leader Kongodin, with Sabana Watara heading a garrison of Dokhosie warriors (Binger 1892, 1:375, 376, 389). Thus, Maubert established these posts because he wanted to hold the Koutiala road, but the positions he selected also corresponded to the late-nineteenth-century residences of Watara and Zara leaders of Sia and environs. In the late nineteenth century, these leaders had turned their face toward the west, whence came incursions of bands launched from Sikasso and from village alliances in Koutiala. Now the direction of the enemy had changed, but the colonial government had basically taken over the former bases of their Watara and Zara allies. These connections were also kept alive by the method of recruitment. The post of Fo was reinforced with many auxiliaries gathered in the Bɛngɛ villages.

On the anticolonial side, a notable presence in the canton of Fo was a large group of fighters of Bwa origin who formed companies taking independent action. We know little about the internal organization of these people, and it is hard to decide whether they had come on their own, responding to some strategic design of their leaders, or if they had been invited to help by local village populations. We know that some came from the cercle of Dedougou and some from across the Muhun River. Since Solenzo is sixty kilometers from Fo, Sara about eighty kilometers east across the river, and Sanaba a hundred kilometers northeast, most of these Bwa fighters were three or four days' walk away from their place of origin, not a commuting distance in war conditions. Therefore, besides the circulation of leaders, propagandists, and war strategists, in this case there was an entire mobile army operating in foreign land and having an impact on the progress of the conflict. Between February 2 and 4, the post of Fo was attacked by a large anticolonial force, including these Bwa fighters, but was able to defend itself.

A SERIES OF DISCONNECTED SORTIES

The anticolonial forces closing in on Bobo-Dioulasso in February consisted of two or perhaps three distinct blocs acting autonomously. The opposition in the cercle, therefore, did not have as much coordination as that under the leadership of the Datomo-Bona area. Combined with the French strategy in Bobo-Dioulasso—the absence of a strong expeditionary force—the war in this cercle took on the character of a series of continuous but disconnected sorties. Maubert was obsessed with the developments in the western, Sambla, front, probably not because they presented more danger than the ones elsewhere, but because he had decided that this would be where he would obtain his victory.

The confrontations in January took the form of duel-like combat—Maubert and his auxiliaries against the various anticolonial forces that surrounded the city on three sides. Maubert organized six expeditions, some to establish his posts, others to relieve friendly villages, with bloody battles in each that cost Maubert several fatal casualties. Where he could not go himself, he sent his auxiliary forces to reverse the advances that his adversaries made.

Sometimes Maubert stretched the definition of "strictly defensive," but many of these tactics were responses to moves of the enemy. On December 29 and January 6 he gave battle in Kofila and in Satiri to establish posts, and on January 10 in Bosora. Between January 14 and 23, when anticolonial forces besieged the canton chief of Kari in the ward of Lankuy (as they had laid siege to the chief of neighboring Wakuy two weeks before), Maubert attacked Dankari to draw some of the Bwa combatants away from Kari. Under the leadership of Kohere Tiano, the anticolonial fighters at Dankari killed 35 of Maubert's men and wounded 21, but lost 665 of their own.[10] Maubert was able to rescue the chief of Kari and escort him to Bobo-Dioulasso. Kari was besieged again a few weeks later, and the partisans dominating its Lankuy ward were not defeated until early June. On January 26, Maubert attacked Molokadon. Some time in mid-January, anticolonial partisans cut the telegraph line between Bobo-Dioulasso and Diebougou.

In Sambla country, a daring assault was organized against a colonial target on February 12 and 13. Approximately 1,500 men led by Sa-Kono attacked the post of Tiara, where the canton chief Si-Boro had a house. They set fire to Si-

Boro's house, but the village chief had alerted Si-Boro, who managed to flee to Bobo-Dioulasso. Some auxiliaries ran away, leaving their guns behind; 43 of them were killed. Today this attack is one of the best-remembered events of the war among the Sambla, and it was a major defeat for the government. After this success, the partisans cut the telegraph line between Bobo-Dioulasso and Sikasso. Northern Tusia villages showed support for the anticolonial Sambla, and the Tusia of Tusiana (southwest of Bobo-Dioulasso) left their villages to live in the bush, awaiting further developments.[11] Closer to Maubert's headquarters—only ten kilometers away from it—Lorofereso joined the anticolonial movement.

Facing an increasingly bold enemy, Maubert sent messages of alarm to his superior. He asked for men and authorization to engage in more repressive action, especially against the Sambla insurgents to the west of the city, who were far from the operation zone of the Molard column and out of its reach. On February 15, Maubert sent a telegram to the lieutenant governor in Bamako: "Need immediate action against Sambla rebellion that threatens to extend the movement to entire south and west and puts in danger the city of Bobo itself."[12] In a later telegram, he warned, "In case of an attack on Bobo-Dioulasso, it is not certain that its population will defend the city." He added that if his superiors refused "an action against the Sambla, which is the only way to prevent the rebellion from expanding to the west and south, it will be necessary to contemplate withdrawing from Bobo-Dioulasso."[13]

During this same period, the administrators of San and Koudougou were in the same predicament, and the chief of staff in Dakar, intent not to countenance the security needs of one cercle over another in this tight situation, for two months refused to grant Maubert's request. Some small leeway was given to Maubert. A company under Captain Amalric, on its way from Guinea to join the Molard column in Dedougou, arrived in Bobo-Dioulasso on February 18 (see p. 192). Maubert obtained authorization to detain the company for nearly two weeks so that it could participate with his guards and auxiliaries in some sorties he planned. The most important of these was on February 26—an attack on the Sambla village of Tukoro that left many dead among the defenders. On March 2, Maubert organized an expedition eastward to relieve the pressure on Kofila. He did not attack the base of Boho, but targeted smaller villages. He lost 7 men and had 18 wounded, but killed 140 enemy and wounded many more.

· The Amalric company left Bobo-Dioulasso on March 3.[14] It marched from Sara to Warkoy through a region at war and was constantly ambushed by Nienegue combatants. Mostly armed with bows and arrows, the Nienegue could not stop the company. Three important anticolonial war chiefs died in these ambushes, including the renowned Tembe, from the village of Maro. Farther north, in the cercle of Dedougou, the administration had not confiscated arms as Maubert did in Bobo-Dioulasso, the combatants who attacked Amalric used guns (p. 193). Amalric's company arrived in Dedougou on March 9, having spent a large amount of ammunition but with few casualties.

Maubert had wrested permission to keep forty of Amalric's soldiers in Bobo-Dioulasso, and in February he received reinforcements of auxiliaries from Sikasso and Koutiala. Now he had under him 50 guards, 40 mounted soldiers, and 1,800 auxiliaries and archers,[15] but as the conflict drew out, some of the auxiliaries either wearied and deserted to their villages or refused to obey orders.

The anticolonial forces kept the initiative, continuing to exert pressure on colonial posts by scheduling attacks in a variety of places.[16] On March 11, there was an important battle in the Sambla village of Surukudinga. The partisans, led by Si-Ju, had 140 people killed and numerous wounded; 2 colonial soldiers were killed.[17] This amounted to a massacre, but the Sambla organizers stepped up their attacks. On March 13 they sacked the Bobo village of Bama as punishment for providing food to the auxiliaries stationed in the post of Kumi. The movement was expanding southward. In mid-March, the Tusia villages of Banfulagwe, Gindie, Gwena, and Sidi—closely linked to the Sambla through exchange of shrines, kinship, and a military alliance in the 1890s against Tieba of Sikasso—openly joined the movement, as did Tien and the Tusia ward of the village of Peni a few days later (map 20).[18]

Maubert responded to this relentless thrust with exceptional energy. On the eastern and northern fronts, his feverish activity was still aimed primarily to keep the conflict away from the city, but the new reinforcements allowed him to step up his activities. His schedule for a few days in mid-March shows his nearly superhuman capacity for action. On March 13, the day Bama was attacked, he was in Wahani, some ninety kilometers northeast of the city on the road to Dedougou. The next day he attacked the mobile Bwa army near Kundugu, some seventy-five kilometers from the city on the road to Fo. On March 15, Maubert attacked Banfulagwe, fifty kilometers due west of the city, as punishment for Bama. On March 16, for a second time he attacked Lena, a Bobo-Ule village fifty kilometers due east of the city. In these four days he traveled at least 530 kilometers on horseback to give uninterrupted battle.

The anticolonial forces continued the pressure without respite. A few days after Maubert went to Banfulagwe, the inhabitants of this village marched against the canton chief Mango Traore, near the post in the village of Sidi on the Sikasso road. The chief and his men were able to drive them back and reciprocate

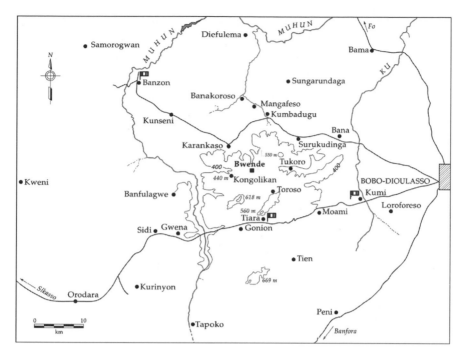

Map 20. Sambla and Tusia conflict zone.

by destroying part of Banfulagwe.[19] In the north, on March 21 forces combining local Bobo men and Bwa combatants from Dedougou attacked the post of Fo for a second time. It did not go well for them; they lost 206 men and had a large number of wounded, whereas the auxiliaries in the post had only 7 men wounded.[20] A few days later, another engagement took place in the northeast, in Wabara. In the south, a detachment of auxiliaries sacked Peni on March 26, but the chiefs of the two Tusia cantons of Gwena and Kwini—both appointed by Maubert in the administrative reform because of their supposed roots in the local population—were now completely isolated in a region swept away by anti-colonial mobilization. On April 3, anticolonial forces in the east organized an-other major assault against the post of Kofila, and the following day the villages of Kukuruma and Dorosiamaso declared for the anticolonial side.

In early April, Maubert's request for authorization to launch a grand expe-dition to squash the anticolonial movement in the Sambla-Tusia zone (map 20) was finally granted. This came at a time when Molard's first campaign in the cer-cle of Dedougou had ended inconclusively, and during its forced inactivity the anticolonial movement had become invigorated, spreading by leaps and bounds in San and Koutiala. Perhaps the colonial government had become receptive to

Maubert's argument that he could crush the poorly armed Sambla with the means at his disposal. On the horizon was the possibility of stronger connections between the Koutiala movement and the one to the west of Bobo-Dioulasso.

THE REPRESSION IN THE SAMBLA-TUSIA ZONE

Maubert set out against Sambla villages with a group of 58 guards (including 7 former tirailleurs), 358 mounted soldiers (60 of them equipped with breech loaders), 375 auxiliary soldiers with muskets, and 61 archers. He took with him about 19,000 cartridges, 250 kilograms of black powder, and 10,000 rounds of other ammunition. Instrumental in the success of the operation was the dispatch to Maubert of an 80-mm mountain cannon; he was sent shrapnel shells to dislodge people hidden in riverbeds and caves and explosive shells to destroy fortified houses. All the canton chiefs of the region accompanied Maubert as guides; these chiefs remained behind after their respective cantons were "pacified."[21] The interpreter Diaman Bathily was also part of the expedition.

Maubert approached Sambla country through the flat northern land, the southern region being protected by steep slopes. The decisive battle took place on April 6 in Maganfeso. The anticolonial combatants had chosen the location of the battlefield, and prisoners later told Maubert that Mori-fin Watara, the deposed head of state, had helped in the decision and had given firearms to the Sambla insurgents. Each Sambla village was represented with a contingent led by a war leader of their own, and these leaders are remembered today as heroes. People from Karankaso say that their men were led by Fie-Dubu, Fie-Kato, and Si-Sado Gegnie. Sambla forces as a whole were organized by Sa-Dagahuru and his companions. Maubert estimated that the Sambla had gathered four to five thousand men, many of them from Karankaso and its neighborhood. Having few guns, they were armed mostly with bows and arrows.

This battle shows the difference between the strategy of Marka leaders, who refused open-field confrontations, and the Sambla, who accepted it—a disastrous choice made worse by the disparity in armament between the two sides. Today some Sambla maintain that during the battle Maubert wanted to retreat but the canton chief Si-Boro dissuaded him. Maubert's diary gives a different picture. The battle was fierce, but lasted only an hour. In that short time more than eight hundred Sambla were killed and many more were wounded. Maubert reported: "They have many wounded as indicated by the ground that is stained with blood everywhere. In their flight—truly a rout—the rebels left behind large numbers of weapons: one musket and more than 400 quivers of reserve holding about 150 arrows each, whistles, and war horns, and even their drums."[22]

Although the Sambla weapons were no match for the breechloaders, they represented a gigantic production effort, even if most of the arrows were purchased, as they probably were. In one day, a blacksmith could forge at most fifty arrow tips. If we assume that the reserve quivers left behind represented half of the weapons that the combatants took to the battlefield, the part of the arsenal present at this engagement alone was the equivalent of several thousand workdays. Maubert attributed his quick victory to his rifles. After the battle, he used his cannon to destroy the wards of Maganfeso, which had been transformed into fortresses, and the village was burned to the ground. That evening, the neighboring village of Kumbadugu, whose inhabitants had fled, was also demolished.

The next day, Maubert's men attacked the central village of Karankaso, where they met little resistance. Most inhabitants had fled. Colonial forces quickly repelled a counterattack by a contingent of about one thousand men from the villages of Bwende and Toroso, again killing more than one hundred Sambla. Maubert noted that "the rebels had such confidence in their strength that they did not even think about removing their possessions. As a result, the losses for Karankaso are considerable."[23] Over the next two days, Maubert systematically destroyed Karankaso and all villages, agricultural encampments, and grain stocks within a radius of about twenty kilometers—the food reserve for the rest of the dry season and the approaching farming season.

On April 8, Maubert moved to the villages in the southern mountainous area of Sambla country. He attacked Bwende, Toroso, Kongolikan, and Tukoro.[24] The Sambla death toll in each incident was one hundred or more. The assaults ended with the systematic demolition and burning of the villages. On April 14, Maubert sent a party to attack and destroy the Sambla and Tusia villages situated south of the Bobo-Dioulasso-Sikasso road: Tiara, Gonion, and Tapoko. Again, enormous supplies of grain were destroyed, and, as had become routine, women were taken hostage. In precolonial years, captured individuals could be reduced to slavery and sold, but colonial administrators treated them as hostages who would be returned to their people once the villagers started to follow orders. On April 13 and 14, Karankaso, Diefulema, Kumbadugu, Banakoroso, Toroso, and Maganfeso surrendered to Maubert. Delegations from these villages brought great quantities of bows and arrows that they had hidden in the bush.

In spite of these formal capitulations, Sambla resistance continued. Sambla resisters—including people from the villages listed above—had taken refuge with their families, their goods, and their cattle on a rocky hilltop near the village of Kongolikan. Maubert attacked them on April 16 and met strong resistance. Two hundred Sambla died, and Maubert took hostage eighty-five women and children. The next day, Sembleni, Moami, and Tien surrendered. Part of the "booty" (Maubert's term) — cattle and other animals and Sambla leaders — was sent to Bobo-Dioulasso.

Maubert and the representatives of the Sambla villages that had not yet surrendered — Bwende, Kongolikan, Tukoro, and Surukudinga — spent the next three days in talks *(palabres)*. In spite of the extraordinarily brutal repression, the Sambla were still arguing and resisting unconditional surrender. Unhappy with the outcome of these talks, Maubert sent his men on April 20 to pursue the rebels in their hideouts. All four villages then capitulated and handed to Maubert large quantities of bows and arrows. Like the other Sambla villages, they were fined (the fines to be paid in cattle) and had to turn over their leaders. Maubert imposed further conditions that had been decided on by the government-general in Dakar to facilitate future French control. These obligated villagers to rebuild their houses as separate units with thatched roofs (a demand that was not met), to provide wide avenues in each village, and to dig wells at precise locations. Traces of these requirements still survive in today's village layouts.

On April 21, Maubert moved on to Tusia villages. Tiara, which is Sambla, surrendered. Between Tiara and Gonion, the column found the Bobo-Dioulasso–Sikasso road littered with the corpses of men and animals left there from the battles dating back to February. Maubert destroyed the villages that did not formally surrender. In Gwena, he met Tusia and Syemu delegations, including people from Tusiana and Takoledugu. Their attitude had previously been hesitant, but they now professed total support for the administration. Maubert's column returned to Bobo-Dioulasso on April 23.

Maubert reported that this campaign cost the column two lives and resulted in twelve hundred deaths for the Sambla and Tusia resisters. A final count of approximately two thousand deaths seems probable. Sambla villages and food reserves had been almost totally destroyed, and the high number of wounded undoubtedly led to many more deaths. The very reproduction of village life was threatened. A 1917 report recommended new population censuses for the Sambla and Tusia because the villages in some cantons had lost half of their populations: "The population, particularly from seventeen to thirty years old, underwent a worrisome decline in the districts that participated in the revolt. . . . The Semblas and Tousya districts . . . have been hit harshly in their adolescent population by the repression of the revolt and also by the recruitment of tirailleurs."[25]

Many people escaped to the west, across the upper course of the Muhun River, into what became in 1919 the new colony of Soudan (now Mali). Maubert executed the main Sambla leaders (including Si-Kugeka and Sa-Kono) and sentenced many to long jail sentences in Soudan and Senegal, from where they never returned. This left the canton chief Si-Boro with no opposition. But in spite of the formidable punishment inflicted on the Sambla and Tusia, pockets of resistance continued to exist for many more months. In January 1917, Maubert attacked Bure, a ward of the Sambla village of Bwende, which is still in ruins today. One hundred or so Sambla combatants, led by five Sambla leaders and by leaders from Lahiraso, had withdrawn to the bush, where they continued to operate as a band. They were captured after the rainy season in 1917—that is, about a year and a half later.[26]

Maubert's bloody campaign in Sambla country did not greatly improve the situation for the colonial government on the northern front. In April, under the leadership of the Marka leader Siaka, wards of the large village of Siankoro joined the movement. In late April, a few days after the Sambla campaign, a coalition of Bwa people from the cercles of Dedougou and Bobo-Dioulasso attacked and burned the small village of Kogwe near Fo.[27] By the end of April 1916, the official count of total losses in the cercle of Bobo-Dioulasso was, on the colonial side, 2 guards and 416 auxiliaries killed and fewer than than 200 wounded, and, on the insurgent side, 3,561 killed and a much larger number of wounded.[28]

THE HECATOMB OF BOHO

Maubert next turned to the Nienegue region in the east, hoping to achieve the same success there as he had with the Sambla and Tusia. This expedition was part of a larger plan and was coordinated with Molard's second campaign. While the Molard column was active near Bagasi, in the cercle of Dedougou, Maubert's was supposed to engage in a parallel campaign not far away, among the southern Bwa of the cercle of Bobo-Dioulasso.

He commanded essentially the same column as earlier: 55 guards, 14 former tirailleurs, 339 cavalrymen, and 351 auxiliaries. Maubert's campaign started on May 5, but because of the risks he took it was cut short by his superiors; it amounted to one major battle against Boho.

Maubert had not dared attack Boho before Molard's column came into the vicinity. Boho was defended by Bwa and Marka leaders and by combatants from all the villages of the cantons of Wakuy and Bereba—thirty-six villages in all. Besides the imposing walls, the surrounding terrain was prepared with great care to enhance the defenses.[29] The small pits dug around the village, lined with poisoned arrows, were only about two to three meters apart.

Maubert attacked on May 6. The Bwa fighters, who had few firearms, acted with utter contempt for their own lives. The initial shelling of the village walls inflicted unusually high losses to the defenders, who tried to fill the gaps created in the fortifications with their bodies, to no clear military benefit. The assault that followed the shelling of the village was driven back, provoking the flight of some of Maubert's men. Reinforcements of two groups of one thousand men each came to the help of Boho. Maubert's mounted auxiliaries panicked and refused to obey his order to attack these reinforcements without a preliminary shelling. The reputation of the town inspired so much fear that at midday, all but twenty-four auxiliaries had fled, and the cavalry remained prudently away from the battle site, leaving Maubert and his guards to take the brunt of the attack. The dangerous military situation and the shortage of water forced Maubert to call a retreat to the post of Kofila. During the night, the Marka and Bwa defenders evacuated Boho. Maubert returned the next day to demolish what was left of it. Then, as his men pillaged and burned the village, he discovered the reason for the abandonment of the village and the full measure of the preceding day's disaster for the defenders.

Maubert's men found that the seventeen collective tombs of the village had each been filled with hundreds of bodies of men, women, and children. In several houses, up to forty bodies had been piled up. A few hundred bodies had been carried outside the village. The defenders' losses were about three thousand. Among the people who had fallen were Kanda, the chief of Boho, and Digo, Niabati, and Beremave, who were the leaders of the movement in Dankari, Maro, and Boyere, respectively.

The battle of Boho stands out among all engagements in the entire colonial campaign of repression. There were more deaths on that day there than in any other single encounter. Nazi Boni wrote that the entire population of the village waited for the enemy in the village and bore the attack inside of it because the village elders had sworn not to outlive "the profanation of the 'land of the Ancestors.' Rather *Humu*—death—than *Wobamu*—slavery" (Boni 1962, 233). For the colonial forces, too, the losses (ten men killed and seventy wounded), though small compared with the massacre of the defenders, were higher than in other engagements. The battle could not be claimed as a victory for either side.[30]

Maubert's superiors blamed him for exposing himself to dangers that could have necessitated the diversion of troops from the Molard column to rescue him. That could have disrupted Molard's campaign plans in the neighboring cercle. In his defense, Maubert pointed out that this battle had pushed the line of insurgent villages back to more than seventy kilometers away from Bobo-Dioulasso. Maubert was ordered by the governor-general to end his campaign and return to Bobo-Dioulasso.[31] Two weeks later, the Molard column arrived in this same area of the cercle of Bobo-Dioulasso (see pp. 265–67).

FINAL CONFRONTATIONS AND THEIR SEQUEL

The Molard column left the Nienegue region in ruin, and yet the war continued for a few more months under the leadership of prominent local figures, most notably Plenza from Karaba.[32] Particularly active in this late resistance were the villages of Karaba, Hunde, Koho, Wani, Dohun, Tiombini, Pe, Boni, and Dosi. Maubert returned to the Nienegue area for an expedition that lasted from July 8 to July 17. People deserted their villages at the approach of colonial troops, and Maubert was able to obtain submission only of the village of Pe. He failed to capture Nienegue leaders. In late July, Maubert headed toward the southwest of Bobo-Dioulasso to attack the Tusia village of Tien.

As the eastern front collapsed, the main area of resistance shifted west of the Muhun River, an area especially inaccessible in the rainy season, when it was difficult to cross the swollen river and the many shallow ponds that form in its flood valley. Many Bwa and Marka combatants who had fled the repression of the Molard column and their destroyed villages in the cercle of Dedougou were welcomed by the mostly Bobo population of this region. Under their influence, in the vicinity of Siankoro, Fo, Lahiraso, and Badema, the war even intensified (see map 19).

In Molard's third and last campaign, his column visited the part of the cercle of Dedougou to the west of the Muhun River, reaching south to the northern sector of Bobo-Dioulasso, as far as Fo. Molard arrived in Fo in mid-July, at the same time that Maubert was leading his campaign in Nienegue country. The villages of the cantons of Siankoro and Fo submitted at the approach of the column. But once again, these acts of submission carried little meaning for the anticolonial combatants. The Bobo villages of Kiebani and Yelentoba surrendered to Molard, but later fired on porters of the column who were looking for food supplies. The column eventually destroyed these two villages.[33] The inhabitants of Yelentoba escaped to the cercle of Dedougou, only to return and ask for peace in September.

After his return to Dedougou, Molard detached a company in August 1916 to establish a post in Hunde, to supplement those of Bondokuy and Boromo. The troops stationed in Bondokuy and Hunde successfully broke up the last centers of resistance of the Nienegue in the east and also in the territories west of the Muhun River. The Bobo villages in the river valley—Bosora, Syoma, Molokadon, Lahiraso, Kimini, Jigwema, Badema, and Segere—surrendered at the end of the rainy season. On September 27, a detachment from the post of Bena (five kilometers north of Siankoro) captured seven important anticolonial leaders from the village of Kiebani in the canton of Fo. These leaders had been hiding in small villages atop the cliff that dominates that region. Following these arrests, many villages surrendered, but Kiebani still refused to submit.[34]

In the Nienegue region, the villages of Boni and Dosi also continued to resist. In September, Dosi even attacked a visiting colonial company.[35] In December 1916, the ward of Manduna in the Bwa village of Tiombini also refused to surrender, even though the major anticolonial fighting had been over for a few months.[36] These last resisters were attacked by troops from the posts established by Molard in the cercle of Dedougou, and by Maubert in the cercle of Bobo-Dioulasso. In February 1917, shortly before being removed from the cercle, Maubert launched an assault on the Bobo village of Lahiraso, which had surrendered in August 1916 but had taken up arms again since then. The colonial administration considered the defeat of this village the last incident of the war.

The central role of individuals in promoting the anticolonial war was not lost on the colonial administrators. They sentenced most of the leaders to long prison terms, and many of them died in jail. The chiefs that helped in the suppression were rewarded.[37] Some important figures of the anticolonial movement, called by administrators rebel murderers (rebelles-assassins), were sentenced to death because they had killed colonial representatives. Gwele was executed in Bobo-Dioulasso on September 6, 1919; Lamisa, from the village of Sara, was executed in 1920 because he had tortured to death two guards and eight auxiliaries who had tried to join Maubert in Bondokuy in December 1915. Lamisa was one of the last to be executed.[38]

While individual leaders of the movement were being eliminated, the communities that had been important military centers during the war were also heavily punished. In addition to paying their taxes, which had become much more difficult to raise in the new circumstances because of population loss and the destruction of property during the campaigns, heavy fines were imposed on them. In the communities most closely watched by the new military posts, the administration was able to collect these fines.

The conditions of surrender uniformly imposed on the villages also included, as we saw above, the rebuilding of villages to suit the French. Hubbell (1997, 280–83) writes that in the north of the cercle of Dedougou, an important program of village rebuilding was implemented in 1917 and 1918, although it has left little trace in oral memory: villagers later reverted back to the old style. In the cercle of Bobo-Dioulasso, the administration had great difficulty in having villagers comply with the building instructions. The population everywhere resisted, and remarks in the reports of following years show that only armed companies could coerce them to obey. The chronic shortage of personnel and the fear of provoking another uprising often led administrators in the direction of "leniency and flexibility," alternating with brief authoritarian shows of force. Moreover, the wide adoption by the colonial army of hand grenades made the invasion of blocks of contiguous houses easier, reducing the administrators' fear of the local labyrinthine architecture.

Another part of the program was to relocate villages from difficult-to-reach hilltops onto lower ground; and dispersed wards were consolidated into larger agglomerations near main roads. This latter measure was extended even to villages in the southern part of the cercle of Bobo-Dioulasso, which had not taken part in the war. When the administrator of Bobo-Dioulasso presented his program of relocation, he cautioned that the "task . . . will be arduous and unpleasant. It is not without some reluctance that we recommend means of intimidation and coercion, but we are convinced that no other method can be used with success."[39] For example, it took three years to convince the villagers of Kongolikan, in an area that had been beaten to submission by both Maubert and then the Molard column during the war, to move their habitations from a cliff to the plain below.

Commentators of the war have taken little notice that military conscription continued in the cercle of Bobo-Dioulasso in 1917, 1918, and 1919, which is surprising, given that some highly placed civilian administrators thought this was the cause of the anticolonial uprising in 1915. The compulsory enlistment of soldiers seems to have been used as another way to punish the rebels. In the 1917 conscription campaign, the subdivision of Hunde, which included the three insurgent Nienegue cantons, was made to give 311 enlisted men. Taking the colonial population figures, this comes out to one man for each 106 people, a rate of recruitment almost seven times higher than that of the larger central subdivision, which gave only 191 men, one for every 700 people. The Banfora subdivision gave none, presumably because there was no colonial military presence there, but it is worth noting that it had not taken part in the uprising.

Possibly, some of those enlisted in Hunde were war captives. In December 1915, as Colonel Molard was organizing his column, the lieutenant governor wrote, "Prisoners would make excellent tirailleurs. In the course of future operations we could make a great number of prisoners."[40] If it is true that the 1917 enlistees were partly or wholly selected from among the prisoners that Molard made in 1916, this would be an interesting throwback to the practices of the precolonial period, when the sofa of the local strongmen included a proportion of captured slaves.[41] In the massive 1918 recruitment campaign, for which the famous Blaise Diagne was brought on tour from Senegal, the disproportion in recruitment between different cantons was reduced, and in 1919 it turned to favor the Nienegue cantons.

One of the central concerns of the administration was to continue the disarmament campaign started by Maubert. It was scheduled to end in 1919, but it persisted for many more years. The cercle commandant blamed the profusion of muskets on the arms trade in the British Gold Coast, where it was legal, and on trade with the cercle of Sikasso, where there had been no disarmament campaign.[42] With time, the disarmament campaigns became less systematic and were conducted on an ad hoc basis during the relocation of villages or the visits of administrators to sensitive regions.

Sequels of the 1915–16 War were also felt in the disarray that struck the administration of the cercle. Following Maubert, in 1917 Bobo-Dioulasso had a quick succession of three administrators, Hummel, Muller, Froger, and then early in 1918 there was a fourth, Mornet—an extraordinary turnover even by the standards of West Africa. Commandant Maubert was replaced in March 1917 and transferred to Bamako to respond to various charges. Maubert's actions during the repression had been extremely bloody. His attacks had caused the greatest number of casualties of the entire war, not only among the enemy but among his own troops as well. On January 16, 1916, in Dankari, 665 enemy died on the battlefield, and 34 died and 21 were wounded among Maubert's own troops. The battle of Maganfeso on April 6 was nothing less than a massacre, and the attack of Boho was the single most murderous day of the entire war. Maubert was not summoned to answer for these wartime excesses, however, but for his abusive practices in times of peace and for irregularities in the trials that followed the repression. The nature of the charges against Maubert are indicative of the unquestioned acceptance of violence in the repression of resistance, and also of the desire to keep the violence of the anticolonial war out of the public eye.

The most serious charge against Maubert concerned the court judgment he passed on November 2, 1916, in Bobo-Dioulasso. In one hearing, seventy-two people had been charged with armed rebellion, incitement to revolt, and murder. Six people received death penalties, thirty-six were condemned to life imprisonment, and thirty others received prison terms. It was impossible, the central administration noted, to hear the seventy-two accused men—in addition to twenty-four witnesses—through the intermediary of an interpreter all in one day. One of Maubert's assistants denounced Maubert for allowing into the hearing confessions that the accused did not make and evidence that witnesses did not formulate; Maubert also, said his accuser, allowed the suspects to be beaten in order to obtain confessions from them or to prevent them from giving explanations.[43] The case against Maubert was dismissed in May 1918.

An atmosphere of intrigue beset the appointment of indigenous chiefs in the cercle after the departure of Maubert (see chap. 4, pp. 116–18). For many years, administrators operated in an atmosphere of fear that the fighting would resume. The acting lieutenant governor of Haut-Sénégal-Niger appointed in 1917, Louis Eugène Périquet, favored an iron-hand policy that was a far cry from the *apprivoisement* approach advocated before the Volta-Bani War. He argued that it was better for administrators to be seen as present everywhere, and not avoid contact with people: "We must give everyone the most vivid impression of our force, and show our most definitive intention to break down and punish in the most dreadful manner any impulse to revolt."[44] His successor Charles Brunet, the last lieutenant governor of Haut-Sénégal-Niger, adopted the opposite policy of extreme prudence. Administrative policy in the cercle of Bobo-Dioulasso reached a semblance of stability only with the establishment of the colony of Upper Volta in 1919 (see conclusion).

CHAPTER 9
The Pilgrim and the Shrines
The War in Koutiala, San, and Bandiagara

A NOTABLE FEATURE OF THE WAR around San and the neighboring areas of the two other cercles is that it flared up at a late date. Anticolonial activities reached their height in this cercle in April 1916, when the Molard column was immobilized in Dedougou for lack of ammunition, and continued on a high note until June, when refugees from the repression in Dedougou came to join them. The vigor of the movement forced the government to create a second column in San, modifying its original plan to focus its energies on the Molard column in Dedougou. Another striking incidence in San and Bandiagara was the participation of high-profile Muslims in the anticolonial side, made even more spectacular by the fact that they accepted a subordinate status in the overall movement, deferring to the non-Muslim leaders from Bona and their representatives in the secondary center of Sanaba. For these reasons, the organization in San and Bandiagara broadens our understanding of the character of the 1915–16 anticolonial movement.

Many links exist between San and areas east of the cercle of Koutiala, as well as part of Dedougou west of the Muhun River (see map 21), and for this reason this chapter considers the developments in these places together. The anticolonial movement began in the cercle of Koutiala much earlier than in the cercle of San. But further north, too—for example, in Sofara in the cercle of Bandiagara—Marka propagandists were spreading their message as early as December 1915. It took a few more months, however, and the adhesion of a few influential local leaders, for the movement to really take off in this cercle,

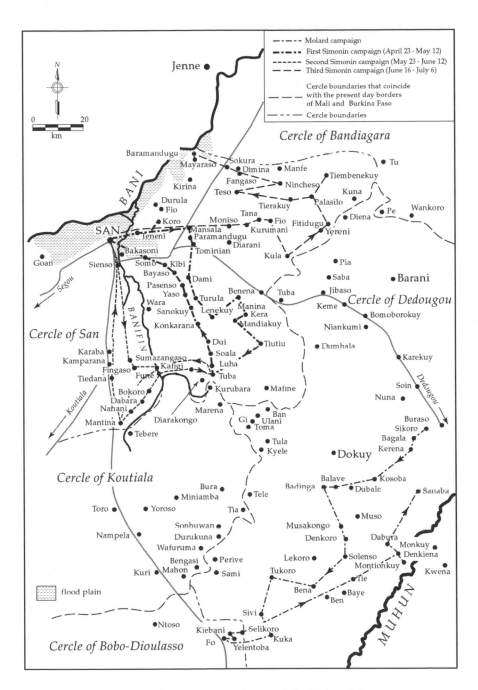

Map 21. San, Koutiala, and the region northwest of the Muhun River.

whereas in the eastern part of Koutiala, villages declared allegiance to it from the beginning.

The influence came to Koutiala from the mostly Bwa villages lying west of the Muhun River, in the cercle of Dedougou. The movement spread from Monkuy and Kwena to the area of Sanaba, Montionkuy, Denkiena, and Dabura. After the failure of the Simonin column in Yankaso in late December, it spread further west to the area of Solenzo. On June 18, the canton chief of Solenzo fled to Donkuy to take refuge with the procolonial Sangare. A few days later, the canton chief of Kuba also tried to escape to Dokuy, but he was stopped and killed in Bena, near Solenzo. In January it was reported that farther north, in the cercle of San, "numerous rebels from Dedougou make irruption." Large villages such as Mandiakuy and Tiutiu passed to the anticolonial movement.[1] Marka emissaries from near Bona found fertile ground in this entire region. A return to the events of the early colonial period will help in understanding how the lines were drawn.

RESISTANCE AND ACCOMMODATION IN THE EARLY COLONIAL PERIOD

To simplify a complicated ethnolinguistic situation, we can describe the territory lying between the Bani and the Muhun Rivers as inhabited by Bobo speakers in the south, Bwa speakers in the north, and Senufo speakers called Minyanka in the west. The city of San is situated at the meeting point of the last two populations. Marka and Fulbe communities are dispersed throughout the region. These ethnic labels do not indicate homogeneous categories. For instance, the Marka of the Bani valley have always been associated with Islam (Pageard 1961, 86), unlike the people called Marka within the bend of the Muhun River (see discussion pp. 78–80). Among the Fulbe, some converted to Islam only in the nineteenth century, influenced by the Qadiriya and the Tijaniyya Sufi orders propagated respectively by the religious and military movements of Seku Amadu and of Umar Tall (who displaced Seku's followers).

Many Fulbe pastoralist communities maintained peaceful economic relations with villagers, but a few Fulbe houses of military vocation influenced this history. In the late nineteenth century, three conflicting Fulbe war houses had settled in the region east of San: the Sidibe around Barani, the Sangare in Dokuy, and Amadu Abdul, the son of Ba-Lobbo (who was successor of Seku) in Fio, east of San.[2] After a long rivalry that split the Sidibe house, Adama Gnobo, known as Widi, a young man who belonged to the branch that lost power in its opposition to the partisans of Seku, returned to prominence in the 1880s as an ally of Tijani, Umar Tall's son, who was established in Bandiagara (see chap. 2, p. 61).

Widi settled in a place that he called Barani, from where he traded slaves and horses. He had clients as far as the Bobo villages of Satiri, Kuruma, and Kotedugu and in the Bwa villages of Yaho, Wakara, Bondokuy, and Warkoy, which in the late nineteenth century became the most important slave-trade market in the Volta region. The Sangare of Dokuy raided the communities on the western bank of the Muhun River and looted the Jula caravans, but their rival Widi was presumably on friendly terms with the Watara and Zara houses of the region of Bobo-Dioulasso.

All of these Fulbe centers had allies and enemies among the Bwa, Bobo, Marka, Dogon, and some Samo communities. In Barani, Youssouf Diallo (1997) was told that "they never made war against the local people to obtain their subjugation" and that "contingents of archers" from villages took part in Fulbe armies, supporting cavalry and infantry that consisted of captives. For example, the Marka of Tisi and the Bwa of Wanikoro supported Widi, but "the balances were extremely precarious . . . and everywhere the alliances contained the germs of their reversal."

In the early, quasi-indirect rule period of colonization, the French chose three heads of state: Widi Sidibe, of Barani, Amadu Abdul (son of Ba-Lobbo), of Fio, and Salum Sangare, of Dokuy; they also appointed a king of Masina — Aguibu, a son of Al Hajj Umar. When Aguibu and Widi quarreled over the right to collect taxes in contested villages, the dispute was arbitrated by Colonel Pineau, commandant of the Niger-Volta Territory. He drew a boundary to separate their territories, and this became the boundary of two cercles; it survives today as part of the international border between Mali and Burkina Faso. As for Fio, when a coalition of Bwa villages forced Amadu Abdul to take refuge in Dokuy, the French annexed his territory to Aguibu's Masina.

In 1905 these states were abolished and their heads demoted to the status of canton chiefs; they continued, nonetheless, to provide mounted auxiliaries to the colonial columns. Idrisa Sidibe (Widi's son) provided most of the cavalry for the Molard column (chap. 7), and as we will see below, Aguibu participated in the repression of the cercle of Bandiagara, and the Sangare proved a very helpful ally to the French in the southwest of the cercle of Dedougou.

The attitude of Bwa communities toward the French often depended on preexisting ties with these Fulbe centers.[3] The French used the city of San as a logistic base for their occupation of the Volta region in 1896, as they did again during the repression of 1916. The villages of Sienso, Teneni, Tominian, and Benena, had close ties with the Fulbe warlords and did not oppose the occupying colonial troops, but the villages farther south in the area of Tiutiu fiercely resisted them. In 1896, the French appointed Salum, of Dokuy, to fight these villages, and in 1897, Caudrelier, commander of the Niger-Volta region, organized a major punitive expedition against them (chap. 2). Important engagements took place in Tiutiu (with high casualties on the French side) and Mafine. The actions of various French missions and their African allies threw this region into a chaos that created a sharp spike in the raiding and trading for slaves (Hubbell 1997). Eventually, the French sacked all of these villages and made the largest of them canton headquarters. In 1916, these villages once again took a position against the French.

The turmoil started with World War I. The French arrested Burahima, the imam of Teneni, along with a few other clerics, for announcing the imminent massacre of all white people. A search of this man's house led to the discovery of portraits of the empress Augusta Victoria and of the crown prince of Turkey (see chap. 4, n. 9 p. 331). The secretary-general replacing Lieutenant Governor Clozel believed that this incident confirmed reports from Ouagadougou and Dori indicating a vast Muslim conspiracy, thus enabling Maguet and Haillot to pursue the affair of the marabouts.[4]

In 1915 and January 1916, violent opposition was rare, but widespread resistance occurred against the military conscription campaigns. In December 1915, the village of Fio refused to present recruits and resorted to arms; a colonial company was sent against this village (Michel 1982, 101). More commonly, people simply evacuated their villages and moved to the bush. In January 1916, in the Minyanka canton of Kamparana (southern San) recruiting agents found only empty villages.[5] In this volatile atmosphere, the news of the anticolonial successes in Bona was received with great hope and a leadership quickly emerged to direct the movement in the San region.

Farther south, where the borders of three cercles, Koutiala, Bobo-Dioulasso, and Dedougou met, the hilly landscape allowed some communities to escape the control of the administrators somewhat (chaps. 7 and 8). The permanent centers of opposition were the villages of the cantons of Kuri and Yoroso in Koutiala cercle, the village of Ntoso, in Bobo-Dioulasso, and the villages of Sami and Perive in Dedougou. From 1902 to 1904, a number of villages under the leadership of Ntoso had refused to pay taxes and chased away tax collectors. The political angle was less evident in other popular manifestations. A prophetic cult centered on a shrine in Ntoso urged people to sell their goods at lower prices and to reduce the amounts of bridewealth (bridewealth here, unlike in the Volta region, involves large resources), attracting visitors from far-off villages to make sacrifices on the cult shrine. In the following decade, several other incidents with colonial representatives occurred.

The year before the anticolonial war, government forces were drawn to this area again. In September 1913, the administrator of Bobo-Dioulasso, Georges Chéron, led a company that destroyed the village of Ntoso for insubordination. In April 1914, a column marched against the villages of Sami and Perive under the command of Cléret, the administrator of Dedougou and predecessor of Maguet. Cléret invited the village dignitaries of Perive to accompany him back to Dedougou "to see for themselves the workings of our institutions and the benevolence we express toward our subjects."[6]

Cléret had avoided a violent engagement against Sami and Perive, and this was considered a success by Lieutenant Governor Clozel, who had strongly advocated "domestication." In late 1914, the war in Europe made the apprivoisement policy increasingly difficult to apply: both military personnel and civilians were departing, and simultaneously there was the entry of new, forceful administrators in the cercles of Dedougou and Bobo-Dioulasso. Tension rose again, and one of the first actions of the new commandant in Dedougou, Edgard Maguet, was to organize, from November 1914 to January 1915, another military expedition against Sami, Perive, and neighboring villages.

The adjoining villages of the canton of Kuri and Yoroso were also unsettled. In November, four months after France declared war on Germany, Bokari Turumbo, a marabout from Kona, in the cercle of Mopti, who was engaged in trade on the Bobo-Dioulasso–San road, announced that the French had left Africa and urged people to stop paying taxes. He claimed that in Dakar he had seen the last Frenchmen embarking on a boat to join the war in Europe. According to Turumbo, the war had started because the French had not been able to pay for the weapons they had purchased from the Germans. Bokari was arrested and sentenced to ten years in prison.[7]

Bokari made this statement at a time of widespread resistance to military conscription in the cercle of Koutiala. In November 1914, the recruiting commission was able to gather only ten men in the canton of Yoroso, and they later escaped. Emerit, the only European aide of the administrator of Koutiala, was looking for the fugitives when he found himself besieged for two days in a house outside Nampela. He was saved by a goum from Koutiala and auxiliaries gathered by chiefs of neighboring cantons.[8] The chief of Nampela, who was involved in the action against Emerit, fled to Ntoso to elude pursuers. This was the occasion for the order given to Maubert, who had just arrived as new administrator in Bobo-Dioulasso, to go to this border region (chap. 4 p. 110). On his way, Maubert discovered that the whole northwest region of his own cercle (the Nanergue and Tagouara regions) was in a "state of insurrection."

The events in Yoroso resemble those of Bona a year later. According to Ernest Bleu, the commandant of the cercle of Koutiala, the rebellion had been "carefully premeditated." Combatants of at least nine villages, armed with firearms, had gathered in Nampela to wait for Emerit to kill him. Had they been successful, Bleu felt that the rebellion would have spread rapidly to the cercles of Koutiala and Bobo-Dioulasso. Why did it fail in Nampela and not in Bona, where preliminary events started in a very similar way? Part of the answer may be better preparation, the role of the Marka military perenkie organization, and the personal qualities of the leadership of the Bona alliance. When the anticolonial movement spread from Dedougou in 1916, the population of the region of Nampela and Yoroso joined it enthusiastically.

THE ANTICOLONIAL LEADERSHIP IN SAN AND NEIGHBORING CERCLES

The important center that spread the movement west of the Muhun River was the Bwa village of Sanaba. From there the movement went west to Koutiala and north to San. The leader Wane Faha and Batieri, the chief of Sanaba, acted as relays between Bona and the villages in the cercle of San. Dignitaries of the villages that joined the movement went to Sanaba to submit to Batieri, offering the traditional presents of a white chicken and a white sheep (Maïga 1937, 277). Valuable objects taken in battles were handed over to Batieri; some of these were sent all the way to Bona. This leadership role of Sanaba was a continuation of its position during the initial French occupation fifteen years before. In December 1901, too, "a wind of revolt" that had originated in Sanaba "blew all over Bobo [Bwa] country as far as Bangasi and Pa."[9]

News from Bona also spread in the north by emissaries from the canton of Datomo. These men arrived directly in the San region to announce that "force" was now on their side and to invite the population to join the anticolonial cause. The most active Marka emissary was a man named Dasa, who hailed from the vicinity of Bona. Dasa remained in the San region, where he served as a military commander. The French held him in high esteem for his "remarkable qualities of energy and tenacity."[10] Another important Marka leader, Nutie Kulibali, also exerted great influence in the region.

The outstanding Bwa counterpart to Dasa in the San region was Niaka Tera, from the village of Dami. Badiani Tera, the canton chief of Turula, later recounted that he joined the insurgents after a visit in Dami. There, a man called Dofini told him "that we had to replace our bonnets with the dafu because that headdress would make us stronger against the French, and that we should not fear the whites, as all those of the west had been killed."[11] Clearly, the emissaries from Bona promoted the dafu cord outside its area of origin as a sign of participation in the movement and as an object with supernatural properties. By emphasizing its magical dimension, they fetishized it to compensate for its lack of cultural significance in these foreign parts.

Dofini seems to have won over many canton and village chiefs to the movement, but he avoided positioning himself as an overt leader. Those he could not persuade, he tried to eliminate by whatever means available. In February, when the chief of the important village of Tiutiu refused to rally to the anticolonial movement, Dofini denounced him to a French officer in Benena as a perpetrator of the rebellion. The officer took fifty tirailleurs to Tiutiu where they shot at people who tried to flee and committed other acts of violence. The inhabitants of Benena followed the tirailleurs and pillaged Tiutiu. After that, the population of Tiutiu did join the anticolonial movement, and one of its first targets was Benena (see below).

Another important leader of the anticolonial movement in the cercle of San was El Hajj Adama Dembele. He joined the ranks of the movement in early March 1916 after being in contact with Marka emissaries from near Bona. Dembele, a Muslim cleric, lived in Kula (on the present-day Malian-Burkinabe border), where he exercised great influence on the canton chief. He had twice been a pilgrim to Mecca, and it is said that on his return from his last pilgrimage there in 1914, he had initiated contacts with influential Marka and Bwa leaders of his own region in preparation for a revolt against the French.[12] In March 1916, Batieri of Sanaba (who was not a Muslim himself) recognized Dembele as the leader of the war in the San region. Dembele carefully situated himself within the moral hierarchy of the movement. He first sent the traditional sheep and chicken to Batieri, who accepted the presents and in return encouraged Dembele's emissaries to wear the dafu, saying it would help to fight the French and would deflect French bullets. This agreement was followed by a visit by the Marka leader Dasa, accompanied by another Marka man, Konguri, to Dembele's residence in Kula. Tiekoroni Dembele, the chief of the canton of Kula, later recounted his first meeting with Dasa: "My father offered him hospitality. He told us that in Dedougou there were no more whites, Senegalese, or servants for the whites, and that the buildings of the residence had been destroyed."[13] Dasa made known throughout the country that Dembele would command the revolt in the north and that he, Dasa, would operate in the south. In April, Dembele sent to "the Marka of Bona" the conventional gifts that are made to a senior partner in the code of war ethics—an embroidered robe (*dulokiba* in Jula) and sixty-four hundred cowries—by the intermediary of Batieri of Sanaba. Batieri announced that from then on Dembele was his surrogate and that booty and presents in the region of San were to be forwarded to Adama and no longer to him.

One of the great achievements of the leadership in the cercle of San was the organization of an army of several thousand men whose different units corresponded to different geographical areas. The first attacks were directed against villages where guards and auxiliaries were stationed and against villages whose leaders had maintained their alliance with the French.

THE EARLY ANTICOLONIAL SUCCESS (FEBRUARY TO MARCH 1916)

The first major actions of the anticolonial movement in the cercle of San took place in February, at about the same time the Molard column set out from Dedougou for its first campaign. When Molard arrived near Monkuy on February 17, many villagers there chose not to engage his column and fled across the Muhun River to Sanaba, Dabura, and to Denkiena. The news these refugees brought was not at all discouraging because the formidable Molard column had been marching through abandoned villages and had had only one important success, in Pundu (chap. 7 p. 181). The first important actions of the anticolonial partisans occurred further north, in the cercle of San. The telegraph line between Dedougou and San was cut,[14] and on February 21 a force of several thousand combatants attacked the village of Luha.[15] Then the anticolonial fighters achieved a more substantial success on March 1 against Benena.

Benena was an important town. In the nineteenth century, Mose merchants had established an important market there, and it included Fulbe, Bwa, and Mose wards. In 1894, Benena had sided with the French, which earned it an attack organized by its important enemy Mandyakuy in alliance with Tiutiu, Tuba, and Dui (Dakono, 1976). The French made Benena the residence of the canton chief. Its former enemies were heavily represented in the anticolonial army of 1916, particularly Tiutiu, which had been pillaged in February by people from Benena after the French expedition provoked by Dofini's scheme. The anticolonial army—estimated at 6,000 men, one-third of them armed with guns—burned down the village, killed about 150 people, mutilated many others, and took captive a large part of the remaining population.[16] In July, the Molard column found Mose captives from Benena one hundred kilometers away in Kosoba, and on September 2, Bleu and Maguet brought back from villages bordering the two cercles 262 more women and children who had been taken captive in Benena.

Three days after their success in Benena, the anticolonial army attacked Tominian. Situated thirty kilometers east of San, this town had been transformed into a defensive post to protect the city of San. The French had placed the post under Verdier, a civilian commissioner for indigenous affairs. With fifteen guards and a force of auxiliaries, Verdier tried to organize the defense in a camp outside the village. The assailants consisted of approximately six thousand Bwa villagers.[17] They had come from the surroundings of Turula, Dami, Benena, Mandyakuy, and Tiutiu (Capron 1973, 105).

Before the assault, the guards, doubting the value of Verdier's defensive dispositions, withdrew into a compound of the village, leaving him with the auxiliaries. The attackers quickly overwhelmed the defense—most defenders fled—and Verdier was barely able to escape on his horse with the help of two guards and three auxiliaries. The assailants then attacked the guards and auxiliaries in Tominian, who defended themselves under the leadership of the formidable canton chief Mama Diasana. After he was killed, the anticolonials took the village by storm and seven of the fifteen guards were killed. Ibrahima Maïga writes that "the clothes of the dead were removed, their left hands severed and circulated as trophies; the weapons that were seized were sent to the chief of Sanaba" (Maïga 1937, 278–80). Mama Diasana's left hand was sent to Sanaba with his gun and his saber. Under the orders of Niaka Tera, the mutilated bodies were hung on a baobab tree at the entrance of the village. A few days later, on March 9, the chief of the village of Bakosoni, only a few kilometers from San, was taken to Dami because he had refused to join the anticolonial fighters. There he was killed by Niaka and Nutie and his body was displayed on a mound near the village.[18]

An anecdote related to the battle of Tominian illustrates how support for the anticolonial movement found followers in this region even among local employees of the administration. An assistant to the telegraph operator of Tominian had disappeared with a case of equipment during the attack of the town. The colonials feared that he might have been killed. A few days later he appeared in the evening at his compound in San to persuade his wife to join him and the insurgents in the bush. His wife refused to go with him and they had a loud discussion. Fearing capture, the man ran away, but he was pursued and eventually caught, wearing no clothing. A search of his house yielded a newly made war fetish and a dafu headdress (Maïga 1937, 279). The man probably believed that his nakedness would make him invisible. The account by Maïga, a local schoolteacher, reveals the colonial view of the contrast between salaried employee in European dress and naked warrior with his charms and obscure rituals, as well as horror at discovering the first having changed into the second.

The growing daring of the anticolonial movement displayed in the attack of Tominian inspired solidarity and awe in the rest of the population. The anticolonial movement seemed to be in total control of the right bank of the Bani River as far as the border of the cercle of Bandiagara. The administrator of San, Jeannet, went with a party to look for Verdier and get him safely to San. Recruitment of local auxiliaries became extremely difficult even in other parts of the cercle where there was no organized opposition. In early March, most auxiliaries recruited by the canton chief of Goan in the west of the cercle fled before they reached San. To avert the collapse of the city, all the guards, auxiliaries, weapons, and ammunition available in Segou, Bandiagara, and Jenne were sent to San, and a detachment arrived under warrant officer Goudelou.[19] Administrator Jeannet and Inspector Vidal—who was held up in San while on his way to Dedougou for the official mission of inquiry into the origins of the crisis— organized the defense of the city with the reinforcements and with the tirailleurs, guards, and auxiliaries already there. They made contingency plans for evacuation toward Koutiala.

The village of Sienso, only seven kilometers from San, was the advance base of the anticolonials, and Goudelou and Jeannet thought that the troops gathered in San were now sufficiently strong to take this place. This judgment was based on Goudelou's past experience and involved a mistaken assessment of the movement that had already led to a series of defeats in the cercle of Dedougou.

Goudelou attacked Sienso on March 9 with a force of forty tirailleurs, reinforced by mounted auxiliaries. He inflicted heavy losses on the combatants. The Fulbe mounted force killed at least two hundred people who were trying to escape the village (Michel 1982, 104). Yet under the leadership of the village chief, Kabaye Traore, assisted by Mukoro Traore from the village of Somo, Sienso offered extraordinary resistance: Goudelou was killed during the fighting, one of the few French military to die in the Volta-Bani War, and Bamana auxiliaries and even tirailleurs deserted the battlefield. Marka leaders were able to claim the battle as a victory.[20] Goudelou's handgun and rifle were paraded as trophies in villages that had not yet taken sides in the conflict, and many (including Lere, Kanoni, and Kansere) decided to join the anticolonial side.

The battle of Sienso was the movement's first confrontation around San with regular colonial troops and strengthened the military situation in its favor. In response to this unexpected extension of the movement, the government-general decided that a second large expeditionary force had to be built in the region. In mid-March, a detachment of sixty-four tirailleurs and two French officers was detailed from Kati to reinforce the defense of San. However, most remaining troops available in West Africa were stationed in Senegal and would not be able to reach San for many weeks. Unexpectedly, reinforcement came in the second half of March, from Dedougou, where the Molard column was waiting for new supplies and ammunition. Molard detached two companies under Carpentier's command to meet in San with the Stefanini company that was expected to arrive from Saint Louis, Senegal, by way of Bamako, with supplies.

The Carpentier column was a considerable force.[21] Columns of similar size had been sufficient to repress the 1915 Beledougou revolt and later the 1916 opposition in the Borgou region of Dahomey. Yet Carpentier avoided the direct road from Dedougou to San controlled by anticolonial forces. He opted for a more northerly course, through Barani, home of Idrisa Sidibe.

Barani had become a refuge for colonial partisans in the region. Past Barani, the Carpentier column fought its way through an uninterrupted series of attacks (in Saba, Tuba, Koro, and Sadinian). The Marka leadership had spread the word that the Carpentier detachment was a remnant of the main Molard column that had been defeated by them; it was trying to escape to San and should be stopped at all costs. In some cases, the Marka and Bwa warriors simply blocked the road to stop the column, acting as if victory was beyond doubt; however, they were decimated by gunfire. When Carpentier finally arrived in San, he discovered that the Stefanini company was not yet there. At the request of the lieutenant governor, Carpentier's detachment was sent to the southern part of the cercle of San to assist in the effort to contain the westward expansion of the movement in the cercle of Koutiala that administrator Bleu had carried out by himself for the past month.

A STOPGAP REACTION: THE CARPENTIER COLUMN

Most villages in the eastern part of the cercle of Koutiala that were close to the border with the cercles of Dedougou and Bobo-Dioulasso had taken up arms in early February, under the influence of the news of the war in the cercle of Dedougou and urged by their Bobo neighbors of Perive (see map 22). Commandant Bleu set out a line of small defensive posts to stem the movement's advance,

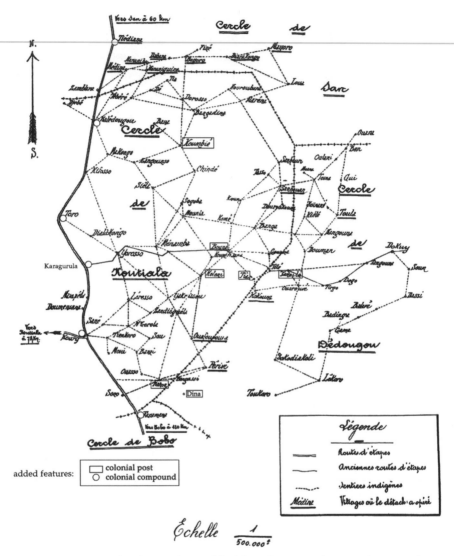

Map 22. Eastern cercle of Koutiala. Modified from "Rapport du Sous-Lieutenant à titre temporaire Grégoire . . . sur les opérations effectuées par le détachement du 9 Février au 5 Septembre 1916," Kati, October 1, 1916 (SHAT 5 H 196).

but they were quickly absorbed into the war zone. In March, the telegraph line between San and Koutiala was cut, and a group of men twice attacked a village used as a post by auxiliaries, killing many each time. Anticolonial combatants from villages of the cercle of Dedougou and of Koutiala converged in the village of Sonhuwan (in the cercle of Koutiala) to attack villages of the canton of Mini-amba (also in the cercle of Koutiala) who had refused to join them.

Bleu attacked Wofurma, Perive, and Bangasi with his guards and auxiliaries. When he was stopped in Sanhuwan he called to his aid the tirailleurs of the recruitment commission. In early March he received more reinforcements from Kati, which allowed him to form a small company under Second Lieutenant Grégoire.[22] He also provided ammunition to the Fulbe of Dokuy, who in mid-March raided villages in the Tele and Tia area, on the border of the cercles of Koutiala and Dedougou. In one documented engagement, this group from Dokuy killed 150 people.[23]

To help Bleu, late in March the governor sent the Carpentier column south to Minyanka country. The villages on the borders of the cercles of San, Koutiala, and Dedougou, which were being used as bases by the anticolonial forces of Minyanka, Bobo, and Bwa, had not yet been attacked by the colonial soldiers; the ones on the Dedougou-Koutiala border were too strong (in Kyele, for example, on the Dedougou side of the border, men from sixty villages had gathered). Carpentier avoided this zone and followed instead the road that led straight south and then forked toward the cercles of Koutiala, on one side, and Bobo-Dioulasso, on the other. On March 22, he destroyed the Minyanka wards of the leading villages Karaba and Kamparana (see map 21).

The most serious engagement took place the next day, in the village of Tiedana, where combatants from the entire region had gathered, most of them armed with guns. In spite of heavy artillery shelling three costly assaults were necessary to penetrate the village, and it took the whole day for Carpentier to gain control. He wrote in his diary, "[The village's] defensive organization is perfect. There is not one alley or passageway not covered by several loopholes. One has to set the siege to every single house, making progress through cavities opened in walls. At dusk, the rebels held on to only one house, from which they escaped at nightfall."[24] Seven tirailleurs were killed, and two officers and thirty-one tirailleurs were wounded. The people who defended the village suffered a heavy death toll, including the chief of the village and his sons.

The overall military situation did not change much with Carpentier's activities. His destruction of a few centers of resistance did not upset the broader regional organization of the anticolonial movement. Some of the men who fought against Carpentier had come from as far north as the cercle of Bandiagara. In fact, the French had hoped only that this expedition would divert the attention of the insurgent Bwa and Marka villages until the second column could be constituted to campaign in the cercle of San, meantime allowing the Molard column to continue its task in the cercle of Dedougou.

That the anticolonial leadership, despite their remarkable organization, could not match the logistical and technological support enjoyed by the French became evident when more important reinforcement started to arrive in San. The company commanded by Lieutenant Stefanini arrived on March 24 after a forty-five-day journey from Saint Louis, in Senegal. It included more than two hundred tirailleurs, a dozen French officers, and a machine-gun platoon;[25] it also brought much-expected food, ammunition, and medicine for the Molard column. A few days later, another company (13 French officers and 250 tirailleurs), under Captain Megnou, arrived in San from Dakar.[26]

The Megnou company had left Dakar on February 2, and their two-month journey shows how lack of transport infrastructure slowed down the colonial administration's response. The Bamako railway existed only up to Kayes, and for large-scale transportation to the inner savanna, the French depended essentially on waterways, which were low in this season. The 263 men of the Megnou company had traveled from Dakar to Conakry by steamboat, then taken the train to Kurusa on the Niger River, where they boarded thirteen barges and two dugout canoes for a nine-day trip downriver to Bamako, then four more days to Segou. There the company recruited 920 porters and finished its journey to San with a six-day march.

The Carpentier column left San to return to Dedougou, 220 kilometers away, on April 1, reinforced by the Stefanini company, the machine-gun platoon, and the Megnou company, and accompanied by Chief Inspector Vidal. A trail of blood marked the eight-day journey back to Dedougou. Many villages, some of them already attacked by Carpentier on his way to San, were burned down. One such village was Tuba. Combatants ambushed the column just outside the village, and after battling them Carpentier found in the village some of the wives of the chief of Benena, captured when anticolonial forces had sacked Benena on March 1.

After Tuba, the column encountered people from Mandyakuy and Tiutiu waiting to attack it in the open field. It took only a few minutes for the column's machine gun to cause enormous losses in their ranks. Similar engagements took place in Keme (where Idrisa Sidibe joined the column with the chief of Keme, who had sought refuge in Barani), in Ulani, in Karekuy, and in Biri. In this area, unlike in the Volta region, the anticolonial combatants chose to fight outside of their villages, perhaps because of a more heterogeneous leadership. More than a thousand anticolonial combatants, coming from all over the region west of the Muhun River, fought in some of these battles, and at least a hundred anticolonial warriors died in each engagement. In all, the column lost eleven men; the anticolonial forces suffered a thousand fatalities.

The succession of massacres did not diminish the resolve of the anticolonial combatants. In late June, almost three months later, some of the villages that had been attacked by Carpentier defied an important company of 160 tirailleurs that escorted back to Segou wounded and sick soldiers and French officers, including Ozil, Colonel Molard's assistant. The inhabitants of Niankumi blocked access to the wells inside their village, declaring that they were still determined "to make war against the whites." They attacked the soldiers, then dispersed into the countryside. In retaliation, the company burned the temporary straw roofs that had been built in place of flat adobe roofs destroyed in Carpentier's attack. A frustrated Ozil reported that there was nothing else left to burn;[27] the French military had no solution other than demolition. But leaving behind them villages in ruin, they were still denied victory.

THE CERCLE OF BANDIAGARA

In late March, Adama Dembele had developed a large following in the northern part of the cercle of San and in the Bwa and Marka villages of the cantons of Fakala and Bobo-Fakala, in Bandiagara (map 24). It was mostly non-Muslim people who followed this Muslim cleric, twice a pilgrim to Mecca. Dembele did not in any way try to suppress the rituals and power objects of his followers. The situation in this area is one of the clearest examples showing that the anticolonial coalition was based on the shared political goal of ending French presence, and not on a common religious or ethnic identity.

In the important market town of Sofara on the Bani River, Marka emissaries had been advocating fighting the French since January 1916.[28] But only when Dembele stepped in did the movement become dominant, bringing trading activities to a halt.[29] Sanibe Kamate, a Muslim Marka, who was the charismatic chief of the canton of Bobo-Fakala, joined Dembele's cause in the first days of March, assuming leadership of the movement in the cercle of Bandiagara.

Dembele reproduced within the region the hierarchical organization expressed by sacrificial rituals and gifts that linked him and the other leaders of the San region to the leadership of Bona.[30] In mid-March, Dembele and his entourage had concluded an alliance with village leaders in the cercle of Bandiagara that was consummated by slitting the throat of a white sheep placed on top of a bull and by successive gifts of seven thousand, seven hundred, seventy, and seven cowries. Curses were called down for ten generations upon the first village that would surrender to the French. Dembele also spread the use of the headdress of *da* (Hibiscus) fiber worn by the Marka of the Bona region; he did,

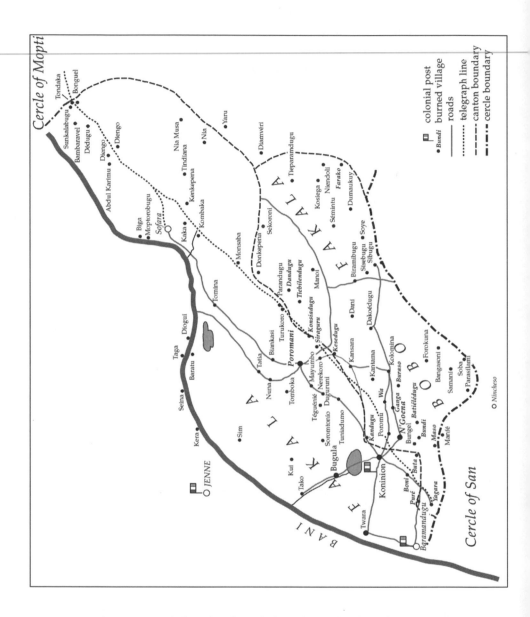

Map 23. The cantons Fakala and Bobo-Fakala in the cercle of Bandiagara. Redrawn from "Compte-rendu sur les opération de police du Cercle de Bandiagara du 27 Mars au 29 Juillet 1916," L'Adjudent-Chef Puget, Sofara, July 31, 1916 (SHAT 5 H 196).

however, transform it into a helmet-like head covering on which hung a false beard, made of the same material. The adornment was supposed to confer invulnerability on warriors by causing colonial troops to flee and by preventing their guns from firing.

Under the directive of partisans from the cercle of San, the telegraph line between San and Bandiagara was cut. Kamate refused to collect the colonial tax due at that time of the year and instead exhorted people to join the war. Each village in the cantons of Fakala and Bobo-Fakala was asked to send a few combatants as reinforcements to the anticolonial units gathered in the cercle of San. Most of these men died in the battles with the Carpentier detachment. Kamate attempted to draw Fawtier, the commandant of the cercle of Bandiagara, and his guards into an ambush by sending an urgent call for help, claiming that he had almost been killed by the insurgent inhabitants of the Bwa village of Parasilami, near the San border. This was the first of many instances of deceit that characterized the conflict in the cercle of Bandiagara. Kamate was actually in Sofara, telling people that "the white man would never see" the tax money from his canton; those who paid the taxes were fools, he added, because "we are going to throw the whites out of the land." Uncommitted people had to assess the balance of forces quickly, and choose a side.

Administrator Fawtier, receiving Kamate's letter on March 17, immediately dispatched twelve men, all the guards that were available at the time, to the region of Poromani, a large Marka and Fulbe village about twenty-five kilometers south of Sofara, in the canton of Fakala. He also assembled a small company of Tukulor auxiliaries from Bandiagara and, with four more guards, on March 20 himself went to Sofara. He found the town in turmoil. Most Marka and Bwa villages of the cantons of Fakala and Bobo-Fakala had joined the anticolonial movement, while the Bamana were staying in their villages, and the Fulbe herders were crossing the Bani River with their cattle to seek safety in neighboring Jenne. The chief of the canton of Fakala, whom Fawtier had charged with recruiting auxiliaries, had been able to enlist only fifteen men; these were sent as reinforcements to Poromani. With auxiliaries also being recruited in the Dogon cantons of Seno Togol, Barasara, Bankas, Ende, Guinini, Tongurury-Bonzon, Timiniri, and Pignary-Maku, as well as the Fulbe canton of Gondo-Senso, Fawtier asked the lieutenant governor to quickly send a detachment of tirailleurs to the cercle.

Kamate's ploy seemed to work in the beginning. While Fawtier was waiting in Sofara for reinforcements, the guards and auxiliaries sent to Poromani found themselves besieged by anticolonial forces. About four hundred combatants armed with guns and bows and arrows had gathered in Konsiadugu, some four kilometers away; six hundred others were in Kesedugu. The inhabitants of Poromani informed them about the colonial presence in the village. In the following weeks, military information was regularly fed to the anticolonial fighters by porters and even fighters in the colonial camp; on the colonial side, Fawtier resorted to "political agents" and prisoners to spread misinformation. Just before the attack on Poromani, Fawtier was able to send his guards a reinforcement of thirty-one horsemen.

The two base camps of anticolonial fighters had planned a joint attack on Poromani, but on March 25 the four hundred combatants in Konsiadugu attacked Poromani by themselves, without waiting for those at Kesedugu. After two hours of furious battle, the assailants withdrew, leaving at least one hundred dead. On the colonial side one guard and one auxiliary had been killed. The war in the cercle of Bandiagara could have taken a different course if one thousand instead of four hundred Bwa and Marka had participated in this attack and had been able to take Poromani.

The next day, Fawtier himself went to Poromani, where he received the reinforcements he had been waiting for. The goumiers who had been sent earlier to defend San returned to join him, and more guards and goumiers arrived from the Dogon areas. The detachment of tirailleurs that he had requested from the lieutenant governor also arrived. This gave him another 2 French officers and 29 men, and although some of these soldiers were very inexperienced, Fawtier and Puget, the senior warrant officer in charge of the tirailleurs, now commanded 313 well-equipped men.[31] Tijani Tall, a son of "King" Aguibu of Masina (who had died in 1908) and nephew of his namesake Tijani Tall (Umar's son), commanded the Tukulor goumiers. As his illustrious grandfather had done, Tijani Tall was going to fight over the Fakala region, and like his father he was fighting for the French, albeit as simple auxiliary, not as "king."

In the aftermath of the attack on Poromani, the people of the region had evacuated their villages. The men had sent many women to the cercle of San, and fighters gathered in the village of Kesedugu. Fawtier burned empty villages (Siraguru, Tiebilindugu, Danduguni, and Turukoro), where he found great quantities of telegraph wire woven into clubs. On April 1, Fawtier attacked Kesedugu (map 24), whose chief was one of the main leaders of the anticolonial coalition.

Approximately 700 warriors from the villages of the cantons of Bobo-Fakala and Fakala defended Kesedugu. Most of the defenders were armed with guns and wore the dafu in the modified form espoused by Al Hajj Adama Dembele. They arranged themselves in a double-line formation outside of the village, lying on the ground in a shooting position, under the command of men standing up behind them. As Fawtier's forces advanced, the anticolonial partisans tried to

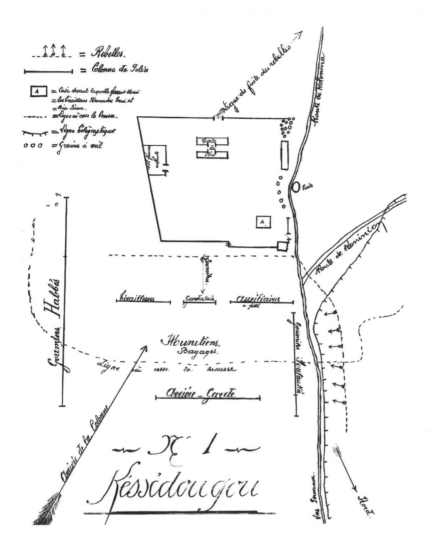

Map 24. The attack of Kesedugu. "Rapport de l'Adjudent-Chef Puget" Baraman-dougou, September1, 1916 (SHAT 5 H 196).

surround them but, failing, they slowly retreated inside the village. Seeing this formation and tactics, Fawtier thought that the insurgents had been trained by former tirailleurs. After a four-hour-long battle, most surviving defenders were able to escape the village in spite of Fawtier's order to the goumiers to pursue them. The latter, too frightened to engage in such a chase, were much more interested in pillaging. A few defenders remained inside the village and fought until the last man. The anticolonial fighters lost more than 200 men. Fawtier's troops used 7,800 cartridges, and here, as in Konsyadugu, the amount of ammunition available to colonial forces was probably responsible for their success.

The defeat suffered by the Bwa-Marka coalition in Kesedugu disoriented the organization of the fight against the French in that region. After burning several deserted villages in the area,[32] Fawtier moved on April 1 to the large village of Koninion, which under the canton chief of Fakala had remained on the French side. The colonial troops used Koninion as their base of operations until April 19. Koninion was strategically located near already demolished important anticolonial villages and also only ten kilometers from the village of Twara (home of the Bozo, fishermen of the Niger system) on the Bani River, which could offer a retreat in case Fawtier needed it (map 23). On April 4 he received further reinforcements: Dogon auxiliaries and a few guards arrived from Sanga with a large quantity of ammunition, guns, and powder. On April 7, Sanibe Kamate surrendered to Fawtier and this was followed by the submission of a few villages.

The day Fawtier moved to Koninion, Casanova, the administrator of Jenne, was trapped with a handful of guards and partisans in Baramandugu, a Bwa village on the Bani River with a large Marka population that had transformed it into an important market center. Casanova sent a distress signal. Fawtier's reserve of ammunition was insufficient to allow him to relieve his colleague, and he called on Captain Megnou's company, which had just been sent to San to ensure the communication between Molard and Bamako. The Megnou company had arrived in San only the day before and was exhausted. It set out again on April 2 with administrator Jeannet of San and two hundred locally recruited partisans to rescue Commandant Casanova. En route, Megnou had clashes in Fio and in Mayereso, but anticolonial partisans reoccupied Mayereso as soon as the colonial troops left.

The north of the cercle of San harbored large numbers of anticolonial fighters. At the village of Fangaso, near Mayereso, there were two thousand, and another important gathering was at Dimina (see map 21). The Dimina forces were pressuring the villages of the cercle of Bandiagara to continue the fight against the French. Megnou and Fawtier visited this area again, but lacking a cannon, they chose to retreat without engaging Dimina. Megnou obtained the submission of a few villages, and he returned to San on April 13 with hostages, but most of his opponents had escaped to the bush. Although Baramandugu was relieved, Megnou was skeptical about the value of the submissions he had received, and this feeling, plus his reluctance to attack the reinforced villages without artillery support, were signs that the situation was still totally different from the customary troubles of a colonial administration. The resolve of the people was so strong that when the inhabitants of the Bwa village of Durula learned that the Megnou detachment was approaching, they destroyed their village before abandoning it.

Meanwhile, Fawtier's campaign had been partly successful. The telegraph line was repaired, and market activities in Sofara slowly resumed, but the anticolonial movement had not yet been crushed in the southern tip of the cercle of Bandiagara. When Fawtier returned to Sofara, he was replaced by Cornet, who had been appointed commandant of Bandiagara a few months earlier. The new administrator organized the small number of auxiliaries at his disposal into cavalry groups capable of rapid movement, placing them under the command of his aide Barrietty. In April, Barrietty conducted short campaigns out of the cercle of Bandiagara to the northeast of the cercle of San, near Kuna (straddling the present-day Burkina-Mali border). He also operated farther east, around Wankoro (see map 21). This is also a border region for Dogon and Bwa people who live side by side, in the same village or in neighboring villages and it is a region heavily populated by Marka people (Capron 1973, 61–64). The administration was concerned that the movement might spread north to the Dogon throughout that region.

In the attack on Kuna, the auxiliaries retreated in panic, leaving the remaining colonial forces in difficult straits. Barrietty and his guards were able to turn the situation around and Kuna lost ninety-two combatants, whereas the French had ten dead and twenty wounded. In spite of their heavy losses, the anticolonial combatants maintained control of the Kuna area after Barrietty's departure. Barrietty returned to the area between April 11 and 16. He attacked the villages of Diena, Se, and Gra—three important centers of the anticolonial movement—provoking the dispersion of the Marka and Bwa combatants into mountainous areas.

Farther east, near Wankoro, villages attached to the cercles of San and Dedougou had also joined the war against the French, even though the Molard column had marched through Wankoro in early February on its way from Kati to Dedougou. One of the main centers of opposition in this region was Tiu. Barrietty moved his men into that area out of fear that the movement would spread to the neighboring Fulbe and Dogon villages, which had so far been quiet.

ANTS INTO WARRIORS: TRADITION AND ISLAM IN THE ATTACK OF KORO

The anticolonial forces organized their major offensive in the region of San against the Marka village of Koro (see map 21). Koro, only twelve kilometers from San, had refused to join the movement. After the fall of Tominian, the village had received a great influx of Fulbe and Marka refugees uncommitted in the conflict. A large number of auxiliaries defended Koro.

The anticolonial assault took place on April 19. Maïga (1937, 284) describes the organization of the anticolonial army, its multiethnic composition, and its religious pluralism. All the great Bwa and Marka anticolonial war leaders of the region were present. The famous Dasa led the attack, but contingents from different regions had their own leaders. Assisted by Tahiru Dembele (a son of El Hajj Adama Dembele), Yerike Dani, a Bwa leader from the eastern part of the cercle, headed the Marka of that region. Yabaso Dembele led the men from the north, which included a few Mose, Bwa, and Dogon people. The great leader Nutie Kulibali, assisted by Badiani Tera (the canton chief of Turula) commanded the people from the south.

Whether accurate or not, the account that Badiani Tera provided later to his French captors gives some idea of the moral persuasion of the combatants and of the pressure exerted on them by those advocating the war. Marka and Bwa emissaries had advised Badiani Tera

> [to] hit tamarind trees with a stick and warriors would come out of them, that if we encountered ant hills and hit them with a stick warriors would come out of them. They also said . . . that we should expel from the village all the people who had been designated chiefs by the French and put them to death because they were toads [the author of the report inserts a note here to explain that these Bwa have as a fetish the hornbill, which feeds on toads]. Nutie told us that we would march against Sanu [the city of San] where there are still a few whites and that we will capture them and have fun with them.
>
> When we came near Koro [to attack the town] I told people to stop. I took a war club and hit a tamarind tree. I hit an anthill, but in vain—warriors did not come out. I said then that what we had been told was not true since I had just hit a tamarind tree and an ant hill three times, all in vain. They replied that it would be impossible for me to bring out warriors, because I, Badiani, was a toad.[33]

The battle began around 9:00 A.M., and near 2:00 P.M. the besieged forces in Koro started to retreat. Last-minute help came from San, and with that the assailants—who were about to win—retreated in panic. The battle left hundreds of dead on both sides. Maïga's description of the attack brings out the startling blend of Islamic and non-Islamic cultural elements among the partisans:

> Around 6:00 A.M. the rebel army took position in a wooded area and was organized into four lines. One could make out a forest of spears, guns, clubs,

bodies that were naked or covered with vegetal fiber, birds' feathers that undulated, or porcupine quills placed in braided hair. . . . In order to take the village more easily, a chicken with amulets hanging on its neck was thrown in the direction of the mosque. Then the rebels shouted in unison: "We defeated the French in Tominian. The white who commanded the garrison fled to San! The great Mama [Mama Diasana] reputed invulnerable and invincible . . . has been killed." . . . They sang loudly as they whirled around: "Demeno, father and master of the universe, help us; our corpses must resuscitate in the next rainy season! [possibly a reference to the dafu headband] . . . Koro, god of war, to whom we continuously make offering! Koro, king of the genies and angels, help us. Destroy the village of Koro that bears your name but in which some inhabitants betrayed you by converting to Islam." . . . Dasa had decided that he would drink mead in the mosque. (Maïga 1937, 284)

What is of particular relevance here is that, although a son of El Hajj Adama Dembele served as a section commander in the attacking army, another commander in that army felt unconstrained to declare that the mosque was his target and that he intended to profane it in the most provocative symbolic manner by consuming alcohol in it. Side by side with the amulets, non-Muslim fighting lore was prominently displayed: the invocation of Koro; the naked bodies; the birds' feathers; the porcupine quills that are among the paraphernalia of cult associations.

THE SIMONIN COLUMN IN THE CERCLE OF SAN

At the end of April, the military authorities were finally able to create the second column in San. This column was placed under the command of Simonin, the major who had led the unsuccessful battle of Yankaso. It was to operate only within the boundaries of the cercle because in Koutiala and Bandiagara cercles the administrators had checked the extension of the war with the guards, partisans, and tirailleurs at their disposal.

The size of the column and the large number of French officers implies that strong opposition was expected. The column included the Tenth and Eleventh Companies of the Fourth Senegalese Battalion. The Tenth had 242 tirailleurs under the command of Captain Megnou, with 12 other French officers. The Eleventh which had arrived from Dakar via Conakry, had 185 soldiers under the command of Captain Thiebaut, also with 12 French officers. The two companies carried 127,952 cartridges (model 86). In addition an artillery platoon, staffed with nine French officers and ten indigenous officers and artillerymen, disposed of 201 high-explosive melinite shells. Three hundred eighty-six auxiliary troops (including 300 goumiers from Segou) and 760 porters completed the column. The Simonin column, though smaller than the Molard column, must nonetheless have seemed a terrifying military force to the villagers.

A third company under the command of Lieutenant Guillermain arrived in San on April 22. It was to protect the supply lines from San to the Molard column. The region between San and Dedougou had been outside the control of French forces, and to some extent it remained so after that date, Molard often complaining that supplies took too long to reach him. He did not hesitate to criticize both Simonin and Guillermain for inaptitude, lack of initiative, and even cowardice. Molard later blamed Simonin for destroying villages — sometimes twice — on the road between San and Dedougou and still not being able to send supplies to Dedougou.

In these charges are intimations of the internal pecking order in the French military. Guillermain, a reserve officer who had been an accountant, had no military experience. When transporting ammunition that was badly needed by Molard's troops, in order to avoid risks he took detours — with Simonin's approval — that stretched the eight-day trip to Dedougou into a twenty-six-day trip.[34] In one case, the lieutenant governor sent medicines, urgently needed by the Molard column, by automobile, but they were kept in San for two months before being forwarded.

Four days after the failed anticolonial attack on Koro, on April 23, the Simonin column left San in the direction of Koro and Tominian, which was then abandoned by the enemy.[35] The resistance in this first campaign in the vicinity of San turned out to be weaker than expected. The first major engagement took place on April 24, in Paramandugu, very near Tominian, where a strong group of anticolonial combatants had gathered. Simonin, disregarding the experience of the Molard column, started the assault in the afternoon, a few hours before dusk, shelling the defensive walls. Help from neighboring villages was unable to reach the defenders, but as in most of the following engagements, the besieged forces were easily able to escape after nightfall. Simonin attacked the villages of Turula and Tiutiu, where the defenders retreated from house to house without truly putting up a fight before fleeing their village. Marching almost to the border with the cercle of Koutiala, he demolished abandoned villages (Dami, Lenekuy, Manina, Kera, Mandyakuy) and encountered strong resistance only in Luha, on May 5 (map 21).

In the heat of the dry season, the column was exhausted, constantly searching for drinkable water as fleeing villagers spoiled their wells with refuse. The column marched back to San in five days, destroying on its way abandoned villages (see map 21).[36] The column rested in San between May 12 and 22 while new porters were found to replace those who were worn out. Politically, Simonin's demolition of villages did not seem to have accomplished much. In its inability to eradicate the major war centers near San, this campaign was somewhat like the first Molard campaign, two months before in Dedougou, that had been heavily criticized by the civilian administrators for not yielding results.

Simonin undertook a second campaign from May 23 to June 12, east of the San-Koutiala Road, reaching as far south as the border with the cercle of Koutiala. The village of Sumazangaso put up the fiercest resistance, led by Pangolo, the son of the village chief. The resisters possessed many guns. Pangolo and his men fled the village during the night, taking their dead with them.

The Simonin column united with Bleu (the administrator of Koutiala) and a detachment under Grégoire that was conducting uninterrupted "police rounds" in the eastern part of the cercle of Koutiala. The detachment had fifty tirailleurs, two 65-mm cannons, twenty-five guards, and an extremely high number of auxiliaries (seven hundred horsemen and a thousand foot soldiers), but had been forced to stop because of the strength of the opposition. On April 29, before meeting with Simonin, Bleu had attacked Perive, the famous center of resistance that had already been attacked in the past.[37] On May 16 he had tried to take the war center of Mantina, but facing a very strong resistance he stopped the assault and waited for the Simonin column. With the help of Simonin, Mantina was finally taken. About 130 defenders from the village and neighboring communities were killed.

The Mantina battle marked the start of a new phase of destruction. The column traveled in a loop to the region of Tuba and Luha, which had been destroyed in the previous Simonin campaign (see map 21). Villages attacked two months earlier by the Carpentier company or by Bleu were pillaged and destroyed again. Rather than use the impressive defensive structures they had built, people chose to evacuate their villages and to return to the ruins after the column's departure. Simonin obtained a few submissions, but several villages readopted an anticolonial stance once the column left.

In addition to the engagements of the Simonin column, very bloody battles occurred between anticolonial combatants and people loyal to the French. They are barely noticed in administrative reports, but they assumed a particular significance in this cercle, perhaps because of the historically entrenched antagonism between groups that fought with the French and those against them. As

we saw earlier, the most important fighters for the colonial side were the followers of the Sangare of Dokuy, to whom Bleu provided ammunition from
March onwards. Some Mose migrants who lived in this area had also joined
them. On June 4 and 5, they won two battles against the villages of Mandyakuy
and Dumbala (Mandyakuy was just recovering from an attack by the Simonin
column). The anticolonial party took revenge two days later. Combatants from
Solenzo, who already had an older grudge against Dokuy, where their canton
chief had found refuge in the beginning of the conflict, trapped a large group
of Fulbe fighters who had been unable to reach Dokuy. They killed a large
number of them — 118 according to one account, 200 according to another.[38]

During the night of May 18/19, the anticolonial forces staged a major attack against the camp of Cornet, the administrator of Bandiagara, in Twara, on
the Bani River. Cornet had been moving from village to village with a mobile
company of twenty-nine soldiers, with Dogon and Fulbe auxiliaries; between
April 20 and 28 they had razed abandoned villages in the Kolomina area and,
arriving in Twara on April 29, had set up camp right outside the village (see
map 23). The concentric organization of the camp reflected the hierarchy of
the colonial army, both social and military (map 25). At the center, small huts
were built to house the Europeans and the ammunition. Around this center was
a protective semicircle of tirailleurs and, further away, guards and auxiliaries in
an outer curve. This defensive disposition, which was replicated, with small
variations, in other camps, explains the wide disparity between the number of
casualties suffered by the different categories of men.

The anticolonial attack outside Twara was a surprise. Taking part were
about five hundred warriors, most of them Bwa. They were led by Tahiru (a son
of El Hajj Adama Dembele), Tiekoroni, the canton chief of Kula (Dembele's
home), and Marka leaders from Kula and villages near Baramandugu. After two
hours, the attack was driven back, the assailants leaving behind more than seventy dead. The colonial side lost three auxiliaries. Cornet wrote in his report
that "the rebels displayed forceful spirit, and fifteen or so came to a sure death
a few meters from the houses."[39] The assailants achieved some success by taking
with them a large herd of cattle — a feat whose significance was greater at that
time of the year because grain reserves were low.

After this battle, Cornet established posts in Baramandugu, Twara, Koninion,
and Samani — a defensive line that would stop the movement from advancing
northward in the cercle of Bandiagara until the Simonin column could arrive
(map 23). The most important post, in Baramandugu, had 30 soldiers, 19
guards, and 127 auxiliaries (most of them armed with guns), in "spacious

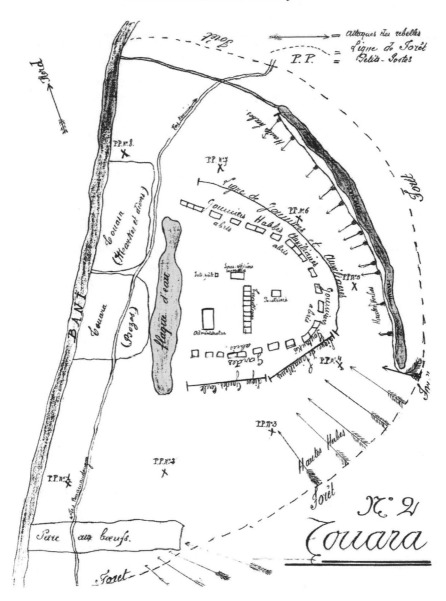

Map 25. The disposition of the camp of Twara and the anticolonial attack. 2e RTS, 4e Co., Détachement de Police du Bobo-Fakala, Bandiagara, "Rapport sur les opérations auxquelles ce détachement a pris part," November 20, 1916. Signed Puget (SHAT 5 H 196). *Goumiers Habbès auxiliaires* = mounted Dogon auxiliaries; *Goumiers Foutankes* = Tukulor mounted men; *poudrière* = powder room; *gardes* = guards; *interprète* = interpreter; *sous-officiers* = noncommissioned officers; *Bozos* = Bozo ward; *Marka et divers* = ward of the Marka and others; *flaque d'eau* = pond; *hautes herbes* =tall grass; *parc aux boeufs* = cattle pen; *forêt* = forest; *attaques des rebelles* = rebel attacks; *petits postes* = small posts; *mare* = pond.

blockhouses with very good defense works." All villages south of that defense line, having joined the movement, now stood abandoned by their inhabitants. The villages of Sokura, Nincheso, Kun, Manfe, and Fangaso in the cercle of San were transformed into important bases of operation for the anticolonial forces (map 21). Undeterred by the French military posts, on May 27 they attacked the Fulbe village of Bangasi, just a few kilometers from Baramandugu, took all the millet reserves, and burned the village.[40] On June 17, a small anticolonial force attacked Ngoena, the headquarters of the canton of Bobo-Fakala and the home of Sanibe Kamate, which had submitted back in April after Fawtier's attack (map 23). But the assailants were dispersed by troops who quickly arrived from the Koninion post.

It was the second half of June before the Simonin column finally arrived in this Bandiagara-Jenne border region. In a three-week-long campaign (June 16 to July 7), the colonial troops were able to shed their defensive posture (this was around the same time, from June 23 on, that the Molard column was conducting its third campaign—described in the next section—not far away in southwestern Dedougou; map 21). But though on the offensive, the Simonin column engaged in few battles during this time because people left their villages as the column approached. Simonin did receive the submission of the important Marka village of Teneni, and he attacked and destroyed Kansere, Moniso, and the surrounding villages of Tana and Fio.

On June 21, the column arrived in Kula, Dembele's village. The Muslim leader had transformed his mosque into a strong fortified structure, but before the column arrived he fled with a large retinue, including his son Tahiru and the canton chief Tiekoroni.[41] After Kula, the column marched northward and demolished more villages (see map 21 for the column's route). As it advanced, the column found remnants of the organization of the anticolonial army. In Teso, large quantities of the dafu headdress and cut telegraph wire had been left behind. In Fangaso, the most important anticolonial center for this region, the column recovered important stocks of foodstuffs. After reaching Baramandugu, where warrant officer Puget's detachment was stationed, the column returned to San on July 6. Puget, who remained in the region, started to receive—in the aftermath of the destruction of Kula—submissions from villages in the cercles of Bandiagara and San. Even at this point, after the systematic destruction and pillage of the area northeast, villages that surrendered only partially met the conditions imposed on them, and the acting governor-general, Angoulvant, doubted the military success of the column.

Angoulvant criticized Simonin for moving from village to village so quickly, without securing full submission of the defeated villages. This fear now haunted the high ranks of the government; they remembered the history of Molard's first campaign in Dedougou. The governor-general, in Dakar, cited the case of the village of Kansere, whose inhabitants had fled before it was demolished by the Simonin column (he still had to fire eighteen shells to overcome the remaining resistance). After the column left, the villagers returned to the ruins—as had happened elsewhere—and they attacked a courier carrying messages from San to Simonin, thus cutting communication between the column and its base.[42] Where the column did find resistance, Angoulvant suspected that the anticolonial combatants were simply luring the colonial troops into expending ammunition before leaving the fortifications at night with only light losses. A report on the political situation of Haut-Sénégal-Niger, dated June 21, stated that the cercle of San in its entirety and the part of the cercle of Dedougou west of the Muhun River were still in open revolt.

MOLARD'S CAMPAIGN WEST OF THE MUHUN RIVER (JULY 1916)

While the Simonin column was in the north of San, Molard left Dedougou for a third campaign across the Muhun River, targeting the villages that had spread the movement to the region of San (map 21, p. 237). The part of the cercle of Dedougou west of the river is historically and ethnically close to the populations of the San region. The simultaneous action of the two columns, following the repression within the bend of the river, finally succeeded in ending the anticolonial movement as an organized force, although it still did not bring all resistance to a halt. With the destruction of hundreds of villages in Dedougou and San, the most important anticolonial leaders were on the run and could be captured more easily.

For this month-long campaign, Molard took two companies, plus a machine-gun platoon and an artillery platoon. Molard had decided that a full column was not necessary. News of the repression in San and Dedougou had of course reached this area, and even though it had not yet been visited by a French column Molard expected little resistance. He applied the new military strategy that had been adopted in June, avoiding demolition of villages except as a retaliatory measure (chap. 7).

The column, made up of troops that had participated in the previous campaign, left on June 27 after only a four-day rest. A reconnaissance patrol was assailed by combatants from Bagala two days later, but when the column arrived, the village surrendered after a brief resistance. Molard captured Nutie (referred to in this document as Niantu) Kulibali, the most important leader in the area, who told him that the village of Sanaba had exerted pressure on his village to join the anticolonial movement.[43] The column went south on July 1 and in Kosoba freed captives that had been taken by anticolonial forces, including many Mose from the village of Benena. In Dubale, the column met a friendly contingent of thirty Fulbe men led by the son of the canton chief of Dokuy, who had taken control of that village (Hébert 1970, 43).

On July 2, the column attacked the important Bobo village of Balave. In 1915, a political agent from Dedougou had terrorized the notables of this village; two of them died after being tortured. When anticolonial emissaries visited Balave a few months later, its inhabitants joined the movement with enthusiasm,[44] and against the Molard column they put up extraordinary resistance. They fought the whole day from behind the walls, then fled by night. The column fired 111 shells and lost four soldiers.[45] The village was burned down the next day. The thunder of the cannon in Balave was heard as far as the cercle of Koutiala, alerting the Grégoire detachment there that the Molard column was nearby.[46] This did not deter anticolonial partisans from Musakongo from attacking Molard. The soldiers drove them back and attacked the village on July 4, meeting strong opposition before they could demolish it. On July 7, Denkoro—a village with Bwa and Bobo wards—was burned down without resistance, and in the following days many villages (Solenzo, Tie, Baye, and Lekoro) surrendered and were spared. On July 10, the Marka ward of the village of Bena surrendered, but its Bwa and Bobo wards refused to do so, choosing instead to flee.[47]

Faced with unforeseen resistance, Molard feared that the column might not be strong enough and called for another company and 250 more cannon shells. He received further reinforcement from troops sent earlier by the commandant of Koutiala to Dokuy. The column then attacked the Bwa village of Tukoro.[48] On July 13 it arrived in the post of Fo, in the cercle of Bobo-Dioulasso.

The solidarity between the Marka villages that were the cradle of the movement (Bona, Monkuy, La, Warkoy) and the area west of the Muhun came into sharper focus in this late phase of the conflict. On July 14 the column started back on a northerly course and destroyed the Bobo villages on its route (see map 21), but met strong resistance in Denkiena on July 19. Denkiena had received reinforcements from Marka villages that were within the bend of the Muhun River (Gnankambary 1970, 85). Showing uncanny resilience, these people had crossed the river after their villages had been destroyed during Molard's second campaign to offer their experience to villages on the western side.

Denkiena was defeated, leaving more than a hundred men on the battleground, and the nearby village of Montionkuy was torn down. Continuing north, the column destroyed two wards of Sanaba, home of prominent opposition figures Batieri and Wane Faha who had been so influential in the spread of the movement to the San region. In keeping with the new military strategy, the wards that surrendered were not destroyed even though they belonged to a major anticolonial center. The column returned to Dedougou on July 24.

The column had fought against forces that it had already met in Molard's first two campaigns. The anticolonials, when their homeland could no longer sustain the resistance, had found the strength and courage to continue the struggle in the neighboring region. Despite this remarkable tenacity, drawing the Molard column into an uninterrupted series of battles had cost the combatants the loss of their bases, the physical structures on which their military efficacy had rested. Destruction of the core anticolonial areas was completed by small groups of auxiliaries and guards put together by the French administrators. Such unceasing though less spectacular activity became essential in the pacification phase of the repression.

THE PACIFICATION (JULY TO AUGUST 1916)

On July 17, it was decided to initiate the second phase of the plan: "pacification." Military opposition was not completely crushed, but all the centers of the anticolonial movement—several hundreds of villages—had been effectively destroyed. Molard's troops were exhausted and the operations of the columns could cease.[49]

A report from Bamako, dated July 24, indicated that the war in the cercle of Dedougou could be considered over, although rebellious activities still occurred in northern Bobo-Dioulasso, in the cantons of Siankoro and Fo, in most parts of the cercle of San, in Nienegue country, and in the region between Koudougou and the Muhun River valley. The commander in chief of the military forces in French West Africa sent the following directive:

> The repression must now take the form of a methodical and progressive pacification, using the "oil stain" method. First, occupation of the Volta-Bani region by military posts with well-defined sectors attributed to them. Each of these posts must combine military and political force to gain new ground only after the complete submission of the one left behind. Submission entails complete disarmament of the rebels, imprisonment or death of the leaders, destruction of the fortified walls, repossession of houses, and return to agricultural work.[50]

"Pacification" marked the completion of the campaigns of destruction led by the Molard and Simonin columns, but it did not signify the end of all military campaigns. It entailed making sure that all anticolonial leaders and their last strongholds surrendered—by force, if need be—and the application of the conditions imposed on the defeated populations.

In the cercle of Bandiagara, submission proceeded slowly throughout July. Each ward of each village surrendered separately, disclosing few weapons. A detachment under the command of warrant officer Puget and the new cercle administrator Guitard made a two-week "police round" through the cantons of Bobo-Fakala and Fakala, seeking submission of villages that had not yet surrendered and collecting weapons from villages that Fawtier had destroyed in April. In late July, the people in these cantons were moving back to their villages, but most conditions for submission remained unfulfilled, especially those related to the rebuilding of villages and the payment of fines and of taxes for 1916.

Farther south, the Simonin column remained stationed in San from mid-July to mid-September. On July 16, a detachment with an artillery platoon was sent on a two-week campaign to the area between Tuba and Kurubara, on the Koutiala border. The Simonin column had destroyed that area two months earlier, but Pangolo, chief of the village of Sumazangaso and war leader for the area, had not yet given up. Threatening villages that surrendered, his forces were concentrated in the village of Diarakongo (map 21). They evacuated before the detachment arrived. The pacification of the area was mostly the work of the three commandants of the cercles of San, Koutiala, and Dedougou, who coordinated their efforts to crush the remaining opposition.

Maguet retuned from Samo country on July 27 and joined the pacification effort in the San-Koutiala-Dedougou border region. On July 30 Wane Faha surrendered to Maguet. Administrator Bleu of Koutiala and the Grégoire detachment joined Maguet on August 1 in Dokuy for a campaign that combined negotiation and military action; their most significant engagements were against Tula, Toma, and Ban villages where many insurgents had sought refuge from the Simonin column.

Tula had capitulated before, but, like many other places, had reneged on its surrender. The village had grown into an even larger center of opposition by welcoming combatants from three cercles: from Sonhuwan (destroyed by Bleu in February) and Durukuna, in Koutiala; from Wara and Mafine, in San; and from nearby Kohimane, Gi, Ban, Felehue, Ulani, Kyele, and Kera, in Dedougou. A reconnaissance mission sent to the village by the two administrators was met with gunshots. On August 12, Bleu and Maguet attacked Tula, and Maguet had all

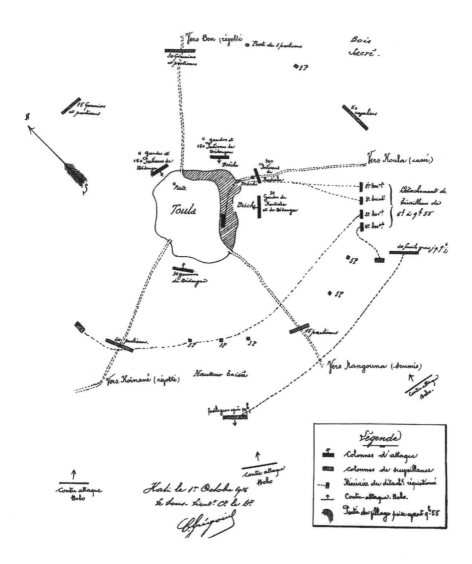

Map 26. The battle of Tula. "Rapport du Sous-Lieutenant à titre temporaire Grégoire … sur les opérations effectuées par le détachement du 9 Février au 5 Septembre 1916" Kati, 1er Octobre 1916 (SHAT 5 H 196).

roads blocked to prevent escape from the village (see map 26). The defenders, each with a gun, put up fierce resistance. Anticolonial reinforcements sent to Tula were repelled by the colonial forces. The troops took control of the village after an all-day battle and burned it to the ground. The anticolonials lost 250—including most of their leaders in the region—and 438 women and children were made prisoner.[51]

The battle of Tula was the last major military engagement of the Volta-Bani War. With the fall of Tula, the Dedougou-Koutiala road was reopened to the colonial administration. But military activity did not cease. Two companies, each with a cannon, operated for another month, joining forces with Ponzio, San's new administrator.[52] The first was sent by Molard to Tula because of the challenge Bleu and Maguet had met there. The second was a detachment from the Simonin column under Captain Thiebaut that operated in the Tiutiu-Mandiakuy area from August 12 to September 10. The activity of these two companies allowed Maguet and Bleu to continue their pacification campaign and confiscate three thousand guns within a few days. On August 24, the government deemed that the cercle of Koutiala was completely "pacified," and Bleu returned to cercle headquarters, but Maguet continued the rounds and did not return to Dedougou until September 15.

On August 24, a military detachment captured El Hajj Adama Dembele in the village of Diarani (cercle of San), along with fifty-one members of his family. The imam, after escaping to the cercle of Dedougou with a large entourage, including his son Tahiru, the former Kula canton chief Tiekoroni Dembele, and captives, had returned to the imam's hometown of Kula, but had been poorly welcomed.[53] Maguet captured Tahiru Dembele in the village of Pia.

In late August and early September, the remaining leaders of the anticolonial movement in the region were arrested, among them Niaka Tera, "war chief" of Dami.[54] These arrests did not signal the end of all opposition, however. At the end of August, centers of resistance were still active in southern San and in Koutiala.[55] But in the following months, most of the country was pacified, and the government-general in Dakar set as a priority the disarmament of the population. This resulted in an astonishing number of confiscated firearms.[56]

Chapter 10

East of the Volta

The War in the Cercle of Ouagadougou

THE PEOPLE OF THE RESIDENCY OF KOUDOUGOU were among the first to establish contact with the Marka centers of Dedougou and in December 1915 to massively join the anticolonial movement. In fact, anti-French stirrings had begun in this region spontaneously much earlier, during the March 1915 conscription campaign. Serious opposition continued from that date until December, when the Marka leadership organized and integrated them into the larger anticolonial movement. Several factors helped shape the movement in this area: the relations of Gurunsi communities with the Mose *naabas* (chiefs); their ties with the Marka centers within the bend of the Muhun River; and the role of Islam, which was in many ways similar to, but in some other ways different from, that of Islam in the region of San. In order to provide a better understanding of the forces that acted on the anticolonial movement, we start with a brief account of French occupation of the territory and the administrative regime they established.

Most of the land between the eastern stretch of the Muhun River and the Nazinon (formerly, the Red Volta) River is inhabited by groups collectively called, in the colonial period, the Gurunsi. The term was borrowed by the French from the Mose political vocabulary. It refers to a number of small populations (today totaling about three hundred thousand people) that share a common cultural and linguistic foundation and occupy a north-south corridor of about two hundred kilometers between the two rivers. On the basis of language, ethnographers usually distinguish in this cluster the Winye (or Ko, in Jula), of the region of Boromo; the Nuna (often called Awuna by English administrators and ethnographers),

271

between Koudougou and Leo; and the Lyela, or Lela, also called northern Nuna, to the north and northwest of Koudougou.[1] These populations had remained outside the grip of Mose chiefly hierarchies that organized political space in territories east of the Hazinon River, but had many connections with them.

THE GURUNSI AT THE TIME OF CONQUEST

As in the other regions further west discussed in previous chapters, matrimonial alliances, religious links, the history of settlement, and armed conflicts in this region led to the construction of loose confederations between villages.[2] Among the Nuna, a category of chiefs called *pio* or *peo* initiated a distinct type of inter-village alliance. According to some authors, this institution had its origin in the southeast and the Mose region (Capron 1973, 54–57; Duperray 1984; Duval 1985; Bayili 1998, 22). Until the colonial period, these chiefs were associated with the domain of warfare and are described as having extended their authority over several villages, in contrast to local chiefs and ritual experts who descended from the first settlers. The French administration invested many pio as village chiefs. The Winye people had a figure equivalent to the pio, the *inu,* whose origin has also been traced to the east, particularly to the Sisala region (Jacob, 1988). In Winye villages that fell in the sphere of influence of the Karantao, the lineages of the inu were allied to the Karantao.

The Mose chiefdoms to the east of the Nazinon River influenced the Gurunsi region through raids organized by Mose chiefs and the migration of Mose strongmen. The latter were often men of junior status from chiefly lineages who had lost out in the competition for office and decided to emigrate rather than stay as subordinates to their more fortunate agnates. When the French conquered the region in the mid-1890s, they integrated Mose chiefly hierarchies of places such as Yatenga and Ouagadougou in the colonial administration. This was the most successful case in the Volta region of incorporating African officeholders as colonial underlings. It motivated the French to claim that the Gurunsi, too, were dominated by Mose princes, include the regions of Koudougou and Leo as residencies in the cercle of Ouagadougou, and appoint Mose chiefs there. This development generated a new and bigger influx of Mose migrants in the eastern part of the Gurunsi cultural area. The conflicting relations between Mose and some Gurunsi people evolved into a joking relationship, or *rakire* (Bayili 1998, 66), but it is difficult to know if this relationship emerged in the pre- or postcolonial period.

Besides these ties to the east, Gurunsi villages had important relations with the Samo, and with Marka and Bwa populations living west of the Muhun River. They included economic and cultural flows as well as military alliances. The dispersion of Gurunsi communities to the north and west reinforced these connections. This history of these affinities and conflicts constitutes the backdrop for the events of 1916. Nuna colonies existed in the area of Ula and Cheriba, and this explains why the most influential Marka leaders in the Gurunsi region came from the surroundings of these two villages. North of Boromo, Winye villages had established an alliance with the Marka of the villages of Da and Jinakongo against the Karantao of Wahabu, who were allied with the Zaberma. However, other Winye communities in the vicinity of Wahabu and Boromo had joined the Karantao. The Winye also had close connections—particularly through the central Winye cult of Lane—with their southern Nienegue neighbors (Capron 1973, 26). These precolonial alliances in the region of Boromo played an important role in the 1915–16 anticolonial war, and in late April 1916 the French established a military post near the Muhun River, in part to prevent contact between the Nienegue and Winye populations living on either side of the river. In the north, populations of Gurunsi origin migrated to southern Samo country, and, as we will see, Samo and Gurunsi combatants established contacts in June 1916.

The settlement of Muslim communities, known collectively as Dagara-Jula or Kantosi, in Gurunsi villages also created connections between the east and west banks of the Muhun River. Many of these Muslim communities had migrated from the region of Wa, in present-day Ghana. In 1915, the most important Kantosi center was To, north of Leo. Most Muslim communities, however, lived in their own quarters at the edges of Gurunsi villages, where they conducted some trade and provided local people with religious services (mostly by selling them protective charms). The Kantosi were also involved in regional trade, traveling from the Marka communities in the north to the Muslim centers of northern Ghana. An important West African trade route joining Kumasi to Jenne in the Niger valley, through the towns of Boromo and Safane, crossed the Gurunsi region. The Kantosi had close relationships with the Karantao of Wahabu and Boromo, whose influence (as explained in chap. 2) penetrated as far as Sati and even farther east.

THE MARABOUT AFFAIR IN KOUDOUGOU

The indirect administration that the French established at the turn of the century rested on the Mose chiefs' claims that they controlled a large part of the north and east of the town of Koudougou, a region they called Kipirsi (a name later adopted by the French). The villagers denied the reality of these claims and resisted the chiefs. In the first years of the colonial period, both old-established leaders and new ones, using the power bestowed by their colonial administrative positions, continued to have conflict-ridden relationships with many Gurunsi communities.

At the beginning of World War I, the reduced French military and administrative presence brought to the surface the contradictions inherent in their interstitial role. The situation in Gurunsi country was similar to that of most of the west Volta region, where the Watara or Fulbe houses or other intermediaries employed by the colonial administration had little success or interest in enforcing the orders of the new colonial overlords. According to Tauxier (1924): "the *Naaba* . . . send from time to time a representative to bring back order. But these envoys rush to return when their job is finished, and their appearance has no serious consequences. These same people actually give a good welcome to the passing European who asks for nothing, but he better have a good escort when he goes to ask for taxes, which is far from being accepted as legitimate." The French had reshuffled the Mose administrative organization after the death of the Mogho naaba in 1905 and, in 1908, an armed opposition of two thousand armed men from Ramongho, led by a Muslim. In the Koudougou region, Laarle Naaba Pawitraogo was appointed to maintain order in the name of the French.[3]

The Laarle naaba and Henri d'Arboussier, commandant of the cercle of Ouagadougou, now played a central role in the 1914–15 marabout affair.[4] As we saw in chapter 4, in mid-December 1914 d'Arboussier met the Laarle naaba, who informed him that Muslim leaders from Wahabu and Boromo, in collusion with Amaria, the chief of Leo, and Koreish, the imam of To, had called on people to rise up against the colonial authorities.[5] D'Arboussier alerted his colleagues of the cercles of Dedougou and San and the lieutenant governor of the Haut-Senegal-Niger about a possible large-scale Muslim conspiracy. A massive campaign of repression and arrests followed in the cercle of Dedougou. D'Arboussier arrested minor Muslim figures and the imam of To and people close to him for "anti-French propaganda." Pursuing his inquiry in the early months of 1915, he disclosed that Amaria and his entourage had engaged in the systematic pillage of the region of Leo. Amaria was arrested, and in April 1915 a twenty-year sentence was pronounced against him. The imam was given a ten-year sentence.

The marabout affair evolved very differently in the cercles of Ouagadougou and Dedougou. At the end of the anticolonial war, administrators of the cercle of Dedougou were charged for the abuses they committed in the course of this inquiry, and all the Muslim suspects that they had convicted were released. In the cercle of Ouagadougou, however, the arrests of the Muslim leaders were never reversed, and a few months after his arrest Amaria died in jail in conditions that have remained unclear.[6] Administrative reports reveal the denunciation of the Laarle naaba as the starting point of the campaign of arrests of Muslim leaders in Koudougou and Dedougou. Duperray proposed that, behind the whole affair, lay the power struggle between Mose chiefs and other chiefs appointed by the colonial administration (Duperray, 1984).[7] However, it is hard to consider the French administrators only as their duped instruments. The strong anti-Muslim paranoia of French colonial circles in those years and d'Arboussier's eagerness to find Muslim agitators need to be taken into account. It is likely that the two colluded in fleshing out the story of an elaborate conspiracy.

The only material evidence presented by d'Arboussier to support the charges against Amaria and the Muslim dignitaries were two letters. D'Arboussier claimed during the trial that

> toward the end of August and at the beginning of September 1914, two letters arrived from Wahabu through different paths to Amaria. The first of these was a call to holy war. It invited all good Muslims to be ready for the struggle that Islam, with the support of the Germans, would wage against the French in this country. It announced the triumph of the cause of Muhammed and the certain annihilation of all Frenchmen.[8]

The French translations of the two letters that d'Arboussier eventually supplied when his superiors requested them are reproduced here in the appendix. The content of these letters does not in any way substantiate d'Arboussier's claims. Neither these two letters nor a third one used as evidence in the trial of Dedougou include seditious propaganda (see pp. 92–95). They were standard exhortations and recommendations to the listeners to be good Muslims and avoid misfortune.[9]

The widespread arrests left the Laarle naaba as the only major power figure on the side of the French in the Koudougou region, a turn of events that affected the organization of the activities against the anticolonial movement. More so than in the other areas where the anticolonial movement took hold, French and colonial authorities lacked full understanding of what happened in this region. Guided by Mose chiefs who were foreign to the cultural world of the Lela, Winye, and Nuna, administrators in the post of Koudougou could not completely comprehend the contradictory intelligence reports they received.

D'Arboussier's interpretation of the letters, the sudden revelation of Amaria's abuses, the condemnation of Amaria for participation in the Muslim plot and not for these abuses, and his death a few months later raise many questions. Is it possible that d'Arboussier resented Amaria's growing power or had another reason to eliminate him? In the current state of knowledge, this is difficult to answer. What seems clear is that Amaria and his entourage were specifically targeted.

THE BEGINNINGS OF THE MOVEMENT AMONG THE GURUNSI: THE LEADERSHIP

The March 1915 conscription campaign appears to have been particularly trouble-ridden in the Gurunsi territories. Young men—and sometimes entire village populations—hid in the bush. Villagers attacked the recruitment agents sent by the Laarle naaba. In March, approximately three hundred armed men attacked the chief of Nanoro and freed the recruits gathered in the colonial compound of the village.[10] These acts of insubordination were not quashed in the following months and the area was never quite "settled." In the midst of this agitation, in late October 1915, came news of a second round of military conscription. It provoked fresh acts of resistance in the residency of Koudougou. To evade the military draft, young men armed with bows and arrows fled their villages to live in the bush, where they organized themselves into groups that regrouped five or six villages. Others crossed the border to the Gold Coast. Blacksmiths everywhere were manufacturing weapons. In the first days of November, messengers sent by naabas and chiefs appointed by the French were attacked; some were killed.[11]

Alarmed by these signs of unrest, the commandant of the cercle of Ouagadougou tried to take matters into his own hands. On November 20, the day after the first battle of Bona in the neighboring cercle of Dedougou, commandant d'Arboussier summoned the canton chiefs of his cercle to inform them that they were to present a total of 12,500 men to the recruiting commission, from which the cercle quota of 2,500 was to be selected. In spite of all the turmoil caused by military conscription in the cercle of Ouagadougou and of the events unfolding in the region of Bona, Governor-general Clozel had ordered the continuation of conscription until the colony was "seriously threatened. One needs to carry on regardless of local incidents and revolts."[12] Under this appearance of intransigence, local colonial authorities had little choice but to continue. The resident of Koudougou, Michel, had been asked to recruit 1,000 men, but when he encountered strong resistance, this number was reduced to 750 (Duperray 1984, 184). The response to the recruitment campaign is described in a report by the commandant of the cercle: "Toward November 25 the young men of the region of Koudougou were leaving the villages in large numbers and waiting in the bush in arms. They all declared that they preferred to die in their country rather than become soldiers. . . . Everywhere, weapons were being readied. Many representatives of the chiefs were killed. . . . In Koudougou itself, sorcerers were openly preaching rebellion."[13] The report states that in the cantons of Ipala and Kayao, people escaped to the bush, and that in the canton of Kokologo (only fifty kilometers from Ouga-dougou), a young man shot an arrow at the head of the canton chief.

At the end of November, news of the outcome of the Bona battles intensified the acts of insubordination to the point where the colonial administration lost all control. The six hundred young men that the resident of Koudougou had been able to recruit at great pains all escaped on November 28—an event that marked the true beginning of armed resistance in this region. The administration was unable to prevent this massive evasion, and the young men returned to their villages, where they joined others who were preparing to fight the colonial government.[14] People identified as Mose took the brunt of the anger of the Gurunsi villagers. Mose messengers and chiefs—and even long-time Mose residents in Gurunsi villages—were threatened; some of them were killed. The alliances between Mose villages and Gurunsi villages collapsed. According to Bayili, "the killing of a Moaga was greeted as an act of honor, a patriotic gesture of the highest level" (1998, 232).

In early December, delegations accompanied by whistle players traveled from village to village, inviting people to join the anticolonial movement. Trade in arms was brisk. A musket was selling for one steer. The pace of ritual activities quickened, and in the hopeful mood of the initial stages of the movement, events confirmed their efficacy. A man whose brothers had been taken away as recruits had an ox sacrificed to obtain their freedom. Eight days later, the recruits escaped, and a note in the diary of the resident of Koudougou indicated that "the indigenous people saw the 'force' of this sacrifice."[15]

Following the successes at Bona and Yankaso, the Marka leaders of the war against the French made the same great efforts to win to their side the populations living east of the Muhun River as they did for those to the west of it. To show that they had truly defeated the French, Marka emissaries brought to Gurunsi villages the colonial objects that were captured during the second battle of Bona (Bayili 1983). Several Marka leaders stayed in Gurunsi country to organize and motivate the local population. But there is evidence indicating that strong support for an anti-French movement antedated these efforts. Already before the battles of Bona, people in the two regions seeking leadership roles in the opposition against the French had established contacts.

The travel of leaders of some Gurunsi villages to Marka villages seeking help in their struggle against the French preceded the arrival of Marka leaders to Gurunsi country heralding the armed opposition. For example, Apediu, a dignitary of Didir who later became a leading figure of the anticolonial movement, in the last days of October sent a man from his village to the region of Durula to request the purchase of a shrine. Following the normal procedure for the transfer of replicas of such shrine material, a Marka man went to Didir to install the new altar. During the festive ceremony organized for the installation, an ox was killed; the man returned to his village with many gifts.[16] O Sabwè Ji Oyo, from the village of Tio, was another person who went to Marka country "to buy the revolt with a ram in Dahounan" (Bayili 1983). Eventually he became one of the most important Lela leaders. In chapter 5 we concluded that the preparations for the anticolonial war in the cercle of Dedougou had started long before the battles of Bona and were led by a determined and dedicated circle of men who became its leaders. This development was not limited to the neighborhood of Bona. A network anticipating the links of the anticolonial war had started to take shape through ritual exchange in the months preceding November between territories to the east of the Muhun River and the Marka villages within the bend of the river.

The local leadership divided the villages of the Gurunsi region into two broad zones. The northern region of Didir (or Didisi) was put under the general command of the Marka leader Dahuda; the central region—with the meeting points of Zula, Tio, Tialgo, and later Zawara and Puni—was left under the command of the local leader Yombie. This military division of the territory was flexible; at times, Marka leaders lent a hand in the southern villages. For example, Dahuda and another Marka leader, Lasana, were present in Zawara (Duperray 1984, 189). Dahuda's origin and identity remain enigmatic. While most reports indicate he was from Ula, others trace him to Biforo or Cheriba. Also, some references to a Marka leader called Buninga, and sometimes Morbal, may in fact be to none other than Dahuda.

The confusion that the French and their Mose chiefly allies had about the identity of these leaders was purposefully cultivated by the Marka active in the Gurunsi region. They maintained a cloud of uncertainty and mystery about their origin, identity, and religious affiliation, among both their Gurunsi followers and the colonial authorities. One report mentions that "a Marka from Dedougou (the chief of Ula) was leading the movement, and presenting the image of a mysterious being, he succeeded in rousing people to revolt by fear of persecution."[17] Some Marka leaders also presented themselves as Muslims.[18] These same leaders participated nonetheless in sacrificial rituals that acknowledged the power of the shrine of Bona, which offered mystical protection to warriors.

The religious ambiguity attached to Marka leaders was reflected in the names given to the conflict and to its leaders. The conflict has been called *mura-twa* in this region, from *twa* (bow, as in bow and arrow—and, by extension, in the Nuni language, war) and *mura* (Muslim); *mura-twa* could then be translated as "war of the Muslims." Similarly, the name Morbal that was attributed to Dahuda had an Islamic connection. *Mor* is a variant form of *mura*, and *bal* means man.[19] These names simply confirm that the anticolonial movement of this region had a Muslim dimension, but, as we will shortly see, devotion of the combatants to Islam should not be exaggerated. It is possible that Morbal was not the name of a specific leader but a title given to different leading figures of the movement. The term projected an ambiguous religious dimension on Marka leaders.

As in the other areas where the movement spread, in addition to the visiting leaders mostly of Marka origin, each Gurunsi village generated its own leaders. Two important Gurunsi leaders in close contact with Marka guides were Beyon, from Tio, and Koso, from the village of Tialgo. Some people who rose in this context were familiar with the colonial military. A former tirailleur named Roerga, from the village of Paologo (southwest of Zula), conducted fighting in the region of Nabidure (Leo residency), and another war leader, Basana, from the village of Ipendo, was a former sergeant in the British army in the Gold Coast.[20] We do not encounter similar cases in other regions; there, the former tirailleurs were more likely to be recruited by the French for the repression.

The most famous Gurunsi war leader was the above-mentioned Yombie. Known also by the nickname Dugbenga (or Dugubenga), he has become a legendary figure in Gurunsi country. Yombie was born in a village between Puni and Zawara, in a region regularly raided by Mose from the village of Tiu, home of one of the few Mose chiefly lineages that had settled in Gurunsi country (Duperray 1984). Yombie spent a large part of his life in the village of Tiu as a groom for Naaba Sarba, who was chief of the canton, and was trained as a soldier. Oral tradition maintains that Yombie was able to raise an army armed with bows and arrows, muskets, and breech-loading rifles, and that he created a hierarchical structure that appears to be modeled on Mose practices (Tiendrébéogo 1968). He also fed his army—again conforming to Mose campaign conventions—with boiled cowpeas (*benga,* in More), a practice that explains his nickname.[21]

Captain Cadence, who conducted the repression in Gurunsi country, wrote in his report that Yombie had lived in the cercle of Dedougou and that he had claimed to be the envoy of Siaka of Datomo. According to one author, Yombie received from the Marka leader Dahuda, in the village of Biforo, the horse and sword of the goumier Kamene (Bayili 1983). O Sabwè Ji Oyo challenged Yombie's authority by saying that the latter was only a former slave, but Yombie prevailed due to his qualities as a leader and warrior. For a person of servile status to attain a position of military and political power is not unheard of in the region's history (other examples are Amaria and Tieba of Sikasso at the end of the nineteenth century). Yombie advocated war as much against the Mose chiefs as against the colonial power. He aspired to become the new ruler of the Gurunsi region. He declared that after the victory, he was going to take up residence in Ouagadougou in place of the Mogho naaba.[22] Some Marka leaders in the Dedougou region made similar pronouncements.

Like the Marka leaders, Yombie was surrounded by an enigmatic and mystical aura. A man who had been Yombie's prisoner later told colonial authorities that Yombie spoke neither More nor a Gurunsi language and that he communicated through an interpreter who had been a prisoner of the Zaberma. Another informer reported to colonial authorities that no one could see Yombie because he addressed people through an intermediary. This intermediary was Beyon, from the village of Tio, and even Beyon could not see Yombie; Beyon was informed of Yombie's orders by a Marka who was in permanent contact with Yombie.[23] Yombie's religious beliefs, like those of Marka leaders, also led to contradictory comments. Lieutenant Marotel, who found "fetishes" left behind by Yombie in a village that the war leader had recently abandoned, noted that "although a Muslim, Dougoubenga also uses gris-gris."[24] Three weeks later, an informer announced Yombie's presence in another village, adding that the Gurunsi leader was widely known as a *féticheur*.[25] At the same time, d'Arboussier noted in a report that "Yombie executes the Muslim prayers conspicuously" (Duperray 1984, 189).

It seems that Marka guides always accompanied Yombie. This continued until the critical situation in their home area after the second campaign of the Molard column urged them to return to their villages. For example, in the battle of Zula in March 1916, two Marka leaders were with Yombie. Colonial authorities were confused because of this and often mistook Marka leaders for Yombie, as well as the other way around. Yombie moved frequently from village to village and never established a permanent base; news of his presence in a village was often announced as that of a Marka leader.

The ties between the Gurunsi anticolonial movement and the Marka leadership was symbolized in the use of the dafu fiber headdress. Like anticolonial fighters in other regions far from the canton of Datomo, Gurunsi fighters seem to have believed that when they wore this cord it protected them or could bring them back to life if they were killed. It is improbable that such thaumaturgic power could be attributed to the cord at opposite ends of the area dominated by the anticolonial movement without the approval of the Marka leaders active in these places. Among the Marka of Dedougou, the cord, like all articles worn in battle, can be ritually treated with special substances to invest it with protective qualities, but it does not have such properties inherently.

As the cord turned into a marker of anticolonial fighter identity, its physical appearance was regionally modified, as we saw in the case of the region of San (chap. 9, p. 253). In Gurunsi villages, a dog bone was hung from the headdress. The sacrificed dog seems to have become a distinctive sign of the movement only in this region.[26] When Yombie fled the village of Naton, the most important gris-gris among the items he left behind was reportedly dog fat, which was smeared on people. It is probable that Yombie included the sacrifice of the dog as a protective ritual in addition to that offered by the headdress—another irony of the religious indeterminacy of the anticolonial movement in Gurunsi country: the dog is anathema to Muslims, who often deride non-Muslim locals as dog eaters.

Another element that the Gurunsi region had in common with the canton of Datomo was the use and symbolic significance of the whistle in inviting communities to join the fighting. Again as in Bona, the fighters planned to disrupt communication between the colonial forces and their posts. In mid-March, when the conflict extended to the region of Leo, they took control of the road Koudougou–Leo, deliberately to stop the mail, because they believed that "it is papers that are at the origin of the force of white people."[27]

The military strategy of the anticolonial partisans in the Gurunsi region was similar to that of the Marka areas. They chose villages as meeting points for hundreds of warriors to gather at before launching attacks. Gathering points moved as necessitated by the military situation; in some cases, villages that had been destroyed by the colonial forces were used again as bases of action.

The number of warriors who gathered in such places never reached the thousands, as in the Marka and Bwa equivalents. But even in the order of a few hundred, Gurunsi forces largely outnumbered colonial troops. Rarely, however, were they able to take advantage of this fact. Colonial authorities in Koudougou refrained from attacking anticolonial formations for lack of sufficient troops and ammunition during the longest portion of the conflict. Yet the

French officers also noticed that despite this restraint the Gurunsi leadership hesitated to attack. The anticolonial forces felt more confident in defense than in assault, and although in the cercles of Dedougou and Bobo-Dioulasso they took bolder initiatives more frequently, everywhere leaders came more or less to the same conclusion in the end. The root cause of this lay in the disparity in firepower. In situations of defense, thick walls could compensate for the shorter range of the muzzle-loading muskets, but in an attack situation, they did not find a comparable substitute.

PREPARATION FOR WAR

In December, the separate acts of opposition spontaneously occurring in the villages of northern Gurunsi country entered a phase of coordinated preparation for war. The number of armed foreigners coming from the region of Dedougou had increased sharply, and much time was spent on meetings to establish and consolidate coalitions of villages and to decide on the gathering points to confront the colonial forces. One of these coalitions included the villages to the west of Koudougou: Tiogo, Tenado, Kukuldi, Zono, and Batolyiri. In the north, Dasa and Didir arose as two important centers under the command of Marka leaders. In the northeast, Lela villages in the area of Nanoro joined the movement, which was promoted particularly by the village of Kuria.[28] East of Koudougou, the Gurunsi and Mose villages of Poa, Ramongho, Kasum, Vili, Nandiala, Godin, and Wolorotenga also prepared for war — as much against the Laarle naaba as the colonial administration, and to the south of Koudougou, the villages of the region of Surgu also prepared (map 27). These preparations were undertaken with the clear understanding of belonging to a larger movement guided by the leadership of Bona in the cercle of Dedougou. We know, for example, that at this time the village of Diergo, near Surgu, sent a sheep to the region of Dedougou.[29] Koudougou was surrounded on all sides by insurgent villages, and most inhabitants of the town itself sympathized with the movement.

In this time of preparation, ritual experts were as conspicuous as military strategists. Everywhere sacrifices were conducted to ensure personal protection and the departure of the Europeans. Throughout the region, ritual specialists (*féticheurs*) from different villages consulted each other and exchanged objects, prescriptions, and recipes. Ancestors sanctioned the decision to take up arms. The chief of the village of Wolorotenga declared, "I am in relation with a man from Reo who speaks to the ancestors at night and they told him that the whites were finished, that they were on their way out."[30] While local shrines and ancestors were consulted in oracles to make the major decision to resist, once this decision was made people went to the marabouts who sold *sebenw* (amulets) for personal protection or as aggressive devices targeted at the French resident and at Mose chiefs. A large number of animals and cowries circulated in the ritual sphere for the acquisition of objects and for sacrifices, and as currency in the booming trade of weapons and arrow poison.

The French, made aware of these preparations by their chiefly allies, responded to them to the best of their ability under the circumstances. On December 13, a company of forty tirailleurs headed by the Lieutenant Marotel mentioned above was dispatched to Koudougou from Sansanne-Mango in Togoland, where French and British troops had met to divide the newly occupied German territory.[31] Marotel and his men constituted the only colonial military force in Koudougou, but none of these tirailleurs had yet experienced combat; six of them had never shot a gun—a characteristic situation that illustrates the state of the colonial army in French West Africa.

Because it became impossible for colonial personnel to circulate in the area, the military conscription campaign came to an end. On December 18, the resident of Koudougou decided to set off on a round in the western and northwestern parts of his post. He was attacked near Tio. The villages of Dasa, Didir, Tialgo, Tio, Tiogo, and Bisanderu planned another attack against his company, but the resident cut short his round and returned to Koudougou.[32] In the last days of December, an anticolonial force of 260 men from the area of Bisanderu, which was the home area of Dahuda, crossed the Muhun River and burned down the colonial compound in Tiogo (map 27). Colonial compounds were also burned farther north, in Didir and neighboring villages, under the leadership of a Marka (probably Dahuda).

By the end of 1915, the administrator of the cercle of Ouagadougou lost nearly all control of the so-called Kipirsi region. In late December, Ouagadougou was further isolated by the extension of the Tuareg resistance (which was not connected to the events in Dedougou) in the cercle of Dori, at the northeast border of Ougadougou. From January to May, Henri d'Arboussier, the administrator of Ouagadougou, seconded by Michel, the resident of Koudougou, and Lieutenant Marotel, organized the defense of the post of Koudougou with a few tirailleurs. His primary aim was to prevent the contagion of the anticolonial movement to the Mose villages, which so far were obedient. Together they launched brief attacks on villages in the vicinity of Koudougou, a strategy similar to that followed by Maubert during those same months in the cercle of Bobo-Dioulasso.

Because all the military forces available in French West Africa were directed to Dedougou, Governor-general Clozel recommended that d'Arboussier not take risks that could force him to ask for reinforcements.[33] In February, Marotel and his 40 tirailleurs from Togo received a few reinforcements: 25 tirailleurs, also from Togo, and the help of the 32 men who protected the recruiting commissions in Leo and Koudougou. D'Arboussier also was able to put together a small number of guards and about 130 Mose mounted auxiliaries, only 25 of whom were armed with guns. In this region, considered secondary for the repression campaign, the contribution of Mose chiefs became essential for colonial defense.

FIRST PHASE OF THE GURUNSI CONFLICT (JANUARY TO MARCH 1916)

In order to loosen the anticolonial movement's clench on Koudougou, d'Arboussier and Michel, with twenty guards and fifty auxiliary Mose infantry, on January 15 and 16 attacked and razed the villages of Tio and Tiogo.[34] This attack surprised the defenders of Tio, but the people of Tiogo, though unable to prevent the destruction of the village, put up strong resistance. At this stage, the destruction of villages had little immediate military significance because the anticolonial partisans, like those in the cercle of Dedougou, moved from village to village or fled and returned to their villages after the battle. On January 22, the people of Reo chased away the Roman Catholic missionaries who were established there (the missionaries took refuge in Koudougou), destroyed the mission, and carried the church bell to Tio, the village that d'Arboussier had attacked a week earlier (de Benoist 1987, 247; Prost 1971, 107).[35] From Tiogo, the anticolonials also organized attacks against Mose villages in the region of Surgu, stealing horses and inflicting casualties (Bayili, 1983).

On January 23, Marotel left Koudougou for another campaign in the area of Tio and Tiogo with a company of more than 100 men, including 30 tirailleurs and 20 guards. In Kukuldi, eighteen kilometers west of Koudougou, a group of 700 to 800 Gurunsi, many with guns, attacked the column; according to a brief oral account, a band of Gurunsi archers, accompanied by drummers and whistle players, had also arrived from Tio. On the colonial side, canton chiefs of the regions of Yako and Ouagadougou with mounted fighters, assisted the column (Bationo 1996). Although the anticolonials constituted an easy target because they formed a continuous line, the damage inflicted by the inexperienced tirailleurs was not as great as it could have been.

The battle of Kukuldi was largely fought according to Mose practices, the cavalry being used for attack and archers for defense. Marotel had the Mose cavalry charge first, but after moving hesitantly they ran away. We quote from two accounts of the battle, which lasted two hours:

> The indigenous cavalry charged the rebel army, but many of them fell under the blow of poisoned arrows. The horses collapsed in the battlefield; the enemy did not budge. (Tiendrébéogo 1968, 112)

> The rebels advanced, their bows aimed at the target, and shouted: "The tail of the horses! The tail of the horses!" The arrows whistled in the air. (Bationo 1996)[36]

The anticolonial forces lost more than 50 men and had many wounded. Although Marotel lost only 1 man, killed by a bullet, it was enough to make him change his plans and return to Koudougou.[37] In oral memory, the battle remains one of the major engagements of the war in the Koudougou region. The oral descriptions agree with the official account that the issue of the battle remained indecisive. The version conveyed by Bationo mentions a cannon, but this detail must have been imported from later incidents. Marotel had no cannon.

The battle of Kukuldi brought to an end for a while the French effort to organize a systematic repression; in the following weeks, Marotel chose instead to conduct small sorties from Koudougou against neighboring villages. For lack of other troops, Marotel used the same men who had fought ineffectively in Kukuldi. These raids had little effect because the anticolonial fighters mostly avoided contact with colonial troops, but where they had sufficient numbers they engaged the raiding parties in open field.

Throughout January, the Koudougou diary notes the presence of Marka among the Gurunsi forces. The Gurunsi fighters were divided into two armies: one was in the western region of Tio, Tiogo, and Kukuldi, the other in the northern region of Didir, Dasa, Pum, and Reo.[38] Groups of partisans also moved from one area to another, and in early January people from Surgu were at Tialgo under the leadership of Koso. By the end of the month, anticolonial contingents could be seen three kilometers from Koudougou.

On January 31, a few soldiers from the conscription commission of the cercle of Fada N'Gourma arrived in Koudougou, to be joined a few days later by a large number of Mose.[39] Laarle Naaba Pawitraogo (who was stationed in Koudougou), and other Mose chiefs whose compounds had been burned by the anticolonials took part in this mobilization. One of their main tasks was to pillage and demolish defeated villages.

With these reinforcements, d'Arboussier decided to attack the villages of
Gundi and Zula, which had become important anticolonial bases. From these villages, the partisans were launching reconnaissance patrols to the wards of Koudougou. The battle took place at Gundi, a fortified village. Despite the lack of
success of the assault, Marotel resisted calling for retreat, fearing the effect it
would have on the morale of his troops and the trust of the Mose, but after seeing
some of his men killed by bullets and realizing the likelihood of heavier casualties, he withdrew to Koudougou.[40] As usual, the anticolonial forces lost more men
than the French and their allies, in spite of the protection given by their fortifications. Having forced the column to withdraw to its base, they now occupied a
ward of Koudougou, where they received strong support from the inhabitants.

In February, colonial troops initiated a series of engagements, many of them
around the fortified village of Zula. In each case, they were forced to withdraw.
The post of Koudougou was under permanent threat, and the movement was expanding rapidly: it was gaining eastward and among the Mose of the Kipirsi as
far north as Godir; and in the south, the Nuna people of the adjoining residence
of Leo were joining. The lieutenant governor of Haut-Sénégal-Niger acknowledged that "on February 5, all the Gourounsi [country] under the leadership of
the chief of the Marka village of Ula was in open rebellion."[41]

The administrator, hampered by the shortage of ammunition, was helpless
without a cannon. Although on February 7 a new detachment of twenty-five
men, headed by Second Lieutenant Boullais, was detailed to Koudougou, it did
not much change the military balance. The French were still limited to making
quick raids on villages just outside of Koudougou and focusing on the defense
of the post. On February 12, anticolonial combatants attacked a ward of Koudougou; the defenders killed one hundred of them and drove them back.

New anticolonial centers emerged in February. Fighters from the villages
of Goden, Batolyiri, Nadiolo, Woro, and Ipendo massed around the procolonial
village of Paologo, southwest of Zula, which was inhabited mostly by Mose
people. Paologo was attacked several times and suffered some losses.[42] Farther
south, Zawara became a prominent center under the leadership of Yombie.

In mid-February, d'Arboussier set up three defense posts, each staffed with
about forty auxiliary horsemen: one was north of Koudougou, in Godin; two
were south of Koudougou, in Surgu and Sabu. The post at Sabu also included a
lieutenant, a doctor, a sergeant, a corporal, and seventeen tirailleurs. The chiefs
of the three villages were asked to provide labor for the rapid construction of
crenellated defensive walls. Mounted auxiliaries protected by thorn bushes were
positioned outside of these. Similar defenses had been erected around Kou-

dougou.[43] Although the posts and the villages around them now became targets of assault, the French were able to use the posts to regularly conduct raids against insurgent strongholds. They were thus able to spoil the planned efforts of the Marka and Gurunsi leadership. Even more effective in preventing the war from spreading into the Mose villages were local political factors. Chief Inspector Vidal remarked in his report that "the authority enjoyed by the Mose chiefs among their people preserved us from a true catastrophe."[44]

Around the posts of Sabu and Surgu, anticolonial forces took position in the villages of La, Ipendo, Dogo, Tiu, and Naton. On February 24, close to eight hundred Gurunsi men gathered in La (sixteen kilometers west of Surgu) and Dogo with the intention of attacking Surgu. Troops in the post led a preventive attack against La and killed approximately twenty combatants. Three days later, the Gurunsi forces in La attacked the post of Surgu, left unprotected while the guards were away at Sabu. The village of Surgu welcomed the combatants, but a colonial detachment from Sabu took back the post.[45] The next day, Lieutenant Marotel, arriving from Koudougou with about 160 men, including 25 soldiers, attacked and destroyed half the village of La. Then he went to Ipendo, whose leader was Basana, the former sergeant and interpreter in the Gold Coast. Men from La and Naton came to Ipendo's help. After violent combat, the defenders fled, leaving behind 60 dead and taking with them many wounded men.

Farther south, d'Arboussier chose to defend the village of Sili, whose chief sided with the French in spite of strong pressure from Dio, a neighboring village. Strategically located, Sili allowed control of the road crossing the Muhun at a ford near Pura; it was a barrier to extension of the conflict to the region of Leo. The post was meant to incommode the Gurunsi of the region of Zawara and inhibit contact with the insurgent Nienegue on the right side of the Muhun. North of Koudougou, near the Godin post, the anticolonial villages of Wera and Ninion on March 1 attacked and burned down the village of Imasorho, which was on the colonial side. Four days later, a punitive expedition attacked and burned down Wera, forcing its combatants to flee.

This geographical dispersion of the conflict was due to the colonial strategy of establishing and being able to hold the new posts. But the threat to Koudougou remained because of the growing number of Gurunsi anticolonial adherents. Sorties were still being launched from Koudougou, particularly against the villages of Zula and Tiogo, which were bases for hundreds of Gurunsi. The post diary notes that in early March many Marka organizers were still going from village to village.

SECOND PHASE (MARCH 7 TO MAY 12 1916)

The uncertainty of the situation was favorable to the anticolonial propaganda of Marka and Gurunsi leaders. Conditions changed, however, with the arrival of eighty-four more soldiers in Koudougou on March 7. Like Marotel and his men, they had come from the Fourteenth Company in Togoland. Now Marotel was able to organize a strong military column and, he hoped, to put an end to the opposition. On March 9, the column left Koudougou to attack the main anticolonial centers in the north and to protect the procolonial villages of Konkistenga, Nanoro, and Sun.[46]

The French effort then shifted to west of Koudougou. On March 17, a detachment of ninety tirailleurs, ten guards, and sixty auxiliary horsemen attacked Zula. Two thousand combatants from Pum, Tialgo, Reo, Gundi, Puni, Boyolo, and Zula itself defended the village. Commanded by Dahuda and other Marka leaders, it was the largest concentration of men ever assembled in the war in Koudougou. Marotel wrote that "the enemy shows a lot of courage . . . as soon as a warrior falls he is taken away by the men around him, who retreat without too much hurry."[47] Nonetheless, the anticolonial forces were defeated. The French counted forty-five enemy dead on the battlefield, and a few days after the battle they estimated that Gurunsi losses were probably greater than that. Zula was demolished. Three days later, the soldiers also demolished the deserted village of Gundi and the neighboring Parapadita and Sisoguin.

The conflict then moved south. On March 21, a detachment from the post of Sabu attacked the village of La, already attacked twice in February. The next day, 400 men based in the village of Naton, where Yombie commanded a large force, attacked the detachment in Sabu. To assist the forces in Sabu against Naton, Marotel left Koudougou two days later with a column of about 150. Marotel's column gave Naton heavy losses and took the village. The troops then went to the neighboring village of Tiu, used as a temporary base by the anticolonial partisans (Tiu was the village in which Yombie had spent a large part of his life in the service of the Mose chief). Inhabitants and combatants abandoned the village before the column's arrival.

In April, Marotel adopted "pincer" tactics — an assault in which two military units from opposite sides converged on the enemy position in order to divide the enemy front and make escape more difficult. After the battle at Naton, the anticolonial fighters had retreated to Dogo, which Marotel attacked on April 2 with two detachments.[48] Dogo was taken after strong resistance and the village was demolished, but three days later the supposedly defeated anticolonial forces gathered in the village of Tiyele. Defiant as ever, they attacked and overran the post of Sabu. Colonial reinforcements were sent again to Sabu, which was re-taken after several hours of battle.

A bizarre set of "police rounds" set out from Sabu on April 13. Troops from Koudougou, headed by Lieutenant Boullais, and troops from Leo, under Re-mond, the resident of Leo, conducted it. First they demolished Ipendo and Tiyele, which they had found deserted. Then, as small contingents of partisans made hit-and-run attacks, the round took a curious turn. The resident of Koudougou, Michel, had advised the column's leaders not to take the risk of attacking fortified villages because the anticolonial movement would consider any failure to be a victory; the colonial troops, therefore, went for five days from village to village (Nabielienayu, Zinu, Bolo, and Dana), but remained at a distance in each instance without engaging in combat. The partisans understood the reluctance to attack for what it was and interpreted it as victory, anyway.

Boullais's description of these villages gives an idea of the kind of defen-sive strongholds that could be found in most of the Volta-Bani region:

> Crenellated outside and walls inside. . . . Dark rooms with little height com-municate through a low doorway, allowing the passage of only one person in an almost crawling position. Each house complex/ward *(soukala)* contains a reserve of millet and water in case of protracted siege. The ground floor com-municates with the flat roof through a man-size hole. On top of the terrace, another structure is built with crenellated walls.[49]

The day after the column ended its rounds, the anticolonial partisans at-tacked a patrol based in the post of Surgu, and on April 23 they attacked the ward of the Mose chief of Tiu, which the column had just visited. Adopting a strategy of continuous harassment, small groups of anticolonial men showed up daily at the post of Sabu without engaging in serious combat. On May 4, ap-proximately three hundred partisans attacked the procolonial village of Velia. They lost many men and were driven back to Tiu.

Despite the demolition of many enemy military bases, the situation had still not decisively evolved in favor of the colonial government. The anticolonial movement was gaining momentum in the residency of Leo, and when colonial forces responded by focusing their efforts in the south, the resisters established new centers of operation northwest of Koudougou in Boyolo and in Pum. These were to be used as bases for an attack on Koudougou. The men in the Boyolo gathering were from villages north of Koudougou (Ninion, Kuria, Bantuli, Wera,

Didir, and Dasa); those in Pum were from the villages of the southwest (Tiogo, Tio, Tenado, Tialgo, Kukuldi, and Zula). What foiled the plans was the bad news arriving from the Marka region, where Molard's second campaign was unfolding. Marka and Gurunsi leaders hesitated. The Nuna and Winye (Ko) villages of the area north of Boromo had begun to surrender after the Molard column destroyed Da on April 22 (see chap. 7).

Combatants led by Yombie, Koso (who was from Tialgo), and Marka leaders left Pum for Tialgo, which thus became an important military center. From April 24 to April 27, d'Arboussier and Marotel led a column of about two hundred men and a large group of Mose allies to that area.[50] Kukuldi was deserted, but attacks from Boyolo and Tialgo interrupted the demolition of the village by Mose auxiliairies. D'Arboussier chose not to attack Tialgo. Thus this strong column, too, achieved little. The French without a cannon, the war was in a stalemate. The anticolonial partisans, however, were growing worried because planting season was approaching; Yombie told them that they had to prepare for a protracted war and that he was waiting for guns that would be sent to him from the other side of the Muhun. The reinforcements finally came, but they were not for Yombie: in early May, the colonial government announced that it was going to send new forces—including an artillery piece—to Koudougou.

At this point Marotel presented an account of what had been achieved under his command since January. This fanciful version of events—approved by d'Arboussier—was reproduced in all the administrative reports of the time, and subsequently in more recent work (Hébert 1970, 45). Marotel reported that first the region around Koudougou had been cleared of enemy forces, but that the insurrection had spread southward in the area of the Leo residency. In reality, in late April the villages of Boyolo (about twenty kilometers from Koudougou) and Tialgo (twenty-five kilometers from Koudougou) housed large concentrations of fighters in anticipation of a major offensive on Koudougou, and the colonial forces in the town did not dare to attack them. The second point made by Marotel was that, by early May, Gurunsi forces did not conduct attacks in open terrain anymore but sought refuge in fortified villages. In fact, small groups continuously harassed colonial forces, and the fortified villages—the so-called refuges— were surely the logical strategic bases for fighting colonial troops that lacked artillery.

Such reports, even allowing for a commander's desire to be self-congratulatory, betray the need to give a rational account of the repression. The action is presented as organized around a plan of action with successive phases. First, the most urgent task, the defense of Koudougou; then, its disengagement by suppressing the proximate enemy centers encircling it; third, the establishment of *postes d'arrêt* to prevent the propagation of the rebellion in Mose country; and finally—yet to be achieved—the suppression of the rebellion by attacking the last strongholds with the support of the incoming artillery.[51] This plan was good on paper, but it did not happen on the terrain. The colonial forces in Koudougou could not follow such a plan because they lacked men and firepower, and because the anticolonial leadership disturbed their plans with unexpected counter-moves. And when, for phase four (see the next section), a much-better-supported column went south, the partisans moved their activity to the undefended north, and the town of Koudougou came very close to being invaded. The column rushed back north, and it was back to phase one. In early May, the military situation was anything but clear.

THE CADENCE COLUMN (MAY TO AUGUST 1916)

The new force sent to Koudougou was the company under Captain Cadence detached from the Molard column, which arrived from Boromo on May 12 (see map 27). In early June, it was reinforced with the Breton company, which came with a cannon.[52] Cadence followed the strategy that was adopted by Molard. He divided his troops into two, the first group to attack and destroy the major military centers in a delimited zone, and the second to follow, achieving "pacification" and receiving submissions. In the pacified areas, temporary posts were established to prevent anticolonial fighters from reoccupying the defeated villages. Cadence wrote in his report that his main objective was at any cost to prevent a failure—a real risk because at first he did not have a cannon.[53]

Augmented by Marotel and d'Arboussier's troops, the Cadence company marched on May 18 to a point near Sabu, the Rock of Kola, a large rocky prominence where the inhabitants of Tiu, Gumorho, Naton, and other smaller villages, men, women, and children, had sought refuge. After three days of siege and a hit-and-run attack from Yombie (who attempted to rescue his besieged brother), the defenders ran out of water and surrendered to Cadence. He took 440 prisoners. The defeat resounded because the rock had the reputation of being a mystical sanctuary.[54] In the following days, the column destroyed and burned down some of the wards of Tiu and the deserted villages of Goden and Woro. It then removed from enemy control a section of the road from Koudougou to Leo, between Sabu and Gao. Many villages of the areas of Gao and Dalo surrendered. In late May and early June, the Cadence column operated in

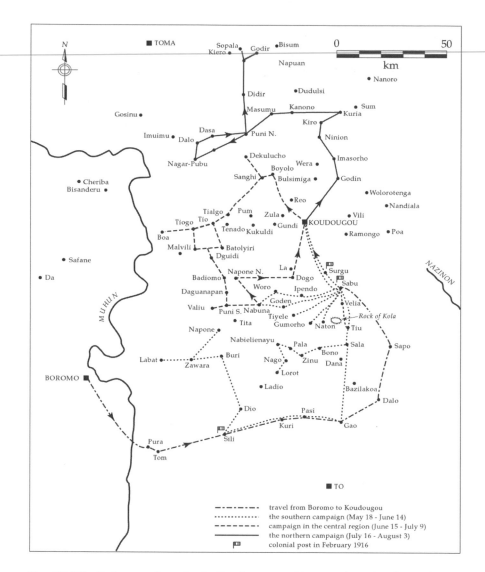

Map 27. The Cadence column in the Koudougou residency. Adapted and completed from "Rapport du Capitaine Cadence sur les opérations de la colonne secondaire Koudougou-Léo du 1er Mars au 15 Octobre 1916," Ténado, October 15, 1916 (SHAT 5 H 196).

the region bordering the residences of Leo and Koudougou, where it destroyed the deserted villages of Bono and Nabielienayu.

By attacking the strongholds, the Cadence column for the first time brought to the war in this region the patterns of the cercle of Dedougou. The village of Nago received the column with gunshots. Under the leadership of a man described by d'Arboussier as a féticheur, "not averse to selling amulets with Arabic text bought from wandering marabouts" (Duperray 1984, 189), Nago had become the region's major center of resistance to the French. Cadence had been told that Nago was "a fetishist center, a gris-gris factory. This village has confidence in its fetish, in its walls, in its multistory houses."[55] After a one-day battle, Cadence controlled part of the village, and during the night its defenders evacuated the rest. A military post was installed in Nago, and other villages of the region (Pala, Zinu) were demolished.

Cadence hoped that, because of Nago's reputation for its military and spiritual defenses, this successful attack — which had been conducted without artillery — would discourage resistance — a hope that proved to be vain. When the column arrived in Dio, another important anticolonial center, Cadence's surrender proposal was rejected by the village chief with the statement that "he did not want to have a single white man before his eyes anymore."[56] Dio was attacked on June 9, taken, and systematically demolished.

The last and most important stronghold in the region was Zawara. By now, the Breton company and its cannon had joined the column. Following the usual pattern, the assault, made on June 13, lasted all day, and at night the defenders left the village. Zawara and neighboring Buri, Napone, and Tita were demolished by the column. Then the column returned to Koudougou because of the urgent developments in the north, but it had destroyed the major centers of resistance in the south, to the Boromo-Sabu road. It left behind small detachments in posts scattered throughout the region (Sabu, Nago, Labat, Sili, Dio, Ladio, and Pura); they could proceed with the pacification phase. The destruction of the villages forced the large Nuna forces to seek protection in the bush.

The emergency in the north was that, while the Cadence column was in the south, partisans had moved back to some of the villages north of Koudougou that had been destroyed earlier; they even occupied a ward of the town. The column turned on the villages near the city. The abandoned villages of Boyolo and Sanghi were destroyed by what Cadence called "our looters." On June 25, the column attacked the village of Dekolocho, whose very existence had so far been unknown to the French administration. The troops then moved west and south, pursuing Gurunsi forces, which were moving quickly from village to village. En route, the column demolished deserted former strongholds of the movement (Tialgo, Tio, Batolyiri, Tiogo, and Malvili).

In the first week of July, the column was back near the Boromo-Sabu road. While the column was west of Koudougou, anticolonial contingents under Yombie had used the village of Puni-south as a base, regularly attacking the "pacification" detachments left behind in the south by the column. Yombie even attacked the post of Labat.

Cadence attacked Puni on July 7, finally coming face to face with Yombie. The resistance was fierce. In spite of the large number of guns the defenders possessed, Yombie, who had been wounded in an engagement in Bagana a few days before, was unable to retain control of the village. He lost 60 of his men and was himself captured, along with his brother and 298 other men. The column returned to Koudougou after establishing the posts of Sanghi and Napone in the central zone. These were expected to receive many submissions after the capture of Yombie, but the movement was not yet vanquished. Malvili, Diudiu, and Batolyiri refused to capitulate.[57] The French may have overestimated Yombie's influence in the anticolonial coalition, and underestimated that of other Gurunsi leaders.

On July 16, the column left Koudougou with administrator d'Arboussier for the far north of the residency. The area had not yet seen the action of colonial troops. The column met little resistance, as Dahuda and other Marka leaders had left some time earlier and local war leaders now had far fewer followers. At the news of the column's approach, the population destroyed the bridges and abandoned the villages (Kiro, Kuria, Ninion, Mozumu, and Didir). In Puninorth and Dasa, forces of a few hundred men fled after briefly engaging the column. In Dasa, the anticolonial forces had gathered under the leadership of the chiefs of Yayo and Tiogo.[58] After the surrender of the villages in this area, on July 25 the column moved northward to Godir. While in Godir, the Breton company was called back to Dedougou because the higher command deemed that the situation in Gurunsi country was now stabilized.

The relation between the anticolonial movement in Gurunsi country and the territories lying to its north was facilitated by the presence of many Gurunsi communities among the Samo. The Samo communities in the north had received emissaries from Pundu across the Muhun River (chap. 7, p. 209), but the Gurunsi combatants in the south provided for them a further connection to the broader anticolonial movement. The latter started contacts with villages in the region of Toma in June 1916. In July, Gurunsi resisters used the village of Sapala, northwest of Godir, as a base for raids against the Samo villages that had surrendered to Maguet. On his way back to Dedougou from Samo country, Maguet had attacked Sapala on July 9 with his company of guards and auxiliary soldiers, reinforced by the tirailleurs of the post of Toma. After a fierce battle, in which Sapala lost ninety-one men, Maguet had seized the town and made two hundred prisoners. It was not until twenty days later, however, when the Cadence column arrived, that the village officially surrendered.[59] Other villages of the area also surrendered and the column returned to Koudougou on August 3.

These submissions were not readily offered to the military. In many cases, they were the object of long negotiations between village representatives and the French administrators—d'Arboussier and the resident of Koudougou. Even the unexpected and extremely violent military campaign had not changed the villagers' attitude toward people of power. The whites were treated as equals—an attitude that still exists. Most villages surrendered many weeks or even months after their destruction. Even then, people stayed away from their villages as long as colonial troops remained in their area, and they rarely respected the conditions that the administration imposed on them.

In late July, Gurunsi armed groups—reported as hiding in the bush—were still "very active" in the region between the Muhun River and Koudougou.[60] Even in August, as in the cercles of San and Bobo-Dioulasso, pockets of resistance existed. Military posts staffed by the men of the Cadence column were scattered throughout the Gurunsi country (Puni, Nago, Labat, Sanghi, and Tenado) to ensure the pacification, but Bayoko, Tio, Batolyiri, and Malvili had not yet sent surrender delegations. In September, in the area of Puni-north, across the Muhun River, and Samo villages, leaders of the movement who were at large still maintained some influence, but the repression had effectively ended the period of large military confrontations. In his report written in mid-October, Cadence concluded, "Of course, it will not be easy. People display an attitude of indifference. It is even possible that they entertain the hope that we will grow weary. It will be necessary to push them—to push them constantly." Most war leaders had not been arrested, but what worried Cadence most in reestablishing control, more than the eventuality of renewed fighting, was the fear that had been instilled in people by the brutal repression.[61]

If we compare the Gurunsi front of the anticolonial war to the main stage within the bend of the Muhun River, we see that the difference between the two was due as much to the nature of the French response as to the local effort. Most battles in the Koudougou residency involved smaller numbers of combatants (usually fewer than five hundred) and casualties (about fifty per engagement). But the main reason why fewer major battles happened in this zone was the waiting attitude of the French, who decided that the Marka and Bwa areas had to be subdued first. They refrained from committing the military resources that were necessary to attack the major strongholds in Gurunsi country. When they did so with the Cadence column, the movement had already been weakened by months of a war of attrition and by the demoralizing news of the repression in the cercle of Dedougou. In the few major battles that did occur, the defense tactics were similar to the ones employed in the Marka and Bwa areas—which is not surprising since the leaderships were in close contact.

The role of Islam in the two regions was different due to the ways in which the alliances around the French were built. In the Marka areas, the established Muslim houses supported the suppression, at the cost of alienating some of their historical village allies, partly because some of them were unreconcilable enemies of the leadership in the Datomo area. This was not the case in the cercle of San or in the Koudougou residency, where the mixture of Islam and non-Islam was present both on the colonial side and within the resistance. Furthermore, around Koudougou the main allies of the French happened to be the Mose chiefs who had initiated the anti-Muslim crackdown, and this naturally generated Muslim sympathies in the anticolonial camp. As we saw earlier, the ties and conflicts that channeled these choices can be traced back to the initial colonial occupation and even to the nineteenth century. Islam as a religion, however, or the groups that identified with it, fitted within the rest of the society in similar ways in all these regions.

The colonial administration estimated that the war in the Gurunsi region involved about one hundred thousand people,[62] and Marotel calculated that from January to May 1916 (that is, before the campaign of the Cadence column) the number of deaths was slightly over one thousand.[63] Taking into consideration the very large number of wounded, which can be gauged by the staggering amount of ammunition used by the colonial troops, the actual final count was undoubtedly much higher. From January 23 to August 3, the officially distributed and spent gun cartridges of the colonial forces added up to 38,072 rounds; in addition, the Cadence column used 46 explosive shells.[64] Gurunsi country had a very low demographic density. Relative to its population, the Koudougou residency and northern Leo suffered as many losses as the cercle of Dedougou or the northern part of the cercle of Bobo-Dioulasso.

As in the other cercles, one of the final actions of the French in the cercle of Ouagadougou was the execution of rebels who had been involved in the killing of colonial soldiers. On November 21, 1917, almost one year after the end of the fighting, eight anticolonial combatants were shot in Ouagadougou: Nebila of Bantuli, Bavuru of Napone, Nyendebin of Zinogo, Banela of Natu, Bamu and Zemze of Malvili, and Lalle and Kudebi of Batolyiri.

Conclusion

THE VOLTA-BANI WAR STARTED IN LATE 1915 after nearly two years of profound disturbances and recurrent local movements of opposition to the colonial administration. This study argues that it was different from all these earlier movements, although it absorbed some of them, in that it was a coordinated regional effort to conclusively terminate French colonial rule. The anticolonial war was not a collection of localized resistances that happened to occur simultaneously and were inspired by each other; even less was it a desperate attempt to deal a blow to an omnipotent colonial government at whatever cost. One often encounters the assumption that anticolonial opposition was a reaction to the strengthening of colonial domination and to political oppression that makes the subject population lose all hope and embark on a suicidal revolt. The evidence gathered in this book makes clear that this view is not valid for the Volta-Bani War.

Colonial control in this region had been tenuous, patchy, and episodic. Most importantly, far from strengthening, with the start of World War I in Europe it showed signs of weakness, raising hopes that it could be ended soon. The majority of the population participated in the resistance movement, reactivating regional intervillage links that were part of the legacy of the nineteenth century and that had survived the colonial occupation. They sustained the staggering losses of the repression because they carried the conviction that in the end, with their organization and their conventional warfare techniques, they could obtain victory against the colonial regime.

The most important development that promoted the perception that France was weakened and could be driven out as colonial power was the massive pullout occasioned by wartime mobilization in Europe and the withdrawal of the military contingents from their bases in the colony. The two conscription campaigns of 1915, and the crackdowns that the commandant of Dedougou carried out the year before the start of the anticolonial war, especially the one that led to the elimination of the Karantao of Wahabu, strengthened the hopeful prognosis that colonial domination was withering. Finally, the initial victories of the anticolonial movement, first in Bona, then against administrator Maubert in Bondokuy, and then again against the large repression column in Yankaso, provided further confirmation of this local view of the balance of power.

The Volta-Bani War was prepared by a group of leaders who were responsible for the organization and the declaration of war. They based their organization on the links provided by village leagues and the broader groupings of villages that emerge around important regional shrines. After their initial successes, following well-established nineteenth-century patterns of communication, they sent emissaries to nearby and distant communities to invite them to join the movement and to explain their arguments of why the resistance was going to be successful. The Datomo area in the cercle of Dedougou provided this leadership and constituted the focus of the ensuing organization for the longest part of the duration of the war. The shrine in the village of Bona, the reputation of Yisu Kote, and the headdress made of *da* fibers were the central components of the emerging movement. Participants in the different areas of the war zone sent to Bona sacrificial animals, gifts, and at least a token portion of the goods captured in successful confrontations. The leadership reciprocated by returning ritually treated objects, by coordinating the movement, and by processing the information and reshaping it through active propaganda work. Military leaders from the core area traveled to distant fronts, disseminated tactical innovations, and often took command of the battles.

As the movement spread, other leaders rose in different areas. Most of these men assumed a position subordinate to the original leadership in the district of Datomo. This elaborate hierarchical arrangement was the product of the anticolonial war itself; it came into existence gradually. It was partly the product of a preexisting political cultural logic, but it was nonetheless a new historical development that emerged in response to colonial government and to the opportunities that presented themselves. The voluntarily assumed hierarchy of the anticolonial movement was different from the strict ranking method of the colonial army and the civil administration, but it was effective in providing the anticolonial movement's coherence and successes.

With tireless and skilled effort the original leadership of the movement managed to crystallize the will of the majority of the local population to end the colonial occupation. In the initial stages of planning, these leaders marshalled the defensive resources of the age-grade perenkie organization and revitalized intervillage alliances. They were able to give a wider extension to the movement by bringing a number of alliances together using the channels of communication made possible by the hierarchies established between the earth shrines of the area. This achievement made it possible for them to stand against the first expeditions of the colonial government, and the early military successes in turn gave credibility to their claims of strength and persuaded partisans from a much wider circle.

The central shrine of Bona and many ritual practices that accompanied anticolonial action owed their intelligibility to non-Islamic conceptions, but Islam also played an intricate role in the movement. In the Koudougou residency and in the cercle of San, situated on the two opposite peripheries of the core area of Dedougou, some important Muslim figures participated in the movement or, alternatively, some leaders were attributed Islamic credentials by both anticolonial partisans and colonial administrators. The relations that Muslims maintained with farmers in the region, as well as some particular events that happened in the months preceding the outbreak of the war, are necessary to understand this development. In this region the Muslims did not constitute a separate sector with its own interests and its own political instruments to express them. As persons and houses, they variously established relations of support and exchange, but also conflict, with the different constituents of the local scene. These relations continued with varying intensities during the anticolonial war, already lending the war a degree of religious ambiguity that is clearly revealed in the mixture of spiritual devices employed by the anticolonial armies.

In the cercle of Dedougou, the anti-Muslim campaign conducted by the French administration considerably weakened an important Muslim center; it was in opposition to this center that the Datomo alliance spearheading the anticolonial movement had established its identity in a long-standing conflict in the nineteenth century. The French thus unwittingly contributed to the rise of the anticolonial movement, but because of the deep-seated animosity, some of the leading Muslim houses of the cercle still allied themselves with the French despite the earlier crackdown against them. In Koudougou, in contrast, the network of Mose chiefs were involved in the inception of the anti-Muslim campaign and heavily invested in it afterwards. These chiefs were also the main participants in the repression of the anticolonial movement. In opposition to them, the anticolonial partisans assigned a greater symbolic role to Islam by ascribing Islamic attributes to their leading figures.

In the region of San there were Muslims both on the colonial side and anticolonial side. In Bandiagara, Aguibu and his son Tijani Tall, who had important Muslim credentials since their pedigree went to Sheikh Umar (although they were not known as religious scholars themselves), remained strong supporters of the French. On the anticolonial side, Adama Dembele was a cleric who carried all the prestige of a haji. The French also made an effort to keep the influential Muslims on their side, mostly by threat and intimidation, which had perhaps an effect in making the Muslim community adopt at least a general attitude of accommodation. In this respect, the quiet pro-French attitude of some Muslim houses of Dedougou was part of a broader trend, while the anti-French position common in the cercle of San was exceptional for the time. The core leaders of Datomo were the sworn enemies of some Muslims in their own area, but they accepted these distant Muslim allies into their fold and bestowed honors upon them. Some of the Marka leaders who went from the Datomo area to help the Gurunsi anticolonial organization may even have taken account of local dispositions by assuming opportunistically a Muslim persona.

The French were eventually able to defeat the anticolonial movement by bringing together the largest military force ever deployed in colonial West Africa. The size of the army that was necessary to achieve the repression implies that the anticolonial leaders were not totally deluded in their assessment that they could be successful, but also that they had miscalculated the logistical capacities of the French and the vast material resources that the latter commanded despite the demands of World War I. The colonial army extinguished the armed opposition by concentrating all its efforts in the Bwa and Marka areas of the cercle of Dedougou. Because of this decision, the fighting in other areas was less intense and lasted longer.

The weapon that gave superiority to the French was the cannon, which was used to open breaches in the thick defensive walls that surrounded the fortified villages. The cannon did not make obsolete the resisters' strategy of giving battle only from behind fortifications, but it forced them to modify this strategy in ways that were less effective and more wasteful of the labor that went into constructing these structures. Without artillery, it seems that the colonial government would not have been able to hold on to this region. Even the advantage provided by artillery was not decisive. Ultimately, the determining factor seems to have been the ability of the French to move in troops and materials from the distant parts of their West African empire. This transportation was accomplished against great difficulties, but it proved to be what the anticolonial leadership had not anticipated. The French columns ran out of ammunition and supplies several times during the seven-month-long repression campaign, but the anticolonial expectation that the moment of evening out the score would eventually arrive was not fulfilled.

The French military campaign in the Volta-Bani region ended in September 1916 without succeeding in gaining the complete submission of the population. Isolated movements of opposition continued for a few more months, particularly in Bobo villages in the north of the cercle of Bobo-Dioulasso.[1] In the devastated core area inhabited by the Marka and Nienegue people, the organized armed movement came to an end, but the population resisted in other ways. There was no true surrender, no resignation to domination. According to the commandant of the cercle of Bobo-Dioulasso, the attitude of the populations in 1917 was the same as in 1915 prior to the revolt, "independent and fierce."[2] The project of "pacification" of the area ran into the same problems encountered by the local colonial administration since the conquest, noncompliance to orders, flights from villages, and unfulfilled promises. In September 1916, some doubt even remained in the mind of the French officials whether hostilities had ceased or had been only suspended by the farmers because they wanted to plant their fields before the end of the rainy season.

In his final report, Colonel Molard felt compelled to prove by argument to the military and civilian hierarchy that his action had indeed snuffed out the rebellion:

> It seems that the column has obtained its desired result. The country has submitted, and the hostilities have ceased. As a warranty of what I am asserting I have the unanimous testimony of the three administrators of the cercles most involved, Dedougou, San, and Koutiala, who in their respective telegrams affirm with the greatest conviction that the pacification is completed and that the return of the rebellion to an offensive is inconceivable.[3]

Yet the attitude of the population made it impossible to claim a definite victory. Another passage in the following page of the same report shows that for Molard some uncertainty persisted:

> Does this mean that in the revolted region from now on everything will be just fine? I would like to be able to maintain that, but having witnessed the confusion, the panic—to say the least—that took hold of everyone, military

and civilian, in the beginning of the movement, and the paralysis that followed among some, having witnessed the explosion of hate against us and
the fierceness of the resistance that we encountered, having observed the intelligence, thoroughness and the true tactical knowledge that our adversaries
displayed, having been unable to prevent myself from admiring the persever-
ance that they maintained till the end despite bloody and repeated failures, I
find it impossible [to assert]. The rebellion has been broken up. That is true.
But is it really smothered? That is something else. Only the future will tell us.
. . . We have to understand that what the natives did they can do again, and
do it better with the experience that they gained, and that disarmament, even
if total, is not sufficient to give us the certainty of absolute quiet among our
adversaries.[4]

This inconclusive outcome of the campaign and the persisting fear on the
colonial side of a resumption of armed struggle opened the door to another manifestation of the perpetual tension between the military and civilian sectors of the
colonial administration. What was to be done now in this region?

MILITARY OCCUPATION

Molard proposed at the end of his long report an extensive and "tight" military
occupation plan for the zone that had participated in the war. His proposal included the presence of a senior officer in the region—a suggestion that avoided
going into detail about the relationship of this officer with civilian administrators. The solution was clear to Molard: the region had to be put back under
military administration.

The civilian administrators vigorously opposed a return of the military.
Edgard Maguet, the commandant of the cercle of Dedougou, had already
brought forward a different proposal—one that involved less extensive use of
military personnel. In a letter to the governor of the colony, he dismissed the
entire rebellion as a freak accident.[5] For Maguet, the only cause of the revolt
was the conscription campaign. A few unfortunate mistakes of the colonial administration in the early stages of the movement, especially the defeat of the
Simonin column in Yankaso in December 1915, had given the uprising a scope
totally unanticipated by its instigators. Now, according to Maguet, the government had proved its strength and the population would not dare to engage in
another armed confrontation. The civilian administration was perfectly capable

of keeping things under control and proceeding with "pacification." Civilian administrators also objected that the repressive nature of the proposed military apparatus would make it more, rather than less, difficult to win over the population after the catastrophic experiences of the war.

The question of military versus civilian administration turned out to be a short-lived debate because, with the world war continuing, France did not possess the resources, military or civilian, to indulge in "tight" military control. France needed soldiers from Africa at the European front, not at home, organizing a backwater territory. Financial considerations also made it difficult for the army to adopt Molard's positions.

Another debate had started earlier at the highest level of political hierarchy, between President Gaston Doumergues in Paris and Governor-general Marie François Clozel in Dakar. This disagreement provides a side commentary to our decision to describe these events as a war. It was sparked by the need to determine which administrative body should pay for the unplanned expenditures occasioned by the military columns deployed in the Volta-Bani region.

The colonies were supposed to be self-financing; they were expected to maintain balanced budgets. Were the confrontations in the Volta and Bani region to be considered a war, the army, and therefore the central government of France, would have to pay for the expenditures; were they, to the contrary, to be considered a civil disturbance, the repression was an internal matter of the colony and the expenses would have to be paid from the budget of the colonial government. Governor-general Clozel maintained that this was a war and that France should pay for the expenditures. President Doumergues and General Pineau, the commander in chief of West African troops, argued that "as in the case of Beledougou it was not a matter of a war operation whatsoever, calling into question the principle of sovereignty, but of simple police operations in a region conquered and organized for a long time." Doumergues added that he could not even mention to the French chamber the resistance to military conscription in West Africa because to do so would instill doubt in French public opinion about the loyalty of "our African populations."[6] Thus budget considerations and propaganda vis-à-vis the domestic public, as well the international one, became factors in the desire to demote the Volta-Bani conflict to civil disturbance.

The issue of a military administration was dropped and the populations of the Volta-Bani region remained under civilian rule, but there was an exceptional deployment of troops to support this rule. In a region where the military had not been stationed since 1914, new military posts were created to constitute a "true network of military protection over the recently subjected populations."[7] Posts

were established in the cercle of San (at San and Benena), in the cercle of Dedougou (with a machine-gun platoon and an artillery platoon at headquarters,
and posts temporarily at Boromo and in Bondokuy), in the cercle of Bobo-
Dioulasso (at Hunde, with two hundred men), in the cercle of Ouagadougou (a
company of 350 at the base in Ouagadougou, with posts at Koudougou and To),
and in the cercle of Gaoua (at Diebougou). A total of seven companies were initially assigned to "the occupation" of the Volta-Bani region.[8]

The officers in charge of the posts were given political, administrative, and
judicial powers, and military posts were themselves gradually transformed into
administrative centers, thus perpetuating the uneasy relations between the civilian administration and the military. The cercle administrations continued to be
beset by shortages of personnel even after the end of World War I and they
could hardly refuse help from the military. In November 1916, the lieutenant
governor of Haut-Senegal-Niger expressed his concern to the governor general: "I will not go over the difficulties and dangers presented by this situation.
It is obviously the duty of everyone to hold out as long as necessary, but it is in
the interest of the administration to plan the relief of the personnel whose
health is running out."[9] Two years later, the end of the world war did not solve
the problem: "We should not wonder at the rumors that we are leaving defini-
tely the region when we see, for example, that the cercle of Sikasso is inhabited
by 230,000 people and administered by one European, who is an agent for Indigenous Affairs."[10]

This second occupation of the Volta-Bani region with the repression campaign and the posts set up after it became the occasion to redraw the administrative borders in order to ensure more effective political control. The overall
borders of the cercles of San, Dedougou, and Bobo-Dioulasso remained unchanged, but new cantons and subdivisions were created and others abolished.
In the spirit of the "*races* policy," new subdivisions were created to bring within
the boundaries of one administrative unit populations of the same ethnic background. In the cercle of Bobo-Dioulasso, the three Nienegue cantons were made
into a separate subdivision to facilitate a careful watch over them. In the cercle
of Dedougou, a new subdivision called Samodougou was created in 1918; it included all the Samo people—"who form an ethnic bloc perfectly homogeneous
but who found themselves scattered over three different cercles; [this new subdi-
vision] will allow us to penetrate the Samo and overcome their spirit of independence."[11] Still, many Samo continued to refuse to pay taxes and to obey the
orders of the resident, based in Tougan, and the new commandant of the cercle
in Dedougou. They would flee to the bush at the time of conscription campaigns.

To control the Samo, a military post had to be established in the village of Lankwe for a period of four years.[12]

THE NATIVE COMMAND

The impossibility of increasing the number of troops or even having civilian officials in sufficient numbers to carry out routine tasks made the administration focus its hope on the native chiefs. Once again, as in the early years of the century, in order to maintain a rule that was rejected by the population, "native command" became the device from which miracles were expected. The policy swung, as is explained in chapter 3, between maintaining the large états placed under local strongmen, who the French wanted to believe had the right of conquest, and dissolving them in the name of the *races* policy. The latter option had been designed by Governor-general Ponty and then adopted by Clozel under the guise of "respect for local traditions." By stipulating that each ethnic group should be ruled by a chief of the same ethnic background, this policy seemed to imply a move toward greater local autonomy. The contrast between the two policies was, however, complicated by other considerations.

The large territorial units called états constituted an intermediate layer between the French administrator and the villages and increased the distance between the two. It was this system that came to be known, in French colonial parlance, as indirect administration. Thus, while, in the arguments, local autonomy was valued in favor of *races* policy, breaking up the états in its name shortened the distance between the administrator and the villages and implied a move toward direct, rather than indirect, administration. In reality, both of these policies sought to establish easier and less costly political control of the population, even though they were justified with loftier aims. The different arguments were about which one of the two was most expedient to achieve that end.

In the more homogeneous cercle of Ouagadougou, the *races* policy did not come into contradiction with that of strong chiefs, and it was applied with some success in Mose chiefdoms. The administration was able to achieve a leverage on the population with its appointed chiefs. The anticolonial movement put to the test the *races* policy in the so-called Gurunsi cantons, where the population rejected the French-appointed Mose chiefs. Nonetheless, the Mose chiefs as a coherent political body proved to be invaluable to the colonial administration in the defeat of the anticolonial movement within the cercle, and they came out of this episode greatly strengthened.

The situation was very different in the core of the war zone. In the cercle of Dedougou, disregarding the *races* policy, the administration promoted the chiefs who supported the repression, or their immediate descendants. The cantons of Datomo and Tunu, the birthplace of the anticolonial movement, were abolished and added into that of Safane, whose chief was thus rewarded for having taken risks to remain on the French side. The Muslim leaders, who had been condemned in 1915 in the marabout affair but whose followers had sided with the French during the war, were pardoned and restored to a position of respect. In the cercle of Bobo-Dioulasso (see chap. 5), the rapid turnover of cercle administrators gave the chiefs demoted by Maubert in 1915 some hope of regaining positions of power. The demoted chiefs made the already difficult work of the new canton chiefs almost impossible by participating in every maneuver imaginable to unsettle them, particularly at times of transfer of administrators. Frequent changes in chiefly appointments came to an end in this cercle only in 1919.

THE "IMPULSE TO REVOLT"

The violence of the war had broken the illusions that the French might have entertained about their "civilizing mission." Froger wrote that he was telling the people of the cercle that it was futile to revolt against "a force like ours that relies on the power of the bayonets and of the cannon."[13] He advised the governor that "in that country for many years we will have to be careful not to ask for anything that we cannot obtain by the strength of arms."[14] Lieutenant Governor Périquet was in agreement: "We must give everyone the most vivid impression of our force, and show our most definitive intention to break down and punish in the most dreadful manner any impulse to revolt."[15] Five years later the feeling had not changed, even if pugnacity was now moderated by caution: "Only force keeps the populations within the bounds of these rudimentary states, which the current cantons are. . . . The mass of the population does not like us. It is only resigned and this should be sufficient for us. To make this state of mind continue is our duty, and we should steer at equal distance from a policy of excess that would push to rebellion those who were resigned and from a policy of weakness that would give the impression that resistance to our orders is possible without taking risks."[16]

Coming to terms with this reality, however, took away the confidence that the French had so far maintained in the superiority of their weapons. The continuing anxiety that a violent anticolonial movement would flare up again finds expression in periodic reports of the cercle of Bobo-Dioulasso. In the dry season of 1917, Froger wrote to his superiors: "While in my opinion the current situation cannot lead to a rebellion in the country, it is also true that we are going through a period of disorder that, in the historical development of the peoples, is comparable to the ones that precede revolutions."[17] The blacksmiths of the Nienegue region were once again rapidly producing arrow tips and other weapons; the inquiry into the matter concluded that these arms were produced for export to "Lobi" populations, but this finding did not totally allay the fear of renewed uprising. At the same time, the Nienegue region was experiencing a massive flight, especially of women and children, to the regions of the south, and investigation revealed that the reason was a widespread belief that fighting would resume. "Weapon factories that are active in many villages . . . the exodus of women and girls . . . cannot be taken as definitive signs of an impending rebellion. Nonetheless, these two observations necessitate that we keep constant watch on the natives of the station of Hounde."[18]

The dry season passed and the fears proved to be unfounded, but in 1918 a similar apprehension took hold of the next administrator. Always prefacing his remark with the obligatory assuaging incantation, Mornet wrote: "Even if at present an uprising appears to be unlikely, we still have the pressing obligation to reduce the risks for the future. Too much confidence in our strength would be reprehensible."[19]

That dry season, too, passed without a new war, but in 1920 there were again "rumors" of trouble ahead, originating from the cercle of Dedougou. The cancellation of the military posts of Bondokuy and Boromo "was a subject of discussion for certain natives, who even said that the French had no longer the force necessary to occupy them and that even the post of Hunde would soon be evacuated . . . a movement of rebellion was about to break out to permanently drive us out."[20] Some of these rumors may have been cultivated by the different local parties always planning intrigues against each other, trying to provoke the administrator against their rivals. They may also have been exaggerated by the administrators themselves in order to obtain leeway for questionable moves from their superiors. But the recurrence of such reports also indicates that the memory of the war of 1916 was never far out of the colonial awareness.

THE CREATION OF UPPER VOLTA

With the end of World War I, the political situation of French West Africa evolved rapidly. The highest colonial administrators indulged in a profusion of new political and economic projects and grandiose plans to reorganize these colonies. Most of the plans remained on paper, with a notable exception: the one plan that succeeded was the division of the enormous territory of the Haut-Sénégal-Niger into two colonies. The history of this division, which led to the current nation-states of Mali and Burkina Faso, shows how the fear instilled by the Volta-Bani War provided an opportunity for some administrators in the higher echelons of the colonial hierarchy to finesse an economic agenda presented as political reorganization grounded in cultural differences.

At the request of the acting governor-general, Gabriel Angoulvant, a preliminary report for the division of the Haut-Sénégal-Niger was written in February 1918 by Maurice Delafosse, head of the Civil Affairs Department. Even though Delafosse had not been one of Angoulvant's favorite subordinates, the publication of his three-volume magnum opus *Haut-Senegal-Niger* in 1912 had established his reputation as a scholarly figure in larger colonial and anthropological circles, and he could lend great legitimacy to the project. In this short report, Delafosse insisted on the unmanageable size of Haut-Sénégal-Niger and wrote:

> We remember the events that took place since 1914 and particularly in 1915–1916 in the Bend of the Niger that almost jeopardized our authority in this part of the colony. There is no doubt that these events could have been anticipated and probably reduced to inconsequential incidents, had the lieutenant governor not found himself in the material impossibility to keep up with the political life of a whole region, to oversee the actions of his subordinates, to take the necessary actions required by the circumstances.[21]

In a previous pioneering article, Delafosse had proposed for the first time the existence of a "Voltaic family" of languages, noting that these languages were spoken in a circumscribed area, a "geographic domain" shown in a map that accompanied the article (1911, 392). The limit of Voltaic languages in that map largely overlaps with the western boundary of what eventually became Upper Volta. What remained unsaid in that article is that this "domain" did not include only languages of the Voltaic family (more commonly called Gur in the English literature). Besides the Bobo of Sia, which Delafosse acknowledges in a parenthesis not to be Voltaic, many other languages within these boundaries belong to the Mande family (Marka, Jula, Sambla, Samogho, Bolon, Syemu, Samo, Bisa). Delafosse did not consider Senufo a Voltaic language, but until recently many people did, and this created a difficulty in the opposite direction.[22]

Delafosse's language boundary in 1911 went between Sikasso and Bobo-

Dioulasso, north toward San, straight through areas speaking Senufo dialects, also dividing speakers of different Mande languages and dialects, following roughly the watershed line in the highlands where the Muhun and Bani Rivers take their sources. Undaunted by these difficulties due to this interpenetration of language families, in his 1918 report Delafosse followed the same boundary as in his earlier language-family article, and he proposed a partition that would leave the "Mande speaking" populations in Haut-Sénégal-Niger, while the "Voltaic populations" would constitute a new colony. This distinction of Delafosse's conflated linguistic/cultural/territorial factors between what was Mande and what was Voltaïc, but it became expedient to many other colonial interests.

The ensuing debate in colonial administrative circles added an economic dimension to what had started as an administrative project in response to the Volta-Bani War and had been turned into this somewhat chimerical "cultural" proposal by Delafosse. Delafosse was mildly criticized for his exclusively ethnic approach. The new lieutenant governor of Haut-Sénégal-Niger, Charles Désiré Brunet, and Angoulvant pointed out that ethnic groups were already so intertwined that new borders, wherever they were, would not create additional ethnic problems. As it often happened in colonial French West Africa, the preponderant voice was that of the governor of Ivory Coast. He developed an argument in favor of the division that was essentially economic and that focused mainly on Ivory Coast, but followed in its rough outline Delafosse's proposal of taking as boundary the watershed line between the Muhun and Bani River basins.

In December 1918, Angoulvant proposed to the minister of the colonies the division of Haut-Sénégal-Niger into two colonies, reiterating some of Delafosse's arguments, and the minister decreed in March 1919 the creation of the colony of Upper Volta, repeating in turn all the reasons given by Angoulvant. In an article written in 1922 entitled "Why Did I Create Upper Volta," Angoulvant stresses the political reasons.[23] He explains that Ouagadougou was chosen as the seat of the government of the new colony because it was the center of a country whose Mose population "has always given us, particularly during the war, continuous demonstration of its loyalty." From Ouagadougou, it would be easy to control surrounding populations. Angoulvant developed yet another political argument suggested by Delafosse. Because of the size of Haut-Sénégal-Niger, the isolated administrators had acted in almost complete independence and had committed serious misdemeanors, a clear allusion to the commandants and other administrators of the cercles of Dedougou, Bobo-Dioulasso, and Dori. The newly established administration in Ouagadougou would allow efficient political control at two levels—control of the populations and control of the administrators.

The memory of the 1916 Volta-Bani War thus acted as the major justification for the creation of the Upper Volta colony, but it also became a convenient argument for those whose real aim was to link Ivory Coast with a larger labor base. In his December 1918 letter to the minister of the colonies, Angoulvant also explained that the proposed territorial reorganization aimed at creating a new commercial axis so that "the countries of the Volta will no longer look towards Bamako but towards Bassam [then the capital of Ivory Coast]." Angoulvant maintained that before French occupation the Volta region had no historical, cultural, or economic ties with the Soudan. As the former lieutenant governor of Ivory Coast, Angoulvant was credited with having opened up the north of Côte d'Ivoire to colonial control. He now envisioned a new north-south flow that would replace the commercial and military channels of communication established during the initial colonial occupation and connecting the Volta region to Bamako through San or Segou. The border of the two new colonies was drawn east of San, coinciding with the border of the cercles of Dedougou and Bobo-Dioulasso on one side and Sikasso and San on the other. It left Koutiala and the region of San in Haut-Sénégal-Niger (which was now renamed Soudan, as at the end of the nineteenth century), even though Bwa populations lived on either side of it.

The first governor of Upper Volta, Frédéric-Charles Hesling, came with considerable powers, and he put his stamp on the new colony by shaping most of its institutions and by ruling over it for nine of its twelve years of existence. He explained the political significance of the new colony in a letter that he addressed to the administrator of Bobo-Dioulasso—the very first piece of correspondence sent out from the freshly created office:

> The creation of the Upper Volta colony, by bringing about a fortunate decentralization of the authority of the government, first of all proves to the natives that their desire for independence must disappear forever. It will also make it possible to gradually obtain more considerable means of action, which I can make available to you more quickly than the governor of Haut-Sénégal Niger could have done previously. Therefore, in all areas covered by your activities I am hoping that there will be positive effects of this change, most particularly in what concerns the political situation.[24]

Hesling instituted the course of the native policy as "respect for the authority of the chiefs," no matter who these chiefs were or on what grounds they had been initially selected. The term *développement* makes a precocious and frequent appearance in Hesling's correspondence, along with the more typical *mise-en-*

valeur of the colonial vocabulary. For development to take place, political stability was essential: "To maintain in the cercle of Bobo-Dioulasso a calm and tranquillity that are absolutely indispensable for the success of the project of development and progress in which we need to engage."[25]

THE AFTERMATH OF THE WAR

Hesling's development schemes meant little for the populations that had been defeated. The administration imposed on them, at gunpoint if necessary, heavy fines and a multitude of corvées and obligations. Men were forcibly enrolled to porter columns, work crews, the army, and migrant labor with little remuneration. As in the past, their flocks and grain reserves were depleted by the incessant visits of armed companies. They were subjected to unending demands in kind and in money. Life in villages was regulated to the point of dictating to the peasant how he should build his house or organize his farm. People were left exposed to the greed and rapacity of loyalist chiefs who returned to their posts after the war, of guards, auxiliaries, agents, and soldiers. When they ran away to the bush, their property was destroyed and their elders and women were caught and taken hostage and returned to them only after they complied with orders. Still, the administration remained fearful of violent reactions. European officials and African guards who went on tour in the villages, be it for an innocuous sounding mission such as census taking or "making contact with the population," had to be followed by a train of porters carrying ammunition, "as a measure of simple precaution."[26]

Punishments for armed resistance fell upon different communities with varying force. Villages such as Bona, La, and Masala that had distinguished themselves in the anticolonial struggle were destroyed and their inhabitants were forced to move to other places. Their farms were given as reward to loyalist neighbors (if there were such in the vicinity). The populations of these villages could not return to reclaim their land until the early 1940s. Heavy fines were also imposed, and as seen earlier (chap. 8), in the conscription campaign of 1917 the subdivision of Hunde was made to contribute a disproportionate number of recruits.

The requirements set out for the rebuilding of the hundreds of destroyed villages—the noncontiguous houses, thatched roofs, wide avenues, and wells that would be available to troops at a time of siege[27]—were little regarded. People followed them to only a very limited degree, and the administration, not having the means to enforce the directives, quickly renounced them.

The higher administration showed itself increasingly hesitant in implementing such directives. Angoulvant, the acting governor-general in 1916 during the last months of the war, despite his earlier reputation for severity now adopted a much subtler policy. Referring to the stipulations on reconstruction of houses, Angoulvant implicitly contrasted the savanna with the forest region that was familiar to him. He noted that such rules would be difficult to implement because "the mode of construction adopted by a people reflects its degree of civilization and the exigencies of the country . . . in most of the Sudanese region . . . [square houses with flat terrace roofs] are the sign of a relative wealth and of the more advanced social state of their inhabitants."[28] When the lieutenant governor of Haut-Sénégal-Niger softened the prohibition on adobe building, Angoulvant endorsed the proposal, only disallowing the construction of defensive walls (tirailleurs were now increasingly equipped with grenades—a devastating weapon when launched inside closed houses—so this relaxation was, in any case, less threatening to the government).[29] In the field, administrators applied the punitive measures selectively and on a case-by-case basis, not strictly according to recommendations from their superiors. This could go either way: in December 1917, in the canton of Loroferesso, the commandant of the cercle of Bobo-Dioulasso was still trying to enforce the rebuilding of houses with thatched roofs.[30]

Another legacy of the anticolonial war was a permanent campaign of disarmament that lasted until the mid-1920s. Firearms and even arrows were collected systematically. As late as 1922, 2,679 flintlocks, 9,963 arrows, 284 bows, and 520 sidearms were seized in the cercle of Bobo-Dioulasso alone, and it was estimated that 36,460 flintlocks had been confiscated since the first disarmament campaign initiated by Maubert in 1914.[31] Villagers hid their weapons with great ingenuity, and occasionally smuggling rings were discovered ferrying firearms from neighboring districts or from the Gold Coast—and even from the cercle's warehouse where confiscated weapons were stored.[32]

This campaign had a lasting impact. The populations of this region had always been armed, even if firearms were a relatively recent acquisition, and the disappearance of arms from village life led to practical problems as well as contributing to more profound transformations. Weapons were regularly used in hunting, and the presence of wild animals forced the administration to redistribute flintlocks to trusted chiefs and individuals. More importantly, for farming communities that had periodically resorted to arms to engage in local wars or even to resist professional armies (as in 1915–16), disarmament marked the end of a period. Disarmament precipitated the decline of the warrior tradition perpetrated by such associations as the perenkie among the Marka. "The great 1915–1916 Marka and Bobo rebellions constituted the last burst of resistance," writes Jeanne-Marie Kambou-Ferrand; it hastened the creation of the colonial territory of Upper Volta (1993a, 85). It was the start of a new era: the talk of a *races* policy (respect for ethnicity) was superseded by a policy of force and the former was no longer used in justifying the selection of chiefs.

One of the most profound effects of the defeat of the anticolonial movement was in the social texture of communities. The war decimated young men and distorted the demographic make-up of the population that had participated in the war. A 1917 report recommended new population censuses for the Sambla and Tusia cantons: some villages had lost half of their population.[33] Human losses due to the war were amplified by frequent flights of the population in the years that followed the war. The population went to the neighboring cercles, to the Gold Coast, to Ivory Coast, and to the cercles of French Soudan. Thus, many Nienegue fled to the region of Pura in the cercle of Ouagadougou, and many Sambla moved to the French Soudan and even constituted a Sambla community in Bamako. Insofar as many of these places were part of French colonies, the refugees would be subjected, one might think, to the same labor requisitions and taxation, to the same regime of arbitrary rule and hardship. But though the formal structures of French colonialism were similar in all parts of West Africa, their actual application varied, sometimes even within short distances. Furthermore, refugees were not readily integrated into local censuses and therefore for a while could escape forced labor and other colonial demands.

The economy suffered tremendously from the war. The pitiful state in which the agricultural economy had fallen is glimpsed in the anxious comments of administrators facing the inflexible expectations of Governor Hesling's development program. The administrator of the cercle of Bobo-Dioulasso, Martin, wrote in 1922: "The economic situation of the canton of Bouende and of the northern part of the canton of Kotedougou is not without causing worry. The Sambla and the Bobo-Oule who constitute these populations work little and farm such small surfaces that their harvests are insufficient." Then he remarked that these two populations had taken up arms in 1915–16.[34] The Nienegue, like the Sambla, showed little will to work: it was as if they refused to participate in the development programs of the new colony.

The Sambla provided a striking example of what administrators saw as a loss of spirit, which can also be interpreted as passive resistance. As we saw in chapter 8, in 1916 the Sambla fought one of the fiercest battles of the war, standing up, despite their inadequate armament, and attacking Maubert's guards and auxiliaries.

They had, in consequence, suffered extraordinary casualties. In 1917, the commandant of the cercle of Bobo-Dioulasso visited Sambla country and reported that in the village of Karankaso, an important political and ritual Sambla center that had been destroyed completely the year before, people "were hidden at the bottom of the poorly lit mud dwellings. . . . I had to grab them myself out of their den."[35]

This portrait of the Sambla bears a striking similarity to that of Dr. Crozat, the first French explorer to go through Sambla country, in 1890: "They are of an excessively shy nature and of an incredible pusillanimity. They never wander far from their house. . . . They do not fight, never resist whomever attack them, obey anyone, and are frightened by everything."[36] In the years following Crozat's travel confederated Somella villages bravely fought against Tieba of Sikaso who, largely thanks to the support of the French, was on his way to becoming a regional superpower (see p. 342, n. 18), but fifteen years after this first description, in 1905, William Ponty, then lieutenant governor of the Haut-Sénégal-Niger, also upheld the early explorer's opinion: "Our task is to slowly dissipate the natural apprehensions and the innate terror of the indigenous people, for whom it is difficult not to see us as conquerors. . . . It is very delicate to domesticate *(apprivoiser)* . . . these big children, shy and easily offended." The way the Sambla acted in the 1890s and in1916 does not provide support for these images. The shy and fearful Sambla did finally become a reality, in 1917, but only after they were crushed in the most violent military campaign in the colonial history of West Africa.

Appendix

Letters Used as Evidence in the Muslim Conspiracy Trials

Used during the trial of Dedougou starting February 27, 1915 (see pp. 91–96) and included in the "Rapport Picanon: Rapport de détail, no. 51"; AOF/ANS 4 G 22 (figure 2 is a photostat of the original).

According to the "Audience du tribunal du cercle de Dédougou," during the trial Maguet listed all the supposed intermediaries who transmitted this letter from Kong to Safane, where it was read at the funeral of M'Pa Sissako and translated into Marka. A first French translation of the letter was made by Maguet, who could read Arabic, but Picanon had the text translated again by Paul Marty.

Traduction de la lettre en arabe lue à la mosquée de BOROMO par le notable de ce village SIRIBOU SENOU, en Novembre ou Décembre 1914 (Rapport no. 51, pages 32 et 33).

Au nom de DIEU, Clément, Miséricordieux.

Louange à DIEU qui nous donne le papier comme messager et la science comme langue [mistranslation: the translator reads *'ilm* "science, knowledge" what should be read as *qalam* "pen"].

Ce papier émane de notre Cheikh et Maître . . . ABD EL QADER EL DJILANI. . . . Que sa bénédiction nous serve à nous et à tous les musulmans.

315

A toutes les créatures, à l'Orient et à l'Occident, au nord et au sud. —Ce Cheikh a vu dans son sommeil une sorte de lune qui a éclaté avec le soleil (ou bien, qui s'est réunie au soleil) du côté de l'Ouest; sa lumière s'est éteinte. La discorde s'est répandue de l'Orient à l'Occident. Chaque jour un million de personnes mouraient et chaque nuit aussi. Alors tombèrent sur eux la peste, les calamités, la faim, la sécheresse; les maladies de ventre et de tête se multiplièrent, ainsi que la ruine et la mort des enfants. Chaque jour, du matin au soir et du soir au matin, mouraient 70.000 musulmans. Les vers et les sauterelles tombaient sur leur nourriture et la consommaient tout entière et jusqu'aux feuilles des arbres. Il ne restait plus rien de vert sur la surface de la terre.

Alors DIEU fit descendre l'Ange Gabriel vers le Prophète. Il lui dit: "O Mahomet, ton Maître t'envoie le Salut; il veut la disparition de ta race sur la terre; il veut la ruine de la terre avec ses habitants." Le Prophète a répondu: "O Gabriel, mon corps s'est brisé et mon coeur a frémi!" . . . "O Mahomet, les fidèles ont abandonné le Salam [ṣalah], ne font plus l'aumône Zaka, ne pratiquent plus le pèlerinage, font de fausses dépositions, ne se marient pas, s'éloignent de la paix, pratiquent l'adultère, ne lisent plus les livres saints, n'acceptent plus les pieuses exhortations des savants et des hommes pieux. Ils oppriment les orphelins et les pauvres. Les riches méprisent les hommes pieux, les voyageurs, les orphelins. On voit parmi eux les médisances, les calomnies, les faux témoignages, et fort peu d'actes de vertu. Les riches ne manifestent plus la crainte de DIEU, ne font plus le Salam [ṣalah] obligatoire ou supplémentaire, ne pleurent plus les larmes de la crainte de DIEU. Le désordre a paru; ils ne secourent plus les orphelins et les pauvres. Ils ont abandonné l'aumône et les lois divines. Les hommes ne recherchent plus le mariage; ils s'écartent de ceux qui les exhortent au bien. Ils ne se marient plus, et même les hommes pieux. Il desobeissent à DIEU et se mettent aux ordres de Satan.

"L'injustice a fleuri chez les hommes et l'adultère chez les femmes. Ils ont abandonné le mariage et s'adonnent à l'adultère. Ils s'écartent des bons conseils. Ils n'honorent plus les vieillards; ils ne respectent plus la vieillesse; ils ne connaissent plus la vénération de l'âge avancé. C'est pourquoi leur âge a été raccourci et ils ne connasient plus les âges avancés. Les jeunes gens et les hommes mûrs n'honorent et ne vénèrent plus leurs Cheikhs, ne cherchent plus à satisfaire leurs maîtres, c'est pourquoi leurs bonnes oeuvres disparaissent et leurs bénédictions aussi. Ils ne prient plus dans les mosquées; les ignorants sont devenus les vénérés; et leur instruits sont les méprisés. L'injustice domine l'équité et le droit a disparu de leur présence. On ne rend plus les jugements que par l'injustice, la concussion et la haine. L'adultère et les infamies fleurissent sur la terre. On déserte les mosquées. Ils embellissent leurs maisons, mais ne s'occupent pas de la maison de Dieu. Ils ne mangent pas ce qui est permis, mais ce qui et défendu. Tous les hommes libres, comme leurs captifs, sont au bord de l'enfer. On ne juge plus d'après la justice, mais avec iniquité et haine et pourtant Dieu a dit: 'Et même en cas de parenté. . . .' [le reste de la citation du texte coranique manque. Ce début de citation se trouve en plusieurs chapitres du Coran; la citation paraît être ici celle du Chap. V verset 105. 'Nous ne vendrons pas votre témoignage pour quelque prix que ce soit, pas même à nos parents.' Note du Traducteur.]

"Les enfants haïssent leurs parents tandis que ceux-ci ont besoin d'eux. Les maris ne s'attachent plus à leurs femmes, mais à leurs maîtresses. On n'apprend plus le Coran aux enfants; on ne leur enseigne plus le bien; on ne les détourne plus du mal; ils ne leur prescrivent plus les bonnes actions, mais les choses de ce bas-monde; ils ne leur prescrivent plus les chose de la vie future. O Mahomet, ton peuple a abandonné sa famille; femmes et filles sont comme les bêtes; on ne s'occupe pas d'elles.

"O Mahomet, ton peuple a rempli la terre d'oppression. On ne juge pas avec justice; on ne va au tribunal que pour l'injustice et le bien. On ne cherche pas à plaire à Dieu par des prières surérogatoires; on ne jeûne pas en Ramadan, on n'y adore pas Dieu; on n'y fait pas les prières surérogatoires. On s'enrichit de biens de femmes, d'enfants jusqu'à ce qu'on voit la tombe. On ne se repent pas; on n'honore pas le mois de Dieu, le mois du Prophète et leur propre mois."

Certains hommes jeûnent bien pendant le jour, mais vont rompre, le soir, leur jeûne avec l'aliment de l'adultère et passent la nuit avec leur complice.

Certains autres jeûnent, puis s'enfoncent dans l'océan de la médisance de la calomnie et de l'iniquité. On a dans les mosquées des conversations profanes.

"O Mahomet le coeur de ton peuple est plus dur que le caillou et que la roche. O Mahomet, ton peuple ne contracte pas des mariages en toute vérité, mais tous les mariages d'aujourd'hui puisent leurs origines dans l'adultère. On n'observe pas les délais d'attente que nécessite l'adultère de sa femme. Celui qui épouse sa complice détruit la valeur de son mariage. On ne connaît plus la sainteté du mariage; on n'en observe plus les limites ni les conditions.

"Les savants de ton peuple ne font plus l'éducation de peuple que pour des richesses; les élèves n'étudient plus pour Dieu, mais pour des biens terrestres. On ne reconnaît plus le savant qu'à sa belle voix.

"L'erreur s'est répandue; certains sont [comme les] chrétiens, mais personne n'a une conduite pure.

"O Mahomet, les riches traitent avec orgueil les pauvres, les orphelins et les malheureux. Ils sont comme le juif et le chrétien, ils ne sont pas sensibles à la pitié; ils ne pensent pas à la mort, ils n'y songent pas; ils s'imaginent qu'ils seront toujours sur terre. 'Ils persévèrent dans une haine implacable'; ils ne se repentent pas; ils pèchent et en rient. Ils rompent les liens de parenté; ils ne secourent pas leurs parents.

"O Mahomet, ceux de ton peuple qui sont morts après toi, étaient des coupables sur la terre Dieu ne les a pas opprimé. Ce sont eux qui se sont opprimés."

A ces mots, le Prophète pleura dans son tombeau; tout l'espace en fut ébranlé et les gens de Médine vinrent voir le tombeau, pensant que le jugement dernier était arrivé.

Et Mahomet s'écria: "O mon peuple, ô mon peuple. Je suis honteux devant Dieu, et la pitié Divine me fait défaut!" Puis il ajouta: "Revenez à votre Maître, O Gabriel, dites à Dieu qu'Il leur accorde un délai. Je leur enverrai un message. S'ils acceptent encore les admonestations, Dieu patientera avant de les détruire, et s'ils ne veulent pas écouter, il fera ce qu'il voudra."

Le Prophète envoya alors Abd el Qader el Djilani.

Il ajoute: "Un vent soufflera de l'Orient à l'Occident. Toute personne qui se heurtera au vent périra. Ce vent sentira le cadavre infect."

Le Prophète a dit: "O mes Gens je vous ai envoyé message sur message. Vous vous éloignez toujours de moi."

Abd el Qader a dit: "Celui qui veut se sauver lira le verset du Trône 7 fois et la sourate du Salut 12 fois après la prière ordinaire. Il l'écrira, la portera sur lui; et on donnera leur salaire aux écrivains, car l'utilité n'a de valeur que par le payement comptant.

"Les Musulmans liront ensuite la Sourate du Salut 1.000 fois, avec le verset: 'Le Prophète croit' etc. [II.186] une fois, et avec le verset: 'Dieu ne les punit pas, tant que tu es au milieu d'eux; ils ne les punit pas non plus, pendant qu'ils implorent son pardon.' [VIII.33], 70 fois, devant la porte de la mosquée, matin et soir, pendant 7 jour, du Dimanche au Samedi.

"Le chef du pays fera l'aumône d'un cheval, d'un boeuf, d'un boubou et les donnera à l'Imam. Chaque chef de case donnera 44 pains et un mouton et l'égorgera dans sa maison.

"Chaque homme donnera un boubou. Il donnera aux pauvres 100 cauris. Il donnera en plus 7 cauris; les femmes en donneront 4.

"Celui qui ne pourra pas le faire n'y est pas forcé. Qu'il fasse comme il pourra. L'aumône efface le mal et le châtiment. Que ceux qui le veulent le fassent et que ceux qui ne le veulent pas le laissent. Dieu n'a besoin de personne. C'est vous qui avez besoin de lui. Dieu est riche, digne d'éloges. Celui qui accomplira une bonne action, la fait pour lui; celui qui fait le mal, le fait contre lui, et D IEU n'est point l'oppresseur des hommes [L.28] et le Salut soit sur celui qui suit la bonne direction, et qui laisse l'erreur et le mal."

Le Prophète a ajouté: "Celui qui portera ce papier de village en village, de pays en pays, de case en case, jouira de la miséricorde au jour du jugement. Celui qui le portera plus tard de village en village se trouvera à l'ombre du trône Divin au jour du jugement, et il aura le Prophète comme compagnons en ce monde et dans l'autre, et celui-là ne sera pas voué au feu de l'Enfer."

> Il n'y a de force et de puissance qu'en D IEU Elevé, Majestueux.
> Gloire à D IEU, Maître des Mondes. Fin — Exact ./.
> Pour Traduction conforme: Ségou, le 14 Mars 1917
> L'Officier Interprète, Signé: P. M ARTY

The following two letters were presented as evidence in the Ouagadougou trial which took place in April 1915 (see p. 275). They were not, however, included in the report of that trial that administrator d'Arboussier dispatched to the headquarters. Lieutenant Governor Clozel expressly asked d'Arboussier to send a copy of these letters in his correspondance dated August 23, 1915. In response, one of these letters (or perhaps both) was sent to the headquarters in Bamako in October, that is months after the Ouagadougou trial. The originals of these letters cannot be found in the archives, and there is no indication of who made the French translations. The translations are in AOF/ANS 15 G "Cercle de Ouagadougou. Mouvement musulman anti-français 1914–1915."

L ETTER 2

Used as evidence in the Ouagadougou trial, joined to the letter of October 19, 1915, from d'Arboussier to Lieutenant Governor Clozel.

HSN Cercle du Mossi.
Rapport sur l'affaire Hamaria, Imam Koureich, Zakaria Sissac & consorts
Affaire Hamaria Mayac & consorts (Gourounsi — Mossi). AOF/ANS 15 G 105.

Au nom de Dieu, le Clément, le Miséricordieux: le salut soit sur le Maître Mahomet. Louanges à Dieu, Maître des mondes.

Le salut soit sur vous ô peuple entier des musulmans et des musulmanes: voici ce que le grand Cheikh a dit aujourd'hui:

"J'ai vu en songe, dans la nuit du vendredi, qu'une époque va venir, où sous le souffle d'un vent accablant, les hommes, les enfants et les femmes mourront en grand nombre, et que cette année des maladies multiples les frapperont. Que chaque homme, que chaque femme verse une aumône soit 700 cauries, soit des vêtements, des moutons des chèvres, etc, qu'ils les donnent aux pauvres et à ceux qui savent. Ceci est la verité et à quiconque la fait connaître de pays en pays Dieu réserve une place au Paradis.

Ecrivez la formule "Au nom de Dieu tout puissant": et que chacun la porte à son cou. Si l'on ne se conforme pas à ce précepte beaucoup de gens mourront cette année et vous aurez à subir le lourd châtiment de Dieu très haut jusqu'à ce que vous prononciez l'acte de foi. Votre salut est dans l'accomplissement de la prière que vous impose votre religion. Vous n'avez aucune pitié pour les pauvres et vous regorgez de richesses qui vous entraîneront en enfer pour l'éternité.

Le Grand Cheikh a dit: O Seigneur, je t'en prie, fasse que ne périssent pas les gens de maintenant. Je t'en conjure par la mémoire sacrée de Mahomet (le salut soit sur lui). Patiente ô Seigneur. Déjà tu as envoyé un prophète au peuple de Mahomet (que le salut de Dieu soit sur lui) et tous se conduisaient alors comme s'ils ne devaient jamais mourir. Et ils acceptèrent le témoignage du Coran.

Et vous, vous pratiquez l'injustice et le mal: vous avez négligé le bien; négligé la prière. O serviteurs de Dieu, sachez que vous êtes indignes de l'enseignement que vous a donné le prophète (Le salut de Dieu soit sur lui).

Ecrivez la sourate des Koreichites (I. Footnote: sourate 106), portez-là sur vous, buvez-là ou lavez vous en: ô serviteurs de Dieu; donnez à celui qui l'écrira pour vous un salaire équitable de 60 cauries. Que chacun en porte sur soi une copie, O serviteurs de dieu, car si l'on transgresse ce précepte le vent deviendra rouge et brûlant (que Dieu nous garde de ce fléau).

Et sachez que tout ceci est vrai et s'appuie sur l'autorité du Cheikh Ahmed Ben Moussa Ben Idriss (que Dieu nous gratifie de la bénédiction de sa science, Amen).

O serviteurs de Dieu, le mal qui vous arrivera, vous l'aurez voulu puisque vous avez négligé le bien et réduit vos aumônes. Quiconque d'entre vous sera frappé par le malheur, l'aura voulu puisque vous avez marchandé vos vertus et vos aumônes.

O serviteurs de Dieu: patientez car Dieu est avec ceux qui patiente [sic]. Et quiconque ne se soumettra pas à ces préceptes ne recevra plus d'avertissement du genre de celui-ci: il sortira à jamais des lieux de délices et ne connaîtra plus que châtiment et douleur.

O serviteurs de Dieu, pensez à Dieu et non à la terre qui est périssable (que Dieu nous en délivre). Suivez ces préceptes sûrs, O gens de l'occident. Vous négligez le mariage juste: vous vous accouplez avec des femmes sans suivre les préceptes du droit: de même vous les quittez en dehors de ces préceptes. Nombre de gens, parmi vous, usent de la calomnie et du mensonge. Leur conduite est injuste et ils n'aspirent qu'à la terre leur coeur est insensible à la miséricorde. O serviteurs de Dieu: Dieu Très Haut a dit: "celui qui fait un mithkal de poussière de bien le retrouvera: celui qui fait un mithkal de poussière de mal le retrouvera également."

O serviteurs de Dieu, Ne quittez pas Dieu pour la terre périssable. Sachez que nous entrons dans une période terrible qu'une famine épouvantable arrivera et un vent dévastateur qui visitera vos maisons jusqu'à ce qu'ils vous ait abattus, O serviteurs de Dieu; vous communiez dans le mensonge, l'injustice et les aspirations terrestres et vous ne vous souciez pas de la vie future.

Et salut à qui suit la voie droite et louange à Dieu, souverain des mondes.

LETTER 3

Second letter used in the Ouagadougou trial, said to have been found in the hands of Salifou Rakay, to whom it was sent by Amaria.

August 23, 1915.
AOF/ANS 15 G 106

"Salut à tous les musulmans et à toutes les musulmanes. Le grand marabout, dont le nom est dans la lettre, a eu dans la nuit de vendredi un songe. De grands malheurs et de grandes maladies vont venir. Tous les chefs de case doivent faire des aumônes aux pauvres. Sept cent cauris, un mouton, une chèvre. Celui qui aidera à répandre la présente lettre aura sa place au paradis. De cette lettre on devra faire des amulettes que l'on portera pendues au cou. Les hommes ne craignent pas Dieu, mais ils verront leur châtiment. Les riches qui ne font pas l'aumône périront. L'auteur de la lettre demande à Dieu de pardonner aux hommes et il prévient ceux-ci qu'ils doivent venir à récipiscence. Les hommes ne veulent plus suivre la loi. Beaucoup d'hypocrisie règne dans le monde. Beaucoup prient mais ce n'est pas du fond du cœur. La colère de Dieu contre les hommes est grande. Dieu sait tout, il connaît les bons et les mauvais. Il faut écrire le verset Lyl Lafi et en faire des amulettes, écrire ce même verset sur des planchettes, laver celles-ci et boire l'eau qui les aura lavées. S'ils ne font pas cela le vent rouge; [?] Ahmadou fils de Brahim, fils de Moussa, fils d'Idrissa. Des étrangers vont venir dans le pays, quand ces étrangers arriveront, ils châtieront tous ceux qui ne suivent pas la loi de Dieu. Les hommes ne doivent craindre personne si ce n'est Dieu [these last two sentences are underlined]. Après cette lettre il en viendra une autre et ce sera le dernier avertissement. Tous les hommes ne pensent plus à Dieu. Ils devraient penser qu'ils vont tous périr. Je prie Dieu de leur pardonner. Croyez ce que je dis dans cette lettre. Les hommes traitent mal leurs femmes et les traitent commme des animaux. Les hommes ont de mauvaises mœurs, l'adultère est une règle et le mensonge règne. Beaucoup se désintéressent de leurs enfants. Les calomniateurs sont nombreux. Les hommes veulent vivre et croient vivre éternellement, ils devraient penser que leur mort est proche. Qu'ils sachent que cette année verra la fin du monde. Une grande famine régnera dans tout le pays, puis un vent terrible s'élèvera qui ravagera tout dans le monde. Les hommes ne pensent à rien."

Notes

INTRODUCTION

1. Presentation notes by Molard, Dec. 4, 1916, to the official report on the Yankaso battle, Oct. 26, 1916; reproduced in Niakate, 1:58.

2. Report by Chief Administrator Vidal, Nov. 1, 1916. This report has been reproduced by many different branches of the administration and can be found in different archives. See, for example, AOF/ANS 15 G 201; also in Niakate, 2:39–69.

3. The colonial government of French West Africa (Afrique Occidentale Française) was organized as a federation, with the governor-general in Dakar as its supreme authority. Under him in 1915 were seven colonies, each headed by a governor. In some colonies, the official title of the governor was lieutenant governor. The Bani and the Volta regions were part of the Haut-Sénégal-Niger colony, which covered what is now the nation-states of Mali and Burkina Faso; it was administered by a lieutenant governor. (From June 1915 to February 1918, Haut-Sénégal-Niger was headed by as many as five acting lieutenant governors.) To each lieutenant governor was attached a secretary-general, who acted in his name when he was absent. When in 1919 Haut-Sénégal-Niger was split into Soudan and Upper Volta, the number of colonies in French West Africa rose to eight. Each colony was divided into cercles (provinces), which were headed by an administrator, who continued to be called commandant after the administration passed to civilian personnel (see glossary). Within a cercle, there could be one or two subdivisions, ruled by a French subordinate of the commandant, called the resident, who lived in a secondary headquarters. The cercles were divided into cantons (districts), each headed by a native chief representing the administrator.

4. AOF/ANS 2 G 17/4 "Rapport du Gouverneur Général Van Vollenhoven," to Minister of Colonies, Sept. 22, 1916.

5. Lt. gov., HSN, to gov.-gen., Oct. 24, 1916, "Compte-rendu de la tournée," AOF/ANS 4 D63.

6. The neglect is almost total with the outstanding exception of Jack Goody, who

in a pioneering essay (1971) brought together the ideas on West African political organization with the types of warfare made possible by armament and ecology.

7. Otterbein (1999) has recently provided a review of anthropological work on
warfare.

8. Summary of the Molard report, in Niakate, 3:79.

9. Person (vol. 3, 1975) describes the west Volta region as *une poussière de peuples*.
These were recurrent expressions in early colonial Africa. Bayart (1989, 21) quotes a
military report of 1900 from the Congo: "We find here only anarchy and bad faith, in
brief a society in infancy, without any organization, a true dust cloud of men."

10. A recent work that greatly inspired us with its explicit attention to the agency
of both local actors and colonial administrators is Peires 1989.

11. These two modes are not mutually exclusive and did not neatly succeed each
other. The rough distinction is still useful because during most of the brief colonial period large sectors of the population in the interior of West Africa remained out of reach
of the discursive practices of the administration. Missionary practice, too, was as likely
to be influenced by local conceptions as it was to be a source of indoctrination.

12. A comprehensive account of the Sahara war conducted by Arab and Tuareg
groups under Sanusi leadership and Ottoman support is provided in the context of a
study of French attitudes toward the Sanusiya brotherhood; Triaud 1995, 781–920. A
major work on the Sahara war is Salifou 1973. See also Fuglestad 1973.

13. One can recall that a large number of African soldiers recruited in West Africa
were fighting in French uniform in Europe at that time. The number usually given for
the duration of World War I is 181,000; perhaps as many as one-fifth of these died in
the trenches. The tragic irony is that a few of these soldiers hailed from districts where
the population had overwhelmingly sworn to throw out the French and were dying for
this cause.

14. Exposition Coloniale Internationale de Paris, 1931.

15. Boni also wrote a pioneering historical work on African resistances to colonial
occupation, covering events until the turn of the twentieth century: *Histoire de l'Afrique
resistante* (1972).

16. There is another thesis that we have not been able to consult: Adama Abdoulaye Toure, "La resistance au recrutement des tirailleurs en Haute-Volta, 1912–1918."
Thesis for Diplôme d'Etudes Supérieures, 1967 Dakar.

17. The Niakate documents, in three volumes of about a hundred pages each, include the Vidal report, the official summary of the report of Colonel Molard, some
cercle diaries, and an important body of telegraphic correspondence, all from the archives of Bamako. Copies of many of these documents are available in other archives;
occasionally we give cross-references since in some West African capitals the collection
may be more readily available than the original documents.

Chapter i

1. Political report, cercle of Bobo-Dioulasso. Aug. 1902, ANCI Haut-Sénégal-
Niger (HSN), 5 EE 21.

2. In the Volta region, the areas of effective matrilineality and patrilineality do not correspond to the boundaries of ethnicity or language. The recognition and uses of these principles of social organization vary with location. One finds the strongest emphasis on matrilineal ties in the southwest of the Volta region. Moving north, one encounters a more balanced application of agnatic and uterine ties, as for example among the Sambla and the southern Bobo, both of which speak languages of the Mande family (Sambla and Bobo speech are very distant to Jula/Manding). Farther north, one is less likely to hear about matrilineages, and ethnographers describe social institutions in strictly patrilineal terms. It is reasonable to assume that patrilineal and matrilineal descent have been in the cultural repertoire of many groups in this region, speaking languages of a variety of families, for a long time and have been made relevant to different aspects of social life, alone or in combination following contingent historical or political factors.

3. For examples of how the house is distinct from a descent unit, see Jean Capron (1973, 216–24). Without distinguishing these two as analytical concepts, Capron nonetheless provides detailed house descriptions from Bwa villages in the district of San. Şaul (1991) presents a discussion of double descent and the house in southern Bobo country and Şaul (1998) its relevance to understanding Watara politics.

4. One special manifestation of the instability of place-names can be found in the maps of the region. Most villages in the west Volta region have two commonly known names. One of them is the name most frequently used by its population; the other is generally in the Manding (Jula) language and serves as official name and appears on the maps. This Manding name is sometimes simply the name of the ward where the Jula traders had established a colony, but because these people had privileged relations with colonial administrators, for government purposes it often ended up becoming the name for the entire village.

5. Only a limited catalog of tricks are encountered in the stories of the "two hunters" type. In the northern part of the west Volta and in many Gurunsi villages, one hunter tries to prove to the other that he came first by showing a rock or some other durable object that he had placed somewhere. The other contender had also placed an object, but he cannot show it because it was impermanent (e.g., a lump from a termite mound placed in a dry riverbed that was swept away when rains started). For similar stories from the Suru area, see Hubbell (1997, 93–95). In southern Bobo country, the contest usually involves inspection of the houses that the two men built to see which one is older. The squalid appearance of the house of one of the hunters, who was a careless builder or less punctilious housekeeper, is taken to mean that he had been there longer than the other.

6. The steps in the constitution of a Bobo village are described in Guy Le Moal (1980, 66–80).

7. This account is simplified for the sake of brevity and clarity. The destruction of villages and forced migrations may mean that a masa lives not in the original village linked to his suru shrine but in a neighboring village. As a result, a village may house two masa, each in charge of a different earth shrine ruling over different territories. T. Quéant and C. de Rouville described this for the Marka and Bwa villages of the Suru valley (1969, 60), and although the terminology of offices and shrines is not identical, Şaul encountered similar cases in southern Bobo country (1993).

8. The names of the villages subordinated to the suru of Banu were given to us as

follows: Kokun, Kongojana, Sirakoroso, Bilakongo, Kongoso, Bwaso, Tuena, Yankaso, Makongo, Koroso, Kiekuy, Sokurani, Nunu, Sodien, Banga, Ta, Ziaso, Sien, Bombula, Nana, Kona, La, Wona, Silaro, Ble, Tunu, Danguna, Somonon, Bana, Dano, Konkulika, Bara-Yankaso, Kyose, Misakongo, Bara, Kira, Pakoro, Datomo, Pakole, Gbasinya, Bona, Soklani, Zinkuy, Biforo, Safane. Interview, June 11, 1998; principal interlocutor Pakoun Oula; present and assisting were, among a few others, Délégué Kone Pakao Vincent, Kone Kedouin, and Kone Bade. In this and all other interviews in Marka country, Lassina Koté, of the University of Ouagadougou, served as guide and interpreter.

9. G. Binger (1892, 1:407 ff.) names separate confederations that were led by the villages of Bondokuy, Wakara, Sara, Bokuy, Pa, and Bagasi.

10. Maguet's report on the origins of the revolt in the cercle of Dedougou, reproduced in Niakate, 1:11-18; quote from 17.

11. This list was provided in a meeting conducted on June 10, 1998. The spokesman of the group of elders was the imam Sidiki Kote. Present in the meeting were Dasa Kote and Konakye Kote, who was the senior elder of the village. The village of Sokurani, which cannot be found on the 1:200000 map of Burkina Faso, is located near Zinkuy. Note that this list is somewhat different from the list of villages provided by Siaka Sombie (1975, 6) as those that participated in the first major intervillage meeting organized by Yisu Kote to declare war on the colonial administration. For more on the meetings, see chapter 5.

12. Son-non is now used as the name of one of the three subregions into which the Marka villages of the Muhun River area are conventionally divided on the basis of dialect and historical affinity. In this sense Son-non refers to the surroundings of Safane, including Bona. It is not certain that Son-non was at any time the name of an actual village, but this detail is not important for our discussion.

13. The narratives in Jean Cremer's book were written from information provided by elders in Dedougou with whom he had established privileged relations and published, unfortunately only in French translation, by his fellow administrator and ethnographer Henri Labouret (see chap. 7, p. 177 and p. 337, note 12).

14. Information on La was obtained principally from Jean-Marie Tamboura and the Délégué André Tamboura; interview, June 12, 1998.

15. The villages in league with Cheriba were Tikon, Ula, Duruku, Kari, Lan, Bankoroso, Sirakele, Kana, Wezela, Banumba, Sao, Labien, Walu, Walubie, Yulu, Munda (now considered a ward of Yulu), Disaso, Gamadun, Tierku, and Zenkuy. Most of the information concerning Cheriba was provided by El Hadj Sanzie Bubakar on July 11, 1998.

CHAPTER 2

1. The standard opening for letters among the Muslims of the Volta region. See letter 1 in the appendix. Compare Wilks, Levtzion, Haight 1986, 202-36.

2. The principal sources for the Karantao are the Tauxier 1912 account (410-12), repeated with slight rephrasing in Tauxier 1924, 147-48; A.-M. Duperray, 1984, 56-60; N. Levtzion 1968; B. Kote 1982; Wilks 1989, 100-103; Launay 1994, 82-83.

3. See Kiethega (1983) for Pura as an important center of gold production.

4. Some of his descendants maintain that Mahamudu's travel to the Islamic heartland lasted thirty years; others say it was ten or twelve years (Kote 1982, 79). In either case, this would be unusually long even if allowance is made for the difficult travel conditions of that time and the practice of interrupting the journey with long stays on the road for study and to earn money. Duperray assesses that Mahamudu's pilgrimage journey took five years (1984, 58).

5. This was the case for Goni, Ye, and Niuwuruni in the region of Durula, and for Urobono, Bandio, Lafara, and Asio in the vicinity of Boromo (Kote 1982, 68).

6. This is more hesitantly stated in the 1912 account: "Then taking as pretext the hostility, real or imagined, of the Ko of Boromo, who, it seems, had made known their desire to chase him"—Tauxier 1912, 410. In the 1924 version, it became: "He lived peacefully in this village, keeping himself busy only to gain followers, when the Ko who then lived in Boromo decided to chase him away"—Tauxier 1924, 147. Between 1912 and 1924, the Karantao had provided support to the colonial administration in the 1915–16 War.

7. Cremer 1924b, 146; Capron 1973, 88; Kote 1982, 85, 89. Granted that terror can be a strong deterrent to other communities contemplating resistance, the full motivation for these mass executions eludes us. One wonders if the conventional agitation of the enemy during the battle—griots hurling insults; charms and shrines taken to the battlefield; and, the most offensive for Muslims, widespread intoxication with sorghum beer—were not read as peculiarly anti-Muslim provocations that prompted such manifestations of violence. Later in the century, Tieba of Sikasso and Samori also performed mass executions following the defeats of especially obstinate and strong enemies.

8. This was the tradition of the jema'a, or jamana, of the Muslims of the Malinke world and of the Niger inner delta to which Mahamudu traced his proximate origins.

9. Interview with Tamboura André and Tamboura Jean-Marie; La, June 12, 1998.

10. Interview with Laji Youssouf Dao; Datomo, June 10, 1998. See also Kote 1982, 88, 101.

11. Duperray 1984, 60, quoting J. Hébert, "Esquisse d'une monographie historique du pays dagara," diocèse of Diebougou, 1976.

12. The sources on the Zaberma include a narrative written in Hausa about 1914 by a man who is said to have been with them: Mallam Abu 1992. The other sources are Tauxier 1912, 182–86; Jean Rouch 1956; J. J. Holden, 1965; Levtzion 1968; M. Echenberg 1971; Yves Person 1975, 3:1579–85, 1707–11; Anne-Marie Duperray 1984, 61–70; Wilks 1989, 103.

13. Interview in Banu with principal interlocutor Pakoun Oula in a meeting attended by many other people, including Kone Pakao Vincent, Kone Kadouin, and Kone Bade, on June 11, 1998; interview in Safane, June 12, 1998, at which the main narrator was the griot Konade Konate—the meeting attended by many young people, including Sere Lonsani, Konate Sidiki, Sere Amadou, and Sakora Piede Pierre.

14. Thus, Person reports that Gazari was a chief, ca. 1874–85 and that the Safane defeat of the Zaberma took place in 1887; this naturally falls in line with Tauxier's view that the latter event must have been conducted by Babato; Person, 1975, 3:1708.

15. Person also discusses another Zaberma leader on the Bandama, Mori Ture, who was a merchant, warrior, and "quite sophisticated Muslim"; ibid., 3:1579–85.

16. Maguet's report, in Niakate, 1:17. This section of the report is extensively paraphrased without reference in Hébert 1970, 18.

17. The principal source for Al-Kari of Buse is Marion J. Echenberg 1969, 531–61. A French version of this article appeared in *Notes et Documents Voltaïques,* 2:1969.

18. The alliances of Al-Kari are given in Echenberg 1969, 550.

19. On the reasons why Aguibu entered into alliance with the French, see Yves St.-Martin 1968. See also Person 1975, 3:1299.

20. The other named enemy was Amadu Abdul (Youssouf Diallo 1997). Amadu Abdul was the son of Ba Lobbo, a successor of Seku Amadu, who fled the Masina when the Tukulor arrived in 1861 and settled in Fio, between the Bani River and Solenso. Amadou Abdul eventually made an agreement with the French, who recognized him as ruler of Fio, but he ended up in exile when the Bwa villagers staged a successful opposition against him in 1896. In 1897, the French administration annexed Fio to Jenne; Person 1975, 3:1790, n. 100.

21. In their exodus to the south, the brothers of Al-Kari gave battles against Samo and Marka villages around Durula and Ye. Then this little army joined the Zaberma leader, Babato, with whom they fought for three years as a separate contingent, and when this area was pacified they became part of Samori's army, continuing to fight the French until 1898; M. Echenberg 1969, 557–58.

22. The standard general histories of the French occupation of western Sudan, focusing on the motives of the French ambition, are A. S. Kanya-Forstner 1969 and John D. Hargreaves 1974 and 1985. Specific histories focusing on what is now Burkina Faso are Kambou-Ferrand 1993b and Madiéga 1981. The occupation of what became the cercles of Diebougou and Bobo-Dioulasso, given in the context of an exhaustive analysis of the competition between the French, the British, and Samori, is described with unparalleled local detail in Person 1975, 3:1913–47.

23. Among these, the two-volume travel account of Binger (1892) stands out.

24. More on political cliques in France at that time can be found in Kanya-Forstner 1969, Hargreaves 1985, 218–38, and in Person 1975, vol. 3, chaps. 2, 3, and 4. Also Newbury 1960.

25. Voulet had no artillery in this campaign, and Kambou-Ferrand (1993b, 129) notes that the number of defenders killed, about one-sixth of the village population, was unusually high under the circumstances. It should be taken into consideration, however, that many fighters had come from other villages.

26. Al Haj Habibou Sanogo of Lanfiera to Youssouf Drame in an interview in 1989, quoted in Drame 1991, 91.

27. Information on Gasan and Suru was provided by Yatou Mamadou Zerbo, délégué of Gasan, in an interview in the village on June 8, 1998. Other information about the region of Gasan was supplied by Banhoro Zama, from the village of Yaba, on June 7, in Ouagadougou, and from El Hadj Sayidou Deme, the imam of Gasan, in an interview on June 8, 1998, in the presence of other dignitaries.

28. For these wars, see N. Boni 1971. Sono was on the Suru River, and after its capture it was chosen as the first headquarters for the region and the landing for the fleet that was to operate on the Muhun River as part of a new transportation line to Mose country.

29. About the treaty, see Duperray, 1984, 124. The text of the treaty is reproduced in Kambou-Ferrand, 1993b, 456, and is to be found in AOF/ANS 15 G 1. This hypothetical language associating Moktar to the French conquest by deeds that were yet to be accomplished was a carryover from the period when the French were experimenting with the use of "African conquerors" to extend their influence inexpensively. Binger had written in his travel account that Moktar's influence extended to no more than a few villages and that he was unable to maintain security even in the immediate surroundings of Wahabu. Binger 1892, 1:418.

30. Boromo was held by the Guira, originally Muslim merchants from Yatenga who had become war captains for Mahamudu Karantao.

31. This incident shaped subsequent relations between the French and Samori, and despite lengthy discussion by historians remains somewhat unclear. The British had broken with Samori, and in April 1897 his son Sarankenyi Mori had attacked and destroyed the British post at Wa and taken Captain Henderson prisoner. It seems that Caudrelier concluded, from an overture made by Samori, that Sarankenyi Mori was about to evacuate Bouna (now in northern Côte d'Ivoire near the border with Ghana). He asked Braulot hastily to occupy the city to forestall the British. On his way to Bouna, Braulot encountered Sarankenyi Mori heading a large column. Sarankenyi Mori acted as if to confirm the instructions received by Braulot, but before entering Bouna, on August 28, 1897, the small French contingent was destroyed in a surprise attack by his soldiers. For a discussion of the details of the event and possible motivations, see Person 1975, 3:1889–94.

32. Monog. cercle of Bobo-Dioulasso, 1920, ANCI 3 Mi 7.

33. This campaign is partly described in the memoirs of General Gouraud, who was then the commander of one of the two columns created by Caudrelier; Gouraud 1939. For a synthetic account see Kambou-Ferrand 1993b, 271–74.

34. Caudrelier was killed in World War I in 1914.

CHAPTER 3

1. "Projet d'organisation de la région de la Volta occidentale," Sept. 14, 1898, ANCI, AOF VII, 4.

2. Hébert (1970, 11), who quotes his remark, adds that the Bwa did find their Vercingetorix in 1915.

3. Monog. cercle of Bobo-Dioulasso, 1920, ANCI; 3 Mi 7.

4. G. Heyte, "Le marché de Baramanadougou" 1958, quoted in Capron 1973, 62.

5. Alteratively, Koulibaly wrote that a Dafing is simply any inhabitant of the area enclosed within the bend of the Muhun River, without regard to language or ethnic identity (1970, 44).

6. The most famous example of such juggling of ethnonyms was the inclusion of the members of the Sonangi war houses of the Kong and Bobo region among the "Jula." This label is still not quite accepted by the elders who claim the Sonangi heritage today. See Şaul 1998.

7. Clozel's letter, referred to second hand by Conklin (1997, p. 178), is actually of May 26, 1916 (during the Volta-Bani war) and can be found in AOF/ANS 15 G 106:

Clozel to Koulouba "Les conditions essentielles à exiger d'un chef indigène sont qu'il appartienne au même groupe ethnique que ses administrés, qu'il professe la même religion que la majorité d'entre eux, qu'il ne soit inféodé à aucune secte à tendances prosélytiques." A last sentence "Il convient que le choix ne porte que sur un candidat dont la famille a des droits historiques" shows that the question was not finding "the" traditional chief, that there might be more than one acceptable candidate for the position. Harrison (1988, 100) gives other quotes showing Clozel's concern with Islam, for example his desire to perpetuate "fetishist societies." According to Deschamps (1953) the inspiration for *politique des races* had come from Madagascar where Joseph Gallieni had replaced the Hova dynasty with chiefs they had supposedly displaced before the arrival of the French.

8. They were Dande, Dasumadugu, Diefula, Karankaso (Vige), Komonos, Kotedugu, Ba, Dakoro, Guendugumi, Karaborola, Kimini, Bala, Faramana, Letiefeso, and Wangolodugu.

9. Those were Kumi, Nienegue, Subaganiedugu, Siankoro, Sidardugu, Deguele, Koro, Dorosie, and Bereba.

10. They were Fulaso, Fora, Karankaso, Kaya, Morolaba, Tusia, Tiamparla, Were, Nanergue, Kwere, and Sungarundaga.

11. Rapport d'Ensemble, sec. 8. Capt. M. Desallais, ANCI HSN 5 EE 21.

12. Order no. 17, June 30, 1903, ANCI HSN 5 EE 21; Kambou-Ferrand 1993b, 386.

13. Rapport d'Ensemble, cercle of Bobo-Dioulasso, 1903, ANCI 5 EE 21.

14. Letter no. 105 to lt. gov., Haut-Sénégal-Niger, ANCI, HSN 5 EE 21.

15. Cercle of Bobo-Dioulasso, political report, Aug. 1902, ANCI HSN 5 EE 21. For similar observations in Samo country see Hubbell, 1997.

16. "Projet d'organisation de la région de la Volta occidentale," Sept. 14, 1898, 6, ANCI AOF VII, 4.

17. Ibid.

18. On Gallieni, see Deschamps and Chauvet 1949 and Deschamps 1953.

19. Cercle of Bobo-Dioulasso, political report, 1903, ANCI HSN, 5 EE 21.

20. The subdivision of Banfora included a cluster of seven contiguous cantons north of the Leraba River (Banfora, Nafona, Téngréla, Séniéna, Bérégadougou, Sindou, Lumana) and many "independant" villages kept outside of any canton. Not included in the new subdivision were the cantons of Karaborola, Diefula (situated on the road to Kong), and, in 1906, the canton of Subakaniedugu, all three remaining in the state of Pintyeba.

21. Cercle of Bobo-Dioulasso, report on pacification in 1904, ANCI HSN 5 EE 21.

22. The popular use of the term Bobo does not correspond to the current scholarly systematization and does not correspond to the distinction between languages. Binger (1892) was the first to realize that the people called Nieniegue spoke dialects that were very similar to those spoken by some of the populations called Bobo. Speakers of this Voltaic linguistic community were later subsumed officially under the label Bobo-Oule; they are now called Bwa in the ethnographic literature.

23. Cercle of Bobo-Dioulasso, pacification report, 1904, ANCI HSN 5 EE 21.

24. Ibid.

25. Quoted in Kambou-Ferrand 1993b, 391.

Chapter 4

1. When Haillot was finally charged for some of his acts in January 1917, an important part of his defense was to explain his impressive pedigree from men in the service of France. His father had commanded a squadron and was an officer of the Légion d'Honneur; an uncle was a grand-officer of the Légion d'Honneur, and another uncle was a general; he was also the cousin of Alexandre Ribot, who several times was a minister in the national cabinet: telegram of Haillot to Dakar, Jan. 29, 1917 (AOF/ANS 15 G 201).

2. "Situation de la colonie au début de la révolte des Bobos" par l'administrateur Périquet, Oct. 13, 1917; in Niakate, 2:21. The major colonial report on the marabout affair is the 216-page document prepared by Inspector-general Edouard Picanon, "Enquête sur les causes de la révolte de la région de la Volta," no. 50, May 12, 1917, AOF/ANS 4 G 21. All later reports make reference to this document.

3. Picanon report, AOF/ANS 4 G 21.

4. Tribunal, cercle of Dedougou, Feb. 27–28 and Mar. 2, 1915, AOF/ANS 15 G 201.

5. The letter itself is found in the "Rapport of detail" of the Picanon report in AOF/ANS 4 G 22. The reading of it is mentioned in "Déclaration faites à l'Inspecteur Général des Colonies, Picanon, Chef of Mission, Cercle of Dédougou," no. 51, 3d cahier, decs. nos. 38, 39, 42, 44, 45, given on Jan. 7, 9, and 13, in Boromo; also in report no. 51, Pièce jointes, 1st cahier.

6. Picanon report, 153, AOF/ANS 4 G 21.

7. After the end of the anticolonial war, in the denunciations that he made to defend himself, Maubert wrote on the basis of information provided to him by the interpreter Bathiby while in detention in Bamako, that Amaria was killed while in jail. Maubert personal file FM EE/ii/1131(1). We return to this matter in chapter 10.

8. Quoted by Harrison (1988, 94). Harrison explains that in 1906 it was Governor-general E. Roume who requested the cercle administrators to establish personal files on the marabouts. The 1911 letter of Governor-general Ponty, from which the quote comes, was written to complain to Clozel that he had received very few files.

9. Périquet report on the situation at the start of the revolt, Oct. 13, 1917, in Niakate, 2:22; telegram from the lieutenant governor of Haut Sénégal-Niger to the governor-general, Jan. 1915, quoted by Duperray 1984, 181. At the same time the French discovered that Syrian traders in Dakar were selling color prints of the Italian and German royal families, of the Ottoman sultan, and of other "political subjects" (Harrison 1988, 125). Yusuf Izzüddin, presumably the person in the photograph in this story, was brother and heir apparent of Sultan Mehmet V. Yusuf Efendi committed suicide on Feb. 1, 1916, and his brother, Vahideddin, became heir, acceding to the Ottoman throne as Mehmet VI in July 1918. The Ottoman monarchy was abolished four years later when the Turkish republic was declared.

10. See Launay 1992, 58–62, and Triaud and Robinson, 1997, 17–21, for the attitude of the other Muslim communities in French West Africa.

11. "Exactions commises par les guardes cercle et les interprètes," Dedougou, Sept. 30, 1915; in Niakate, 1:19–24.

12. "Rapport d'ensemble" no. 50, May 12, 1917; Picanon report, AOF/ANS 4 G 21.

13. These verdicts were annulled after the inquiry following the anticolonial war.

14. "Rapport d'ensemble" no. 50, May 12, 1917; Picanon report, 112, 161. AOF/ANS 4 G 21.

15. Inspection mission report, AOF/ANS 4 G 21, "Rapport d'Ensemble" no. 50, May 12, 1917; Picanon report, 112–13.

16. Picanon report, 120.

17. Haillot also had a mistress of griot origin, who according to the Picanon report "was very much dreaded in the country."

18. There is a large literature on military conscription in the French African colonies and the French Black Army. The principal ones are Davis 1934; Salo 1973; Andrew and Kanya-Forstner 1978; Balesi 1979; Michel 1982; Echenberg 1991; Lunn 1999.

19. See Mangin (1910), where the famous general gathered his various statements in which he lobbied for a larger Black Army.

20. The transfer of the recruits to the headquarters was yet another cause of disagreement between the military and civilian administrations. The army claimed that as long as the recruits had not arrived in Kati, they were not yet military and therefore remained the responsibility of the civilians. The civilian administration maintained that from the moment they were selected in the headquarters of the cercle, the recruits were under the military and that the military should pay the expenses of the trip. Another question concerned who should take reponsibility for the numerous desertions.

21. Excerpts from the diary of the cercle of Dedougou; Niakate, 1:47.

22. Picanon report, 198, AOF/ANS 4 G 21.

23. Périquet report on the situation at the start of the revolt, Oct. 13, 1916; Niakate, 2:20.

24. Described in the diary of the cercle of Bobo-Dioulasso by administrator Chéron. Unclassified archives, Bobo-Dioulasso high commissariat. Not all the troops left the Volta region. A few from the Bobo-Dioulasso brigade were sent in early July to Gaoua as reinforcement for Administrator Labouret, who had difficulties with the bellicose population of his cercle.

25. For this military campaign, see d'Almeida-Topor 1973. For an account of the Togo campaign itself, written by an officer, see Moberly 1931.

26. Quoted in Périquet's report, Oct. 13, 1916; in Niakate, 2:16.

27. Bobo-Dioulasso was placed under civilian administration when Haut-Sénégal-Niger was formed in 1904, but the administrators continued to be chosen from among military officers after that date.

28. Maubert personal file, ANSOM FM EE/ii/1 131 (1).

29. Report by Maubert, Dec. 7, 1914, AOF/ANS 15 G 201.

30. Chéron authored one of the early ethnographies of the Bobo people (1916). He had worked as an attorney at the appellate court in France before entering the African service.

31. Enquête de Jules Vidal . . . sur Maubert, Aug. 12, 14, and 16, 1916, AOF/ANS 15 G 201.

32. This order of 1907 specified that the villagers should go to the colonial compound to perform a welcome—men, women, children, and all, without exception.

"Rapport du Capitaine Castelnova . . . sur la tournée dans les Etats de Morifing et dans le Nanergué," ANCI 5 EE 23.

33. Tribunal, cercle of Bobo, judgment, Nov. 30, 1914, AOF/ANS 4 D 54. On the *campements*, see "colonial compound" in the glossary.

34. Political report, cercle of Bobo-Dioulasso, Jan. 1915, AOF/ANS 15 G 201.

35. "Rapport sur le jugement rendu par le tribunal," cercle of Bobo, Maubert, president of the tribunal, Mar. 10, 1915, AOF/ANS 15 G 201.

36. The cult is still very powerful today. People visit its shrine in Banfora and return to their homes with a miniature replica of the spear. Yoye Karama's grandson was the last chief of the canton of Banfora (Michèle Dacher, personal communication).

37. Maubert's report on the political situation, 7 Dec. 1914, AOF/ANS 15 G 201.

38. Hébert 1970, 5–7; 1976, 13–17. According to Hébert, 1976, 13, the three villages were tied to each other by ritual exchanges.

39. Archives CNRST, "Cercle of Bobo-Dioulasso, 1899–1916," B I/1.

40. Musodugu was one of the many centers (like the better-known Sami and Perive in the cercle of Dedougou) that had never acknowledged European rule and that had a long history of violent opposition to the colonial administration.

41. Cercle of Bobo-Dioulasso, political report, Mar. 1915, AOF/ANS 15 G 201.

42. Cercle of Bobo-Dioulasso, judgment, 10 Mar. 1915, AOF/ANS 4 D 54. Cercle of Bobo, monthly political report, Apr. 1915, ANCI 5 EE 6(3).

43. According to the same lieutenant governor, "the only regime that would be both corrective and humane would be flogging, but it is contrary to our principles of humanity"; lt. gov., HSN (Antonetti), to gov.-gen., AOF, Nov. 1916, AOF/ANS 15 G 201. Flogging was commonly used in the 1890s by the French during the conquest of the Soudan, particularly for prominent local figures, and in 1915 Haillot made it his favorite pastime.

44. Political report, cercle of Bobo-Dioulasso, Mar. 1915, ANCI 5 EE 6(3).

45. Clozel took the position of acting governor-general of French West Africa when Ponty died in June 1915.

46. Telegram from Clozel to Maubert, 2 mars 1915, AOF/ANS 15 G 201.

47. Extract, Maubert recruitment report, Bobo-Dioulasso, AOF/ANS 4 D 54.

48. Political situation report, cercle of Bobo-Dioulasso, 2nd trim. 1918, ANCI 5 EE 1(3).

49. Cercle of Bobo-Dioulasso, political report, 4th trim. 1917, ANCI 5 EE 1(3).

50. 1934 report, unclassified archives, Bobo-Dioulasso high commissariat.

51. Report on political situation, cercle of Bobo-Dioulasso, 2nd trim. 1918, ANCI 5 EE 1(3).

52. "Renseignements pour servir à la rédaction d'instructions destinées à M. Hummel." These hand-written notes are not signed, but a pencilled note in the margin indicates "Rapport fourni par M. Nebout." Archives of the Bobo-Dioulasso high commissariat.

53. Report on political situation, cercle of Bobo-Dioulasso, 3rd trim. 1917, ANCI 5 EE 1(3).

54. Political report, cercle of Bobo-Dioulasso, 4th trim. 1917, ANCI 5 EE 1(3). When Froger was appointed, the Watara leaders started a massive compaign in the cer-

cle proclaiming their very near return to favor and were able to pressure hundreds of villages to make contributions for celebration festivities.

55. The heads of the third Watara house, Mori-fin and his nephew Badiori, were not returned to any office, and Froger in fact charged them with concocting a scheme to make the new canton chiefs appear as if they were fomenting a rebellion.

56. Letter of Maubert to Bamako, Apr. 3, 1918, AOF/ANS 15 G 202.

57. Report on political situation, cercle of Bobo-Dioulasso, 2nd trim. 1918, ANCI 5 EE 1(3).

58. "Notice sur les chefs de canton du cercle of Bobo-Dioulasso," par l'administrateur sortant, Mar. 31, 1917, Bobo-Diuoulasso high commissariat.

CHAPTER 5

1. This account of the events that occurred in four days mid-November is constructed from depositions made by various parties, including M'Pa Adama himself, and recorded in the cercle of Dedougou diary. The statements do not agree on all details, but the outline of what happened is clear. Our description combines the various versions, noting, by language or footnote, where we hesitate because of a contradiction.

2. M'Pa Adama's own account differs somewhat from that found in the declarations of other villagers from Bona. We are following the latter here. Excerpts from cercle of Dedougou diary; in Niakate, 1:46, 47.

3. Excerpts from cercle of Dedougou diary; Niakate, 1:49.

4. Testimony, Sept. 22, 1916. Excerpts from cercle of Dedougou diary; Niakate, 1:50.

5. Picanon report no. 50, AOF/ANS 4 G 21, 198.

6. In 1998, this shrine was in the same place as in 1915 and received ritual attention, despite important changes in religious life and residence patterns. In recent decades most people in the village have become practicing Muslims. Following an urbanization scheme, the residential area has been enlarged and parceled out in square lots; the old concentrated village has disappeared. Consequently, the shrine stands by itself in the open and is no longer in a crowded ward.

7. Some of this information about Bona derives from a meeting we held with some elders of the village on June 10, 1998. The spokesperson in this meeting was Sidiki Kote, imam of the village (Sidiki's father was a teenager in 1915); Dasa Kote assisted him. Also present, among others, were Konajye Kote, senior elder of the village, and Soona, a man of about forty, grandson of Yisu Kote.

8. Elsewhere in the western Sudan, kambele sometimes means unmarried young man. In this Marka area, it is a formal prerequisite that some members of the cohort get married before an age set is admitted to kambele status.

9. This observation leads to a more general question concerning French colonial administration. Colonial records do not mention a masa among the Sambla either, and we think the same is true for other communities that have masas in the Volta region.

10. Excerpts from cercle of Dedougou diary; in Niakate, 1:50.

11. Deposition by prisoner Tebili Kote, June 1916; ibid., 48.

12. Gnankambary (1970, 67), who first published this information, initiated con-

fusion about the village affiliation of these leaders. This is corrected in the Jula version, in Bobo Julaso ni Dedugu Serepeya 1995, 26.

13. In an appendix to his report, Picanon indicates that Haillot was known locally as Musa.

14. "Compte-rendu de la révolte en pays marka et bobo"; in Niakate, 1:33.

15. The rest of the story in this booklet follows mostly Gnankambary's version for the guard M'Pe and Alamasson episodes, but adds the women's protest scene from Cire Ba. The subplot of marabout and sacrifice, derived from current oral tradition, appeared in print for the first time in this booklet.

16. The motif of killing a pregnant woman can be put to different uses. The oldest variant, included in a mid-seventeenth-century manuscript, says this was done by the Songhay ruler Sonni Ali; Houdas and Delafosse 1913–14, 82–83. For the date of composition and authorship of this MS, see Levtzion 1971, 571–93. The cruel act is also attributed to Samori by his enemies (Person 1975, 3:2039). The Muslim literati who report these stories use this motif to tarnish the historical image of a well-known historical figure.

17. Seni published this story in two places: 1981, 59–61; and 1985, 25. The 1985 publication is an abridged version of a longer manuscript on the anticolonial war that the author graciously made available to us.

CHAPTER 6

1. Taxil was a discharged military officer. As a civilian, he had set up a trade factory in Segou, but because of the dearth of personnel he was temporarily mobilized to serve in the conscription campaign at his former rank of lieutenant.

2. "Compte-rendu de la révolte en pays marka et bobo (depuis le commencement de l'affaire de Bouna jusqu'à l'attaque de Yankaso du 17 Novembre au 23 Décembre 1915)"; in Niakate, 1:30; Hébert 1970, 22; Sombie, 1974, 10.

3. Périquet report on the situation at the start of the Bobos revolt; in Niakate, 2:35.

4. "Compte-rendu de la révolte en pays marka et bobo"; in Niakate, 1:33 (Nov. 23; mistyped 21).

5. Maubert's road diary, "Carnets de route de l'Administrateur Maubert, Dec. 14, 1915," is in AOF/ANS 4 D 64; it is also in ANCI 5 EE 69 (2). Another source close to Maubert's point of view is Hummel's "Historique des combats de Bondokui et de Sara, Dec. 25, 1915, Bobo-Dioulasso," in ANCI 5 EE 69 (2).

6. Extracts from Maguet's political journal; in Niakate, 1:45 (May 23, 1916).

7. Hummel, "Historique des combats de Bondokui et de Sara," Bobo-Dioulasso, Dec. 25, 1915; 3, ANCI 5 EE 69 (2).

8. HSN, cercle of Koury, "Compte-rendu de la révolte en pays marka et bobo (depuis le commencement de l'affaire de Bouna jusqu'à l'attaque de Yankaso [Nov. 17 to Dec. 23, 1915])," Jan. 1, 1916; in Niakate, 1:36.

9. Maubert's road diary.

10. See, for example, Labouret's diary, in CHETOM 15 H 39. What the French knew about the organization of the anticolonial movement was gathered very early on

by Maguet's spy network, then repeated by the others. The information ended up in Hébert's 1970 article.

11. Letter of Lt. Gov. Digué, Apr. 1916, quoted in report by Périquet, "Role des administrateurs au cours de la repression"; in Niakate, 2:6–7.

12. "Compte-rendu de la révolte en pays marka et bobo," Jan. 1, 1916; Niakate, 1:36.

13. Political report, HSN, 3rd trim. 1916, 16, signed Angoulvant, AOF/ANS 2 G 16 8. When villagers in the Volta region don't buy cartridges, they still prepare sulfurless powder like this.

14. Diary entry, Dec. 19, CHETOM 15 H 39.

15. HSN, cercle of Koury, "Compte-rendu de la révolte en pays marka et bobo, Jan. 1, 1916"; in Niakate, 1:37–39; Sombie 1975, 17–18.

16. Diary entry, Dec. 20, CHETOM 15 H 39.

17. This was a reference to his serving in the Simonin column during the initial occupation of the Volta region. See chap. 7, n. 14, for Simonin in the initial conquest of the Volta in 1898.

18. Note about the rebellion in Marka and Bobo country, Dedougou, Dec. 14, 1915; in Niakate, 1:37–38.

19. A movement under the joint leadership of the marabout Mamadu Amet (leader of Mididagen Senaceres) and Mamadu Ottu (chief of Wadala) was threatening all the French posts in the distant Sahel, which had never been fully subjugated.

20. A small military column was finally sent to Dori at the end of January; in Niakate, 2:10.

21. Report by Maj. Simonin on the battle of Yankaso, Dec. 23 to 25, 1915; in Niakate, 1:57–65. This report is also available as part of the "Historique du 2e Régiment de Tirailleurs Sénégalais: Colonne de Police Bani-Volta [Nov. 23 to Feb. 9, 1916]," CHETOM 15 H 34.

22. "Compte-rendu de la révolte en pays marka et bobo"; in Niakate, 1:40 (Dec. 22).

23. Lt. gov., HSN, to gov.-gen., "Compte rendu de la tournée effectuée par Gouv. de la colonie dans la région du Bani et de la Volta," Oct. 24, 1916, AOF/ANS 4 D63. This complaint is one of the numerous examples showing that the usual tension between the civilian administrators and the military continued throughout the anticolonial war.

24. These lines may have been written by Molard.

25. Report by Simonin on the battle of Yankaso, Dec. 23 to 25, 1915; in Niakate, 1:64, 65.

26. Idem; in Niakate, 1:58.

27. N. Boni, 1962, 227: (divinité déchue). The verb déchoir implies a fall from grace following a mistake, or a sin, a meaning that dovetails with the common West African perception of a fall, even if the causal chains implicit in the two conceptions are not identical.

28. Extracts from Maguet's political journal; in Niakate, 1:50 (July 22, 1916).

CHAPTER 7

1. Bamako to Dakar, 30 Jan. 1916, AOF/ANS 4 D 64.

2. Molard report "sur les opérations de police dans le bassin de la Volta," SHAT

Fonds AOF 5 H 196. A slightly different version of the Molard report from CHETOM (15 H 34) and an abridged version from Niakate 3: 50–98 are also used in this chapter.

3. AOF political situation, 1916, reports to gov.-gen., AOF/ANS 2 G 17/4.

4. The commanding officers were 2nd Lt. Breton, Capt. Carpentier, Capt. Lucas, and Capts. Ferron and Labouret, who had participated in the Simonin column. They were reinforced in early March with a sixth company based in Guinea under the command of Amalric.

5. The 80-mm cannon was part of the Bange line developed after 1870 as part of the rearmament for the revanche with Germany; the mountain model dated from 1878. By 1914, it was no longer in use in Europe and had been superseded by the M1897 75-mm recoil-controlled field gun. Some of them, however, when trench warfare in World War I became permanent, were brought back, with other outmoded guns, as light "trench cannons," to throw bombs and grenades. Kambou-Ferrand (1993a) has a picture of the cannon without its carriage adapted for this kind of use in Europe.

6. Molard to Pineau, Aug. 10, 1915, AOF/ANS 1 D 211. Instructions from Pineau, high commander for AOF, Oct. 1915, AOF/ANS 1 D 211.

7. Melinite was made by combining nitrocellulose, the first dependable "smokeless" powder, developed by French chemist Paul Vieille, with highly explosive picric acid. Shells filled with this explosive could shatter into a thousand splinters.

8. The British had used the U.S.-made, hand-operated Gatling gun as early as the 1873–74 Ashanti war. They used the Maxim gun for the first time in 1888, in action in Gambia, then in the Anglo-Boer War of 1899–1902, and in the Volta region of northwestern Ghana in police rounds in the first years of colonial rule. The Maxim gun was also used by the Italians, and by the Germans in the repression of independent movements in German South West Africa and Tanganyika (Vandervot 1998, 49). The French reluctance to use machine guns was not because, as it has been argued, of their refusal to adopt a weapon produced abroad, but because they had placed great hopes on this new weapon in the war of 1870 and obtained very poor results. Later the French did use it in some colonial adventures (China, southern Morocco, Algeria) albeit parsimoniously. The model used by the colonial troops at that time was the 1900 Hotchkiss, a sturdy model placed on a tripod (Deville 1913).

9. Gen. Goullet, chief of AOF armed forces, Jan. 31, 1917, SHAT Fonds AOF 5 H 3.

10. A doctor who accompanied the small column that repressed the Tuareg rebellion in the region of Dori (northern Burkina Faso) described how, in March and June 1916, the machine gun decimated the Tuareg in two decisive battles (Déjean, 1970). This column included tirailleurs returning from the expedition to German Togoland. Other tirailleurs from Togo were sent to help defend Koudougou (chap. 10). Also "Note sur les mouvements insurrectionnels dont a été le théatre la colonie du HSN en 1915–16. Touaregs de la Boucle: cercle de Hombori, Dori, Say [May 1915 to July 1916]," Apr. 16, 1917, AOF/ANS 4 D 63.

11. Another new weapon, the grenade, was not used in the Volta-Bani War. Tirailleurs were equipped with grenades only after 1916. In repressive campaigns against the Lobi, these weapons proved to be devastating inside houses.

12. These included dictionaries of the Fulbe and the Kasena languages and two volumes on the social and religious life of the Bwa, based on discussions with informants in the Dedougou area (Cremer 1923; 1924a; 1924b; 1927). All of these works

were published by the Société Française d'Ethnographie, with financial contribution from the colony of Upper Volta.

13. On Lobi country under Labouret, see Kambou-Ferrand 1993a.

14. Marie-François Clozel was governor-general of French West Africa throughout the Volta-Bani War, from June 26, 1915 to May 8, 1917 (Angoulvant served as acting governor in 1916). Clozel had started his West African career as lieutenant governor of the Ivory Coast, before his appointment in 1908 as lieutenant governor of Haut-Sénégal-Niger. In both colonies, he followed Ponty's 'apprivoisement' and 'politique des races' policies in opposition to the military-minded faction of the administration represented by Angoulvant. Pineau conducted pacification campaigns, especially in the Nienegue area, when he was the first commander of the Volta region (see chap. 3). Simonin was commandant of the cercle of Bobo-Dioulasso in 1898, and commander of the Second Military Territory (which included the Volta region) in 1900.

15. Quoted from a report by Lt. Gov. Antonetti to gov.-gen., Mar. 22, 1917, AOF/ ANS 1 D 209.

16. Molard report; in Niakate, 3:54.

17. The problems were created by the same enemies. In 1897, the people of Warkoy had tried to cut off Caudrelier's communication with San, but the village was destroyed. It rose again in 1916 against the Molard column.

18. Digué, in Koulouba, to gov.-gen., Apr. 1, 1916, AOF/ANS 4 D 63.

19. The term *Nienegue* was popularized by colonial administrators. In spite of its colonial connotations, the term is used here for clarity.

20. Molard report; in Niakate, 3:62–63.

21. Bamako to Dakar, Feb. 14, 1916, AOF/ANS 4 D 64.

22. The Molard column spent 217 shells and 13,665 cartridges in La. It used an average of 3,000 cartridges in middle-sized engagements and up to 7,000 to 8,000 cartridges against important military centers.

23. That the burial of Europeans in a village was perceived even more outrageous in this instance will be understood if it is seen in the context of villagers' views about recruitment to the French army: recruits, once they had left the village, were considered to be to all intents and purposes dead; moreover, they would not receive appropriate funeral ceremonies in their home villages.

24. According to Gnankambary (1970, 73) Marka forces had gone to Da (east of Bona).

25. Molard report, SHAT Fonds AOF 5 H 196.

26. Compte-rendu de la tournée effectuée par le Gouverneur de la colonie dans la région du Bani et de la Volta, Oct. 24, 1916; lt. gov., HSN, to gov.-gen., AOF/ANS 4 D 63.

27. Carpentier report, Mar. 11 to Apr. 9, 1916, SHAT 5 H 196.

28. Molard report, CHETOM 15 H 34.

29. Compte-rendu de la tournée effectuée par Gouverneur de la colonie dans la région du Bani et de la Volta, Oct. 24, 1916; lt. gov., HSN, to gov.-gen., AOF/ANS 4 D 63. Amalric report, Dedougou, Mar. 23, SHAT 5 H 196.

30. In comparison, the Carpentier detachment to San conducted a major campaign lasting one month and used 15,300 cartridges; "Colonne de Dédougou, état ré-

capitulatif des munitions d'infanterie consommées pendant les opérations de la région Volta-Bani," SHAT 5 H 196. See also note 27 above.

31. Molard report, in Niakate, 3:90.

32. Upon arriving in his own cercle, Labouret led a vigorous campaign and destroyed the village of Tokona on May 6. His action, however, did not take care of the difficulties in Lobi country, echoing the events of the Volta bend, and in June other police rounds had to be organized against Puguli, Dagari, Birifor, and Lobi villages; HSN political situation report, June 21, 1916, AOF/ANS 4 D 63.

33. Picanon report, "Rapport d'ensemble" no. 50, May 12, 1917, AOF/ANS 765/4 G 21.

34. From lt. gov. in Bamako to Dakar, Mar. 22, 1917, AOF/ANS 1 D 209.

35. Molard report, SHAT 5 H 196.

36. Molard report; in Niakate, 3:65.

37. Idem; in Niakate, 3:64–65.

38. Idem; in Niakate, 3:61, 93.

39. General report, Dakar to Koulouba, AOF/ANS 4 D 64.

40. Quoted in Sombie 1975, 24.

41. Molard report; in Niakate, 3:61.

42. The Stefanini company was of standard composition and size (222 tirailleurs commanded by a dozen French officers and 17 African officers of lesser rank). It was reinforced by a machine-gun platoon with 19 tirailleurs and 7 French and African officers; Lt. Stefanini report, CHETOM 15 H 34.

43. Molard report; in Niakate, vol. 3.

44. Quoted in Sombie 1975, 26.

45. Digué, to Dakar, May 21, 1916, AOF/ANS 4 D 63. The villages destroyed included Pahin, Konkoliko, and, most importantly, Tunu, the home of M'Bien Nienzien, close relative of Yisu Kote of Bona, and the last stronghold of resistance in the Marka region. The Stefanini company was left in Tunu to prevent the villagers from returning and starting their farms.

46. Idem, May 27.

47. Gnankambary, 1970, 84. Molard report; in Niakate, 3:68. Clozel to minister of colonies, June 5, 1916, ANSOM Série Affaires Politiques, carton 2801/6.

48. The source for the Molard campaign in the Nienegue region is "Opérations de la colonne Molard en pays Nienegue," in Niakate, 2:92–98.

49. Molard report, SHAT Fonds AOF 5 H 196.

50. Labouret's diary, CHETOM 15 H 39.

51. From Molard to Maguet, May 5, quoted in the Molard report; in Niakate, 3:67.

52. Idem, May 21; in Niakate, 3:68.

53. AOF/ANS 4 D 63 (emphasis added).

54. Telegram from Digué to Clozel, June 13, 1916, AOF/ANS 4 D 63.

55. Letters from Angoulvant to Digué, June 16 and June 21, 1916, ibid.

56. Angoulvant to lt.-gov., Aug. 19, 1916, ibid.

57. On the Borgou movement, see Crowder, 1978, 181–87; Garcia, 1970.

58. Koulouba to gov.-gen., AOF/ANS 4 D 63.

59. Koulouba to Dakar, June 19, 1916, AOF/ANS 4 D 63.

60. Two of them, the Voulet and the Destenave columns, are mentioned above in this chapter and in chapter 2, pp. 64–67.

61. In the ethnological literature, *Samo* is now often replaced with the term *San* (pl. *Sanan*). Such improvements or "corrections" in labeling (with the claim that "this is the way people call themselves") risk disguising the great heterogeneity of the population and the colonial origin not only of the rubric but of the entire category. The practice entrenches the colonial creation of tribe rather than improving understanding. We remain uncommitted to any of these terms. Toe (1994, 173) indicates that in the Maka language the anticolonial war is called Bodo-zia. Bodo would be a derivative of Pundu, and *zia* means war.

62. Pare (1984, 155) writes that the headdress was called *bosa*.

63. Isa Pare was one of the most notorious colonial figures in the southern Samo region. Isa was an acquaintance of Bere Jibo, the powerful chief of the canton of Kougny, who owed his position to Widi of Barani. In the 1905 overhaul of chiefs in the cercle of Dedougou (then, the cercle of Koury), Bere and Isa were arrested and jailed for several years. Like many other colonial chiefs, Isa was rehabilitated and appointed chief of the canton of Toma in 1915 (Prost 1971, 107). Other sources, however, indicate that he was appointed canton chief in 1916 as a reward for his leading role in the defense of Toma against anticolonial forces. It may be that in 1915 he had been appointed chief of Toma and not of the canton of Toma. In 1933, in the reports of the Sol mission, Colony of Upper Volta, and further inquiries by de Beauminy in the Samo region, Isa Pare and most other colonial appointed chiefs in the region were described as tyrants, and Isa was sent into forced residency in Ivory Coast. Description of the extraordinary economic enterprise run by Isa Pare, including the relocation of Gurunsi people in his canton who worked on his plantations in exchange for tax exemption, can be found in Hubbell 1997.

64. Testimony of Alfred Diban Ki-Zerbo, who was among the besieged, Ki-Zerbo (1983, 54).

65. For years afterwards, the canton chief based in Toma refused government services, such as providing schooling and so forth, to the inhabitants of Zuma and the other villages that took part in these attacks.

66. Excerpts from Maguet's diary quoted in "Role des Administrateurs au cours de la répression, par l'Administrateur Périquet"; in Niakate, 2:1–15.

67. He died in 1949. The colonial administration prohibited his family from organizing his funeral.

68. Lucas report, CHETOM 15 H 39.

69. Niakate, 1:7. Angoulvant, in Dakar, to minister of colonies, AOF/ANS 4 D 63, July 1, 1916. Also in ANSOM Série Affaires Politiques, carton 2801/6.

70. Annex to Molard report, SHAT 5 H 196.

71. Report on recruitment of black troops by gov.-gen., Van Vollenhoven, Sept. 25, 1917, AOF/ANS 4 D 72.

72. In British Somalia, the British resorted to airplanes at the end of World War I in their fight against Mohamed Ibn Abdullah Hassan ("Mad Mullah"), who had initiated military action in 1899 and who was definitively defeated only in 1920.

Chapter 8

1. Vidal inquiry, "Déposition des Chefs de Canton," Aug. 16, 1916, AOF/ANS 15 G 201.

2. "Tableau des combats par Maubert," ANCI 5 EE 6(3/2). Hébert 1970, 13; see also Boni 1962, 228–30.

3. High commissariat archives, Bobo-Dioulasso; also, Vidal inquiry, Aug. 1916, "Déposition de Si-Boro, chef de canton Sambla," AOF/ANS 15 G 201.

4. The dispatch of Sambla auxiliaries to Bondokuy to help the administrative column has been reversed in Sambla oral history as help brought by the Sambla people to the Bwa combatants. Today, some say that the joking relationship *(senenkuya)* that exists between them and the Bwa people was the reason for their participation in the conflict, while in other versions (in "Sanblaw ka muruti," in Bobo Julaso ni Dedugu Serepeya 1992, 5) that special relationship was born as a result of the help that the Sambla resisters brought to the Bwa. It is possible that after the battle of Bondokuy, Sambla combatants fought alongside Bwa resisters, but we have no contemporary testimony to this.

5. Clozel to Koulouba. Jan. 9, 1916, AOF/ANS 4 D 64.

6. A similar opposition divided the Winye (Ko) populations, half of whom supported the Karantao, while the other half fought against them (chap. 2). It is common to find in the region that a population of the same speech community is divided into two opposing camps. We see this to some extent, for example, between the northern Tusia, who during the anticolonial war joined the Sambla, and those of the surroundings of Tusiana, who adopted a wait-and-see attitude.

7. Maubert gave the following description of these men when he met them as reinforcements on his way back from Bondokuy: a "detachment consisting mostly of older auxiliaries, without qualities of resistance and energy." Maubert's poor judgment on the lack of motivation of the people forcibly enrolled in colonial troops is surprising, given that he had just been betrayed by archers, who had also been sent to Bondokuy by the chief of Wakuy (Maubert, "Carnet de route," Dec. 14, 1915, AOF/ANS 4 D 64). It should be noted that these men, since they had witnessed the French occupation of the region when they were in their early twenties, were very aware of the military power of the colonial authority.

8. High commissiariat archives, Bobo-Dioulasso.

9. The dialect differences between the two groups are less easy to summarize at the present level of research because Bobo speech shows great variation within and between these subethnic boundaries.

10. ANCI 5 EE 6(3/2); monthly political reports, Bobo-Dioulasso, Jan. 1916. Kohere Tiano was captured on August 29 and sentenced to death for having immured alive nine men who were former tirailleurs.

11. Tusia people include two main groups, one in the north, mixed with the Sambla, and the people of the Tusiana region, who are later settlers.

12. Telegram from Maubert to Koulouba, AOF/ANS 15 G 201. The lieutenant governor's refusal was largely because of Maubert's lack of foresight in Bondokuy and of apprehension about his impulsive character; Bamako to Dakar, AOF/ANS 4 D 64.

13. AOF/ANS 15 G 201.

14. High commissariat archives, Bobo-Dioulasso; Amalric report, Dedougou, Mar. 23, SHAT 5 H 196.

15. High commissariat archives, Bobo-Dioulasso.

16. ANCI 5 EE 6(3/2); monthly political reports, Bobo-Dioulasso, Mar. 1916.

17. High commissariat archives, Bobo-Dioulasso.

18. In 1892, the northern Tusia villages, with the exception of Banfulagwe, were part of a coalition to resist Tieba of Sikasso, who defeated them in the village of Kaka. Tieba had another encounter with Banfulagwe, which was defended by a great number of Sambla warriors; they resisted for three weeks before being crushed. After this victory, Tieba raided Sambla villages — but not Karankaso, which was protected by a fortified wall and allied to Mori-fin Watara.

19. Monthly political reports, Bobo-Dioulasso, Mar. 1916, ANCI 5 EE 6(3/2).

20. High commissariat archives, Bobo-Dioulasso; also ANCI 5 EE 6(3/2); monthly political reports, Bobo-Dioulasso, Mar. 1916.

21. These chiefs were Mongo Traore of Guena (Tusia), Bali Traore of Kwini (Tusia), Si-Boro of Bwende (Sambla), Mo Ture of the Bobo village of Loroferesso, and Kito Kone of Beregadugu (Turka).

22. Column in Sembla and Tousia country — Maubert, "Carnet de route"; high commissariat archives, Bobo-Dioulasso; also in Niakate, 3:83–91.

23. Ibid.

24. These villages were much larger than the present-day villages. Maubert counted 96 compounds in Bwende and 151 in Toroso.

25. Cercle of Bobo-Dioulasso, political report, 4th trim. 1917, ANCI 6(3/2).

26. High commissariat archives, Bobo-Dioulasso; Hébert (1970, 8); in Niakate, 2:75.

27. Monthly political reports, Bobo-Dioulasso, Apr. 1916, ANCI 5 EE 6(3/2).

28. General report, Koulouba to Dakar, late Apr. 1916, AOF/ANS 4 D 64.

29. The account of this campaign is based on Maubert's "carnet de route," reproduced in Niakate, 2:78–82, and in the high commissariat archives, Bobo-Dioulasso.

30. The following day, Maubert also demolished the deserted village of Kukuruma, nine kilometers away from the post of Kofila.

31. Clozel to minster of colonies, June 5, 1916, ANSOM Série Affaires Politiques, carton 2801/6.

32. The Bobo revolt in the cercle of Bobo-Dioulasso; in Niakate, 2:74.

33. Idem, Niakate, 2:75.

34. Monthly political report, cercle of Bobo-Dioulasso, Dec. 1916, ANCI 5 EE 6(3/2).

35. The Bobo revolt in the cercle of Bobo-Dioulasso; in Niakate, 2:76. Brief account of the revolt by lt. gov., in Koulouba to gov.-gen., Dakar (1918), AOF/ANS 2 G 16/7.

36. Monthly political report, Bobo-Dioulasso, Dec. 1916, ANCI 5 EE 6(3/2).

37. In the last document that Maubert prepared as cercle commandant, in March 1917, he recommended the payment of special bonuses to eight people for their services during the repression. Six canton chiefs 2nd class: Zezuma Millogo (Kotedugu), Si-boro Traore (Bwende), Mango Traore (Gena), Dambio Kulibali (Kari), Kama Bihun (Wakuy, son of Beopa, killed Jan. 2), Woman Dionu (Fo); and two canton chiefs 3rd class: Sanro

Traore (Segedugu) and Bali Traore (Kwimi); "Notice sur les chefs du cercle de Bobo-Dioulasso"; Mar. 31, 1917; high commissariat archives, Bobo Dioulasso.

38. Political reports, cercle of Bobo-Dioulasso. 3rd trim. 1919; 1st trim. 1920, ANCI 5 EE 1 (3). Lamissa, with his partner Diumugu, had cut the bodies of the two guards into pieces and planted their heads on poles on the Bobo-Dioulasso–Dedougou road. The French also commonly practiced the display of enemy heads on stakes; for the Baule pacification, see the frontispiece in T. C. Weiskel 1980; among the Lobi, see Kambou-Ferrand, 1993b.

39. Political report, cercle of Bobo-Dioulasso. 4th trim. 1919, ANCI 5 EE 1 (3).

40. Lt. gov., HSN, to gov.-gen., Dec. 13, 1915, AOF/ANS 4 D 57.

41. The early colonial army had enlisted house slaves or purchased slaves, sometimes disguising the practice by calling the sum paid to the owner "compensation for the loss of a member of the family." Hubbell (1997, 206) describes how in Samo country around 1900 the officers procured soldiers by coercing people recruited as porters.

42. Political reports, 1921, cercle of Bobo-Dioulasso, ANCI 5 EE 1(3).

43. AOF/ANS 15 G 201. In the following months, an extremely bitter Maubert denounced many of his former colleagues of other cercles for various abuses and crimes. Maubert, who had a Senegalese common-law wife, ended his career in Senegal with the support of the minister of colonies but against the advice of Governor-general Angoulvant, who considered him to be a "bush administrator" and to lack the necessary qualities to succeed in an organized colony such as Senegal; Maubert personal file FM EE/ii/1131(1).

44. Bamako to Dakar, Jan. 18, AOF/ANS 1918. 4 D 73.

Chapter 9

1. Administrator Ponzio to governor in Koulouba, telegram no. 682; in Niakate, 2:70.

2. Information on the Sangare of Dokuy and on the Sidibe of Barani can be found in Diallo 1997. Unfortunately, Diallo's excellent presentation is mired in the hopeless task of manufacturing an evidently nonexistent dynastic succession list. Information on the Futanke power in Bandiagara can be found in Barry 1993. A source of information, used by both authors, is Bâ and Daget 1955.

3. For resistance to French occupation in the San region, see Dakono 1976; in the Minyanka region, see Jonckers 1987, 123–37.

4. Périquet, report on the situation at the start of the revolt; in Niakate, 2:16–35. Telegram from Henry, in Koulouba, to gov.-gen., Jan. 11, 1915, AOF/ANS 15 G 106.

5. Recruitment reports, cercle of San, AOF/ANS 4 D 57.

6. Lt. gov., HSN (Clozel), to Dakar. June 11, 1914, AOF/ANS 15 G 198. In the months before the 1915–16 war, Maguet got into the habit of bringing back leaders of rebellious villages to Dedougou, where they were forced into all kinds of drudgery and were at times beaten; Picanon, Paris, May 22, 1919; AOF inspection mission reports, 1916–17, AOF/ANS 765/4 G 21.

7. Judgment, cercle of Koutiala tribunal, Dec. 2, 1914, AOF/ANS 4 D 54; and Koutiala, "Affaire Boukary Touroumpo: Procès verbal d'information," AOF/ANS 15 G 105.

8. Picanon report, "Recrutement des troupes indigènes pendant la première période comprise entre le 1er aout 1914 et le 1er Oct. 1915," Nov. 7, 1916, AOF/ANS 4 D 65.

9. Second Military Territory, Cercle of Koury, political reports, Mar. 1902, AOF/ANS 2 G 2/10.

10. "Compte-rendu de la tournée effectuée par le Gouverneur de la Colonie dans la région du Bani et de la Volta," Oct. 24, 1916; lt. gov., HSN, to gov.-gen., AOF/ANS 4 D 63.

11. Ibid.

12. Cercle of Bandiagara. Rapport d'ensemble sur la tournée de police exécutée du 20 mars au 15 av 1916 contre les Bobo et les Markas révoltés des cantons de Bobo-Fakala et Fakala, AOF/ANS 4 D 64.

13. "Compte-rendu de la tournée effectuée par le Gouverneur de la colonie dans la région du Bani et de la Volta," Oct. 24, 1916; lt. gov., HSN, to gov.-gen., AOF/ANS 4 D 63.

14. Brief account of the revolt by lt. gov., Koulouba, to gov.-gen., Dakar (1918), AOF/ANS 2 G 16/7.

15. Maïga 1937, 277. Also, brief account of the revolt by lt. gov., Koulouba, to gov.-gen., Dakar (1918), AOF/ANS 2 G 16/7; Journal of the Post of Koudougou, in Niakate, I: 90.

16. General report, Koulouba to Dakar, late Apr. 1916, AOF/ANS 4 D 64; lt. gov., HSN, to gov.-gen., "Compte-rendu de la tournée effectuée par Gouverneur de la colonie dans la région du Bani et de la Volta," Oct. 24, 1916, AOF/ANS 4 D 63.

17. Besides the guards, Verdier had under him 335 auxiliaries, of whom twenty were equipped with regular army rifles and the rest with muskets. Telegram no. 182 from Insp. Vidal, Mar. 4, 1916, quoted in "Situation de la colonie au début de la révolte"; lt. gov. Périquet, Dedougou, Oct. 13, 1917, in Niakate, 2:28.

18. Arrested on Sept. 6, Niaka Tera was immediately sentenced to death for the mutilations of the guards in Tominian and for the murder of the chief of the village of Bakosoni; Antonetti, in Koulouba, to gov.-gen., Dakar, Sept. 8, 1916, AOF/ANS 4 D 63; also, Maïga 1937, 282.

19. General report, Koulouba to Dakar, late Apr. 1916, AOF/ANS 4 D 64. The administration easily recruited auxiliaries and porters in Segou because this region had a history of raids and conflicts with the hinterland of the Bani and many warriors who had belonged to the armies of precolonial leaders disbanded by the French.

20. Kabaye Traore was later captured and, like many other important anticolonial leaders, sentenced to death. He was executed Nov. 21, 1917. Quarterly political reports, 2 G 16/8, HSN, "Compte-rendu de la tournée effectuée par le Gouv. de la Colonie dans la région du Bani et de la Volta," Oct. 24, 1916; lt. gov., HSN, to gov.-gen., AOF/ANS 4 D 63; Report "From Ponzio, cercle of San, to gov., in Koulouba, and administrator and colonel in Dedougou", in Niakate, 2:70–72.

21. Carpentier had 240 tirailleurs, 8 French officers, and a cannon under him. Report by Carpentier, operations detachment chief, Mar. 11 to Apr. 9, 1916, SHAT 5 H 196.

22. Bleu attacked Wafuruma, Perive, and Bangasi between Feb. 18 and 21, and Sonhuwan on Feb. 24, where he inflicted heavy casualties. Périquet, "Role of administrators during the repression"; in Niakate, 2:1–15; acting lt. gov., HSN, to gov.-gen. Feb. 28, 1916, AOF/ANS 1 D 211.

23. Molard report; in Niakate, 3:50–95.

24. Carpentier report, Mar. 11 to Apr. 9, 1916, SHAT 5 H 196.

25. CHETOM 15 H 34.

26. Report by Capt. Megnou, commandant, 10th Comp., 4th Regt., Tirailleurs Sénégalais, San, Apr. 15, 1916, SHAT 5 H 196.

27. Report by Maj. Ozil on AOF troops "au sujet de l'incendie du village de Niankoine," June 29, 1916, CHETOM 15 H 39.

28. Bamako to Dakar Jan. 30, 1916, AOF/ANS 4 D 64.

29. "Évènements survenus dans le Bobo-Fakala et dans la région limitrophe de Ouencoro du 16 Av. Au 27 Mai 1916: Région du Fakala," in Niakate, 1:69–73.

30. The following section is based on the following archival documents: "Cercle de Bandiagara. Rapport d'ensemble sur la tournée de police exécutée du 20 mars au 15 av 1916 contre les Bobo et les Markas révoltés des cantons de Bobo-Fakala et Fakala," AOF/ANS 4 D 64; "Compte-rendu sur les opérations de police du cercle de Bandiagara du 27 mars au 29 juillet 1916" by Chief Warrant Officer Puget, Sofara, July 31, 1916, SHAT 5 H 196; "Rapport de l' Ajudant-chef Puget, commandant le détachement de police du Bobo-Fakala, Baramandugu, Septembre 1, 1916, SHAT 5 H 196; "Évènements," in Niakate, 1:69–73.

31. The total composition of the company was 29 tirailleurs, 25 cercle guards, 120 auxiliaries on foot, and a Tukulor and a Dogon goum with a total of 132 men. They were equipped with 78 sophisticated rifles model 74 and 85, 92 flintlocks, 10,600 cartridges, and 140 spears and bows.

32. The deserted villages burned by Fawtier were Ngoena (the headquarters of the canton of Bobo-Fakala), Poromu, Kandugu, Wa, Ganga, Buta, Maso, Pure, and Yagara.

33. "Compte-rendu de la tournée effectuée par le Gouverneur de la Colonie dans la région du Bani et de la Volta," Oct. 24, 1916; lt. gov., HSN, to gov.-gen., AOF/ANS 4 D 63.

34. Ibid.

35. The account of the Simonin campaign is based on "Colonne de San: Journal des marches et opérations. 13 avril–10 septembre — 1916. Par le Chef de Bataillon, commandant la colonne, Simonin," SHAT Fonds AOF 5 H 196.

36. The column encountered resistance only in Sonakuy, on May 7, but easily put it down.

37. By late April, 2 guards and 42 auxiliaries had been killed in these rounds; the insurgents counted at least 650 dead. General report, Dakar to Koulouba, late Apr. 1916, AOF/ANS 4 D 64.

38. For the first number, see the "brief account of the revolt" by lt. gov., in Koulouba, to gov.-gen., Dakar (1918), AOF/ANS 2 G 16/7. For the second number, see Angoulvant, Dakar, to minister of colonies, July 1, 1916, AOF/ANS 4 D 63; the same report can be found in ANSOM/2801/6.

39. "Évènements survenus" (see n. 29 above), in Niakate, 1:69–73. "Rôle des Administrateurs au cours de la répression, par l'Administrateur Périquet," in Niakate, 2:1–15, 5; "Compte-rendu, opérations, 27 mars au 29 juillet 1916," Puget, SHAT 5 H 196. Puget report, Baramandugu, Sept. 1, 1916, SHAT 5 H 196.

40. "Compte-rendu, opérations, 27 mars au 29 juillet 1916," Puget, SHAT 5 H 196. Puget, commandant, Bandiagara, to colonel at Barani, SHAT 5 H 196.

41. Brief account of the revolt, lt. gov., Koulouba, to gov.-gen., Dakar (1918), AOF/ANS 2 G 16/7.

42. Gov.-gen. to gen. cmdnt. supr., Dakar [Goulet], Jul. 9, 1916, AOF/ANS 4 D 63.

43. From Bamako to Dakar, Mar. 22, 1917, AOF/ANS 1 D 209.

44. Picanon report, AOF/ANS 4 G 21.

45. Molard report; in Niakate, 3:50–95. Picanon report, Nov. 7, 1916, "Recrutement des troupes indigènes," Oct 1, 1915 to Apr. 7, 1916, AOF/ANS 4 D 65; also in ANSOM, carton 2762, doss. "Télégrammes."

46. Report by 2nd Lieut. Grégoire, commandant, Kati, Oct. 1, 1916, SHAT 5 H 196.

47. The region of Balave is mostly Bobo and the region of Solenzo is mostly Bwa, but such ethnic classifications do not reflect the actual population diversity of the region. Many villages include Bobo, Bwa, Fula, Marka, and Mose wards.

48. Brief account of the revolt, lt. gov., Koulouba, to gov.-gen., Dakar (1918), AOF/ANS 2 G 16/7.

49. Political situation of the HSN, July 24, 1916; 4 D 63. Goullet, supr. cmdt., AOF troops, to Molard, July 17, 1916, AOF/ANS 4 D 64.

50. Ibid., and Dakar, Goullet, to gov.-gen., AOF, July 18, 1916, AOF/ANS 4 D 63.

51. "Role des Administrateurs au cours de la répression, par l'Administrateur Périquet"; in Niakate, 2:1–15.

52. Brief account of the revolt, lt. gov., Koulouba, to gov.–gen., Dakar (1918), AOF/ANS 2 G 16/7. Molard report; in Niakate, 3:50–95.

53. Maïga 1937, 283–84. Brief account of the revolt, lt. gov., Koulouba, to gov.-gen., Dakar (1918), AOF/A.N.S 2G 16/7.

54. Antonetti, in Koulouba, to gov.-gen., Dakar, Sept. 8, 1916, AOF/ANS 4 D 63.

55. Acting gov.-gen. (Angoulvant), to commander in chief AOF troops, Aug. 28, 1916, AOF/ANS 4 D 63.

56. According to Michel (1982, 105) by October 1916 the administration had seized 19,000 guns and about 8,000 bows in the cercle of San; Capron (1973, 105) gives for the end of the year the figures of 7,000 bows, 230,000 arrows, and 300 knives and spears.

Chapter 10

1. On the different ethnic labels used for Gurunsi groups and the attempts to work out the relationship of the various languages in this region, see Duperray 1984, 13–29.

2. On intervillage alliances among the Gurunsi, see, for example, Tauxier 1912, and Duval 1986. Duval states that the Nuna villages of Buyunu, Kasu, Sapuh, and Sili had been centers of resistance to the French. Sili controlled twenty-two villages.

3. The French thus transformed the essentially ritual position of the Laarle naaba into a function specifically related to a territory, the Laarle, or Lalle, canton north of Koudougou.

4. Baron Henri d'Arboussier was a major colonial figure. In the early 1900s he was the commandant of the cercle of Jenne, and he finished his career as governor of New Caledonia (French Polynesia). His half-African son, too, had a remarkable career. Gabriel d'Arboussier, whose mother's family was close to the family of the great Tukulor re-

former and political leader Al Hajj Umar Tall, was born in Jenne and grew up in Ouagadougou. He became a colonial administrator in West Africa, but in an extraordinary and rather unique turnaround, he renounced his career in 1946 to become one of the founders of the Rassemblement Démocratique Africain (RDA), the political party that became the major force pushing for African independence in French West Africa. After independence, he chose Senegalese nationality, becoming first the minister of justice of Senegal, under Leopold Senghor, and subsequently Senegal's ambassador in Paris.

5. On the marabout affair, see "Rapport sur l'affaire Hamaria, Imam Koureich, Zakaria Sissac, et consorts: Cercle du Mossi," AOF/ANS 15 G 105.

In the mid-1890s, Amaria, a Gurunsi captive who had become a successful leader in the Zaberma army, had led a revolt against his former master, the Zaberma leader Babato, and signed a treaty with the French as "king of the Gurunsi."

6. In a letter to the minister of the colonies, Maubert declared that Amaria had been strangled in jail. He also blamed administrator Rémond for sparking the revolt in the residence of Leo and wrote that d'Arboussier covered up for him: Paris, Aug. 22, 1918, "H. Maubert, Administrateur en Chef de 2ème Classe des colonies, à Mr. Le Ministre des Colonies," FM—EE/ii/1131(1), Maubert personal dossier. See note 7, p. 331.

7. A few months later, in November 1915, the Laarle naaba also warned the resident of Koudougou that the former chief of Ramongho, Tahiru, was spreading the rumor that after the overthrow of the French he would become chief of the Kipirsi. The French had just released Tahiru from jail to use him as an agent.

8. Cercle of Mossi, hearing, April 27, 1915, tribunal of cercle of Ouagadougou, AOF/ANS 15 G 105.

9. Duperray (1984, 184) notes that some people in Leo believe that the letter received by Amaria was planted by d'Arboussier.

10. Rapport d'une tournée par le commis des affaires indigènes Talagrand, Mar. 5–23. Picanon report, "Recrutement des troupes indigènes pendant la première période comprise entre le 1er aout 1914 et le 1er oct 1915," Nov. 7, 1916, AOF/ANS 4 D 65.

11. Post of Koudougou journal; in Niakate, 1:85.

12. From the diary of André Chrestien de Beauminy, adj. administrator, Ouagadougou cercle, quoted in Balima 1996, 208–9.

13. Ouagadougou cercle report, Nov. 25, 1915, AOF/ANS 4 D 57.

14. Post of Koudougou journal; in Niakate, 1:96.

15. Idem; in Niakate, 1:97.

16. Idem; in Niakate, 1:94 (Dec. 13).

17. HSN trimester political reports, 2nd trim. 1916, AOF/ANS 2 G/16/8.

18. D'Arboussier wrote in a report that the Marka leaders presented themselves as "marabouts"; "Note demandée par Monsieur le Gouverneur du HSN sur les causes du soulèvement des Gourounsi," in Niakate, 3:49.

19. Variant forms of *mori* (sometimes *more*) are used to designate Muslim clerics or men of letters throughout the savanna, from the Malinke world near the Atlantic to Mose country in the eastern Volta region. Person writes that this is a southern Malinke form corresponding to *mudu* in northern Malinke (Person 1968, 1:263). Another origin for the word *muratwa*, suggested by Bayili (1983) is that it represents a distortion of the Manding word *muruti* (rebellion). This latter word (which is of Arabic origin) may have

been used at the time in some places, but it is not clear if it was known in the Gurunsi areas, where Jula remains unspoken to this day. From a purely philological angle it seems improbable that *mura-twa* could derive from *muruti,* but a semantic resonance between these two homophonous words is conceivable if the word were widely used.

20. Marotel, "Rapport d'ensemble politique, administratif, et militaire concernant les opérations de dégagement du poste de Koudougou. Troupes du Groupe de l'AOF," 32, May 11, 1916, SHAT 5 H 196.

21. According to Mose traditions, in 1896 Naaba Wobogo fed his army with cowpeas boiled in a stretched cotton cloth during his war against Lieutenant Voulet.

22. Marotel, "Rapport d'ensemble," 48; May 11, 1916, SHAT 5 H 196.

23. Ibid., 22, 47, May 11, 1916, SHAT 5 H 196.

24. Ibid., 41, 47.

25. Ibid., 60.

26. Rituals involving the dog are common in adjacent regions, both on the Mose side and the west Volta side. The sacrifice of the dog is a central practice in shrines of the secret-society type that spread out of Bambara and Minyanka countries, known in the west Volta region by names such as Komo, or Kono; see Jonckers 1993.

27. Marotel, "Rapport d'ensemble," 36, May 11, 1916, SHAT 5 H 196.

28. Post of Koudougou journal; in Niakate, 1:88.

29. Idem, Niakate, 1:99.

30. Périquet, "Situation de la Colonie au début de la Révolte"; in Niakate, 2:19.

31. D'Arboussier, with forces that included five hundred Mose men under command of the Mogho naaba, Amaria and his auxiliaries, and the administrator of Fada N'Gourma, led a short military campaign in Togo between August 6 and 26, 1914. They encountered no opposition. Military control of northern Togoland was left to tirailleurs constituting a portion of the former brigade of Ouagadougou (Fourteenth Company, Second Regiment, Tirailleurs Sénégalais) who remained stationed in Ouagadougou and in Sansanne-Mango, SHAT Fonds AOF 5 H 3. General order no. 19, Pineau, cmdt. sup. AOF troops, 1914., n.d.

32. Post of Koudougou journal, in Niakate, 1:103–4.

33. Clozel to Koulouba, Jan. 9, 1916, AOF/ANS 4 D 64.

34. Post of Koudougou journal, in Niakate, 1:74; Duperray 1984, 185–86; Bayili 1983, 390.

35. The mission in Reo was opened by the White Fathers (Société des Missionaires d'Afrique) in 1912, the first in the west Volta region and only the third in what became the colony of Upper Volta. In Koudougou, the superior of the mission of Reo, Father Viguier, acted as interpreter for the resident and participated in the interrogation of the prisoners. The missionaries were able to return to Reo only in August 1916. The mission was rebuilt under supervision of the guards, using former insurgents as workers.

36. This verbal emblem shouted by the anticolonial side may imply contestation of Mose chiefs' claims. The horsetail, used as fly whisk, is a symbol of chiefly power. As in comparable cases from Asia, it brings out the role of the horse as the formidable tool of warfare in the savanna.

37. Marotel, "Rapport d'ensemble," 5, May 11, 1916, SHAT 5 H 196; Bayili, 1983, 390. In this early phase around Koudougou, bullet injuries were inflicted on colonial troops in many battles.

38. Marotel, "Rapport d'ensemble," 8, May 11, 1916, SHAT 5 H 196.

39. AOF/ANS 1 D 211.

40. "Rapport spécial militaire concernant les opérations de dégagement du poste de Koudougou" (Jan. 23 to May 11), SHAT 5 H 196. Marotel, "Rapport d'ensemble," 9, May 11, 1916, SHAT 5 H 196.

41. Brief account of the revolt, lt. gov. in Koulouba to gov.-gen., Dakar (1918), AOF/ANS 2 G 16/7.

42. Marotel, "Rapport d'ensemble," 17, 42, May 11, 1916, SHAT 5 H 196.13–14, 30.

43. Marotel, "Rapport d'ensemble," 21, May 11, 1916, SHAT 5 H 196. Marotel, "Instructions pour le Lieutenant Tilmont, commandant le poste de Sabu," SHAT 5 H.196. Marotel, "Instructions pour le Lieutenant Boullais, commandant le poste de Godé," SHAT 5 H 196.

44. Vidal report, AOF/ANS 15 G 201, Nov. 1, 1916.

45. Marotel, "Rapport d'ensemble," 25–27, May 11, 1916, SHAT 5 H 196.

46. The column attacked Ninion (defended by four hundred combatants, who suffered twenty-five deaths), Wera (for the second time), Bulsimiga, Zalim, Bantuli, and Reo. The French estimated that the column inflicted a total of fifty deaths. Ibid., 35–36.

47. Ibid., 38.

48. One of them included twenty-five soldiers, five guards, and thirty cavalrymen, and the other, forty soldiers, ten guards, and fifty cavalrymen.

49. Marotel, "Rapport d'ensemble," 59, May 11, 1916, SHAT 5 H 196.

50. Marotel and Cadence report "sur la répression de la révolte dans la circonscription de Koudougou"; in Niakate, 3:42.

51. From Bamako to Dakar, Mar. 23, 1917: "Sujet: de la répression dans la Résidence de Koudougou, et des rapports de MM. les Capitaines Marotel et Cadence," AOF/ANS 1 D 209.

52. Ibid. In May, Breton and Maguet had broken away from the Molard column and followed a road parallel to that of Molard in southern Bwa country (chap. 7, p. 204). Then Maguet went north to Dedougou and to Samo country (p. 211); Breton continued eastward to the Gurunsi region.

53. Cadence report "sur les opérations de la colonne secondaire Koudougou—Léo," May 1 to Oct.15, 1916, SHAT 5 H 196.

54. From Bamako to Dakar, Mar. 23, 1917, "La répression, Koudougou, et rapports de Marotel et Cadence," AOF/ANS 1 D 209. Clozel to minister of colonies, June 14, 1916, ANSOM Série Affaires Politiques, carton 2801/6.

55. Cadence report, 14, SHAT 5 H 196.

56. Ibid., 20.

57. "Opérations de police de . . . d'Arboussier"; in Niakate, vol. 1.

58. Idem; Niakate, 1:78.

59. HSN report political situation, June 21, 1916, AOF/ANS 4 D 63. ANSOM Série Affaires Politiques, carton 2801/6. Dakar to minister of colonies, Jul. 26, 1916, in Niakate, 1:7.

60. HSN, report on political situation, Jul. 24, 1916, AOF/ANS 128/4 D 63, "Opérations de police de . . . D'Arboussier," in Niakate, 1:78.

61. A side note to the anticolonial war in this region is that it inspired opposition in the Zouarugu district of the Gold Coast, the British territory to the south, some sixty kilometers from the operation zone of the Cadence column. The population of this area, which came to be known as Frafra—a cluster including the Gorisi, the Namnam, the Kusasi, and the Tallensi—have cultural and historical affinities with those in the French territory. They also had a similar colonial history of almost uninterrupted resistance to European occupation until 1911; the British had tried to stem this by appointing local "big men" as chiefs. In 1915, the departure of the soldiers stationed in Zouarugu and Navrongo created hopes similar to those in the French territory. The disturbance in this area started following a land dispute in April 1916, when some villages rose against the chief of Bongo. One of the constables that the British commissioner, Louis Castellain, sent was killed. When Castellain led a punitive expedition, the ringleaders fled to the French territory. In May, another constable was killed. In June the rebels planned an attack on Bongo and the conflict spread to the district of Bawku, across the Red Volta. Between 8 and 18 July, the commissioner suppressed this opposition with the substantial reinforcements that he received, including two Maxim machine guns (Thomas 1983, 72).

British authorities thought that this opposition was inspired by what was happening north of the border, but it is not clear if direct communication took place between the leaders on the two sides of the border. The area adjacent to the border on the French side, where the Bongo ringleaders escaped, was considered quiet by the French authorities; it experienced no repressive action from the French. The intensification of the Bongo events corresponds to the period when Cadence undertook his southern campaign. The relation between these events is a topic that can be explored in the future. It is possible that the areas considered "quiet" by the French, in this zone as elsewhere, were not so much outside the anticolonial movement, but were simply ignored because no important colonial targets existed to cause dramatic clashes.

62. "Opérations de police de l'Administrateur," in Niakate, 1:78.

63. Marotel and Cadence report "sur la répression de la révolte dans la circonscription de Koudougou"; in Niakate, 3:45.

64. Second Regiment, Tirailleurs Sénégalais: "Nombre de munitions consommées au cours des opérations de dégagement de Koudougou," SHAT 5 H 196. Cadence report, SHAT 5 H 196.

Conclusion

1. In December 1916, part of the village of Tiombini in Nienegue country and the villages of Bure, Tiebani, and Lahiraso in the cantons of Bwende, Fo, and Kotedugu continued resistance; cercle of Bobo-Dioulasso monthly report, Dec. 1916, ANCI 5 EE 6(3).

2. Political report, cercle of Bobo-Dioulasso, 2nd trim. 1917, ANCI 5 EE 1 (3).

3. Summary of Molard report, in Niakate, 3:73.

4. Idem, in Niakate, 3:74.

5. Maguet to lt. gov. in Koulouba, Sept. 4, 1916, in Niakate, 1:53–56.

6. Minister of colonies (Services militaires), Doumergues to Clozel, Apr. 25, 1916, F. M. Série Affaires Politiques, carton 2801/6.

7. Brief account of the revolt, lt-gov. in Koulouba to gov.-gen., Dakar (1918), AOF/ANS 2 G 16/7.

8. "Note sur les mouvements insurrectionnels dont a été le théâtre la colonie du HSN en 1915–16," Apr. 16, 1917, AOF/ANS 4 D 63. "Organisation militaire du HSN 1915–1917," AOF/ANS 5 D 46. In November 1916, Goullet (who had replaced Pineau as chief of staff in July) warned that the large number of troops in the Volta-Bani region was "an illusion . . . because they will be difficult to administer and handle given the shortage of officers . . . who are for the most part unfit for military campaign or wounded." (Goullet to gov.-gen., Nov. 17, 1916), AOF/ANS 5 D 46.

9. Bamako to gov.-gen., Nov. 21, 1916, AOF/ANS 2 G 17/4.

10. HSN, political report, 2nd semester 1919, AOF/ANS 2 G 17/4.

11. Brief account of the revolt, lt. gov., Koulouba, to gov.-gen., Dakar (1918), AOF/ANS 2 G 16/7. See Hubbell (1997) for a discussion of how arbitrary this characterization was.

12. In 1918, Kolonkwere Sondo (son of the "chief of Lankwe") called people to rise again against the French. Pare (1984, 5) recounts that while the new administrative buildings were under construction in Tougan, the village of Kasan had been chosen as temporary headquarters of the new subdivision. When the administrators finally left Kasan to settle in Tougan, the people of Kasan attributed the move to the strength of an important village shrine. To their mind, two antagonistic powers could not share the same space.

13. Report by Froger on Anzumana, Jan. 28, 1918, AOF/ANS 15 G 202.

14. Cercle of Bobo-Dioulasso political report, 3rd trim. 1920, ANCI 5 EE 1 (3).

15. Lt. gov. Brunet to Gov.-gen. Merlin, AOF/ANS 15 G 202. Périquet also intervened on behalf of Haillot and Lowitz (who were facing punishment for the atrocities they had committed in Dedougou) and the administrator Thomas (who was being charged for illegally executing prisoners during the Tuareg War in the cercle of Dori). "Role des administrateurs au cours de la repressison," Oct. 13, 1917, in Niakate, 2:1–15.

16. Political report, cercle of Bobo-Dioulasso, 4th trim. [marked 2nd trimester in error] 1923, ANCI 5 EE 1(3).

17. Ibid.

18. Ibid.

19. Ibid.

20. Ibid.

21. Reports and correspondence concerning the creation of Upper Volta can be found in AOF/ANS 2193/10 G 8.

22. In the latest effort to work out the genetic relationships of the languages of this region, the long-held supposition that Senufo is a Voltaic language has been abandoned (Williamson and Blanch 2000, 25–26).

23. Angoulvant 1922.

24. Letter from Hesling to commandant, Bobo-Dioulasso, Upper Volta colony no. 1. Response to the political report of 2nd trim, 1919. The copy of this letter, handwritten, corrected, and edited by Gov. Hesling, is attached to a typed copy of the report in ANCI 5 EE 1 (3).

25. Ibid. Published information on Hesling is very dispersed. For his attitude toward

Mose chiefs, see Skinner 1964, 161–72. For his economic policy, see Schwartz, 1993, 210–13.

26. Letter from administrator Martin to Hesling, July 31 1922, ANCI 5 EE 1 (3).

27. These requirements formulated by Dakar could be viewed as an indirect compliment to the quality of the opposition if one remembers that the new urban planning in Paris initiated by Hausmann included the destruction of old neighborhoods and the building of large avenues that facilitated the suppression of the Commune of Paris.

28. Interim gov. to lt.-gov., HSN, Aug. 19, 1916, AOF/ANS 4 D 63.

29. Koulouba to gov.-gen., Aug. 3, 1916, AOF/ANS 4 D 63.

30. Political report, cercle of Bobo-Dioulasso, 4th trim., 1917, ANCI 5 EE 1 (2).

31. Trimester political reports, 1922, cercle of Bobo-Dioulasso, ANCI 5 EE 1 (3).

32. Such a ring involving employees of the colonial administration was discovered in 1922. Political report, cercle of Bobo-Dioulasso, 2nd trim. 1922, ANCI 5 EE 1(2); political report, 4th trim. 1922, ANCI 5 EE 1 (3). The memory of this long-term disarmament campaign surfaces in the villages of the region today. For example, farmers tell anecdotes that some Fulbe herd owners became wealthy at that time owing to their ability to guess where in the bush the villagers hid their prized weapons, stealing them as they grazed their animals.

33. Political report, 4th trim. 1917, ANCI 5 EE 1 (3).

34. Idem, 1st trim. 1922; ibid.

35. Ibid.

36. Crozat 1891, 8.

Glossary of Colonial Terms

AGENT FOR INDIGENOUS AFFAIRS *(commis aux affaires indigènes)*
In the colonial administration of French West Africa, commis were clerks of low administrative rank who could fill different positions. They could be either African or French, depending on their position. The agents for indigenous affairs were all French and were charged with implementing the administration's orders and with the everyday political problems encountered by the administration. Their functions were essentially of a repressive nature. Periodically, agents for indigenous affairs were sent by the commandant of the cercle to villages to make people comply with orders (these agents had an important role in the recruiting campaigns) or to quell minor shows of defiance toward colonial rule.

AUXILIARY TROOPS *(troupes auxiliaires)*
Auxiliary troops consisted of local men temporarily hired by the commandant of a cercle for a military campaign. These men were often former tirailleurs or followers of chiefs allied to the French, such as the chief Idrisa Sidibe of Barani who provided a great number of auxiliary troops to the Molard column. In order to save the tirailleurs' efforts and lives, auxiliary troops were placed in the front lines and bore the brunt of the initial combats. Having less stake in the future of colonial rule than tirailleurs, they could be a liability. When the issue of a combat did not turn in their favor they could run away, and in some cases even turned against the colonial masters.

CANTON (district)
An intermediary administrative unit between the village and the cercle, the canton was an essential unit in the French territorial organization. For that reason it was also the one most frequently subject to modification, through amalgamation or redrawing of boundaries. Each canton included at least ten villages, one of them being the *chef-lieu de canton* (district town). French colonial administration attempted to overlap ethnic or former political boundaries with those of cantons, an approach that was the basis for the *politique des races* after 1908. Cantons chiefs were all African and among the most

hated collaborators of the colonial administration. They owed their position to the French, but many eventually gained considerable power and wealth by combining the coercive means of the colonial administration with their own.

CERCLE (province)
The cercle represented the largest administrative unit within a French colony. Large cercles often included "subdivisions" that, like cantons, were subject to constant modification of boundaries (for example, the subdivision of Boromo in the cercle of Dedougou). The cercle first appeared in Algeria before it was adopted by Governor Louis Faidherbe in Senegal and later in the new territories of West Africa. The French administrative personnel in a cercle of French West Africa included at minimum the commandant (who was normally a civilian), assisted by an *adjoint* (assistant) and by an agent for indigenous affairs (*commis aux affaires indigènes*). The administrator placed at the head of a subdivision was subordinate to the commandant of the cercle.

COLONIAL ARMY *(armée coloniale)*
Of all the European powers, France was the only one to create a colonial army in Africa. The Italians had set up the Corpo Speciale per l'Africa, but it was based in Italy and it was used essentially as an expeditionary force. The French *Armée coloniale* was created in 1900 in the aftermath of the wars of conquest, which were fought by officers of the French marine corps. Administrative control of the *Armée coloniale* went after that to the War Ministry (whereas the marine infantry had depended on the Naval Ministry), and its military headquarters for French West Africa was established in Dakar. The *Armée coloniale* was staffed with the companies of the Tirailleurs Sénégalais.

COLONIAL COMPOUND *(campement)*
A complex of rooms and houses built on the outskirts of villages situated on major roads *(routes d'étapes)*, intended to be used as housing for the traveling representatives of the colonial administration. On the frequently traveled roads of the cercle of Bobo-Dioulasso, they were situated every ten or fifteen kilometers. These structures were built and maintained by villagers. They consisted of square rooms for the European visitors, round rooms for the Africans, and enclosures, or stables, for animals. (In the Gold Coast the British administration constructed similar buildings in the countryside, and the corresponding term they used for them is "rest house.") As part of the effort to promote trade, from the first decade of the colonial occupation these compounds were made available, when colonial employees did not occupy them, to African traders. The colonial compounds became one of the first targets of the anticolonial movement in 1915–16. Today, administrative buildings are still located on the outskirts of villages. Preferred sites are on an elevation.

COLUMN
The military columns were temporary outfits put together for specific military campaigns. A column was commanded by a French military officer (never by a civilian administrator), who gave it his name. The column normally included a few other French officers. The troops were tirailleurs (African regulars), in numbers varying from a few dozen to a few hundred for the largest expeditions. This military component was backed up by scores of auxiliaries, porters, women to do the cooking, and hangers-on.

The latter joined for plunder. For instance, of the thirty-six hundred men of the Archinard column that entered Segu in 1890, only four hundred were tirailleurs. In 1916, the Molard column was still modeled on the organization of columns that conquered West Africa. The columns combined up-to-date armament and mobility. In enemy territory, columns marched in so-called square formation (an elongated rectangle), preceded and followed by auxiliary troops. This formation presented two major advantages: it reduced the length of a column marching in line, and soldiers could open fire at any time without endangering each other; at the same time, it kept porters, who might panic, inside the "square." At night, the camp formation was closer to a true square and was protected by a hedge of thorny shrubs, if possible with one side by a river (see map 25 in chap. 9 p. 264). A sizable train *(convoi)*, which included ammunition, medical supplies, and tableware for French officers, followed each column under the protection of tirailleurs.

CERCLE COMMANDANT *(commandant de cercle)*
The commandant was the administrator who represented the highest authority of a cercle. Normally a civilian official, he was the only person responsible for the cercle to the governor of the colony. By administrative decision, the commandants were frequently moved from one cercle to another to prevent them from setting down roots and accumulating too much power. The cercle commandant combined the functions of administrator, policeman, and judge. He was in charge of political order, of the gardes-cercle and auxiliary troops, and of the economy, agricultural development, public health, and education. He was also census taker, tax collector, bookkeeper, supervisor of labor, builder of roads, urban planner, and organizer of markets. In order to maintain contact, he was expected to be on tour in the villages of his cercle for at least ten days every month—to explain instructions to villagers, receive complaints, arbitrate, motivate, and, if need be, punish. Because of his comprehensive powers, combined with his isolation, the commandant was known in the administration as King of the Bush *(Roi de la brousse)*. He has remained in collective memory as one of the most remarkable figures of colonial society.

FORTIFICATIONS
In the region where the Sudanic style of architecture is prevalent (buildings made of sun-dried clay walls and flat, pressed-earth roofs supported by wood posts, with a second, and sometimes a third, story on top) the defense of villages was ensured by the arrangement of the houses. In each ward *(so-kala* in Bamana/Jula; called *soukala* by the French) of a village, contiguous houses, with entrances toward the inside of the ward, offered a continuous closed facade, broken only by narrow, almost invisible entry paths. In some villages, houses had no doors on the ground floor; people entered through a hole in the first-floor terrace that was accessed by movable ladder. In preparation for an attack, the walls were pierced to make it possible to shoot at assailants. These loopholes were in the shape of a wide isosceles triangle for firing guns and a narrow, vertical rectangle for arrows. Water-supply wells were inside the ward, and reserves of food were stored in the buildings—a maze of dark rooms. Such compact habitats, often called clay castles, can still be encountered today. Villages with a military function were further surrounded by a fortified wall *(tata)* built with stones and a clay mortar. Villages such as Karankaso in Sambla country, one of the defensive sites for the

Watara in their recurring confrontations against Tieba of Sikasso, were surrounded by a tata. In the 1880s, Tieba made Sikasso the most impressive fortified city in West Africa, surrounded by a wall six meters high and about two meters wide at the base. Before the French attacked Sikasso in 1898, Tieba's successor Babemba had built an additional wall, three to four meters from the first, and filled the space between the two. During the 1915–16 war, colonial troops faced mostly villages with back-wall fortifications, not the tata type.

GOUMIERS

A *goum* was an indigenous army unit; *goumiers* were men recruited from within the local population on a temporary basis for a particular purpose. Such recruitment—a colonial tradition imported from Morocco—was done to maintain order in territories conquered by the French army. In Morocco there were infantry and cavalry units of goum; in West Africa, where there were no official goum units, officials used that word to refer only to mounted auxiliaries. The goumiers were a close equivalent of mercenaries.

GUARD *(garde-cercle)*

The gardes-cercle were soldiers hired by the cercle administration. Often they were recruited among former tirailleurs. In the words of W. Ponty, lieutenant governor of Haut-Sénégal-Niger, they constituted "a genuine local gendarmerie force." (Ponty to commandant, cercle of Koury, Jan. 21, 1905, AOF/ANS 15 G 198.) Unlike gendarmes in France, however, the guards were part of the civilian administration, not the army. They were the odd-job men of the commandants, guarding the prison of the cercle, maintaining public order, carrying notifications from the commandant to villagers, assisting village and canton chiefs in tax collection and in the implementation of orders, and ensuring the protection of administrators on tour. Guards committed all kinds of abuses and lived at the population's expense and villagers dreaded them. Because of their long-standing employment they were also one of the significant elements of local level politics in the cercle.

HAUT-SÉNÉGAL-NIGER

Haut-Sénégal-Niger was one of the five colonies created in the major reorganization of French West Africa (Afrique Occidentale Française-AOF) in 1904. It incorporated basically what is now Mali and Burkina Faso. In colonial French Africa each colony had a different relationship with the metropolitan government, based on the history of the conquest. Haut-Sénégal-Niger was administered by a lieutenant governor—not by a governor, as was the case with Ivory Coast and Guinea. This meant that Haut-Sénégal-Niger's top colonial administrator was subordinate to the governor-general in Dakar and that its budget was submitted to him and not directly to the minister of colonies in Paris. (In practice, HSN's lieutenant governor enjoyed great latitude in his decisions and actions and was called "governor.") The reason for this subordinate status was to counteract the great influence that the military had acquired in this colony during its expansion after 1890, when it became a distinct colony named Soudan, headed by Colonel Louis Archinard. In 1898, as French West Africa was reorganized, part of this Soudan was given to the colony of Guinée; the newly conquered regions east of the Bani River were also separated from it and made into three separate military territories under the governor-general (see "Military Territory"). At this point the name was changed from Soudan to Haut-Sénégal et Moyen Niger. In 1902, as the government of French West Africa was moved from Saint Louis to Dakar and its political and financial powers were reinforced, the new colony was renamed Territoire de la Sénégambie et du Niger. In the 1904 reform, when the colony was renamed Haut-Sénégal-Niger, two of the military territories, including the cercles of Dedougou and Bobo-Dioulasso, were again attached to it, and the residence of its lieutenant governor was moved from Kayes to Bamako (on a hill called Koulouba in official documents). The colony was short lived. It was split in 1919 when Upper Volta was established, as explained in our conclusion, and the remaining part assumed, once again, and name Soudan. The name HSN was resented by the military, who often ignored it, continuing to refer to the colony as Soudan, even in official letters, in celebration of the imperialist legacy of Archinard. It became known to future generations mostly in the title of the three-volume work of Delafosse (1912), which remained for many decades the most comprehensive synthesis of what was known in Europe of the history and ethnography of this part of Africa.

MARABOUT

The English word comes from the Arabic *murābiṭ*, an inmate of a Sufi hospice, through Portuguese. In North Africa, a marabout is a Moslem hermit and saint whose tomb becomes the center of pilgrimages, but this practice is not common in West Africa. In colonial West Africa, the term often carried a pejorative connotation associated with magical and divinatory practices. Administrators used the term indiscriminately, for the best-known clerics as well as for a large number of more obscure Muslim figures. The former had great religious scholarship and prestige as well as political influence. Some who were perceived as allies were given the honorific title Grand marabout by the colonial administration. Others (often misleadingly labeled *marabouts errants* in administrative reports) earned a living through commerce and by providing services such as, mostly, the writing of charms. There was a demand for these services among Muslims as well as non-Muslims. The most important clerics performed the hajj, or pilgrimage to Mecca.

MILITARY TERRITORY *(territoire militaire)*

Newly conquered territories were initially administered by the military to ensure pacification before power was transferred to a civilian administration. In the 1898 reorganization of French West Africa (AOF) that followed the fall of Sikasso, the capture of Samori, and the treaty with the British, the newly conquered territories to the east of the Bani River were organized into three territories under military administration (see Haut-Sénégal-Niger). The First Military Territory, based in Timbuktu, included the Mose region of Yatenga; the Second Military Territory, centered in Bobo-Dioulasso, included the Mose region of Ouagadougou; the Third Military Territory was based in Zinder. In 1904, the First and Second Military Territories were placed under civilian rule and united in the colony of Haut-Sénégal-Niger, the former Soudan, which was administered from Koulouba (the administrative neighborhood of Bamako).

Even after the military territory was transformed into a civilian colony, in some cercles the military retained administrative positions for many years. The cercle of Bobo-Dioulasso remained under military command until 1913. Notwithstanding the deep-seated hostility that existed between the civilian administration and the military, for the

native population the difference between a civilian commandant and a military one was
very small. Many civilian cercle commandants spent much of their time in military
campaigns and in making "police rounds." Conversely, in 1917, the officers stationed
in the military posts that were scattered throughout the region after the Volta-Bani War
were officially granted the political, administrative, and judicial powers of the cercle
commandants.

PACIFICATION

So-called pacification was the second phase of the repression campaign of the Volta-
Bani War. This phase followed the main column's destruction of the major centers of
enemy resistance (the column moved on to do the same in another area). Pacification
was conducted by civilian administrators heading groups of guards and auxiliaries. The
administrator accepted submissions from village delegations, took prisoner the anticolonial leaders, and punished communities that did not send submission delegations
or deliver leaders. He was also instructed to ensure that the conditions of surrender
were followed.

Elsewhere "pacification" could be the name of an entire campaign of repression. In
such cases, the distinction between a war and a pacification campaign is hazy: some
wars resulted in fewer casualties than pacification campaigns. Joseph Gallieni (the future general, war minister in 1915–16), the "father of pacification" in French West
Africa, associated pacification with the strategy of the "oil stain" and with "political action and intimate knowledge of the country and its inhabitants" (Deschamps 1953).
Twenty years after Gallieni left West Africa, between 1909 and 1911, the civilian governor of Ivory Coast, G. Angoulvant, led the most notorious pacification campaign and
became known as the theorist of pacification. Although the pacification of Ivory Coast
took on many aspects of a war of conquest, the French could not acknowledge this,
given the prominent position of that colony. In the economically backward Volta-Bani
region, however, many administrators interpreted the 1915–16 events as a new conquest, which suited the sequence and nature of the confrontations.

POLITICAL AGENT *(agent politique)*

Political agents were Africans individually hired by cercle commandants for temporary
missions. They were not members of the administrative body, but their existence was
officially acknowledged. Expenditures for them were accounted for in the cercle budget. In the years leading up to the 1915–16 war, these agents had become one of the
administration's most important sources of information about the population.

STATE *(état)*

At the time of the colonial conquest, the French gave the title *chef d'état* (head of state)
to some of their allies; such allies claimed political control over local populations. The
états, or states, of Seydu Amadu (east of the Suru River), of the Sidibe (west of the Suru
River), of the Sangare (the region of Dokuy), and the three Watara states in the cercle
of Bobo-Dioulasso occupied a large part of the Bani and Volta region. It should be
noted that the state of Seydu had no pretense to historical legitimacy: it evolved from
a military post used to control northern Samo villages.

States included a variable number of cantons; the chiefs of the cantons were named by the head of state. The word for state was often used by administrators in the plural (e.g., "the states of Idrisa Sidibe"), as if to stress their temporary nature. That the French chose the term *état* is intriguing: in the years preceding colonial conquest, the term the French used for their allies was *roi* (king). For example, treaties were signed with Moktar Karantao, "king of Wahabu," and with Amaria, "king of the Gurunsi." Once these regions were conquered by the French, *state* seemed to them to be the politically more appropriate word than *kingdom,* but it did not imply recognition of equality. States had no autonomous structures, and heads of state were responsible directly to the commandant of the cercle. The states were not a device in implementing indirect rule; they were not entities with recognized adjudication and law-making powers, as were British colonies. Contrary to what is commonly suggested, there was thus no fundamental policy shift between indirect and direct rule in French colonial policy. For the administration, hesitant as to what would be the best way to control the region's "anarchic" societies, the role of heads of state was twofold: it ensured a semblance of order, and it facilitated tax collection.

The heads of states themselves held a different view of their position: they often considered themselves to be allies of the French, not subordinates.

TIRAILLEUR
The infantry corps of the Tirailleurs Sénégalais (lit., Senegalese sharpshooters) was created by the governor of Senegal, General Louis Faidherbe, in 1857. The Tirailleurs Sénégalais belonged to the navy until 1900; after that date they were attached to the French Colonial Army (Armée coloniale). Officers of high rank were French, but all other ranks and recruits were African. Tirailleurs were recruited originally in Senegal and later in the newly conquered areas. In April 1915, a decree authorized Senegalese from the Four Communes (the old colonial districts of Senegal where the native residents enjoyed many of the rights of French citizenship) to enroll as regular French troops, but objections by French politicians voided the decree: Africans could thus enroll only in the Tirailleurs Sénégalais.

Avowedly cheaper to maintain and in Africa less prone to disease than white soldiers, the tirailleurs conquered West Africa for the French. The tirailleurs became famous in France for their participation in World War I, but their role in the conquest of West Africa and in the suppression of revolt movements has remained largely unknown. Tirailleurs' stipends came from the French West Africa government's budget; stipends were kept so low that booty was an important incentive for enrollment. Defeated enemies who wished to pursue mercenary activities often enrolled as tirailleurs. Another important source of tirailleurs was through purchase of domestic slaves; however, the status of tirailleur seems not to have been much higher than that of slave, at least in the early years of colonization. In his report on the origins of the Volta-Bani War, Chief Inspector Vidal explained that when the tirailleur enrolled, he almost always changed his name because he was committing treason: one day he may have to fight against his own people, subjecting himself to the wrath of his village's tutelary divinities. Even for a former tirailleur, "the white remains his father and his unique support till his death." Decommissioned tirailleurs who returned to their area of origin resented being treated as any other villager and were often in conflict with canton chiefs.

Archival Sources

AOF/ANS Archives of French West Africa kept at the Archives Nationales du Sénégal, consulted from microfilms in CAOM

ANCI   Archives Nationales de Côte d'Ivoire (Abidjan)

ANM   Archives Nationales du Mali

ANSOM Archives Nationales Section Outre-Mer (in CAOM)

CAOM   Centre des Archives d'Outre-Mer (Aix-en-Provence)

CHETOM Centre d'Histoire et d'Etudes des Territoires d'Outre-Mer (Fréjus)

CNRST   Centre National de la Recherche Scientifique et Technologique (Ouagadougou)

SHAT   Service Historique de l'Armée de Terre (Paris)

Overview of Archival Material

The most important archival collections concerning the history of the war in Burkina Faso and Mali are dispersed in Mali, Côte d'Ivoire, Senegal, and France. This situation is the result of the colonial history of these territories. From 1896 to 1904, Burkina Faso was a military territory dependent on the government of AOF based in Dakar. From 1904 to 1919 it became part of the Colony of Haut-Sénégal et Niger (HSN) with headquarters in Koulouba (near Bamako). In 1919, the partition of HSN gave birth to the Colony of Upper Volta, with its own government based in Ouagadougou. In 1933, the Colony of Upper Volta was itself partitioned between its neighbors. The southwest and the center of the colony—including the cercle of Bobo-Dioulasso, part of the cercle of Dedougou, and the cercle of Ouagadougou—became part of Côte d'Ivoire. The portion of the cercle of Dedougou that lies west and north of the Muhun River was annexed to French Soudan (Mali). In 1947 the colony of Upper Volta was reconstituted and became an independent nation in 1960. At every one of these changes of administrative status, the colony archives and current administrative work were sent to the new headquarters (Koulouba, Ouagadougou, and Abidjan).

Archives in France (ANSOM, SHAT, and CHETOM)

Two important archival collections from the civilian administration concern West Africa. The first are the archives of the Ministère de la France d'Outre-Mer, which were transferred to the National Archives in 1987, as the Archives Nationales Section Outre-Mer (ANSOM) held at the Centre des Archives d' Outre-Mer (CAOM) in Aix-en-Provence. The second collection consists of microfilm copies of the AOF archives kept in the Archives Nationales du Sénégal in Dakar. Two identical sets of microfilm copies of these Dakar materials are available in France, under the rubric Fonds Anciens AOF, one at the Centre des Archives d' Outre-Mer (CAOM) in Aix-en-Provence and the other in the Centre d' Accueil et de Recherche des Archives Nationales (CARAN) in Paris. The classification system into "series" follows that of Dakar. The reference of microfilms in Aix is preceded by 14 mi (*mi* for microfilm) and in Paris by 200 mi, followed by the number of the roll, and the reference of the series. For example, 14 mi or 200 mi/132/4 D 72. In the reference notes, we have skipped these prefixes; they are not necessary to locate the documents.

Two military archival funds including West African material are open to the public. The largest is located in the Château de Vincennes (Service Historique de l'Armée de Terre—SHAT) near Paris. Archives from SHAT contain original field records of military expeditions and operations that are of limited interest for the West African historian not concerned with military matters. The archival sources used in this book come from the "Fonds AOF" 5 H. Another, much smaller, military archival fund, the CHETOM (Centre d'Histoire et d'Etude des Territoires d'Outre-Mer), is of some interest as it holds documents exclusively related to former French colonies. The CHETOM is part of the Musée des Troupes de Marine located in Frejus. It was formerly known as CMIDOM (Centre Militaire d'Information et de Documentation, based in Versailles).

The reports that were required of all commanding officers, including those commanding detachments or companies that were part of larger columns, provide an abundance of archival material. While helpful in establishing a chronology of events, they are repetitive and restricted to descriptions of military engagements, frequently devoid of commentaries on the adversary.

Archives in Senegal (AOF/ANS)

Archival records concerning different colonies of AOF (Afrique Occidentale Française) remained in Dakar after independence as part of the Archives Nationales du Sénégal. Part of the archival fund from Dakar is available in the form of microfilm in France. Archives are organized into "series" that cover the different domains of administration. To each series is attributed a letter. The most interesting series for the history of the Volta region are the G (Administration générale and Affaires politiques) and D (Affaires militaires). We have consulted these archives from the microfilm copies in France at CAOM (see "Archives in France").

Archives in Burkina Faso

In the 1970s, a project for the construction of a center in Ouagadougou under the auspices of UNESCO failed to come to completion. Today, in the absence of a national archives center in Burkina Faso, most colonial archives remain dispersed. A small collection is found in the Centre National de la Recherche Scientifique et Technologique (CNRST) in Ouagadougou, and the headquarters of the former cercles (high commissariats) also contain stacked documents that have not been classified.

Archives Nationales of Côte d'Ivoire (ANCI)

Archival documents, as in Dakar, are organized into "series" that cover the different domains of the administration of the colonies. To each series is attributed a letter and until 1925 the letter was doubled. The most interesting series for the history of the Volta region are the DD (Administration générale), EE (Affaires politiques), and N (Affaires militaires).

Archives in Mali (ANM)

The head of the Archives Nationales du Mali in Bamako, Moussa Niakate, published a collection of archival documents on the 1915–16 Volta-Bani War (Niakate in the bibliography) and a guide to the archives of Mali. See also Conrad in the section below, "Archival and Inventory Guides."

ARCHIVAL AND INVENTORY GUIDES

Charpy, Jacques
1946–58 *Répertoire des Archives (de l'AOF)*. Rufisque: Imprimerie du Gouvernement de l'AOF.

Cisse, Ibrahim
1988 *Répertoire des archives du Burkina Faso (ex Haute Volta) en dépôt aux Archives de Côte d'Ivoire*.

Conrad, David
"Archival Resources in Mali," *History in Africa*, 1976, 3: 175–180

Cordell, Dennis D.
1980 *Documents sur la Haute Volta disponibles aux Archives Nationales de la Côte d'Ivoire (Abidjan)*. Ougadougou: INSD, Ministère du Plan.

International Council on Archives
1971 Guide to the Sources of the History of Africa. Published under the auspices of the UNESCO. 3 vols. Zug, Switzerland, Interdocumentary Co.

Mbaye, Saliou
1990 *Guide des archives de l' AOF* Dakar. Archives du Sénégal.

N'Diaye, Abdoulaye Gamby
1975   Répertoire des Archives. Sous-série 2G. Rapports périodiques mensuels, tri-
        mestriels, semestriels et annuels des Gouverneurs, administrateurs et chefs de
        service. 1ère tranche — 1895-1940. Dakar: Archives du Sénégal.

Niakate, Moussa
        "Répertoire des Archives Nationales du Mali — Koulouba." *Études Maliennes*. Ba-
        mako: Institut des Sciences Humaines.

Nikiema, Jules
1973   Répertoire des archives concernant la Haute Volta dans le fonds de l' AOF aux
        Archives du Sénégal. Ouagadougou: Ministère des Finances et du Commerce,
        Service des Archives.

Porges, L.
1988   Sources d'Information sur l'Afrique Francophone et Madagascar. Paris: Min-
        istère de la Coopération.

Welch, Ashton Wesley
1982   "The National Archives of Ivory Coast," in *History in Africa,* 1982, 9: 377–80.

Westfall, Gloria
1992   French Colonial Africa: A Guide to Official Sources. London: Hans Zell.

ARCHIVAL MATERIALS CONSULTED

I. Afrique Occidentale Française (AOF / ANS)

Série D: Affaires Militaires

Sous-série 1 D 1–242: opérations militaires

1 D 209 [14 mi 301]
        Remarques générales sur la révolte
        Rapports sur les causes de la révolte

1 D 211 [14 mi 301–302]
        Situation politique, HSN, 1915–16
        Beledougou

1 D 213 [14 mi 303]
        Correspondance Koulouba — Dakar

Sous-série 4 D 1–139: Personnel militaire jusqu'à 1920

4 D 54 [14 mi 360]
        Compte-rendu de jugements de leaders de révolte, 1914, 1915
        Rapports sur le recrutement cercle par cercle

4 D 57 [14 mi 360–361]
        Rapports sur le recrutement cercle par cercle
        Compte-rendu de la révolte en pays Marka et Bobo

4 D 58 [14 mi 361]
        Rapports de Koulouba à Dakar sur la révolte (fin 1915–début 1916)

4 D 63 [14 mi 363]
Résumé des mouvements insurrectionnels dans le HSN
Tournée du Lt.-Gouv. du HSN dans la région Bani/Volta.
Journal du poste de Koudougou, 8 Nov.–28 Déc.

4 D 64 [14 mi 363–364]
Tournée de police, 20 mars au 15 av. 1916, cercle de Bandiagara
Carnet de route de Maubert
Rapport de Digué
Journal de Maguet
Rapport Vidal
Correspondance Koulouba—Dakar

4 D 65 [14 mi 364]
Rapport Picanon. Recrutement des troupes indigènes entre le 1er août 1914 et
le 1er octobre 1915 et le 1er oct. 1915–17 av. 1916.

4 D 69/70 [14 mi 366]
Recrutement
Dahomey
Conditions et problèmes des tirailleurs
Description des batailles auxquelles ils ont participé en France
Lettre de Van Vollenhoven sur les risques du recrutement
Informations sur les conditions de vie des tirailleurs en France

4 D 72 [14 mi 367]
Rapport du Gouv. Gén. Van Vollenhoven sur le recrutement et ses effets, 1917
Préparatifs pour la campagne de recrutement de 1918

4 D 72 [14 mi 367]
Préparatifs pour la campagne de recrutement de 1918

4 D 74 [14 mi 368]
Diagne, 1917–18

4 D 75 [14 mi 368]
Recrutement, 1918

Sous-série 5 D 1–73: Défense et organisation militaire jusqu'à 1920

5 D 46 [14 mi 421]
Organisation militaire du HSN, 1915–1917

Série G: Politique et Administration Générale

Sous-série 2 G: Rapports périodiques mensuels des Lieutenant Gouverneurs

2 G 2 / 10 [14 mi 1624]
2ème Territoire Militaire. Rapports politiques mensuels d'ensemble et des cercles,
1902

2 G 16 / 4, 6, 7, 8 [14 mi 1681]
    Rapports sur la situation politique (1914–17)

2 G 17 / 4 [14 mi 1683]
    Rapports sur la situation politique (1914–17)
    Note sur les évènements politiques graves survenus du 2 août 1914 au 20
    février 1918

2 G 19 / 4 [14 mi 1690]
    HSN. Rapports politiques, 1er et 2e Trim. 1919, 2e Sem. 1919

Sous-série 4 G: Mission d'inspection des colonies
4 G 21 [14 mi 765]
    Rapport Picanon. Rapport d' ensemble no 50 du 12 Mai 1917 — Enquête sur
    les causes de la révolte de la région de la Volta

4 G 22 [14 mi 765–766]
    Annexes au Rapport Picanon. Déclarations faites à l'Inspecteur Général des
    Colonies, Picanon, Chef de Mission, Cercle de Dédougou. Rapport no 51

Sous-série 10 G: Affaires politiques, administratives et musulmanes. Haute Volta
10 G 5 — 6 [14 mi 2193]
    Reconstitution de la Haute Volta

10 G 7 [14 mi 2193]
    Années 1920. Haute Volta
    Recensement populations Mossi et Marka

10 G 8 [14 mi 2193]
    Création de la Haute Volta
    Organisation administrative de base: 1916–31

Sous-série 15 G: Affaires politiques, administratives et musulmanes
du Soudan, 1913–20
15 G 105 [14 mi 1025]
    Cercle de Koutiala
    6 déc. 1913. "Rapport sur l'affaire Sompe et consorts Rébellion à main armée
    9 nov. 1914. "Affaire Boukary Tourompo. Procès verbal d'information"

15 G 106 [14 mi 1025]
    Cercle de Ouagadougou. Mouvement musulman anti-français 1914–15. Audi-
    ence publique du 27 av. 1915 tenue par le Tribunal du Cercle de Ouagadougou
    Divers. (Commandement indigène, manque d'administrateurs, réorganisation
    des cantons)

15 G 107 [14 mi 1025]
    Telegrams, 1918

15 G 191 [14 mi 1049]
    Poste de Leo, 1898

15 G 192 [14 mi 1049]
  Région Volta et Mossi, 1898
  Relations avec Allemands et Anglais

15 G 193 and 194 [14 mi 1049]
  Lobi 1898–18

15 G 195 [14 mi 1049]
  Poste de Boromo. Relègue des archives du poste

15 G 196 [14 mi 1049]
  Cercle de Sono, 1898

15 G 197 [14 mi 1049]
  Cercle de Koury, 1899

15 G 198 [14 mi 1049]
  Koury, affaires politiques
  Soumission des villages de Sami et Perive
  Lettre de Ponty

15 G 199 [14 mi 1049–1050]
  Rapports politiques, 1898–99. Cercle de Bobo-Dioulasso

15 G 200 [14 mi 1051]
  Bobo-Dioulasso, affaires politiques, 1903–6

15G 201 [14 mi 1051]
  Affaire des marabouts
  Rapport Vidal
  Enquête Vidal sur Maubert

15G 202 [14 mi 1051]
  Bobo-Dioulasso. Enquête sur tentative de révolte conduite par Ansoumana, 1918

Sous-série 19 G: Affaires musulmanes

19 G 1 [14 mi 1084]
  Questions musulmanes
  Politique des races

19 G 2 [14 mi 1084]
  Questions musulmanes

II. Archives Nationales Section Outre-Mer (ANSOM)

(Classified in CAOM under Fond Ministériel)

Série Affaires Politiques

Carton 2762

Dossier "Télégrammes"
Télégrammes entre Dakar et Paris (années 1915–17)
Rapport Picanon sur recrutement (Nov. 1916)

Carton 2801
Dossier 1: Côte d'Ivoire 1911–12
Dossier 2: Guinée 1911–12
Dossier 3: Côte d'Ivoire (1914–17)
Dossier 4: Mauritanie 1912
Dossier 5: Dahomey — Opérations de police. Pays des Hollis. 1914–17
Dossier 6: Rapports politiques et militaires. Opérations de police
1. Rapports mensuels ou trimestriels — Mauritanie
2. Troubles en Guinée Portuguaise (1915) / Incidents aux frontières libériennes (1914–16)
3. Affaire du Bélédougou (1915)
4. Affaire de Dédougou (1916)
5. Agitation et Opérations de police au pays Touareg
6. Opérations de police au Dahomey
7. Affaire d'Agadès

Carton 5976
Reports and telegrams on 1916 revolts

Carton 3036/1
Reports by Chief Inspector Picanon and reports by Picanon with the assistance of Inspector Kair
The recruiting campaign from Aug. 1 1914 to Oct 1 1915, including the Beledougou and Goumbou revolts
The recruiting campaign from Oct. 1 1915 to Ap. 7 1916, including the Bani-Volta revolt

FM EE/ii/1131(1)
Maubert — Personal File

III. Service Historique Armée de Terre (SHAT)

Fonds AOF Classeur 5 H

5 H 1: 1890–1913

5 H 2: 1914–19

5 H 3: 1914–20
Ordres généraux / Télégrammes

5 H 196: Soudan 11 — Dossier 1. Rapports sur la Colonne Bani-Volta
Rapport du Capitaine Carpentier, chef de détachement sur opérations du 11 mars au 9 avril 1916

Rapport du Capitaine Megnou, commandant la 10ème Compagnie du 4ème Régiment de tirailleurs Sénégalais. San, 15 Avril 1916

Compte-rendu sur les opérations de police du cercle de Bandiagara du 27 mars au 29 juillet 1916. Adjudant-chef Puget, Sofara, le 31 juillet 1916

Colonne de San. Journal de marche et opérations militaires, 13 av.–10 sept. 1916, par le Chef de Bataillon, commandant la colonne, Simonin

Rapport d'ensemble politique, administratif, et militaire concernant les opérations de dégagement du poste de Koudougou. Troupes du Groupe de l'AOF Capitaine Marotel, 2ème Régiment de Tirailleurs Sénégalais. 11 Mai 1916

Rapport du Capitaine Cadence sur les opérations de la colonne secondaire Koudougou-Léo du 1er mai au 15 octobre 1916

Rapport du Capitaine Amalric, commandant la Compagnie de marche du Bataillon de Guinée. Dedougou, 23 Mars 1916

Colonne de Dedougou. Etat récapitulatif des munitions d'infanterie consommées pendant le opérations de la région Bani-Volta

Rapport du Colonel Molard, Commandant Militaire du HSN sur les opérations de police dans le basin de la Volta

IV. Centre Historique et d'Etudes des Territoires d'Outre-Mer (CHETOM)

15 H 34

Colonne de police Bani-Volta. (Extrait de l'Historique du 2ème Sénégalais). 23 novembre au 9 février

Colonne Bani-Volta. Rapport du Colonel Molard, Commandant Militaire du HSN sur les opérations de police dans le bassin de la Volta—1916. 10 février 1916 au 24 juillet 1916

15 H 39

2ème RTS. Compagnie Labouret. Rapport sur les opérations de la Compagnie de marche du 21 novembre 1915 au 1er avril 1916, n.d.

Rapport du Lt. Stefanini, Commandant de la 3ème Compagnie du 1er Sénégalais sur les opérations auxquelles a pris part cette unité, depuis sa formation le 12 février 1916 jusqu'au 23 septembre 1916. Hounde, le 24 septembre 1916

Rapport du Ss-Lt. Breton, Commandant la Compagnie du 13 février au 31 juillet 1916. Dedougou, le 1er Aout 1916

4ème RTS. Rapport sur les opérations auxquelles a pris part la 3ème Compagnie. Capitaine Lucas, Lt. Vallet

V. Archives Nationales de Côte d'Ivoire (ANCI)

Microfiches

3 mi 7 Monographies des cercles de Haute Volta
Monographie du cercle de Bobo-Dioulasso (1920)

Série EE

5 EE 1 (1)	Rapport d'ensemble sur la situation de la colonie de la H V (1920)
5 EE 1 (2)	Rapport d'ensemble sur la situation de la colonie de la H V (1921)
5 EE 1 (3)	Rapports trimestriels du Cercle de Bobo-Dioulasso (1917–23)
5 EE 6 (2)	Rapports trimestriels du Cercle de Bobo-Dioulasso (1917–23)
5 EE 6 (3)	Rapports politiques mensuels du Cercle de Bobo-Dioulasso (1917–23)
5 EE 6 (3/2)	Rapports politiques mensuels du Cercle de Bobo-Dioulasso (1916)
5 EE 21	HSN Rapports du Cercle de Bobo-Dioulasso (juillet 1902–avril 1905)
5 EE 22	HSN Rapports du Cercle de Bobo-Dioulasso (1913–18)
5 EE 48	Cercle de Bobo-Dioulasso, Fiches de renseignements des chefs de canton (1908–37)
5 EE 69 (2)	Révoltes des Markas et des Bobos
AOF VII, 4	Projet d'Organisation de la Région de la Volta Occidentale

VI. Centre Nationale de la Recherche Scietifique et Technologique

(CNRST Ouagadougou)
B II   Cercle de Bobo-Dioulasso

VII. Haut Commissariat de Bobo-Dioulasso

Unclassified papers

Livre-Journal, Cercle de Bobo-Dioulasso (1908–24)

Bibliography

Abu, Mallam
1992 [c. 1914] *The Zabarma Conquest of North-West Ghana and Upper Volta: A Hausa Narrative "Histories of Samory and Babatu and Others."* Ed. Stanisaw Piaszewicz. Warsaw: PWN—Polish Scientific Publishers.

Alber, Erdmute
2000 "Automobilismus und Kolonialherrschaft." *Paideuma* 46: 279 99. To be published as "Motorization and Colonial Rule," in *Everyday Life in Colonial Africa,* ed. Adam Jones.

d'Almeida-Topor, H.
1973 "Les populations dahoméennes et le recrutement indigène pendant la première guerre mondiale." *Revue d'Histoire d'Outre-Mer* 60, no. 219: 196–237.

Andrew, M. C. and A. S. Kanya-Forstner
1978 "France, Africa, and the First World War." *Journal of African History* (special issue, World War I and Africa) 19, no. 1: 11–23.

Angoulvant, G.
1922 "Pourquoi j'ai créé la Haute Volta?" *Encyclopédie Coloniale et Maritime.*

Asiwaju, A. I., and M. Crowder
1977 Introduction to special issue, "Protest against Colonial Rule in Africa." *Tarikh* 5, no. 3.

Bâ, Amadou Hampaté
1987 [1973] *The Fortunes of Wangrin: The Life and Times of an African Confidence Man.* Trans. of *Etrange destin de Wangrin,* by Aina Pavolini Taylor. Bloomington: Indiana University Press.

Bâ, A. H. and J. Daget
1984 [1955] *L'empire peul du Macina* (1818–53). Paris: EHESS.

Balesi, Charles J.
1979 *From Adversaries to Comrades-in-Arms: West Africans and the French Military, 1885–1918.* Waltham, Mass.: Crossroads Press.

Balima, Salfo-Albert
1996   *Légendes et histoire des peuples du Burkina Faso.* Paris: J. A. Conseil.

Barry, Ibrahima
1993   Le royaume de Bandiagara (1864–93). Thèse pour le Doctorat d'histoire sous la direction de E. Terray, Paris, EHESS.

Bationo, Bekouly Joseph
1996   "La Révolte dans le Pays Gourounsi." Paper presented at the *International Colloquium on the History of Burkina Faso,* Ouagadougou, December 1996.

Bayart, Jean-François
1989   *L'Etat en Afrique: La politique du ventre.* Paris: Fayard. Trans. as *The State in Africa: The Politics of the Belly.* London: Longman, 1993.

Bayili, Blaise
1998   *Religion, droit et pouvoir au Burkina Faso. Les Lyele du Burkina Faso.* Paris: L'Harmattan.

Bayili, Émmanuel
1983   "Les populations Nord-Nuna (Haute Volta) des origines à 1920." Thèse de doctorat, 3ème cycle, Histoire des sociétés de l'Afrique Noire, Université de Paris I.

Bazin, Jean, and Emmanuel Terray, eds.
1982   *Guerres de lignages et guerres d'états en Afrique.* Paris: Editions des Archives Contemporaines.

de Benoist, Joseph-Roger
1987   *Église et pouvoir colonial au Soudan Français. Administrateurs et missionnaires dans la boucle du Niger (1885–1945).* Paris: Karthala.

Bernus, E.
1960   "Kong et sa région." *Etudes Eburnéennes* 8:242–323. Abidjan: Direction de la Recherche Scientifique.

Bhadra, G.
1988   "Four Rebels of Eighteen-Fifty-Seven." Reprinted in R. Guha and G. C. Spivak, eds., *Selected Subaltern Studies.* New York: Oxford University Press.

Binger, Gustave
1892   *Du Niger au Golfe de Guinée.* Paris: Hachette. Reissued Société des Africanistes, 1980.

Blegna, Domba
1990   *Les masques dans la société marka de Fobiri: origine, culte, art.* Etudes sur l'Histoire et l'Archéologie du Burkina Faso, vol. 5. Stuttgart: Franz Steiner Verlag.

Bobo Julaso ni Dedugu Serepeya (Centre Régional de Promotion Agropastoral)
1992   "Sanblaw ka muruti." In *Horonyakelew.* Bobo-Dioulasso: Grande Imprimerie du Burkina.

1995   *Bonakaw ka Muruti.* Bobo-Dioulasso: Grande Imprimerie du Burkina.

Boni, Nazi
1962   *Le Crépuscule des temps anciens.* Paris: Présence Africaine.

1972   *Histoire de l'Afrique résistante.* Paris: Présence Africaine.

Bonnafé, Pierre, Michèle Fiéloux, and Jeanne-Marie Kambou
1982   "Le conflit armé dans une population sans état: Les Lobi de Haute-Volta." In Bazin and Terray, pp. 73–141.

Capron, Jean
1973   *Communautés villageoises bwa.* Paris: Institut d' Ethnologie, Musée de l' Homme.

Chauveau, J.-P.
1987   "La colonisation 'appropriée': Essai sur les transformations économiques et sociales en pays baule de 1891 au début de années 1920." In *La colonisation: Rupture ou parenthèse?* ed. M. H. Piault, pp. 57–122. Paris: L'Harmattan.

Chéron, Georges
1916   "Les Bobo-fing." *Annuaire et mémoire du Comité d'Etudes Historiques et Scientifiques de l'Afrique Occidentale Française.* Gorée: Imprimerie du Gouvernement Général.

Ciré Ba, Birahim
1971   *Sya ou Bobo-Dioulasso.* Bobo-Dioulasso: Imprimerie de la Savane.

Conklin, Alice L.
1997   *A Mission to Civilize: The Republican Idea of Empire in France and West Africa.* Stanford: Stanford University Press.

Cooper, F.
1994   "Conflict and Connection: Rethinking Colonial African History." *American Historical Review* 99, no. 5: 1516–45.

Coquery-Vidrovitch, C.
1988   "Revolt and Resistance, Collaboration and Assimilation." In *Africa: Endurance and Change South of the Sahara.* Berkeley: University of California Press.

Coulibaly, Elysée
1997   Savoir et savoir-faire des anciens métallurgistes: Recherches préliminaires sur les procédés en sidérurgie directe dans le Bwamu (Burkina Faso-Mali). Thèse de doctorat, Université de Paris 1.

Coulibaly, Niampégué
1978   La révolte de Baninko et du Minyankala après la prise de Ségou par Archinard en 1980. Mémoire de fin d'études, Ecole Normale Supérieure, Section Géographie—Histoire, Bamako.

Cremer, Jean
1923   *Matériaux d'ethnographie et de linguistique soudanaises,* vol. 1. *Dictionnaire français-peul (dialecte de la Haute Volta).* Paris: Geuthner.
1924a   *Matériaux d'ethnographie et de linguistique soudanaises,* vol. 2. *Grammaire de la langue Kassena ou Kassené.* Paris: Geuthner.
1924b   *Matériaux d'ethnographie et de linguistique soudanaises,* vol. 3. *Les Bobo (La vie sociale).* Paris: Paul Geuthner.
1927   *Matériaux d'ethnographie et de linguistique soudanaises,* vol. 4. *Les Bobo (La mentalité mystique).* Paris: Paul Geuthner.

Crowder, Michael
1971   *West African Resistance: The Military Response to Colonial Occupation.* Africana
         Publishing.
1978   *Colonial West Africa. Collected Essays.* London: Frank Cass.

Crozat, François [Doctor]
1891   "Rapport du Docteur Crozat sur sa mission au Mossi." *Journal Officiel de la Ré-
         publique Française* (Oct. 5): 4797–801.

Crummey, D.
1986   "'The Great Beast.'" Introduction to *Banditry, Rebellion, and Social Protest in
         Africa,* pp. 1–29. London: James Currey.

CRPA
See Bobo Julaso ni Dedugu Serepeya

Dakono, Joachim
1975–76 "La conquête du pays Bô des cercles San-Tominian, 1893–1916." Mémoire
         de fin d'étude, Hist. Géog. Ecole Normale Supérieure, Bamako.

Davis, Shelby Cullom
1970 [1934] *Reservoirs of Men. A History of the Black Troops of French West Africa.* West-
         port, Conn.: Negro University Press.

Déjean, Charles
1970   *Trois ans sous les tropiques africains.* Rodez: P. Carrère.

Delafosse, Maurice
1911   "Les langues voltaïques (boucle du Niger)" *Bulletin et Mémoires de la Société de Lin-
         guistique de Paris,* no. 16: 386–95.
1912   *Haut-Sénégal-Niger (Soudan français).* Paris: Larose. (reissued in 1972 by Maison-
         neuve et Larose)

Deschamps, H.
1953   *Les méthodes et les doctrines coloniales de la France.* Paris: A. Colin

Deschamps, Hubert, and Paul Chauvet
1949   *Gallieni, Pacificateur. Écrits coloniaux de Gallieni. Choix de textes et notes par H. De-
         schamps et P. Chauvet.* Paris: PUF. Colonies et empires. 2ème série. Les classiques
         de la colonisation, no. 13.

Deville [Lieutenant]
1913   "Emploi et organisation des sections de mitrailleuses aux colonies." *Revue des
         Troupes Coloniales* (Feb.):125–34; (Apr.): 406–420.

Diallo, Youssouf
1997   *Les Fulbe de Boobola. Genèse et évolution de l' Etat de Barani (Burkina Faso).* Köln:
         Rüdiger Köppe.

Dirks, Nicholas B.
1992   "Colonialism and Culture." Introduction to *Colonialism and Culture,* ed. N. B.
         Dirks. Ann Arbor: University of Michigan Press.

Drame, Youssouf
1991 "L'évolution de l'Islam à Lanfiera du XIXe au début du XXe siècle." Mémoire de maîtrise, Département d'Histoire et d'Archéologie, Université de Ouagadougou.

Duboc, Général
1938 *L'épopée coloniale en Afrique occidentale française.* Paris: Editions SFELT.

Duperray, A. M.
1984 *Les Gourounsi de Haute Volta. Conquête et colonisation, 1896–1933.* Stuttgart: Franz Steiner.

Duval, Maurice
1986 *Un totalitarisme sans Etat.* Paris: L'Harmattan.

Echenberg, Myron Joel
1969 "Jihad and State Building in Late Nineteenth Century Upper Volta: The Rise and Fall of the Marka State of Al-Kari of Bousse." *Canadian Journal of African Studies* 3, no. 3.
1971 "African Reaction to French Conquest: Upper Volta in the Late Nineteenth Century." Ph. D. thesis, University of Wisconsin.
1991 *Colonial Conscripts: The Tirailleurs Sénégalais in French West Africa, 1857–1960.* London: James Currey.

Exposition Coloniale Internationale de Paris
1931 *Histoire Militaire de l'Afrique Occidentale Française.* Paris: Imprimerie Nationale.

Frèrejean, Louis
1996 *Objectif Tombouctou.* Paris: L'Harmattan.

Fuglestad, F.
1973 "Les révoltes des Touareg du Niger (1916-17)." *Cahiers d'Etudes africaines* 13, no. 49: 82–120.

Gallais, Jean
1960 "La signification du village en Afrique soudanienne de l'Ouest: Essai comparatif." *Cahiers de Sociologie Economique,* no. 2: 128–62.

Garcia, Luc
1970 "Les Mouvements de resistance au Dahomey," *Cahiers d'Études Africaines* 10, no. 37: 144–78.

Gnankambary, Blami
1970 "La révolte bobo de 1916 dans le Cercle de Dédougou." *Notes et Documents voltaïques* 3, no. 4 (July-Sept.): 55–87. Reprinted in vol. 11, nos. 3–4 (Apr.-Sept. 1978): 1–38. Ouagadougou: CNRST.

Goody, Jack
1971 *Technology, Tradition, and the State in Africa.* Cambridge: Cambridge University Press.

Gouraud, Henri Joseph E.
1939 *Au Soudan. Souvenir d'un Africain.* Paris: P. Tisné.

Griffeth, Robert R.
1968   *Varieties of African Resistance to the French Conquest of the Western Sudan, 1850–
        1900.* Ph.D. thesis, Northwestern University.

Hargreaves, John D.
1973   "The European Partition of West Africa." In *History of West Africa,* ed. J. F. Ade
        Ajayi and Michael Crowder, vol. 2. pp. 402–23. New York: Columbia Univer-
        sity Press.
1974   *West Africa Partitioned,* vol. 1: *The Loaded Pause, 1885–1889.* Madison: Univer-
        sity of Wisconsin Press.
1985   *West Africa Partitioned,* vol. 2: *The Elephant and the Grass.* Madison: University of
        Wisconsin Press.

Harrison, Christopher
1988   *France and Islam in West Africa, 1860–1960.* Cambridge: Cambridge University
        Press.

Hébert, Jean
1970   "Révoltes en Haute Volta de 1914 à 1918." *Notes et Documents voltaïques* 3, no. 4
        (July-Sept.): 3–54.
1976   Esquisse de l'histoire du pays toussian. Bobo-Dioulasso: CESAO.

Héritier, Françoise
1973   "La paix et la pluie." Rapports d'autorité et rapport au sacré chez les Samo.
        L'Homme 13, no. 3.

Holden, J. J.
1965   "The Zabarima Conquest of North Ghana." *Transactions of the Historical Society
        of Ghana,* vol. 8, pp. 60–86, 119–20.

Houdas, O. and M. Delafosse, eds. and trans.
1913   *Tarikh el-Fettach, ou chronique du chercheur pour servir à l'histoire des villes, des armées,
        et des principaux personnages du Tekrour.* Paris: Ernest Leroux.

Hubbell, Andrew Frederick
1997   *Patronage and Predation: A Social History of Colonial Chieftaincies in a Chiefless Region—
        Souroudougou (Burkina Faso), 1850–1946.* Ph.D. dissertation, Stanford University.

Hugot, L.
1901   "Un Soudanais. Le journal du Capitaine Hugot." *Bulletin du Comité de l'Afrique
        Française* 11, no. 8 (Aug.): 306–7; no. 10 (Oct.): 340–41.

Isaacman, Allen, and Barbara Isaacman
1977   "Resistance and Collaboration in Southern and Central Africa, c. 1850–1920."
        International Journal of African Historical Studies 10, no. 1: 31–62.

Izard, Michel
1993   "Paysans partisans. A propos de la guerre dans les sociétés burkinabé." *Cahiers
        des Sciences Humaines,* hors série, pp. 61–64 (ORSTOM).
1997   "Petite Guerre, grande guérilla: sur deux modalités d'existence d'un espace
        non-étatique ouest-africain." Paper given at seminar "La Guerre Folle, Journées
        du Laboratoire d'Anthropologie Sociale," Maison Suger, Sept. 26–27.

1999   "Histoire militaire et anthropologie politique: à propos de la conquête du bassin des Volta (Afrique de l'Ouest)." In *Histoire militaire et sciences humaines,* ed. Laurent Henniger, pp. 43–59. Paris: Eds. Complexe.

Izard-Heritier, Françoise, and Michel Izard

1958   *Bouna. Monographie d'un village pana de la Valée du Sourou (Haute Volta).* Service Hydraulique de Haute Volta, Institut des Sciences Humaines Appliquées de l'Université de Bordeaux.

Jacob, Jean-Pierre

1988   "Le sens des limites. Maladie, sorcellerie, religion et pouvoir chez les Winye, Gourounsi du Burkina Faso." Thèse, Université de Neufchâtel (Switzerland), Faculté de Lettres.

1997   "L'administration coloniale comme puissance antisorcellaire." In *Dire les autres: Réflexions et pratiques anthropologiques,* ed. Jacques Hainard and Roland Keehr, pp. 291–308. Lausanne: Payot Lausanne.

Jameson, Fredric

1991   "Immanence and Nominalism in Postmodern Theoretical Discourse." In *Postmodernism, or the Cultural Logic of Late Capitalism,* pp. 181–259. Durham: Duke University Press.

JanMohammed, A. R.

1985   "The Economy of Manichean Allegory: The Function of Racial Difference in Colonialist Literature." *Critical Inquiry* 12, no. 1.

Jansen, Jan

1996   "The Younger Brother and the Stranger: In Search of a Status Discourse for Mande." *Cahiers d'Etudes africaines* 36, no. 4: 659–88.

Jonckers, Danielle

1987   *La société minianka du Mali.* Paris: L'Harmattan.

1993   "Autels sacrificiels et puissance religieuse, le Manyan." *Systèmes de Pensée en Afrique Noire,* cahier 12; *Fétiches 2, puissance des objets, charme des mots:* 65–101.

Kambou-Ferrand, Jeanne-Marie

1993a   "Guerre et résistance sous la période coloniale en pays lobi/birifor (Burkina Faso) au travers des photos d'époque." In *Images d'Afrique et Sciences Sociales: Les pays lobi, birifor, et dagara (Burkina Faso, Côte d'Ivoire, et Ghana),* ed. M. Fiéloux, J. Lombard, and J.-M. Kambou-Ferrand, pp. 75–98. Paris: Karthala.

1993b   *Peuples voltaïques et conquête coloniale 1885–1914. Burkina Faso.* Paris: L'Harmattan.

Kanya-Forstner, A. S.

1969   *The Conquest of the Western Sudan: A Study in French Military Imperialism.* Cambridge: Cambridge University Press.

Kaspi, A.

1971   "French War Aims in Africa, 1914–19." In *France and Britain in Africa: Imperial Rivalry and Colonial Rule,* ed. P. Gifford and William Roger Louis, pp. 369–96. New Haven: Yale University Press.

Kiétégha, Jean Baptiste
1983   *L'or de la Volta Noire.* Paris: Karthala.

Ki-Zerbo, Joseph
1983   *Alfred Diban: premier chrétien de Haute Volta.* Paris: Cerf.

Kodjo, Numukie G.
1986   *Le royaume de Kong des origines à 1897.* Thèse pour le doctorat d'Etat, Université de Provence, Aix-en-Provence, UER d'Histoire.

Kote, Blamami
1982   "Les marka et l'islam dans la boucle de la Volta Noire, du jihad d'El Hadj Karantao aux débuts de la colonisation française, 1820–1915." Mémoire de maîtrise, Université de Ouagadougou (ESLSH).

Koulibaly, Fabégna
1970   "Histoire des Marka de Haute Volta." *Notes et Documents voltaïques* 3, no. 3 (Apr.-June): 43–51.

Kurtz, Donald V.
1996   "Hegemony and Anthropology: Gramsci, exegeses, reinterpretations," *Critique of Anthropology* 16(2): 103–35.

Labouret, Henri
1931   *Les tribus du rameau lobi.* Paris: Institut d'Ethnologie.
1934   *Les Manding et leur langue.* Paris: Librairie Larose.

de Latour, Eliane.
1982   "La paix destructrice." In Bazin and Terray, pp. 235–67.

Launay, Robert
1992   *Beyond the Stream: Islam and Society in a West African Town.* Berkeley: University of California Press.

Le Moal, Guy
1980   *Les Bobo: Nature et fonction des masques.* Paris: ORSTOM.

Levtzion, Nehemia
1968   *Muslims and Chiefs in West Africa.* Oxford: Clarendon Press.
1971   "A Seventeenth-century Chronicle by Ibn Al-Mukhtar: A Critical Study of Ta'rikh Al-Fattash." *Bulletin of the School of Oriental and African Studies* 34, no. 3: 571–93.

Lunn, Joe
1999   *Memoirs of the Maelstrom: A Senegalese Oral History of the First World War.* Oxford: James Currey.

Madiéga, Georges
1981   "Esquisse de la conquête et de la formation territoriale de la colonie de Haute Volta" *Bulletin de l'IFAN* 43, série B, nos. 3–4: 217–77.

Maïga, Ibrahima
1937   "Une page d'histoire locale: Tominian." *Bulletin de Recherches Soudanaises,* nos. 7–8 (Jan.-Feb.): 277–85.

Mangeot [Colonel]
1922   "Manuel à l'usage de troupes opérant au Soudan Français et plus particulière-
        ment en zone saharienne." *Bulletin du Comité d'Etudes Historiques et Scientifique de
        l'AOF,* pp. 590–648.

Mangin, Charles
1910   *La Force noire.* Paris: Hachette.

Marjomaa, Risotto
1998   *War on the Savannah: The Military Collapse of the Sokoto Calipahte under the Invasion
        of the British Empire, 1897–1903.* Helsinki: Finnish Academy of Science and
        Letters.

Meillassoux, Claude
1991   *The Anthropology of Slavery.* Chicago: University of Chicago Press. Trans. from
        Anthropologie de l'escalvage: le ventre de fer et d'argent, 1986.

Méniaud, J.
1935   *Sikasso, ou l'histoire dramatique d'un royaume noir au XIXe siècle.* Paris: Imprimerie
        F. Bouchy.

Mercier, Paul
1968   *Traditions, changements, histoire: les Somba du Dahomey septentrional.* Paris: Editions
        Antropos.

Michel, Marc
1982   *L' Appel à l'Afrique. Contributions et réactions à l'effort de guerre en AOF, 1914–1949.*
        Série 'Afrique' 6. Paris: Publications de la Sorbonne.

Moberly, Frederick J.
1931   *Military Campaigns in Togoland and the Cameroons.* London: H. M. Stationary Office.

Newburry, C. W.
1960   "The Formation of the General Government of French West Africa." *Journal of
        African History* 1: 111–28.

Niakate, Moussa
n.d.   *La révolte des Bobos dans les cercles de Dédougou et San, 1915 à 1916.* A typed and
        mimeographed collection of documents from the Malian National Archives,
        bound in three vols. Bamako: Maison du Peuple.

Norris, Ted
1990   "German Attempts to Incite Insurgency among the Muslims of the French and
        British Colonies during the First World War: The Case of the Campaign in
        West Africa," FU Berlin, Institut für Ethnologie, Sozialanthropologische Arbe-
        itspapiere, no. 32. Berlin: Das Arabische Buch.

Olivier de Sardan, Jean-Pierre
1982   "Le cheval et l'arc." in Bazin and Terray, pp. 189–234.

Osuntokun, J.
1977   "West African Armed Revolts during the First World War." *Tarikh* 5, no. 3.

Otterbein, Kewith F.
1999   "A History of Research on Warfare In Anthropology." *American Anthropologist* 101, no. 4: 794–805.

Pageard, Robert
1961   "Note sur le peuplement de l'est du pays de Ségou." *Journal de la Société des Africanistes* 31, no. 1: 83–90.

Pare, Habana
1984   La société samo de la fin du XIXe siècle et la conquête coloniale francaise. Approche socio-historique: Mémoire de maîtrise 1983–84, Ecole Supérieure des Lettres et des Sciences Humaines (ESLSH), Département d'Histoire et d'Archeologie, Université de Ouagadougou.

Peel, J. D. Y.
1995   "For Who Hath Despised the Day of Small Things? Missionary Narratives and Historical Anthropology." *Comparative Studies in Society and History* 37, no. 3: 581–607.

Peires, J. B.
1989   *The Dead Will Arise: Nongqawuse and the Great Xhosa Cattle Killing Movement of 1856–7.* London: James Currey.

Person, Yves
1968–75 *Samori: Une révolution dyula.* 3 vols. Dakar: IFAN.

Piault, Marc H., ed.
1987   *La colonisation: rupture ou parenthèse?* Collection Racines du présent. Paris: L'Harmattan.

Prost, André
1971   *Les Missions des Pères Blancs en Afrique Occidentale avant 1939.* Paris: Pères Blancs.

Quéant, Thierry, and Cécile de Rouville
1969   "Agriculteurs et éleveurs de la région du Gondo-Sourou." Ougadougou: Travaux du Centre Voltaïque de la Recherche Scientifique, no. 1.

Quiquandon, F.
1891   "Rapport adressé par le Capitaine Quiquandon . . . sur sa mission auprès de Tieba." *Journal Officiel de la République Française* 23ème année: 260:4636–40; 261:4649–53; 262:4678–82; 263:4691–94; 264:4700–702.

Ranger, Terence
1983   "The Invention of Tradition in Colonial Africa." In *The Invention of Tradition,* ed. E. Hobsbawm and T. Ranger. Cambridge: Cambridge University Press.
1996   "Colonial and Postcolonial Identities." In *Postcolonial Identities in Africa,* ed. R. Werbner and T. Ranger. London and New Jersey: Zed Books.

Rondeau, Chantal
1980   *La société senufo du sud Mali, 1870–1950. De la tradition à la dépendance.* Thèse doctorat de 3ème cycle, Université de Paris VII, Département d'Histoire.

Roseberry, William
1994   "Hegemony and the Language of Contention." In *Revolution and the Negotiation*

of Rule in Modern Mexico, ed. G. M. Joseph and D. Nugent. Durham, NC: Duke University Press.

Rotberg, R. I., and A. A. Mazrui, eds.
1970   *Protest and Power in Black Africa.* Oxford: Oxford University Press.

Rouch, Jean
1956   "Migrations au Ghana." *Journal de la Société des Africanistes* 24, nos. 1 and 2: 46–50.

Royer, Patrick
1996   *In Pursuit of Tradition: Local Cults and Religious Conversion among the Sambla of Burkina Faso.* Ph.D. dissertation, University of Illinois.
1999   "Le Massa et l'eau de Moussa: Cultes régionaux, 'traditions' locales et sorcelerie en Afrique de l'Ouest," *Cahiers d'Etudes africaines* 39, no. 2: 337–366.

Salifou, André
1973   *Kouassan ou la révolte Sénoussiste.* Etudes Nigériennes no. 33. Niamey: CNRSH.

Sahlins, Marshall
1991   "The Return of the Event, Again; With Reflections on the Beginnings of the Great Fijian War of 1843 to 1855 between the Kingdoms of Bau and Rewa." In *Clio in Oceania: Toward a Historical Anthropology,* ed. A. Biersack, pp. 37–99. Washington, D.C.: Smithsonian Institution Press.

Salo, P. S.
1973   *Le recrutement militaire en AOF avant la première Guerre Mondiale: Les contingents pour les Territoires Extérieurs, 1907–1914.* Thèse de doctorat, Montpellier, Université Paul Valéry.

Şaul, Mahir
1991   "The Bobo 'House' and the Uses of Categories of Descent." *Africa* 61, no. 1: 71–97.
1993   "Land Custom in Bare." In *Land in African Agrarian Systems,* ed. T. J. Bassett and D. Crummey, pp. 75–100. Madison: Wisconsin University Press.
1997a   "Islam et appropriation mimétique comme ressource historique de la religion bobo." *Journal des Africanistes* 67, no. 2: 7–24.
1997b   "Military Alliance, Personal Submission, and Oaths in Precolonial Sudan." Working Papers on African societies, no. 21. Göthe Universität, Institut für Historische Ethnologie. Berlin: Arabische Buch.
1998   "The War Houses of the Watara in West Africa." *International Journal of African Historical Studies* 31, no. 3: 537–70.

Schwartz, Alfred
1993   "Brève histoire de la culture du coton au Burkina Faso." *Découvertes du Burkina,* vol. 1, pp. 207–37. Paris-Ouagadougou: Sépia.

Seni, L.
1981   "Un vieux de Fakèna se souvient de la révolte de 1915." *Afrique Histoire* (Dakar), no. 4: 59–61.
1985   *La lutte du Burkina contre la colonisation.* Ouagadougou: Imprimerie des Forces Armées Nationales.

Skinner, Elliot P.
1964   *The Mossi of Upper Volta.* Stanford: Stanford University Press.

Sombie, Pierre Siaka
1975   "L' insurrection de 1915–1916 dans les pays de la boucle de la Volta Noire."
        Mémoire de stage, École Nationale d'Administration, cycle B2. Ouagadougou.

St.-Martin, Yves
1968   "Un fils d'El Hadj Omar: Aguibou roi de Dinguiray et du Macina, 1843?–
        1907." *Cahiers d'Etudes africaines* 8, no. 28: 144–78.

Suret-Canale, Jean
1958   *Afrique noire. Géographie, civilisations, histoire.* Paris: Éditions Sociales.
1964   *Afrique noire. L'ère coloniale, 1900–1945.* Paris: Éditions Sociales.

Tauxier, Louis
1912   *Le Noir du Soudan, pays mossi et gourounsi.* Paris: Emile Larose.
1924   *Nouvelles notes sur le Mossi et le Gourounsi.* Paris: Emile Larose.

Thioub, Ibrahima
1997   "Gabriel d'Arboussier et la question de l'unité africaine, 1945–1965." In *AOF:
        réalités et héritages. Sociétés ouest-africaines et ordre colonial, 1895–1960,* ed. C.
        Becker, S. Mbaye, and I. Thioub. Dakar: Direction des Archives du Sénégal.

Thomas, Roger G.
1983   "The 1916 Bongo 'Riots' and Their Background: Aspects of Colonial Admin-
        istration and African Response in Eastern Upper Ghana." *Journal of African His-
        tory* 24: 57–75.

Tiendrébéogo, Anatole
1968   "La révolte des Gourounsi de la région de Koudougou 1916–1919, ou la guerre
        de Dougbeinga." Mémoire de stage 1967–68, cycle B, 2ème année. École Na-
        tionale d'Administration, Ouagadougou.

Toe, P.
1970   "La résistance à l'occupation française sur la boucle de la Volta noire pendant la
        guerre de 1914–18." Mémoire de Maitrise d'histoire, Université de Reims.
1994   "Contribution à l'étude des transformations socio-agraires en Afrique Tropi-
        cale: Une approche anthropologique des politiques d'innovation dans l'agricul-
        ture en pays 'San' meridional." Thèse de doctorat, 1993–94, ss la dir. d'E.
        Terray, Centre d'Etudes Africaines, EHESS.

Tosh, J.
1974   "Small-Scale Resistance in Uganda: the Lango 'Rising' at Adwari in 1919."
        Azania 9: 51–64.

Triaud, J.-L.
1995   *La légende noire de la Sanûsiyya: Une confrérie musulmane saharienne sous le regard français,
        1840–1930.* 2 vols. Paris: Éditions de la Maisons des Sciences de l'homme.

Triaud, J.-L., and D. Robinson, eds.
1997   *Le temps des marabouts. Itinéraires et stratégies islamiques en Afrique Occidentale
        Française.* Paris: Karthala.

Vandervort, B.
1998   *Wars of Imperial Conquest in Africa, 1830–1914.* Bloomington: Indiana University Press.

Weiskel, T.
1980   *French Colonial Rule and the Baule Peoples: Resistance and Collaboration, 1889–1911.* Oxford: Clarendon Press.

Wilks, Ivor
1989   *Islam and Polity in Northwestern Ghana.* Cambridge: Cambridge University Press.

Wilks, Ivor, Nehemia Levtzion, and Bruce M. Haight
1986   *Chronicles from Gonja: A Tradition of West African Muslim Historiography.* Cambridge: Cambridge University Press.

Williamson, K., and R. Blench
2000   "Niger-Congo." In *African Languages: An Introduction,* ed. B. Heine and D. Nurse, pp. 10–42. Cambridge: Cambridge University Press.

Index of Subjects and Persons

Index of Place Names